TEXANS
and
WAR

NUMBER 116

The Centennial Series of the Association of Former Students,
Texas A&M University

TEXANS

and

WAR

NEW INTERPRETATIONS
OF THE STATE'S MILITARY HISTORY

EDITED BY

ALEXANDER MENDOZA

AND

CHARLES DAVID GREAR

Texas A&M University Press
College Station

This paper meets the requirements of ANSI/NISO Z39.48-1992 (Permanence of Paper).
Binding materials have been chosen for durability.

LIBRARY OF CONGRESS CATALOGING-IN-PUBLICATION DATA

Texans and war : new interpretations of the state's military history /
edited by Alexander Mendoza and Charles David Grear. — 1st ed.
p. cm. — (Centennial series of the Association of Former Students,
Texas A&M University ; no. 116)
Includes index.
ISBN-13: 978-1-60344-583-2 (cloth : alk. paper)
ISBN-10: 1-60344-583-8 (cloth : alk. paper)
ISBN-13: 978-1-60344-695-2 (pbk. : alk. paper)
ISBN-10: 1-60344-695-8 (pbk. : alk. paper)
ISBN-13: 978-1-60344-124-7 (e-book-c)
ISBN-10: 1-60344-124-7 (e-book-c)
ISBN-13: 978-1-60344-320-3 e-book-p)
ISBN-10: 1-60344-320-7 (e-book-p)
1. Texas—History, Military.   I. Mendoza, Alexander, 1970–   II. Grear, Charles D., 1976–
III. Series: Centennial series of the Association of Former Students,
Texas A&M University ; no. 116.
F386.T325   2012
355.009764—dc23
2011033347

For Drs. Alwyn Barr, Charles "Chuck" Grear, Rick McCaslin,
Daniel S. Murphree, Steven H. Newton, and David L. Snead.
My friends and colleagues.

Alexander Mendoza

For Marion ("Buck") and Mary Grear.
My parents,
my guidance,
and my examples for life.

Charles David Grear

CONTENTS

ILLUSTRATIONS

FIGURES

MAPS

GRAPHS

ACKNOWLEDGMENTS

I T IS DIFFICULT to pinpoint the genesis for *Texans and War*. Suffice it to say that it came from a longstanding experience of trying to understand the notions and concepts of the martial spirit of Texas and Texans since childhood. It is something I am still working on, in case one is curious. Along the way I have been very fortunate to meet many special friends, and getting to know Chuck in graduate school was certainly an auspicious event, both personally and professionally. I remain eternally grateful to him for his patience in dealing with me (or ignoring me) during the conception, organization, and editing phases of this project. Of course, our contributors are to be commended for their diligence and their professionalism in providing us with some very innovative studies to this anthology. Thank you all.

I am also indebted to the staff at the Briscoe Center for American History at The University of Texas at Austin (CAH), where the bulk of my chapter was researched. Kathryn Kenefick, Catherine Best, Kelli Hansen, and the rest of the CAH staff are a treasure trove of helpfulness and expertise for any scholar. Many thanks also go to the Tejano veterans and their families who opened their doors and spoke to me at length about their experiences serving in the armed forces. *¡Mil gracias a todos!*

Also, a large amount of gratitude goes to my friends and colleagues who provided support in ways they may not realize. Steve Sisson, my former teammate on The University of Texas cross-country team and now the women's cross-country coach at our alma mater, and his better half, Ruth England, have opened their home in Austin for me while I traipsed across town and explored libraries and archives on too many occasions. I owe them—and their dogs (Lupe, Bala, and Cadence)—greatly for accommodating me during my visits. My South Texas crew—or entourage, as my wife jokingly calls them—have provided nothing but laughter and support for far too long. Marc García, Luis Valdez, Rick Valdez, Jesus Quiroz, Robert Cantú, Bertha Benavides, Magda Martinez, "Pistol" Pete Lara, Ale Arreguin, and Adriana Salinas, I thank you for everything, but most of all for your friendship and support of the Mendoza family. Monica McGetrick, the former editor at *LareDOS: A Journal of the Borderlands,* also allowed me the creative latitude to explore a few topics on war and memory that helped me with my chapter.

Thank you for your patience, Monica. My North Texas friends, Damien and Teresa Rosado, also deserve a hearty thanks for their support in my personal and professional endeavors; heaven knows I could not have functioned this fall semester without their assistance. The Rosado clan, including Daniel and Syrah, are truly special. Also at UNT, colleagues Harland Hagler, Todd Moye, Andrew Torget, Gus Seligmann, Walt Roberts, Beto Calderón, and Randolph "Mike" Campbell all provided a wonderful support system encouraging of scholarship and research, as well as having a good time. Thank you, gentlemen. The History Department's administrative staff—Stephanie Friday, Kayla Hunt, and Donna Morgan—also deserve a special thanks for all their help during the school year. I also thank UNT's graduate students.

Astute observers will note that this book is dedicated to several colleagues and mentors. While dedicating this anthology to my collaborator, Chuck, might seem a bit odd, I am certain that mutual friends who know the two of us recognize the rationale behind such a gesture. I also dedicate this work to two very inspirational professors: Alwyn Barr and David L. Snead. I was very fortunate to receive their help while I was a graduate student at Texas Tech University. In the years since I left Lubbock, I have relied on them for advice and support, perhaps more than I should. In the last year both men have shown me what it means to be a great mentor. But more importantly, each has shown me how to be an honorable, selfless man, something I treasure more dearly.

Before he returned to the confines of his adopted home state, my friend and colleague Daniel S. Murphree was on the receiving end of what I am sure he considers too many phone calls and e-mails. Yet he remained my friend. And while I miss him and his family (Mary Beth and Taylor) in Texas, I am happy to know he is basking in all that the Sunshine State has to offer. Steven H. Newton, professor of history at Delaware State University, demonstrated that support can span vast geographical distances through e-mails and phone calls. For everything he did for me, practically a stranger at the time, I sincerely thank him. Finally, at UNT, I must thank Rick McCaslin. Rick—recognized and respected in the fields of Texas and Civil War history—affirmed my faith in academia. I am fortunate to work and laugh alongside him and the rest of our colleagues in the Military History Center.

Finally, and most importantly, I must thank my family for their support. My wife, Punny, and son, Justin, have learned to coexist alongside me and my laptop for what I am certain they consider is an inordinate amount of time. During the final editing stages of this book, we dealt with the loss of a dear family member, but my wife and son remained strong and supportive of this study. They both laughed at my tired jokes and remained uncomplainingly patient as I disappeared for a conference or research trip or chose to read rather than play outside. I am very fortunate, for I believe some people will never truly experience the love and affection I have received from my family. For that, and more, I thank them.

— Alexander Mendoza

TEXAS MILITARY HISTORY has always been a part of my life. My father, though an Ohioan, visited Texas for basic training at Lackland Air Force Base. After his service he decided to remain in San Antonio because he met a pretty red-headed German girl from New Braunfels. Though out of uniform, my father continued to serve the military as a civil servant at Kelly Air Force Base. Also, growing up in San Antonio, one has a vested interest in the military history of Texas because of the numerous elementary school fieldtrips to the Alamo. College furthered my interests through the stories told by Donald Frazier about the lives of Ben McCulloch and Tom Green. But it was Alwyn Barr who took my interest in a different direction by suggesting I research Gano's Brigade for my master's thesis. From that moment on, the fire was fully ablaze, and books like this one continue to add fuel.

Many people helped us develop this book. I first have to give credit to my good friend who has helped me in many endeavors, both professional and personal, Alexander Mendoza. We met at Texas Tech University, where he took me under his tutelage, showing a tenderfoot what to expect in graduate school. Afterward Alex even surprised me by attending the defense of my dissertation at Texas Christian University—a memory I still hold dear. He initiated this project during a very long phone call, during which we hashed out the basic plans for the book; the bulk of the credit for planning and organization of this anthology belongs to him. Others also helped me during the process, such as Kenneth W. Howell, my colleague and friend, who encouraged and advised me during our numerous days on campus. Lastly, I would like to thank Steven E. Woodworth at Texas Christian University. His continual guidance and friendship are invaluable—truly a mentor in every sense of the word.

Without the help of the staff of the Sophienburg Museum and Archives in New Braunfels, Texas—Linda Dietert, Keva Boardman, and Beverly Wigley—I could not have begun to research my chapter. Their patience and knowledge helped me find resources that I did not know existed in our quaint German city. I owe my deepest gratitude to all our contributors. Their cooperation and dedication to this book made it a joy to work on—more importantly, it would not exist without them. Thank you all.

I cannot forget my family, who all supported me throughout this process. My parents, Marion "Buck" and Mary Grear, are the cornerstone of my life. From my humble beginnings on a farm in San Antonio, my parents instilled, by example, a strong work ethic and a steady moral compass. They supported me in all my endeavors, from 4-H and Boy Scouts to football and college. Mom and Dad never missed a stock show, campout, or a single game. Still today they proudly buy my books at the local bookstore and never leave without informing the clerk and everybody else in earshot that the book was written by their son. This collection is my way of exhibiting my pride in them. I would especially like to thank my beautiful wife, Edna, for the patience she displays after I continually say, "let me get this idea down first"; my stepdaughter, Haley, for assistance with the maps and laughs to break the monotony of researching and writing; London for sleeping next to my feet as I work; and KoKo for taking me on runs so I could have time to think. My family, which now includes a new member, Jackson David Grear, is the calm harbor when the storms of life arise. I am indebted to their love.

— *Charles David Grear*

TEXANS
and
WAR

INTRODUCTION

Alexander Mendoza and Charles David Grear

TEXAS IS FOREVER associated with the concept of war. From pre-Columbian Indian conflicts, its inception as a nation and later a state, to modern times, conflict has largely been present in the Lone Star. Battlefields are found throughout the state, from the Battle of Rattlesnake Springs in the trans-Pecos to the Battle of Sabine Pass on the border with Louisiana, and from the Battle of Palo Alto near Brownsville to the Battle of Adobe Walls in the Panhandle. The Battle of the Alamo, one of the most famous events in Texas history, continues to enthrall people across the globe through countless books, movies, and documentaries. Additionally, military terminology is often associated with the fight for San Antonio. For instance, references to the "Alamo" are often attributed to a place or event that will be a last stand or that demonstrate some element of defiance in the face of long odds. Even during World War II, the very first Special Forces unit in American history was known as the "Alamo Scouts." Historians and soldiers alike associate the Alamo to Thermopylae, the renowned battle between the Spartans and the Persians, with phrases such as "drawing the line in the sand." Images of martial Texans, beginning with the Texas Revolution, thus remain strong today, including the stereotype that every resident of the Lone Star State owns a gun.

Even at the turn of the twenty-first century, Texas has many notable military connections. Fort Hood, near Killeen, is the largest army post in the United States and home to the famous 1st Cavalry Division and 4th Infantry Division. Every airman in the US Air Force goes to basic training at Lackland Air Force Base in San Antonio. The American military-industrial complex has also had many homes in Texas, ranging from Boeing in San Antonio to Lockheed Martin in Fort Worth and General Dynamics in Garland.

Texas and Texans have also played significant roles in America's military history. Conflicts in the Lone Star State began with the American Indian tribes fighting for dominance and access to resources such as food, fuel, and water. By the early fifteenth century, Spanish explorers entered the region, sparking a war between the two groups. Additionally, quarrels escalated amid Indian nations to strengthen economic bonds created by new technologies brought by the Europeans. With the French vying for control in the late seventeenth century, conflicts and an escalation of the Spanish military presence followed. Tension remained between Spain and France until the eighteenth century, when the British expelled the latter from North America and created a new concern of Anglo expansion into Texas, particularly after the American Revolution. Texas was not the first Spanish territory Americans wanted, but immigration, both *de jure* and *de facto*, began during the early nineteenth century. This influx reached its peak when Mexico gained its independence from Spain and welcomed Anglos into the region to buffer the bulk of the country from Native American attacks and US filibustering expeditions. Accordingly, cultural and political differences sparked the Texas Revolution. In less than a year, Texas became an independent republic. Thus a nation was forged in war. Yet as historian Stephen L. Hardin has noted, Texans' martial spirit was not unique to those already there. The Americans that arrived amid the Revolution, for instance, "were no strangers to war: they were born to it."[1] These newcomers were descendants of the American Revolution and the War of 1812. And while they might have been far removed from the events of Valley Forge or New Orleans, they staked their own claims to martial glory at the Battle of San Jacinto.

Yet independence from Mexico did not end hostilities in Texas. Over the course of the Republic era, Mexico invaded Texas several times, spawning several retaliatory Texan campaigns, the most noted being the Santa Fe, Somervile, and Mier Expeditions. With the treasury coffers empty and expensive conflicts with Mexico and American Indians continuing, Texas joined the United States with hopes that this union would ease the burden of combat through annexation of the nascent nation. But statehood brought war with Mexico, not only over the indignation of a former state joining another country but also over a dispute regarding the new border between the neighboring countries; was it the Rio Grande (as the United States asserted) or the Nueces River (as Mexico claimed). Texans played a significant role in the Mexican-American War (1846–48) by fighting under Maj. Gen. Zachary Taylor in northern Mexico and protecting Maj. Gen. Winfield Scott's logistical lines in central Mexico. Many gained fame, if not notoriety, in the conflict, and the martial glory won during the Texas Revolution extended to the next generation.

Just over ten years later, Texas became embroiled in another war, this one between the states. Though never extensively occupied nor subjected to a major Union invasion, Lone Star men fought in every theater, from New Mexico to Virginia. The state's martial reputation remained intact—if not bolstered—by Texans' actions and active participation in the Battles of Gettysburg and Vicksburg and the war's other notable campaigns. With defeat, Texans became disgruntled with the New America, resorting to violence against carpetbaggers and freedmen in what historian George Rable has called "political terrorism," thus sparking a lesser-known war during Reconstruction.[2] Throughout this time also was the lingering conflict with the Indians. It was not until the latter half of the nineteenth century that these hostilities ceased, one of the last being with the Chiricahua Apaches led by Victorio. Thus the longest war in Texas history and the last conflict for the control of its vast territory finally concluded on the arid landscape of the trans-Pecos in 1880.

Subduing the American Indians also calmed the frontier, thus speeding it closer to modernity at the end of the Gilded Age. With imperialism becoming popular in the United States, a new war with Spain emerged over control of Cuba, the Philippines, and numerous other Pacific islands. Reflecting on the famous battle cry "Remember the Alamo," Americans instead called out "Remember the Maine" to inspire their martial spirit. Victory came quickly for US armed forces, many of the men training at Fort Sam Houston in San Antonio, including Roosevelt's famed Rough Riders. During the following Progressive Era, US efforts to extend a stronger presence in world affairs ulti- mately dragged the nation and Texas into World War I, during which the Zimmerman Telegram stirred up Mexico's resentment against its northern neighbors. The Great War further expanded Texas' military role with the establishment of several airbases in the state, the most significant, Kelly Air Force Base, in San Antonio. America's entry brought a clear victory for the Allies and thus peace in the "War to End All Wars." That moniker might have been a misnomer, for in 1941 war came to the nation once more. This time Texas was part of the national fabric, the state littered with military bases and an expanding home front effort. A Texas native, Adm. Chester W. Nimitz, led the Pacific fleet against Japanese-held territory in World War II while fellow Texan Audie Murphy carved a name for himself thanks to his heroic exploits on the battlefields in Europe. Thus the martial legacy of Texans endured.

After World War II the Cold War with the Soviet Union began. Amid the burgeoning American military-industrial complex, Texans answered the call for the two largest conflicts during this era. Men like Gen. Walton H. Walker, commander of the Eighth Army, helped pushed the North Koreans back to the Yalu River and held the Chinese Army at bay while UN forces "advanced in a different direction" until the signing of the armistice. Just over a decade later, a Texan in the White House aided South Vietnam in its war against North Vietnam. The United States eventually exited the grueling and unpopular fighting, leaving their southern allies vulnerable to northern invaders. The next two conflicts also had Texans declaring war against Middle Eastern countries. Pres. George H. W. Bush, a transplanted Texan from Maine, evicted the invading army of Iraq from Kuwait. Just a decade later his son, George W. Bush, urged Congress to declare war after the attacks on the World Trade Center and the Pentagon, against terrorist organizations like the Taliban in Afghanistan and Iraqi dictator Saddam Hussein, who was suspected of aiding them. To put the last three American wars into perspective, each conflict had a Texan as president.

The earliest histories of Texas military lore appeared shortly after the Revolution, highlighting the short war as a dramatic struggle for freedom and equality. Of these early works, a clearly Anglocentric tone is evident in this master narrative. Even the most recent historian of the Revolution concedes, "A chauvinistic tone has admittedly marred many earlier studies published north of the Rio Grande."[3] As such, the defenders of the Alamo and the other Texas revolutionaries were transformed from a group of armed land speculators and adventurers into brave, valiant soldiers who died on behalf of freedom and democracy.

Similar patterns followed the histories of subsequent conflicts that Texas was involved in during the Mexican-American War, the Civil War, and the Indian Wars. The early works that focused on the state's military experience were grounded in the narrative of good versus evil. In the case of the Civil War, the early histories framed the conflict in the context of defending Southern homes from Yankee aggression. And while slavery proved a prominent role in the origins of the war, the subject was erased from the historical framework in the postwar era. Early histories of Texas and the Civil War stemmed from the veterans themselves and focused on the state's role in the war's major campaigns in the eastern theater and the Trans-Mississippi.

In contrast, examinations of later wars have emphasized the Texas spirit of individualism and martial bravery to mark the accomplishments of the state's residents. Richard Huff's *A River Swift and Deadly: The 36th "Texas" Infantry Division at the Rapido River* (1989) and Fred L. Walker's *From Texas to Rome: A General's Journal* (1969) accordingly emphasize the bravery and heroism of the Texas-based infantry division that saw service in the world wars. This notion that Texas could produce heroes worthy of the national stage was exemplified by the exploits of Kingston native Audie Murphy, the most decorated soldier in World War II, who was awarded the Medal of Honor for exceptional valor near Holtzwhir, France, where he was credited with killing or wounding approximately fifty Germans. Murphy's later success in scores of Hollywood films—particularly Westerns—only served to solidify the Lone Star State's place in the national fabric.[4]

Yet as histories of the Texas and Texans at war reached their zenith in the latter decades of the twentieth century, the discipline went through dramatic changes. The developments in academia and scholarship revitalized and changed the focus of traditional studies to a broader, more inclusive approach. Historian Peter Karsten noted these changes in his essay "The 'New' American Military History: A Map of the Territory, Explored and Unexplored." Karsten noted that the emphasis on war's effect on society proved to be a new marker in the study of America's military past. His arguments were echoed in Edward M. Coffman's "The Course of Military History in the United States since World War II." Coffman traces the more comprehensive works that university presses have published and the changes to leading scholarly journals as evidence of the changing scope of the field.[5]

Texas military historians have taken heed to the new dimensions of US military history. In *The Texas Military Experience: From the Texas Revolution through World War II* (1995), Joseph G. Dawson's collection of essays exemplifies the changing scholarship of the wars involving Texas and Texans. It provides students and scholars of the Lone Star State and its wars a rich variety of topics, ranging from a reinterpretation of race and the Texas Revolution to the Texas military experience in popular culture. In essence, *The Texas Military Experience* is a major contribution to the study of the state's military past.[6]

As significant as Dawson's study remains, his work leaves room for further exploration. This anthology, for instance, brings together a collection of noted scholars of Texas military history along with burgeoning historians who are contributing to the field. Their research provides a new understanding of the role and reactions of Texas and Texans to military conflicts. A strength of this work is its scope. Contributors to the anthology provide new perspectives on the military experience of Texas that historians have generally overlooked or never explored, ranging from new aspects of individual conflicts to social, cultural, and public history from the earliest quarrels to the modern era. Equally important, attention is also given to the ethnic and gender perspectives of these conflicts. The studies herein present important facets of Texas history that can help us understand how wars affected Texans and how the Lone Star State affected the history of the United States.

The first half of this book explores broad topics ranging from the roles of ethnic and gender groups to concepts such as the quest for "renown." Exploring the military history of all the Indian nations in Texas is an arduous task. In the first chapter, Thomas Britton provides the perspective of the Lipan Apaches of these Indian wars. Archeological records suggest that Indian warfare existed well before the introduction of Europeans to the Americas. After the arrival of European explorers in the New World, conflict in Texas escalated as Spaniards viewed the Lipans as the greatest threat to their settlement and development of their northern frontier. These Indians proved to be a similar risk to the interests of nineteenth-century Mexico, Texas, and the United States. During the Spanish colonial period, government officials attempted to dissolve the Lipans as a tribal unit, an effort that continued well into the establishment of the Republic of Texas in 1836. The Lipans, like some of the Indian peoples, seized upon changing circumstances to bolster their own self-sufficiency and expansion of tribal domains. Accordingly, from their homeland in South Texas, migrant hunter-gatherer bands pushed to maintain their social and cultural traditions amid numerous Indian and non-Indian enemies. During the US period, Lipans continued their struggle for survival, fighting against expanded frontier-army forces and against Indian enemies who made alliance with the Americans as a means of subduing or gaining protection from their traditional enemies. While the Lipans continued to pose a challenge to frontier settlement, Texas officials accused the federal government of failing to fulfill its constitutional guarantee to protect the state from the Indian threat. Following the Civil War, Lipans could no longer resist and fled south of the Rio Grande. Forced removal from their traditional homelands diminished their ability to defend themselves, and attaching themselves to the Mescalero Apaches and the Tonkawas, the Lipans wavered on the brink of extinction by 1884. Britten's chapter thus provides a fascinating window for viewing the region's Indian wars since the Lipans faced off against practically every Indian and non-Indian group that crossed their path.

In the following chapter, Alexander Mendoza broadly examines the role of Tejanos in the various wars and conflicts of Texas and the United States. He looks at the motivations of nineteenth-century Texans of Mexican descent to participate in the Revolution of 1835–36 and the subsequent Civil War for both the Union and the Confederacy. During the Revolution, Tejanos—like the Anglo-American settlers—chafed at the growing political and economic restrictions imposed upon them by Pres. Antonio Lopez de Santa Anna. Accordingly, Hispanic Texans who cast their lot with the Texian Army did so out of longstanding grievances tied to political and economic concerns. Following the Revolution, many Tejanos witnessed the eclipse of their political hegemony as incoming settlers ultimately limited their power. By the time of the Civil War, the nearly 4,000 Texans of Mexican descent joined the Union and Confederate armies for similar reasons: defense of their homes, escape from peonage, and money. Thus this chapter explores how Tejanos altered their framework of patriotism at the turn of the twentieth century and beyond to enlist in the various foreign conflicts of the United States and how their participation affected their lives. While traditional reasons continued to be prevalent, additional factors clouded the landscape of why they volunteered to fight. Foremost among these new reasons was the essence of patriotism. Texans of Mexican heritage, long accustomed to their second-class status as "inferior" individuals, sought to prove their worth and earn their compatriots' respect. The military experience of Tejanos during the First World War, for instance, served as a catalyst for Mexican American civil rights organizations that emphasized the US citizenship and patriotism of these veterans. By the Cold War, Mexican Texans were further exposed to the desegregation of the military and to the idea that they had been excluded from the Fourteenth Amendment's equal-protection clause. Thus by the latter part of the century, Tejanos joined various organizations in championing and recognizing their contributions to the American war effort. As such, many continue to try to commemorate their accomplishments and contributions to the various American wars in which they have participated.

In chapter 3 Melanie Kirkland explores the role of women in Texas during times of conflict. Kirkland focuses on the collective actions and activities of Texas women as well as the contributions of individuals in war. She moves away from the traditional interpretations that emphasize the stalwart defender of home and hearth in the absence of men to demonstrate that women in the Lone Star State were active participants in each conflict, from the Texas Revolution to the wars in the Middle East. Women donated currency and supplies, sewed clothing for men in their spare time, and filled the labor shortages caused by war by working on farms and providing sweat and sacrifice during the state's nineteenth-century wars. Kirkland notes that even though primary sources are limited, the contributions of Texas women to the various conflicts of the 1800s certainly helped these efforts. During World War I, she notes, women enthusiastically volunteered to aid their state and nation during war, despite being rejected in any capacity other than nursing. Yet these Texans also served near the front lines, driving ambulances and working as yeomen in the US Marine Corps, the first women to earn full military status in American history. By the Second World War, they not only provided support on the home front but also joined the military establishment beyond nursing for the army and navy. These gains, Kirkland notes, continued into the twenty-first century, for women now comprise a larger number of the state's military recruits. She concludes that modern Texas women have thus found a way to continue to defend their homeland through military education, military service, and moral support.

Subsequently, Alwyn Barr examines in chapter 4 another neglected facet of Texas military history, the participation of African Americans in the conflicts of the Lone Star

State and United States, and the influence of those wars on the status of black Texans. Free blacks and African American slaves found themselves facing different potential consequences in the Texas Revolution. Thus free African Americans responded in ways that protected their existing freedom, while slaves sought escape from bondage amid the conflict. Similar circumstances and choices existed for African Texans in the Civil War, although Confederates ironically employed slave labor on a larger scale to aid their cause. Beginning in the Reconstruction era, black men had their first opportunity to serve in the state militia, a forerunner of the National Guard. During this late-nineteenth-century period, black soldiers in the US Army served on the West Texas frontier and the border with Mexico. Despite their service in protecting other citizens, these men faced various forms of discrimination in many towns, which might also produce tension and conflict. Early twentieth-century wars raised hopes among African Texans that military service would open the way to more-equal treatment in American society. In World Wars I and II, black Texans achieved limited advances in the military but continued to face segregation until the Korean and Vietnam Wars. Social tensions that resulted from the protests to gain civil rights and reduce poverty in the 1960s carried over to some degree into the military. By comparison with earlier periods, however, progress toward equality and inclusion did occur in Texas and in the national military services during the late twentieth century.

Nineteenth-century American men considered courage, with its strong overtones of manhood and masculinity, essential to their personal and public identity. Men were expected to be brave and aggressive in their daily activities. Whether it was facing the danger of death in battle or proving one's worth through a heroic deed under the veil of danger, a man's reputation and character were clearly defined by his actions and exploits. Jimmy L. Bryan Jr. examines the lives of John S. Brooks, Walter P. Lane, and Samuel H. Walker and maintains that these patriot-warriors were adventurers who incorporated the concepts of duty and renown with violence to serve in the vanguard of expansion. They traveled to confront fear, not to run away from it, and believed that they could shape their world. While economic, political, and diplomatic motives could drive the nation westward during the 1800s, so did the needs and desires of such individuals seeking adventure and hoping to prove their courage.

Charles David Grear concludes the first half of the book by exploring the actions and reactions of German Texans. War stresses a populous, especially one that holds a conflicting view such as the German community of New Braunfels. No two wars tested the patriotism and resolve of the town more than the Civil War and World War I. During the Civil War, Confederates distrusted German communities because of their unionist beliefs and disinclination to the Southern cause. Decades later, as the drums of World War I began to beat, these communities once again gained the attention and ire of their neighboring Texans because of their continued connection to Germany and its customs. Attachments to their culture, their country of origin, and their current residence in the Lone Star State created a paradox: do German Texans stand up for what they believe in or participate to save face with their neighbors and preserve their prosperity? Using New Braunfels as a case study, Grear contests that in both conflicts the citizens initially did not want to participate because of their political and cultural beliefs. Despite their reluctance, the German community severed, if only temporarily, their attachments to culture and ancestral homeland to boisterously participate in a conflict in order to further solidify their attachment to their current state and nation.

The second half of the book provides a more chronological view of the military history of Texas. Instead of examining large groups and concepts in the state, these chapters explore specific conflicts, ranging from the French and Indian War (1754–63) to the modern War on Terror, with an emphasis on the lesser known wars involving Texans. Accordingly, the popular and commonly studied Texas Revolution, Civil War, and Indian battles are not addressed.

In his chapter Francis X. Galán charts a new military topic in Texas' Spanish past. In broader military histories no conflict loomed larger in North America prior to the Revolution than the French and Indian War. Sir Winston Churchill proclaimed it the first "world war" because it was fought on four continents and on several oceans. It also held great significance for Euro-Indian relations in Spanish Texas. The Louisiana-Texas borderlands became the first link to British interests upon New Spain, for the region stood at the end of the Camino Real from Mexico City and included many byways and Indian trails to the Gulf of Mexico. In this area the smuggling of captives, guns, and tobacco spiked among the Spaniards from Los Adaes in eastern Texas, the French from Natchitoches in northwestern Louisiana, and the numerically superior Caddo Indians from the four corners of modern Arkansas, Louisiana, Texas, and Oklahoma. The American Revolution ended British overland access to New Spain from the Louisiana-Texas borderlands and approaches from all along the northern Gulf of Mexico. Comanche aggression against Spanish Texas subsided, meanwhile, through the "trade, treaties, and toleration" policy Spain adopted from its French Bourbon cousins in Louisiana. Following the French and Indian War was a relatively brief "cold war" period in Texas before political, commercial, and cultural boundaries were once again challenged in the aftermath of the Louisiana Purchase and the revolutions of the early nineteenth century.

Kendall Milton examines a better known but still often overlooked war in chapter 8. The Mexican-American War (1846–48) suffers from serious neglect from scholars and public perception, Milton argues, due to its place in Texas (if not US) historiography, being buttressed by the Texas Revolution and the Civil War. Despite serving as a pivotal event in Texas history, there are few memorials to the war in the state. This lack of attention, Milton argues, is due in part to the expansionist legacy and the aggressive policies of the US government. Providing a broad historiographical overview of the major trends of the war, she highlights some of the key problems that have lingered in Texas since the Treaty of Guadalupe ended the conflict in February 1848, including equality for Mexican Americans, land claims, and the issue of further immigration. Yet the legacy for Mexican Americans is not Milton's sole focus. Rather, the author uses the war as a platform to discuss the debate over public history and what Texans could do to improve their efforts toward collective memory.

Introducing a new concept in Texas military history is Kenneth W. Howell's interpretation of the Reconstruction Era in chapter 9. He moves beyond the traditional views of the Civil War (1861–65) and Reconstruction periods (1865–77) as two separate events in US history. Instead, following in the footsteps of historians like George Rable, Leena Keith, and James Keith Hogue, who have examined the violence of the postwar era, Howell maintains that the Civil War and Reconstruction periods should be viewed as a continuous conflict between the North and the South. A tenet of his argument is the southern resistance to the end of slavery and the implementation of legislation designed to protect and advance the rights of African Americans. In Texas, as throughout the South, whites organized terrorist groups and initiated a guerrilla war against the Republican governments and their agents to resist the political and social change that was thrust upon them. Howell explores the concept of guerrilla warfare, logistics, and the challenges of civilian control by military forces in a state that still witnessed American Indian attacks on the frontier population. This "second phase of the Civil War," he argues, proved to be a bloody battleground as white Texans attempted to restrict the newly liberated slaves and to spoil the efforts of the Republican Party in reconstructing the South.

At the end of the nineteenth century, Texans found themselves embroiled in the martial spirit of the Spanish-American War. James McCaffrey examines the role of the Texans who volunteered to take part in the conflict as members of the 1st US Volunteer Infantry Regiment. The unit was also known as the 1st Immune Regiment because authorities believed that it was necessary to recruit men who had already been exposed to tropical diseases, particularly yellow fever. Thus, troops who were to be included in any occupation force in Cuba would have built up immunities to these diseases and be free from the dangers of further illness. As such, on May 11, 1898, Congress authorized the raising of ten regiments of such men. McCaffrey examines these Texas "Immunes" and their motivations to take part in this war. Under the command of Col. Charles S. Riché, these Texans, like many other volunteers, readied themselves for a battlefield they never saw. Instead, as McCaffrey outlines, these men faced other struggles at the end of the 1800s. Yet their experience reveals a great deal about Texans and their martial spirit since ex-Confederates and local political leaders encouraged their enlistment and organized companies to fight in Cuba.

The centennial of World War I has brought new attention to that conflict. José Ramírez provides a innovative interpretation by bringing the war to the Texas-Mexico border in chapter 11. Ramírez highlights the problems facing the Tejano community in the wake of America's entry into the First World War. Almost immediately, the state's Mexican American population became prime targets for government surveillance as doubts about their loyalty and nationalism proved prevalent. This stemmed from concerns over the possibility of German-Mexican collusion and a general anti-Mexican sentiment, which was further sparked by the lawless raids and subversive activities of Mexican revolutionaries and Tejanos on both sides of the Rio Grande. Native Tejanos, frustrated with their deteriorating political and economic status, would lend their support to both banditry and separatist movements such as the Plan of San Diego Rebellion (1915), which called for an all-out war against the United States. These isolated cases of disloyalty served as the impetus for the government surveillance. Ramírez traces these wartime fears and demonstrates how they culminated with a general sense of hysteria that led to US intelligence forces not only conducting operations in Mexico but also keeping track of Mexicans and Mexican Americans on the home front.

In chapter 12 Kelly E. Crager follows the plight of Texan prisoners of war. In March 1942 nearly one thousand members of the 2nd Battalion, 131st Field Artillery Regiment, 36th ("Texas") Division, along with the sailors and marines who survived the sinking of the USS *Houston*, became prisoner of the Imperial Japanese Army on Java in the Dutch East Indies. Remarkably, 90 percent of them survived brutal conditions and torture to return to Texas, where they received a hero's welcome from Gov. Coke Stevenson, who declared October 29, 1945, as "Lost Battalion Day." Combing through a multitude of newspapers, archival sources, government records, and oral histories, Crager sets out to discover the rationale behind the high survival rate of these men compared to other prisoners of the Japanese. He maintains that a strong factor in explaining this positive variance was an underlying sense of camaraderie rooted in a common Texas heritage and identity that helped these servicemen bond closely and commit to care for one another. Thus when other POW communities broke down, these men proved resilient, despite the miserable conditions imposed by the Japanese. Crager analyzes key elements of the Texas military experience, including labor, morale, and unit cohesion.

In the subsequent chapter James Smallwood provides a new perspective of Lyndon B. Johnson's views of the Vietnam War. With regard to his domestic policies, Johnson was a reformer. He wanted to create a "Great Society" and fight a "War on Poverty." The Vietnam War and the lobbying of his closest advisors, both civilian and military, who urged on the conflict rather than his domestic policies ruined him. Originally, Johnson questioned the war in Vietnam and believed that the United States should withdraw, but advisors who claimed to know more about foreign policy than he swayed him. Their lies led him into expanding the war in hopes of triumph where there could be no victory. Eric Goldman, a historian who was an advisor to LBJ, entitled his book on the president, *The Tragedy of Lyndon Johnson*. The tragedy was Vietnam, and it ruined what might have been.

Concluding this anthology is Ronald Goodwin's quantitative analysis of black Texans enlisting in the US military before and after the terrorist attacks of September 11, 2001. Social historians examining the early years of the civil rights movement argue that service in the military contributed to the burgeoning black middle class of the 1950s and 1960s. Nonetheless, the social upheaval of the 1960s, the Vietnam War, and the end of the military draft challenged the black community's perceptions of military service in the post-Vietnam era. Nonetheless, the military has traditionally had a strong presence in Texas, and many blacks view military service as a positive alternative to college enrollment. With the end of segregation in Texas' colleges and universities, however, blacks became less and less dependent upon military service as a means of achieving middle-class status. Goodwin seeks to determine if the terror attacks on September 11, which serve as his benchmark, resulted in an increase or decrease in Texas' black enlistees and identifies the regions from which these enlistees came. He then compares this data to black enrollment in the state's four-year colleges and universities during the same period. Goodwin's findings illustrate the degree to which the black community currently views military service as opposed to educational attainment as a means to achieving middle-class status.

These essays display the wealth and breadth of the military history of Texas. Although historians have studied the state's and Texans' roles in war for well over a century, there is still a plethora of topics that deserve greater attention, among them Tejanos in World War II, the common soldier's interaction with foreign enemies, the perception of Texas warriors throughout the world, the role of religion among Texans, the controversial paramilitary groups in the state, and obscure conflicts involving Texas and its people. Only through continual research can the true extent of Texas' role in military conflicts be revealed. It is our hope that *Texans and War: New Interpretations of the State's Military History*, the largest collection of original research on Texas and Texans in war to date, will serve as a stimulus for future studies.

NOTES

1. Stephen L. Hardin, *Texian Iliad: A Military History of the Texas Revolution* (Austin: University of Texas Press, 1994), 5.

2. George Rable, *But There Was No Peace: The Role of Violence in Reconstruction* (Athens: University of Georgia Press, 2006), ix.

3. Hardin, *Texian Iliad*, xiii.

4. See, for example, the biographies of Murphy by Harold B. Simpson, *Audie Murphy, American Soldier* (Hillsboro, TX: Hill Junior College Press, 1975); and Don Graham, *No Name on the Bullet: A Biography of Audie Murphy* (New York: Viking Penguin, 1989).

5. Peter Karsten, "The 'New' American Military History: A Map of the Territory, Explored and Unexplored," *American Quarterly* 36 (1984): 389–418; Edward M. Coffman, "The Course of Military History in the United States since World War II," *Journal of American Military History* 61 (Oct. 1997): 773–74.

6. Joseph G. Dawson, ed., *The Texas Military Experience: From the Texas Revolution through World War II* (College Station: Texas A&M University Press, 1995).

PART I

Texans Fighting through Time

Thematic Topics

1

The Indian Wars of Texas

A LIPAN APACHE PERSPECTIVE

Thomas A. Britten

THE AMERICAN INDIAN wars of Texas began centuries before Francisco Coronado led his expedition of Spanish explorers, treasure seekers, and missionaries across the Texas Panhandle en route to Quivera. The archeological record suggests that Indian violence was common in the Southwest and Great Plains, and archeologists have recognized its occurrence in human skeletal remains dating back to A.D. 400. Anthropologist Clayton A. Robarchek writes that pre-contact warfare was a "regional cultural institution, a complex of values, ideas, and behaviors that persisted for at least two thousand years."[1] Scholars examining skeletal remains unearthed on the southern plains, and in the Texas Panhandle in particular, have determined that violence in the area was frequent during much of the fifteenth century. Disarticulated remains indicate that fifteenth-century combatants took trophy skulls, dismembered bodies, and burned the dwellings of their enemies. Although the specific causes of warfare remain unclear, scholars speculate that competition over valuable commodities such as bison hides and meat or over the use of the Alibates flint quarries (north of Amarillo) may have been precipitating factors.[2]

Following European contact and the subsequent introduction of guns, horses, and manufactured goods, Indian warfare in Texas intensified as native peoples jockeyed for advantage in the ever-changing political landscape. Some tribes sought new commercial opportunities and to gain access to high-status trade items like horses and firearms, while others desired to make alliances with the Europeans as a means of subduing (or gaining protection from) their traditional enemies. As time passed and the new imperial powers shifted their attention to and from Texas, some Indian peoples seized upon changing circumstances to bolster their pursuit of self-sufficiency, independence, and the expansion of their tribal domains. Others watched helplessly as their traditional economies, cultures, and homelands evaporated in the face of intense competition by powers both larger and stronger than they had ever encountered. That being the case, there was no monolithic "Indian perspective" on the various conflicts that raged across the region during the eighteenth and nineteenth centuries, but a collage of conflicting attitudes and interests. The experiences of the Lipan Apaches provide a useful window for viewing the Indian wars of Texas since they faced off against practically every Indian and non-Indian group that crossed their path. A fiercely independent and remarkably adaptable people, the Lipans were the dominant tribe in Texas during the seventeenth century. By the end of the eighteenth century, however, the consequences of frequent warfare, epidemic disease, and near-constant displacement led to demographic collapse. And when the Indian wars of Texas finally ended in the 1880s, the Lipans wavered on the brink of extinction.

The factors that compelled the Lipan Apaches to engage in warfare were typical of most other Indian peoples inhabiting Texas in the three centuries following European contact. The Lipans, for example, possessed a rich oral tradition that featured cultural hero Killer-of-Enemies (or Enemy Slayer). They looked to Killer-of-Enemies as the originator of raiding for horses, making weapons, scalping, and of warfare itself. To follow his example was a lifelong goal of all Lipan men.[3] A host of more-mundane causes and motivations also led Texas Indians to make war. In general, these fall into two broad categories: Those attributed to various material and socio-cultural concerns—the de facto causes of war, and those credited to the various psychological needs or motivations of individual warriors. The former group included competition over critical resources (bison herds, fertile soils, water, wood, pasturage, and holy places), defense of homeland or territory, and a variety of economic issues such as gaining access to or control over commerce, high-status trade items (European weaponry and manufactured goods), and other valuable commodities such as horses and enemy captives. The psychological motivations that help explain why individuals were willing to engage in warfare include their desire for status, prestige, respect, and social mobility. Warfare also provided opportunities for men to fulfill familial obligations to exact revenge on enemies who had killed or captured relatives.[4]

During the eighteenth and early nineteenth centuries, control over the bison lands of northern and central Texas provided the crucial impetus for a ferocious war that pitted the Comanches and various Wichita tribes (whom the Spaniards called *Norteños,* or Nations of the North) against the Lipan Apaches. The Comanches, who entered Texas in the early 1700s, soon carved out an empire on the southern plains that rivaled that of Spain or France. Bison hides and meat were crucial trade

Lipan Apache warrior on horseback. Courtesy Prints and Photographs Division, Library of Congress, Washington, DC (LC-USZC4-5368).

commodities that these Indians traded with Pueblos and Spaniards in New Mexico for corn, blankets, and a host of highly desired articles such as horses, guns, hatchets, and metal blades. In 1747 the Comanches and Wichitas forged an alliance in an effort to expand their commercial activities. The Comanches found the Wichita villages a convenient market for trade and probably expected their new allies to help them connect with French traders in Louisiana. The Wichitas, meanwhile, traded their surplus agricultural produce to the Comanches. Various Norteño tribes such as the Taovayas and Iscanis became middlemen in the Comanche-French exchange network, trading the Comanches' hides, horses, and captives to the French for weapons, gunpowder, and other coveted items. Like the Tonkawas and Caddoan-speaking tribes of the Hasinai Confederacy, the Wichitas and Comanches viewed the Lipans as an attractive source of horses and slaves.[5]

Taking captives served as a significant precipitant for violence and warfare. Both Indians and Europeans considered these individuals as spoils of war and bartered them as they would any other commodity. During the seventeenth and early eighteenth centuries, Apache, Wichita, and Comanche raiders preyed on one another to acquire captives that they could sell or barter at trade fairs for horses and weapons. Lipans also took captives (usually women and children) to exchange at trade fairs, to hold for ransom, or to adopt into their bands to bolster declining populations. But over time this trade worked to the Lipans' disadvantage. The Comanches' patrilineal kinship system and patrilocal residence permitted them to assimilate outsiders into a particular band with comparative ease. The Lipans, in contrast, were a matrilineal people with matrilocal residence, which made it more difficult for their men to take captive women as wives as the latter had neither relatives nor kinship connections so vital to that society.[6]

Weapons

As is the case with any organized group of people that has made the decision to go to war, careful preparation is essential for success. Among the first orders of business is the preparation of weapons. The most important weapon to the Lipan Apaches, as well as most other plains and Southwest tribes, was the bow and arrow. Lipan bows measured over five feet long since, with one end of the weapon resting on the ground, the other reached as high as its owner's head. To ensure discharged arrows flew straight and with accuracy, warriors fluted them with feathers from eagles, hawks, turkeys, and crows. They transported their arrows in cylindrical quivers constructed from the skins of deer, mountain lions, wildcats, or peccaries, which warriors carried at their side, under their arm, or slung across their back. Texas Ranger Noah Smithwick recollected that the Lipans "could discharge a dozen arrows while a man was loading a gun," while Lipan captive Frank Buckelew maintained that a warrior "could present and string his bow, then shoot an arrow almost as quickly as we can shoot our modern rifles today."[7]

Additional Lipan weapons included the lance, which may have been ten feet long and required two hands to throw. The lance shaft was usually eight to nine feet in length and tipped with a two-foot-long straight blade or saber made of iron or steel. Warriors also used pikes, spears, war clubs, slings, hatchets, knives, and even sticks for close-order fighting. Lipans carried circular shields with a convex front, possessing a diameter of approximately two to three feet, constructed from layers of dried bison or cowhide stretched around a wooden frame. They cut two slits into

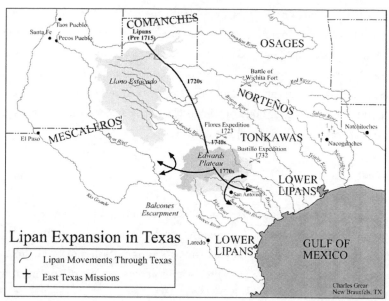

Lipan Territory. Courtesy Thomas A. Britten.

either side through which they inserted buckskin straps so that the warrior could wear it on his forearm, thereby shielding his body from arrows and bullets. During the seventeenth and early eighteenth centuries, warriors wore protective leather "armor" constructed of layers of bison hide that they had glued or sewn together, and they fitted their horses in similar gear, although they abandoned these accessories with the introduction of firearms.[8]

Lipan Apaches probably acquired guns at some point in the eighteenth century. Although early firearms were not always dependable, many Indians preferred them to bows and arrows. The loud explosion and smoke inspired fear and awe on the part of enemies, giving gun owners a psychological advantage. American Indians also understood that bullets traveled faster than arrows, were more lethal, and were less likely to be deflected by brush.[9]

The members of Lipan raiding and war expeditions observed a set of rituals that they believed would protect them from danger and confer important advantages over their enemies. Before conducting a raid, for example, warriors performed rituals directed at enhancing successful concealment and thwarting pursuit. Ritual preparations for war, however, were more elaborate. On the eve of battle, Lipan warriors may have burned sage to ward off evil spirits, bathed themselves with yucca suds to achieve purification, fasted, and consulted various amulets or fetishes, summoning their power and influence for success and bravery in combat. They also participated in dances of incitement to recite the enemies' misdeeds, to enlist the support of Killer-of-Enemies, and to prepare warriors emotionally for inevitable hardships and perhaps injury or death. Warriors consulted shamans to conduct ceremonies and lead prayers, puffing smoke or blowing pollen to the four cardinal directions. Shamans might also apply sacred paints of red ochre, yellow ochre, and white to the head, face, or body of warriors, while special clothing was prepared to ensure that combatants returned home safely.[10]

Tactics

Most Lipan engagements were small-scale episodes involving war parties of twenty or fewer participants. Campaigns were generally short in duration, given the fact that the Lipans were unable (due to ammunition and food shortages or because their families were nearby) to sustain active combat or continual maneuvering for any appreciable length of time. Warfare was also seasonal as warriors had to transition to hunting during annual bison harvests, although the congregation of several bands at this time provided opportunities for conducting larger campaigns. All the same, large war parties were uncommon—raids, ambushes, and skirmishes were the norm. Raiding operations conducted for horses, captives, or supplies were relatively commonplace occurrences that satisfied the varied cultural, social, and psychological needs of warriors. That is not to imply that these engagements were little more than "stylized sporting events" or that deadly fighting did not take place. More often than not, these small-scale operations provided the catalyst for larger campaigns.[11]

The most frequent and effective Lipan tactic was the raid, often followed up with an ambush of the pursuers. If the opposing force was small and the raiders enjoyed a numerical advantage, a favorite battle formation was to advance in a crescent-shaped line with ends thrown forward to outflank and surround the enemy as rapidly as possible. In September 1731, for example, a small group of Lipans stole sixty horses from the presidial herd at San Antonio. The Spanish commander sent five men in immediate pursuit and shortly thereafter led a second group of soldiers out in support. As the Spaniards rode into battle, an estimated five hundred Indians came out from their hiding places and encircled the soldiers, who hastily dismounted to make a stand at the foot of a tree. The warriors pressed the attack, but then much to the Spaniards' astonishment, they began to flee, perhaps worried that additional reinforcement might come from the presidio or possibly content with keeping the horses they had stolen. At any rate, this clever luring of a small group of Spanish troops into ambush probably accomplished all that the Indians had hoped for, leaving fifteen enemy casualties.[12]

The observations of Col. Don Antonio Cordero provide crucial firsthand insight into the detailed preparations required to conduct a raid. According to Cordero, once a band of Lipans had decided to launch an offensive expedition and selected leaders, the warriors found shelter for their families and then set out in small groups toward the target. The leader placed one group at a good ambush site and sent the others ahead to lure away the enemy by stealing some cattle or horses. Communicating with one another via smoke signals, waving buckskin, or through animal calls, the raiders coordinated their actions. At the given moment, warriors seized the herd, the victims gave pursuit and were lured into the ambush site, where the Lipans launched their surprise attack. The Indians then withdrew, leaving in place a rear guard with fast mounts. If they became aware that their enemy was in pursuit, they waited in a pass and committed a second ambush, repeating this trick as often as their good luck and the inexperience or foolishness of their opponents made it possible.[13] Thus, Lipan raids and ambushes required extensive preplanning, knowledge of the terrain, timing, communication, and flexible leadership that was willing to make quick decisions as circumstances merited.

The Spanish Period

During the eighteenth century, the Spaniards launched several campaigns into Lipan Apache territory in hopes of putting a stop to relentless raiding and attacks. In the early 1720s, warriors from the various Lipan bands residing in south central Texas conducted frequent raids on the presidial horse herds of San Antonio Béxar. One stormy night in August 1723, one raiding party made a daring foray on the herd. Despite the fact that the horses were under a ten-man guard and enclosed in a locked corral, the Indians managed to break in and run off eighty animals. In response Capt. Nicolás Flores led a force of soldiers and mission Indians to follow the Lipans' trail. On September 24, over a month after leaving their presidio, they came on an Apache ranchería of two hundred people near present-day Brownwood, Texas. According to Spanish reports, a six-hour battle ensued in which soldiers killed thirty-four Indians and captured twenty women and children. The Spaniards "recovered" about 120 horses together with a large quantity of plunder, suffering only three light casualties (including the captain, who lost a tooth).[14]

An important reason why Spaniards seized Lipan captives was to gain useful intelligence and to use them to encourage their families and leaders to make peace. Following his return to San Antonio, Captain Flores dispatched a captive woman to her own people astride a horse loaded with gifts to entice the Indians to discuss peace and gain the release of their relatives held in San Antonio. In late December a party of thirty Lipans arrived in San Antonio to begin negotiations, but talks broke down amid rumors that they were not at all interested in peace but only in securing the release of the captives.[15]

A decade later Texas governor Antonio de Bustillo conducted a similar campaign against Lipan raiders. In December 1732, Spanish scouts located hostile encampments on the banks of the San Saba River, with an estimated four hundred tipis and seven hundred warriors. The ensuing battle lasted five hours. The well-disciplined Indians, mounted and wearing leather breastplates, fought tenaciously, timing their attacks to coincide with the interval after the Spaniards had discharged their firearms. Perhaps fearing that the Spaniards would desecrate the bodies of fallen warriors, the Indians threw their dead into the San Saba. Fighting at close quarters against superior firepower, the Apaches slowly retreated, leaving behind an estimated two hundred dead kinsmen and thirty women and children captives. The Spaniards seized seven hundred horses and one hundred mule-loads of hides and other plunder. Remarkably, the attackers suffered only seven casualties and one death. Bustillo's party marched back to San Antonio amid persistent Indian sniping, arriving home a few days before Christmas.[16]

Far from curbing attacks in south central Texas, the Bustillo campaign ignited a decade-long period of retaliatory strikes, murders, kidnappings, and theft. Having pierced the Apache heartland, the Spaniards struck a nerve that must have resonated strongly among Lipans who had been feverishly fending off Comanche and Norteño attacks along their northern and eastern peripheries. The slaughter of two hundred warriors (albeit a probable Spanish exaggeration) must have been as shocking as it was demoralizing to the Lipans, prompting warriors to question what they had done—or not done—to offend the supernatural forces that controlled their lives.

In the 1750s the Spaniards adopted a different tactic in their dealings with the Lipans. After much debate, authorities approved the construction of a mission (Santa Cruz de San Sabá) and a presidio (San Luis de las Amarillas) on the San Saba River in the heart of Apache country. The apparent Lipan-Spanish alliance infuriated the Comanches and Norteños, and in the early morning hours of March 16, 1758, a large force of mounted, well-armed Norteños, Comanches, and perhaps smaller numbers of Bidais, Tonkawas, and warriors from other East Texas tribes (estimated at more than two thousand total) gained entrance into the mission stockade and began pillaging the various buildings. The attackers took what supplies they could carry off, killed the livestock, and then set fire to the buildings. Final casualty reports differ but place the total number of Spaniards killed at between eight and twelve, with four people wounded. The number of Indian attackers reported killed was seventeen.[17]

In retaliation, a large Spanish and Indian force under the command of Col. Diego Ortiz Parrilla set out from San Antonio in late September 1759. On October 2 they encountered a Yojuane (a Tonkawan tribe) village on the north side of the Brazos River and attacked, killing fifty-five warriors and taking 149 captives.[18] The captives stated that they knew the location of a Norteño encampment (perhaps containing Taovayas and Iscani Wichitas), and Parrilla selected a couple of them to serve as guides. On October 7 the Yojuanes alerted the colonel that they were very close to the enemy. After traveling about fifteen miles farther, the Spaniards came under attack by a group of sixty or seventy warriors, followed closely by a second wave of attackers. Parrilla quickly formed his men in a line, charged the Indians, and killed three of the enemy before the warriors disappeared into the woods. The colonel's men gave pursuit, rushing into the trees before their quarry could alert reinforcements. When the Spaniards emerged on the far side of the woods, however, they were astonished to discover on the north bank of the Red River a large fortification, which included several oval-shaped huts and a wooden stockade complete with firing ports, all surrounded by a moat.[19] The large coalition of Norteño and Comanche warriors inside, confident in the impregnability of their position, laughed and taunted the Spaniards to attack. During the ensuing Battle of Wichita Fort, Parrilla ordered several frontal charges but was unable to gain entry into the palisade. Spanish cannon fire proved equally ineffective, the balls bouncing harmlessly off the sturdy timber walls. As night closed in on the combatants, Parrilla abandoned any hope of taking the fort and ordered a retreat. At a hastily convened council that night, the Spaniards took stock of their situation. The troops were completely discouraged, having suffered losses of nineteen dead, fourteen wounded, and nineteen missing, a total of fifty-two men. In addition, they had abandoned their two cannons to the enemy and had lost a significant number of horses and mules. Convincing themselves nonetheless that a "glorious military exploit had already been attained" and Spanish honor restored, Parrilla and his officers decided to return to San Antonio.[20]

Emigrant Tribes and the Texas Period

Complicating the relationship between Spaniards and the indigenous peoples of Texas was the arrival of increasing numbers of "emigrant tribes" from the southeastern United States—peoples who had been either pushed south by hostile northern tribes or forced west by the expanding American frontier. In its ongoing efforts to both populate and protect its northern frontier, the Spanish government had extended invitations to various tribes to settle in northeastern Texas. During the first decade of the nineteenth century, Gov. Antonio Cordero had encouraged Kickapoos, Shawnees, Delawares, Choctaws, Chickasaws, Coushattas, and Cherokees to reside in his province, and by 1820 there were approximately 2,000 "immigrant Indians" residing there. Over the course of the next decade, that number swelled to nearly 10,000 persons.[21]

These Indian newcomers, of course, did not settle on vacant lands but on territory claimed by indigenous peoples, who viewed them as invaders, not much different from the Americans who were crossing the Sabine River from Louisiana. By the early 1820s, prominent Caddo chief Dehahuit, recognizing that his people were incapable of restraining both Indian and non-Indian invaders from settling on Caddo lands, attempted without success to establish a pan-Indian confederacy of native and immigrant tribes to withstand US encroachment. Instead of allying with the Caddos, however, bands of Osages, Choctaws, and other newcomers raided their villages. New Cherokee settlements in northeastern Texas, meanwhile, sparked both Caddo and Wichita resentment, and before long a vicious cycle of horse thefts and revenge killings entangled the Caddos, Wichitas, and Cherokees, all teetering on the edge of all-out war.[22]

By virtually all accounts, the scattered bands of Lipan Apaches who periodically hunted and traded in East Texas enjoyed a comparatively good relationship with the newly arrived Texans of the Austin colony. They mingled peacefully with the American settlers on the lower Brazos River, pleased to have found an indiscriminating trade partner with whom to conduct business—and perhaps obtain assistance against the Comanches. Texan militiamen aided the Lipans and Tonkawas in scrapes with Tawakonis and Kichais, while Lipans and Tonkawas reciprocated by helping the Texans ward off attacks from Comanches, Tawakonis, and Wacos.[23]

Details about the activities of the Lipans during the period immediately preceding the Texas Revolution are sparse. Lipan raiders were reportedly active along the lower Rio Grande frontier, and together with the Tonkawas jointly plundered settlements between the Brazos and Colorado Rivers. Some served as auxiliaries of the Mexican Army. In February 1832 as many as fifty Lipan and Tonkawa scouts and trackers rode alongside Mexican troops from Tamaulipas and Nuevo León, militiamen from Béxar and Monclova, and Austin's colonists in an ambitious campaign to drive out the Comanches from Texas altogether. Led by Capt. Manuel Rudecindo Barragán of the presidio Rio Grande, the campaign netted meager results in several small skirmishes with the Comanches.[24]

The Lipan Apaches made peace with the Republic of Texas in January 1838 and sided with the Texans in several of their military campaigns against tribes intent on preserving their own land and way of life. Verne Ray asserts that the Lipans' close friendship with Sam Houston played an important role in their decision, as did the opportunities that campaigns offered to take booty and weaken various tribal foes. Having spent decades fighting the Spaniards, Comanches, and Norteños, the Lipans also may have determined that allying with the Texans was simply the best mode of protecting their interests and ensuring that they preserved their access to firearms, powder, ammunition, and other crucial supplies.[25]

For a variety of reasons, therefore, the Lipans served as scouts and auxiliaries for Texas frontier troops. In late December 1839, for example, Gen. Edward Burleson employed Lipan and Tonkawa scouts in a successful campaign against Cherokee holdouts at the Battle of Pecan Bayou. The Texans dispersed the Cherokees, seized over twenty captives, and killed Chief Bowl's son John and another chief known as The Egg.[26] The Lipans also served in several expeditions against the Comanches. Angry that their treaty with Texas did not delineate a clear boundary line between their lands and those claimed by the republic, the Comanches continued to harass the settlements, stealing livestock, taking captives, and killing residents. General Burleson responded by calling out the militia to conduct raids on the Comanches in the fall of 1838.[27] In the winter of 1839, Capt. John H. Moore led three companies of volunteers and a contingent of Lipans under Chief Cuelgas de Castro on a campaign of chastisement against Comanches under the leadership of Chief Maguara (Muk-wah-ruh). On February 11, Lipan scouts reported the presence of a large Comanche encampment near Spring Creek in present-day Archer County, and Moore called for a daylight attack the next morning.[28] The Texans tasked eight of Castro's warriors with stampeding the Comanches' horse herd while the remaining Lipans accompanied Moore's men on an assault of the encampment. In the wild fight that followed, the Texans killed some thirty to forty Comanches and wounded the same before reinforcements compelled Moore to retreat.[29] According to participant Noah Smithwick, one Comanche warrior laid on his back shooting arrows straight up so they would come down on the Texans. A young warrior named Flacco—the son of Chief Flacco—killed the archer with a lance and captured his shield. As the Comanches regrouped and received reinforcements, however, the Texans quickly found themselves on the defensive, and many of the attackers lost their mounts and had to walk home. Castro, meanwhile, rode away with over ninety horses and mules, perhaps assuaging his disappointment at not achieving total success over his hated enemies.[30]

In the aftermath of the infamous "Council House Fight," where Texas troops killed over thirty Comanches during a wild melee in March 1840, outraged Comanches led by Chief Buffalo Hump (Potsanaquahip) retaliated by raiding deep into Texas. In early August hundreds of warriors attacked southward along the Guadalupe River valley, focusing their wrath on the towns of Victoria and Linnville. In what became the largest of all southern Comanche raids, Buffalo Hump's men seized hundreds of horses, thousands of dollars' worth of supplies, and several captives. Warriors slaughtered cattle, plundered homes, and set fire to buildings, shooting at virtually anything that moved. After a week of such activities, and with their vengeance spent, the Comanches rode back north, leaving behind over twenty people dead.[31]

Following closely on the heels of the retreating Comanches was a hastily assembled army of Texas volunteers. On August 11 and 12, 1840, they engaged the Indians near Plum Creek, inflicting over eighty enemy casualties and forcing the Comanches to move north toward the Colorado River. Texas authorities organized a second campaign in October under the leadership of John H. Moore. The second Moore expedition consisted of approximately one hundred Texas volunteers and many of the same Lipans who had participated in the winter campaign of 1839 (including Castro and Flacco the Younger). After a long pursuit up the Colorado, Lipan scouts located the Comanche encampment at the river's Red Fork—about three hundred miles northwest of Austin. In a brief battle that took place on October 24, Moore's men routed the Comanches, killing 140 and capturing 34. The Texans burned everything in the camp, including tipis and food, and recovered as many as five hundred horses, pelts, as well as some of the remaining plunder from the Linnville raid, which they divided among themselves. Their remarkable success at the "Battle of the Comanche Village" (Moore's force suffered only two casualties) apparently stimulated a series of new campaigns directed against the Comanches later that spring, as Texas Ranger companies rode out in pursuit of glory and plunder.[32]

The US Period

The Treaty of Guadalupe Hidalgo ended the Mexican-American War in February 1848, but the return of peace did not translate into improved conditions for the Lipan Apaches. Two tragedies occurred in the months following the conclusion of the war that devastated the affected Lipan bands, but more significantly they ushered in a renewed era of conflict that would last for the duration of the nineteenth century. The first occurred after surveyors and settlers began pushing into the upper Guadalupe and Medina River country northwest of San Antonio—the region where Texas authorities had relocated the Lipans just two years earlier. The Indians responded by staging raids on the settlers' livestock herds, but in one instance they absconded with some animals owned by a Texas Ranger named William "Big Foot" Wallace. In the spring of 1848, Wallace assembled a posse of about thirty Rangers, set off in pursuit of the Lipans, and located their encampment on the headwaters of the Frio River northwest of San Antonio. After surrounding the ranchería, the heavily armed Texans attacked on horseback and, within a half hour, had killed over a dozen people. Wallace's men then began sizing up the plunder, which consisted of kegs of gunpowder, sacks of lead, blankets, robes, and some 170 horses. Wallace later reflected: "The Lipans never recovered from the fatal blow we gave them on this occasion. From having been, up to this time, a formidable tribe, able to send six or eight hundred warriors into the field, they rapidly dwindled away until now they scarcely number a hundred souls, men, women, and children, all told."[33]

While land speculators, settlers, and Texas Rangers were responsible for the first disaster that befell the Lipans in 1848, the second calamity came at the hands of the Comanches and the US Army. A Comanche war captain named Carnebonahit had been on his way to Mexico with a raiding party when a company of US soldiers attacked him and dispersed his men. Carnebonahit followed the soldiers and, catching them off guard, managed to steal seven of their horses. He rode northward with the horses until he came to the camp of the Lipan chief Chiquito. Chief Chiquito, whose name meant "Little One," was actually a tall, thin man who, according to one contemporary, had the appearance of one possessing "more than ordinary powers of endurance." The old chief eyed the branded horses with concern and rebuked Carnebonahit for leading the stolen animals to his encampment, thus focusing the suspicion of American authorities on his people. "I don't care," Carnebonahit responded indifferently. "You and your people have piloted the Americans to the Comanche camps." Shortly thereafter, Capt. William G. Crump and a company of soldiers, having tracked their stolen horses to Chiquito's encampment, attacked the Lipans and killed over twenty people. Chiquito later explained that he had seen the soldiers coming and had tried to stop them, but the Americans were too mad to listen. They went on to kill several innocent people and seize two hundred horses.[34]

Facing starvation, frequent and involuntary relocations, declining trade opportunities, and sporadic but deadly clashes with soldiers who were well armed (although not necessarily well trained or disciplined), the Lipan Apaches of the 1850s were in the most desperate position in their history—they were, in essence, teetering on the brink of extinction. That being said, their scattered, fragmentary bands that resided along the Rio Grande frontier during the second half of the nineteenth century maintained a disproportionately strong presence in South Texas, one that could not—or would not—be easily ignored. Between the years 1849 and 1881, for instance, the US Army participated in 219 "actions and skirmishes" against hostile Indians in Texas. The Lipans (who could field a total of perhaps 50 to 100 warriors) accounted for nearly 30 of them—about 13 percent of the total and second only to the far more numerous Comanches.[35]

Stories of Indian attacks, robberies, and murders along the Rio Grande frontier reached new heights in 1867 and 1868 as Texas officials struggled with post–Civil War demobilization, economic restructuring, and complying with the various Reconstruction policies emanating from Washington, DC. Providing substantial numbers of soldiers to patrol the southwest Texas frontier against small bands of marauding Indians, consequently, was not at the top of anyone's priority list. John H. Evans, a soldier who served along the Rio Grande border during the late 1860s, reported that a "portion of the frontier [between Eagle Pass and Laredo] was constantly overrun by bands of Lipanes and Kickapoos" who "pillaged and murdered indiscriminately" before stripping the area of its cattle and horses.[36]

Texas state officials, meanwhile, clamored that "something be done" about the Kickapoos and Lipans, going so far as to accuse the federal government of failing to make good its constitutional guarantee to protect the state from "invasion" and requesting that a commission be established to investigate the Indian problem. During the summer of 1872, therefore, Secretary of State Hamilton Fish sent a three-man commission to Texas to hear testimony and collect evidence about the border problems with Mexico. The commissioners concluded that much of the blame for escalating violence could be attributed to Mexico's chronic instability and powerlessness (or unwillingness) to enforce its laws and to suppress the lawless bands that operated from south of the Rio Grande.[37]

Meanwhile, top military officials huddled together at Fort Clark, plotting their own solution to the Indian problem. On April 11, 1873, Secretary of War William W. Belknap and Lt. Gen. Philip H. Sheridan met with Col. Ranald Slidell Mackenzie, a talented leader and experienced Indian fighter who had only recently arrived in South Texas with several companies of the 4th US Cavalry Regiment.[38] Although no written minutes of their meeting exist, most scholars believe that Belknap and Sheridan ordered Mackenzie to put a stop to the border raids that had been plaguing Texas for nearly two decades, but they left the timing and details to the colonel. Over the course of the next month, Mackenzie prepared for his secret mission, gathering intelligence about the various Indian encampments in northern Coahuila and training his troops for the task ahead. By mid-May, civilian scouts had discovered the exact whereabouts of Kickapoo, Lipan, and Mescalero encampments at Remolino, located northeast of the Burro Mountains about forty miles south of the border. Mackenzie's force of 360 men set out toward the Rio Grande on May 17 and crossed the river later that evening. Riding all night, the force drew up to the outskirts of Remolino on the morning of the eighteenth and, once in position, charged the grass lodges that composed the Kickapoo village. As the terrified Indians fled for their lives, the soldiers set fire to the settlement, "the fierce crackling of the flames," 1st Lt. Robert G. Carter later recalled, "mingled strangely with the carbines, rifles, cheers, and yells." In a matter of minutes, the "battle" was over, and the troopers rode on to the other villages. The occupants of the Lipan encampment, which was located less than a mile away, had taken flight at the first sound of shots, and the soldiers moved unopposed among their deserted dwellings to set them afire. In minutes the soldiers had destroyed all three villages (around 180 lodges). Mackenzie later reported nineteen Indians killed and forty women and children taken prisoner. Costilietos, the elderly chief of the Lipans, and his daughter Teresita were also among those captured, although most of the Lipans had managed to escape before the army could corner them. Mackenzie lost one man killed and two others wounded.[39]

Following up on his Remolino campaign, Colonel Mackenzie scoured the countryside in search of Indian raiders. In 1874, US soldiers in Texas traveled 19,000 miles in search-and-destroy missions, and a year later they rode an additional 40,000 miles in an effort to locate and expel hostile Indians. Large-scale expeditions (such as Mackenzie's raid) were common in the years following the Civil War, and military leaders waged a war of attrition (or exhaustion) against Texas Indians. The tactics employed included the constant search and pursuit of Indians year round, staking out their watering places, invading favorite hunting and camping sites, and destroying (or seizing) the Indians' horses, weapons, equipment, and stores of food. State forces further ratcheted up the pressure by undertaking their own military actions against the Apaches.[40]

The Lipans also remained the prime targets of numerous army campaigns conducted on the south side of the Rio Grande. Following the deaths of twelve people in clashes with the Lipans during April and May 1876, officials at Fort Davis dispatched Lt. John L. Bullis across the border to launch a retaliatory strike on a Lipan encampment. On July 29 Bullis, with twenty Black Seminole scouts and twenty African American cavalrymen (often referred to as Buffalo Soldiers), crossed the Rio Grande about twenty-five miles above the mouth of the Pecos. After riding all night, they reached the San Antonio River near Zaragoza, and in the early morning hours, Bullis's men struck the sleeping Lipans. In an intense struggle that lasted for fifteen minutes, the Americans found themselves "in a wild, confused melee in which the two parties were so intermingled that the fighting was chiefly hand-to-hand—clubbed carbines against the long Lipan lances." When the struggle ended, fourteen Lipans lay dead and four women were taken prisoner. The soldiers also seized the Lipans' sizeable horse herd before setting the village on fire. The Indians retaliated a couple months later, however, by crossing the Rio Grande and killing thirteen men and one woman.[41]

On April 14, 1881, a small party of seven Lipans committed the "last important Indian raid on Texas soil" when they attacked and killed a fourteen-year-old boy named Allen Reiss (Allen Lease) and Mrs. John McLauren while they were out working in the garden at the McLauren's home near the Frio River. Two weeks later Lieutenant Bullis and thirty Black Seminole scouts received orders to pursue the killers. The Lipans had made rawhide "shoes" to cover their tracks, but the sharp-eyed scouts were still able to pick up their trail. Bullis and his men followed the Indians across the Rio Grande and trailed them to their encampment in the Sierra del Burro. On May 2 they attacked the Lipans, killing four warriors and capturing a woman and child along with twenty-one horses. In 1882 twelve expeditions set out from various Texas posts and covered 3,662 miles, though without finding the slightest trace of Indian raiders.[42] The Texas Indian wars had ended.

Consequences

As W. W. Newcomb observes in his study of Texas Indians, during the various intertribal conflicts of the eighteenth and nineteenth centuries, the "Lipans had little choice in the matter: it was be warlike or perish." They fought to defend their homelands and to save themselves from destruction. This was true for both offensive and defensive actions. Their offensive thrusts, adds Verne Ray, "were for the purpose of dulling the enemies' power so as to make possible the retention of their homes and property and saving their lives."[43]

The Indian wars of Texas also provided the Lipan Apaches with tremendous opportunities to advance the social and economic status of individual warriors and undoubtedly enjoyed the sanction and approval of both men and women, young and old. But the maintenance of a persistent culture of war—albeit necessary at times—came with a price. Death, injury, fear, and constant flight were constant reminders that the excitement and joy of one day's victory dance could be followed the next by the agonizing news that one's son, brother, father, or husband had not survived the enemies' reprisal. Warfare during this time ate away at the demographic structure of the Lipans: the number of males declined, leaving a gender imbalance with far-ranging consequences. It was common among Lipan women, when a warrior died in battle or on a raid, to shave their heads, dress in their particular robes of mourning, and go to some secluded spot, where they would spend several days weeping for their loved ones.[44]

The culture of war that the Lipans so tightly embraced also contributed to the eventual breakdown of the very thing that they cherished most—their independence and cohesiveness as a people. When powerful enemies combined to destroy them, the very fabric of Lipan life and culture unraveled. The Lipan Apaches struggled to find new groups with which to identify during the nineteenth century. Some attached themselves to the Mescaleros and Tonkawas, while others fled to Mexico and attempted to carve out new lives and identities for themselves. But by living as small fringe groups on the periphery of more numerous and powerful peoples, they surrendered the cultural distinctiveness and independence that made them Lipan. Thus, the Indian wars of Texas exercised a decidedly negative influence on them, and the Lipan Apaches vanished from the historical record at the turn of the twentieth century.

Notes

Portions of this chapter are excerpts from Thomas A. Britten, *The Lipan Apaches: People of Wind and Lightning* (Albuquerque: University of New Mexico Press, 2011), used with permission of the publisher.

1. Clayton A. Robarchek, "Plains Warfare and the Anthropology of War," in Douglas W. Owsley and Richard L. Jantz eds., *Skeletal Biology in the Great Plains* (Washington, DC: Smithsonian Institution Press, 1994), 312–13; Christy G. Turner and Jacqueline A. Turner, *Man Corn: Cannibalism and Violence in the Prehistoric American Southwest* (Salt Lake City: University of Utah Press, 1999), 2.

2. Robert L. Brooks, "Warfare on the Southern Plains," in Owsley and Jantz, *Skeletal Biology in the Great Plains,* 317–21; Susan C. Vehik, "Conflict, Trade, and Political Development on the Southern Plains," *American Antiquity* 67 (Jan. 2002): 37, 42–43.

3. Morris E. Opler, *Myths and Legends of the Lipan Apache Indians,* Memoirs of the American Folklore Society, vol. 36 (New York: J. J. Augustin, 1940), 16–19, 36–37.

4. See Steven A. LeBlanc, *Prehistoric Warfare in the American Southwest* (Salt Lake City: University of Utah Press, 1999); and W. W. Newcomb, "A Re-Examination of the Causes of Plains Warfare," *American Anthropologist* 52 (July–Sept. 1950): 317–20.

5. Elizabeth A. H. John, *Storms Brewed in Other Men's Worlds: The Confrontation of Indians, Spanish, and French in the Southwest, 1540–1795* (College Station: Texas A&M University Press, 1975), 314–17; Pekka Hämäläinen, *The Comanche Empire* (New Haven, CT: Yale University Press, 2008), 55–57; F. Todd Smith, *The Wichita Indians: Traders of Texas and the Southern Plains, 1540–1845* (College Station: Texas A&M University Press, 2000), 25–26; Elizabeth A. Harper, "The Taovayas Indians in Frontier Trade and Diplomacy, 1719–1768," *Chronicles of Oklahoma* 31 (1953): 272.

6. Timothy G. Baugh, "Ecology and Exchange: The Dynamics of Plains-Pueblo Interaction," in *Farmers, Hunters, and Colonists: Interaction between the Southwest and the Southern Plains,* ed. Katherine A. Spielmann (Tucson: University of Arizona Press, 1991), 123; Michael L. Tate, "Comanche Captives: People between Two Worlds," *Chronicles of Oklahoma* 72 (1994): 234–37; Donald E. Worcester, "The Apaches in the History of the Southwest," *New Mexico Historical Review* 50 (1975): 27.

7. T. S. Dennis, *Life of F. M. Buckelew: The Indian Captive* (Bandera, TX: Hunter's Printing House, 1925), 48; Edward W. Gifford, *Culture Element Distributions: Apache-Pueblo,* Anthropological Records, eds. A. L. Kroeber, R. H. Lowie, and R. L. Olson, vol. 4 (Berkeley: University of California Press, 1940), 29–32; Andrée F. Sjoberg, "Lipan Apache Culture in Historical Perspective," *Southwestern Journal of Anthropology* 9 (1953): 88–89; Percy Bigmouth Interview, Morris Edward Opler Papers, Collection 14–25–3238, Subseries D, Box 44, Division of Rare and Manuscript Collections, Cornell University Library, Ithaca, NY; Noah Smithwick, *The Evolution of a State or Recollections of Old Texas Days* (Austin, TX.: Steck-Vaughn, 1968), 215.

8. Sjoberg, "Lipan Apache Culture," 89–90; Gifford, *Culture Element Distributions,* 32–33; Jean Louis Berlandier, *The Indians of Texas in 1830,* ed. John C. Ewers, trans. Patricia Reading Leclerq (Washington, DC: Smithsonian Institution Press, 1969), 130.

9. Thomas F. Schilz and Donald E. Worcester, "The Spread of Firearms among the Indian Tribes on the Northern Frontier of New Spain," *American Indian Quarterly* 11 (Winter 1987): 1–4; Armstrong Starkey, *European and Native American Warfare, 1675–1815* (Norman: University of Oklahoma Press, 1998), 21.

10. Morris E. Opler, "An Application of the Theory of Themes in Culture," *Journal of the Washington Academy of Sciences* 36 (May 15, 1946): 142–44; Gifford, *Culture Element Distributions,* 71; Grenville Goodwin, *Western Apache Raiding and Warfare,* reprint edition, ed.

Keith H. Basso (Tucson: University of Arizona Press, 1994), 264–69; Percy Bigmouth and Stella La Paz Interviews, Opler Papers.

11. Frank R. Secoy, *Changing Military Patterns of the Great Plains Indians* (Lincoln: University of Nebraska Press, 1992), 24–25.

12. Ibid., 26; William Dunn, "Apache Relations in Texas, 1718–1750," *Texas State Historical Association Quarterly* 14 (1911): 226–27.

13. Don Antonio Cordero, "Cordero's Description of the Apache, 1796," *New Mexico Historical Review* 32 (Oct. 1957): 345–46; Gifford, *Culture Element Distributions*, 71–72; Elizabeth A. H. John, "Views from a Desk in Chihuahua: Manuel Merino's Reports on Apaches and Neighboring Nations, ca. 1804," *Southwestern Historical Quarterly* 95 (1991): 158–60.

14. Carlos E. Castañeda, *Our Catholic Heritage in Texas, 1519–1936,* 7 vols. (Austin, TX: Von Boeckmann-Jones, 1936), 2:190–201; Curtis D. Tunnell and W. W. Newcomb, *A Lipan Apache Mission: San Lorenzo de la Santa Cruz, 1762–1771* (Austin: Texas Memorial Museum, 1969), 154–55; Dunn, "Apache Relations in Texas," 207–209.

15. Dunn, "Apache Relations in Texas," 209–16; Thomas Schilz, *The Lipan Apaches in Texas* (El Paso: Texas Western Press, 1987), 8–9; Castañada, *Our Catholic Heritage in Texas,* 2:193–201.

16. Dunn, "Apache Relations in Texas," 230–34; Schilz, *Lipan Apaches in Texas,* 10; Robert S. Weddle, *The San Sabá Mission: Spanish Pivot in Texas* (Austin: University of Texas Press, 1964; reprint, College Station: Texas A&M University Press, 1999), 13–15; Tunnell and Newcomb, *Lipan Apache Mission,* 154–56. Tunnell and Newcomb state that the "Apaches" were Mescaleros, while the "Ypandis" were Lipans.

17. See Weddle, *San Sabá Mission;* Lesley Byrd Simpson, *The San Sabá Papers: A Documentary Account of the Founding and Destruction of the San Sabá Mission,* rev. ed. (Dallas: Southern Methodist University Press, 2000); William Edward Dunn, "The Apache Mission on the San Sabá: Its Founding and Failure," *Southwestern Historical Quarterly* 17 (1914): 379–414; and Juan M. Romero de Terreros, "The Destruction of the Mission San Sabá Apache Mission: A Discussion of the Casualties," *Americas* 60 (Apr. 2004): 618–26.

18. Weddle, *San Sabá Mission,* 137.

19. The name of the fortified village was Tawehash. See Ralph H. Vigil, Frances W. Kaye, and John R. Wunder, eds., *Spain and the Plains* (Niwot: University of Colorado Press, 1994), 16; and Harper, "Taovayas Indians in Frontier Trade and Diplomacy," 282–83.

20. Henry Easton Allen, "The Parrilla Expedition to the Red River in 1759," *Southwestern Historical Quarterly* 43 (July 1939): 64–69; Simpson, *San Sabá Papers,* 155; Stan Hoig, *Tribal Wars of the Southern Plains* (Norman: University of Oklahoma Press, 1993), 67; Weddle, *San Sabá Mission,* 119–23.

21. Gary Clayton Anderson, *The Conquest of Texas: Ethnic Cleansing in the Promised Land, 1820–1875* (Norman: University of Oklahoma Press, 2005), 26–28; Anna Muckelroy, "The Indian Policy of the Republic of Texas," *Southwestern Historical Quarterly* 25 (Apr. 1922): 247; A. M. Gibson, *The Kickapoos: Lords of the Middle Border* (Norman: University of Oklahoma Press, 1963), 143–45.

22. David LaVere, *The Texas Indians* (College Station: Texas A&M University Press, 2004), 160–67; Castañeda, *Our Catholic Heritage,* 6:228; "Referendum on Indian Relations," Sept. 28, 1825, in *Papers Concerning Robertson's Colony in Texas,* ed. Malcolm D. McLean, 18 vols. (Fort Worth: Texas Christian University Press, 1974–93), 2:373–75.

23. Sjoberg, "Lipan Apache Culture," 79; Schilz, *Lipan Apaches in Texas,* 42–43; Dorman H.. Winfrey, ed., *Texas Indian Papers, 1825–1843,* 4 vols. (Austin: Texas State Library, 1959), 1:1; William B. Gannett, "The American Invasion of Texas, 1820–1845: Patterns of Conflict between Settlers and Indians" (PhD diss., Cornell University, 1984), 264–68; F. Todd Smith, *From Dominance to Disappearance: The Indians of Texas and the Near Southwest, 1786–1859* (Lincoln: University of Nebraska Press, 2005), 132–33.

24. William B. Griffen, *Utmost Good Faith: Patterns of Apache-Mexican Hostilities in Northern Chihuahua Border Warfare, 1824–1848* (Albuquerque: University of New Mexico Press, 1988), 28–29; Andrée F. Sjoberg, "The Culture of the Tonkawa: A Texas Indian Tribes," in *Ethnology of the Texas Indians,* ed. Thomas R. Hester (New York: Garland, 1991), 357–58; "Campaign Plan Drawn up by Manuel Rudecindo Barragán," Feb. 25, 1832, in McLean, *Papers Concerning Robertson's Colony,* 7:134–37; Smith, *From Dominance to Disappearance,* 143–44.

25. Verne F. Ray, "Ethnohistorical Analysis of Documents Relating to the Apache Indians," in *Apache Indians,* 12 vols. (New York: Garland, 1974), 10:59.

26. John Henry Brown, *Indian Wars and Pioneers of Texas* (Austin, TX: State House, 1988), 69; John H. Jenkins and Kenneth Kesselus, *Edward Burleson: Texas Frontier Leader* (Austin, TX: Jenkins, 1990), 216–18; Helen Burleson Kelso, "Burleson, Edward," *Handbook of Texas Online,* accessed Nov. 8, 2005, http://www.tshaonline.org/handbook/online/articles/fbu40; Gerald S. Pierce, "Burleson's Northwestern Campaign," *Texas Military History* 6 (Fall 1967): 195–97. Pierce states that the battle occurred three miles below the mouth of the San Saba River at a place known as Molasses Hollow.

27. Jenkins and Kesselus, *Edward Burleson,* 169–70; "From Texas," *Atkinson's Saturday Evening Post* 18 (Jan. 26, 1839).

28. The location of Moore's raid on the Comanche winter encampment is unclear. According to Moore's report to Secretary of War Albert Sydney Johnson in March 1839, the fight occurred at Spring Creek. Winfrey, *Texas Indian Papers,* 1:57–59. Noah Smithwick, who also participated in the campaign, recollects that the battle took place on the San Saba River. Smithwick, *Evolution of a State,* 215. According to J. M. Morphis's *History of Texas,* the battle took place at Wallace's Creek, located seven miles from San Saba.

29. Enrique Gilbert-Michael Maestas, "Culture and History of Native Peoples of South Texas" (PhD diss., University of Texas, 2003), 327. Carl Coke Rister writes that the Lipans killed all of the Comanche prisoners. Rister, *Border Captives: The Traffic in Prisoners by Southern Plains Indians, 1835–1875* (Norman: University of Oklahoma Press, 1940), 85.

30. Winfrey, *Texas Indian Papers,* 1:57–59; Smithwick, *Evolution of a State,* 215–20; "Moore's Defeat on the San Saba," *Frontier Times* 3 (Feb. 1926): 1–2; Robert S. Reading, *Arrows over Texas* (San Antonio: Naylor, 1960), 73–74; Smith, *From Dominance to Disappearance,* 174.

31. Craig H. Roell, "Linnville Raid of 1840," *Handbook of Texas Online,* accessed Nov. 8, 2005, http://www.tshaonline.org/handbook/online/articles/bt101; Mildred P. Mayhall, *Indian Wars of Texas* (Waco: Texian, 1965), 31–33.

32. Anna Muckelroy, "The Indian Policy of Texas," *Southwestern Historical Quarterly* 26 (Oct. 1922): 145; Hoig, *Tribal Wars of the Southern Plains,* 161; Mayhall, *Indian Wars of Texas,* 39–40; Anderson, *Conquest of Texas,* 190–91; Brown, *Indian Wars and Pioneers of Texas,* 83–84.

33. Anderson, *Conquest of Texas,* 221–22; John C. Duval, *The Adventures of Big-Foot Wallace: The Texas Ranger and Hunter* (Macon, GA: J. W. Burke, 1870), 150–62. According to

Charles Howard Shinn, thirty-five Lipans later attacked and tried to kill Wallace at his ranch near San Antonio—perhaps in retaliation for his role in the battle on the Frio River. Shinn, "Tales of the Mexican Border," *New Peterson Magazine* 1 (June 1893): 600.

34. John Salmon Ford, *Rip Ford's Texas*, ed. and with an introduction by Stephen B. Oates (Austin: University of Texas Press, 1963), 449–50; Kenneth Franklin Neighbours, *Robert Simpson Neighbors and the Texas Frontier, 1836–1859* (Waco: Texian, 1975), 43–48; John C. Cremony, *Life among the Apaches* (1868; repr., Alexandria, Va.: Time-Life Books, 1981), 18.

35. Thomas T. Smith, "U.S. Army Combat Operations in the Indian Wars of Texas, 1849–1881," *Southwestern Historical Quarterly* 99 (Apr. 1996): 503, 506, 512.

36. US Congress, House, *Testimony Taken by the Committee on Military Affairs in Relation to the Texas Border Troubles*, 45th Cong., 2nd sess., 1878, H. Misc. Doc. 64, serial 1820, 16 (hereafter cited as *Texas Border Troubles*); Winfrey, *Texas Indian Papers*, 4:167–68, 173–74, 177–80, 262–64.

37. US Congress, Senate, *Resolution of the Legislature of Texas*, 42nd Cong., 1st sess., Mar. 28, 1871, S. Misc. Doc. 37, serial 1467. The three commissioners were Thomas P. Robb, F. J. Mead, and Richard H. Savage. See US Congress, House, *Report of the United States Commissioner to Texas*, 42nd Cong., 3rd sess., 1872, H. Exec. Doc. 39, serial 1565, 35, 39.

38. For additional information about Mackenzie's military career, see Michael D. Pierce, *The Most Promising Young Officer* (Norman: University of Oklahoma Press, 1993); and Lessing H. Nohl Jr., "Bad Hand: The Military Career of Randall Slidell Mackenzie, 1871–1889" (PhD diss., University of New Mexico, 1962).

39. Robert G. Carter, "A Raid into Mexico," *Outing* 12 (Apr. 1888): 1–9; Testimony of 1st Lt. John L. Bullis, *Texas Border Troubles*, 187–88; Ernest Wallace, *Ranald S. Mackenzie on the Texas Frontier* (Lubbock: West Texas Museum Assoc., 1964), 103–104; Allen Lee Hamilton, "Remolino Raid," *Handbook of Texas Online*, accessed May 15, 2006, http://www.tshaonline.org/handbook/online/articles/qfr03.

40. Morris E. Opler, "The Lipan and Mescalero Apaches in Texas," in *Apache Indians*, 10:299–301; Smith, "U.S. Army Combat Operations," 519, 529; "How Two Lipans Met Death on the Saline," *Frontier Times* 4 (Aug. 1927): 40.

41. Frost Woodhall, "The Seminole Indian Scouts on the Border," *Frontier Times* 15 (Dec. 1937): 122; Kenneth W. Porter, *The Negro on the American Frontier* (New York: Arno, 1971), 484; Opler, "Lipan and Mescalero Apaches," 302; Testimony of Bullis, *Texas Border Troubles*, 188, 202.

42. Robert Wooster, "The Army and the Politics of Expansion: Texas and the Southwestern Borderlands, 1870–1886," *Southwestern Historical Quarterly* 93 (Oct. 1989): 162; "Last Indian Raid in Southwest Texas," *Frontier Times* 4 (Aug. 1927): 58–59; Porter, *Negro on the American Frontier*, 489–90.

43. Maria F. Wade, *The Native Americans of the Texas Edwards Plateau, 1583–1799* (Austin: University of Texas Press, 2003), 161, 207; W. W. Newcomb, *The Indians of Texas: Prehistory to Present* (Austin: University of Texas Press, 1961), 125; Ray, "Ethnohistorical Analysis of Documents," 10:31.

44. S. E. Banta, *Buckelew: The Indian Captive or the Life Story of F. M. Buckelew while a Captive among the Lipan Indians in the Western Wilds of Frontier Texas* (Mason, TX: *Mason Herald*, 1911; repr., New York: Garland, 1977), 81; Jeffrey P. Blick, "Genocidal Warfare in Tribal Societies as a Result of European-Induced Culture Conflict," *Man* 23 (Dec. 1988): 660.

2

TEJANOS AT WAR
A HISTORY OF MEXICAN TEXANS IN AMERICAN WARS

Alexander Mendoza

O N SEPTEMBER 12, 1918, Pvt. Marcelino Serna, part of the 89th Division, IV Corps, First Army, received orders to move toward the German Army's lines at a salient near St. Mihiel. The main assault focused on the German 1st Division and was to attack the small town of Vigneulles, about twelve miles behind the enemy's position. Serna's division stood on the corps' right as they made their way against the southern face of the St. Mihiel salient. The Americans surpassed the goals of the offensive's first day by midafternoon. Serna's unit came across a German machine-gun nest that had already killed twelve in the Argonne Forest. Serna, the scout for his company, received permission to probe the enemy position. He soon came under fire, bullets piercing his helmet. Yet he was not deterred, continuing to move along the enemy's left flank. "When I got close enough," Serna recollected, "I threw four grenades into the nest. Eight Germans came out with their hands up. Another six were in the nest dead. I held my prisoners until help arrived." The private was not done. In the Meuse-Argonne offensive two weeks later, Serna followed a German sniper to an enemy bunker. He then single-handedly captured twenty-four soldiers and killed twenty-six others with his rifle, handguns, and an assortment of grenades. The American Expeditionary Force's (AEF) offensive ultimately led to the Armistice on November 11. But four days before the ceasefire, Serna was wounded by a German sniper. As Serna recovered in a French army hospital, Gen. John J. "Black Jack" Pershing, the commander of the AEF, awarded him the Distinguished Service Cross, the second-highest American combat award. A few days later Field Marshal Ferdinand Foch, supreme commander of the Allied armies, awarded him the French Croix de Guerre for bravery.[1]

In 1919 Serna received his discharge papers and returned to his adopted home in El Paso, becoming one of Texas' most highly decorated soldiers of the First World

War. But Serna was not a US citizen. Born in Chihuahua City, Chihuahua, Mexico, on April 26, 1896, he crossed the Rio Grande at the age of twenty and came to El Paso in search of a better life. He found work in the railroads and agricultural fields of the American Southwest. A year after Serna arrived in El Paso, however, the United States entered World War I. At about the same time that Congress declared war on Germany, federal officials detained Serna and a group of men in Colorado. Risking deportment, he volunteered to enlist in the US Army. After three weeks of training, the young Serna traveled to England as part of the army's "Middle Wests" Division (most of its soldiers came from the region between the Canadian border and the Rio Grande) before participating in the bloody offensives of 1918. Yet for all his bravery, Serna apparently had no chance to receive the Medal of Honor, much less a promotion. An army officer, according to Serna, told him that the Medal of Honor was not awarded to "buck" privates. Adding insult to injury, the officer also told him that because of his difficulty with English, he would not be promoted. Nevertheless, Serna became a US citizen in 1924 and lived a long life on the Texas-Mexico border before his death on February 29, 1992, at the age of ninety-five. Attempts to have the Medal of Honor posthumously awarded to him failed.[2]

The exploits of Serna symbolize how Texans of Mexican descent have labored to receive recognition for their service on the battlefield. These Tejanos struggled to overcome the discrimination and attitudes of Anglo-Americans following the Texas Revolution.[3] Accordingly, they straddled their loyalties in the various American wars of the nineteenth century, uncertain what side to take while at the same time remaining loyal to their native Mexico. By the turn of the twentieth century, additional Mexican immigrants kept the accommodation of Tejanos somewhat limited as the burgeoning middle class still retained cultural markers with the land of their birth. Yet by the 1930s, Tejanos related to American ideology more clearly than ever. By extension, many saw their participation in the various wars of the United States as a way to demonstrate their form of patriotism, which focused on the Mexican cultural emphasis of the warrior tradition while maintaining a desire to obtain equality in the social, political, and economic realms. In the process Tejanos have played a major role in the nation's wars through their military service. And while feelings that Texans of Mexican descent were lazy and cowardly permeated the ideology of the nineteenth century, Tejanos managed to carve a place of respect in the history of Texas through their actions on the fields of battle.

The legacy of the Tejano military experience was already present when American settlers first arrived in Texas during the early part of the nineteenth century. In their efforts to establish a successful entrepreneurial and social existence in Mexico's far north, Tejanos were familiar with the military presence required to keep the frontier safe from

Indian attacks. After Mexican independence, Tejano men assumed duties with the various militia detachments designed to protect the population through military forays and to provide a buffer against Indian incursions. As historian Andrés Tijerina points out, due to early Texas' isolated frontier, Tejanos established what they called a *compañía volante,* or flying squadron, to defend the region with their "special knowledge of offensive cavalry tactics." These organizations later laid the groundwork for the militia structure in Texas, even being used to apprehend criminals during the 1820s. The flying squadrons ultimately had an influence on the Anglo settlers as they adopted the offensive nature of the cavalry for military advantage. By the time of the revolution, Anglo-Americans had adopted many of the principles of the Tejano militia.[4]

Tejanos played a significant role in the Texas Revolution (1835–36). Anglos who chafed at the Mexican government's stricter collection of tariffs, proposals to ban slavery, new commerce taxes, and cultural/racial differences launched an organized resistance against the federal authority. Tejanos joined the Anglos in these protests. After an initial clash against the Mexican Army's forces at Gonzalez in October 1835, the Texans decided to advance against San Antonio de Bexar the following month. Joining the expedition were more than sixty Tejanos. The contributions of the Mexican Texan population were best articulated by William T. Austin, who wrote, "These Mexicans being well acquainted with the country, were of important service as express riders, guides to foraging parties, &c." Two prominent Tejanos who joined the ranks of the Texian Army were Victoria alcalde Plácido Benavides and Bexareño Juan Seguin, the latter receiving a commission as captain with the authority to raise a company of vaqueros.[5] As the Texians laid siege to the Mexican garrison in San Antonio, the skill of the Tejanos was evident to their Anglo colleagues. "[W]e were all I supposed pretty good horsemen, as the term is understood in the 'old States,'" one Anglo Texan volunteer noted, but the Tejanos "are unsurpassed by any people in horsemanship." For all their skills, the Mexican Texans did not excel during the siege and the street fighting that ensued in San Antonio. Nevertheless, they assisted the Anglo Texans in wresting the city from Mexican hands on December 11. With the departure of the federal force, the Texians established a garrison at the Alamo complex and awaited Mexico's response.[6]

The role of the Tejano population at large in the rebellion against the Mexican government was mixed. Some clearly identified with the broader issues and concerns of the Texas region. Others remained loyal to Mexico. Meanwhile, an additional group of Tejanos tried to remain neutral during the conflict's early stages, perhaps hoping to later align themselves with the winning side. More importantly, there were various degrees of loyalty that moved beyond simply supporting or rejecting the notion of a Texas secession movement. As historian Raúl

Ramos notes, characterizing "Tejano identity . . . needs to take into account the multiple roles played by Tejanos and their underlying role as mediators in a culturally complex place."[7]

The ambivalence of the neutral Tejanos stemmed in part from Antonio López de Santa Anna, who had recently assumed power in the Mexican capital when hostilities were about to erupt in Texas.[8] In May Santa Anna's forces defeated an uprising in the state of Zacatecas in central Mexico. When news reached the capital of the unrest in Texas, Santa Anna moved north with a force of over 6,000 men, determined to crush the rebellion. On February 23, 1836, the Mexican Army reached the outskirts of San Antonio, its first objective. By that point the Texian forces had undergone a few changes in their leadership and were now led by Col. James Bowie and Lt. Col. William B. Travis in a dual-command structure borne out of necessity. Captain Seguin had repeatedly warned Travis about the pending Mexican attack. Seguin and two of his Tejano cavalrymen were ordered to obtain help from Goliad but were unable to return with any viable assistance before Santa Anna decided to attack the beleaguered garrison. While some of Seguin's men reluctantly left Bexar to serve as scouts for Gen. Sam Houston in Gonzalez, seven remained behind and fell at the Alamo when Santa Anna stormed the mission on March 6.[9]

Even though as many as fifteen Tejanos left the Alamo garrison prior to the Mexican advance, Seguin led a detachment of nineteen Mexican Texans east toward Houston's army, then maneuvering against Santa Anna near the San Jacinto River. Despite being excused from combat duty, these men joined the ranks of the Anglo Texans who sought revenge for their fallen comrades at the Alamo and at Goliad. Houston accepted Seguin's help, yet insisted that the Tejanos wear pieces of cardboard in their hatbands in order to differentiate them from the Mexicans. In the ensuing Battle of San Jacinto on April 21, 1836, the Texian Army wrecked havoc on the Mexicans. Seguin's men participated in the battle, yelling, "Recuerden el Alamo" (Remember the Alamo) along with the Anglo Texans. The battle, which lasted less than twenty minutes, was a decisive rout of the Mexican Army. Santa Anna's force suffered more than 650 deaths and over 200 additional casualties as the Texians continued the slaughter well into the night. For his exploits at San Jacinto, Seguin was promoted to the rank of colonel. The men under his command, the 9th Company, 2nd Regiment of Texas Volunteers, could return to Bexar now that the Mexican threat had been expelled and Texas independence agreed upon with Santa Anna's capture.[10] In sum, 183 Tejano men fought in the Texas Revolution.[11]

The Treaty of Velasco signed by Santa Anna was quickly repudiated by the Mexican government. As such, even though Texas would remain an independent republic for almost a decade, it came at the price of uncertainty for the Tejano population. They had cast their lot with their Anglo counterparts only to have fear and mistrust take hold. In fact, some of the Tejanos in Seguin's company made claims against the Republic of Texas for their services in the war, only to have those demands rebuffed.[12] The problems being faced by these veterans of the revolution were not unique. During the next few years, the Tejano population experienced a transformation of their native land. As historian David Montejano notes, "the spirit of revenge" remained present as Anglo Texans began to claim the lands of the Mexican Texans, "ally and foe alike," in the following years.[13] Some Tejanos attempted to resist the encroachment into their holdings through armed force, but the majority lost their land in East and Central Texas. While some of the elite might have staved off complete displacement through economic partnerships and intermarriage, others were not so fortunate.[14] Others, like Texas Revolution veterans Juan Seguin and José Antonio Navarro, continued to ply their positions of leadership as they straddled their dual identities as Texians and Mexicans. While Seguin remained integral to Texas politics, serving as the only Tejano in the Texas Senate, Navarro also advocated for the recognition of Tejano rights. His support of the Mirabeau B. Lamar administration ultimately led to his selection as part of an ill-fated expedition to annex Santa Fe, New Mexico, in the summer of 1841, an attempt to wrest the upper Rio Grande into the republic's control. Even though the Texas party ultimately surrendered to Mexican authorities without firing a shot, the incident suggests that some Tejanos still believed that they could have the best of both worlds. It would be an uphill battle as animosity and mistrust based on race and greed forced many Mexican families to flee south into Mexico despite their citizenship in the nascent Republic of Texas.[15]

By 1845 the Tejano population had another challenge to deal with: annexation to the United States and a potential war with Mexico. Despite some US trepidations about absorbing the Lone Star due to slavery, the election of James K. Polk to the presidency in 1844 on an expansionist platform added a sense of urgency to the brewing conflict between Texas and Mexico. In May 1846 the presence of Bvt. Brig. Gen. Zachary Taylor's force on the Rio Grande led to the clash that the authorities in Washington had sought in order to pursue additional Mexican territory. After news of a cavalry skirmish reached Washington, President Polk declared that "American blood had been shed upon American soil" and asked Congress for a declaration of war against Mexico, which he received on May 13. The ensuing conflict placed the Tejano population in an unenviable position. Among the more than 8,000 Texans who volunteered to fight in the war were those who still had scores to settle from the revolution. They made little distinction for the Mexican Texans as they made their way to the Rio Grande and points south. Despite General Taylor's orders for volunteers to conduct themselves properly, instances of looting and violence were common throughout southern Texas and northern Mexico. Some Tejanos volunteered to fight in this latest conflict, while others served in the capacity of guides and spies, such as Chapita Sandoval, who moved freely from Corpus Christi to Matamoros with information. Yet as the majority of the Tejano population chose to await the latest outcome of hostilities, some Mexican-born Texans joined the fray in the numerous state volunteer units that made their way to the Rio Grande. Some of those men included two members of Company E, 2nd Texas Volunteers, Pvts. Francisco Acosta and Anasta[cio] Barrilla. More than a dozen other Spanish-surnamed volunteers served in the ranks of Texas forces, all of them in the enlisted ranks.[16]

Because of Tejanos' Mexican cultural heritage, Anglos viewed them as Mexicans. Accordingly, most Tejanos chose to remain on the sidelines for this latest conflict. That did not mean that Mexican Texans would remain idle to threats—real or perceived— from the Anglo Americans making their way south to join the war against Mexico. In one case Tejano ranchers attacked a US supply train making its way from Corpus Christi into the Rio Grande Valley at the war's onset in 1846.[17] Retaliatory raids, murders, and other atrocities from volunteers, Texas Rangers, and Mexican bandits all kept Texans embroiled in violence. The Rangers' role in the bloodshed and in the intimidation of Tejanos is exemplified by the nickname given to them, "Los Diablos Tejanos" (Texas Devils). In the years prior to and after the war, the Rangers administered their own version of justice with impunity. Mexican-born Texans also retaliated, making South Texas and northern Mexico a veritable hotbed of guerrilla activity during this period.[18]

The notion of divided loyalties between the Tejanos' national identities and the fears that retaliation would only lead to further bloodshed kept the population in a state of flux, not easily discernable during the war with Mexico. There is another reason why Tejanos welcomed, in part, the American invasion. According to historian Douglas Richmond, by the early 1840s, Mexico's far north and, by extension, the disputed land of Texas had witnessed additional Indian attacks on homes and ranches. Consequently, the presence of US soldiers promoted the notion of joint operations against hostile Comanches and other tribes.[19] Yet the presence of troops did not mean that Mexican-born Texans could join the volunteer ranks; the Old Army held strong prejudices against any soldier with dark skin.

The end of the Mexican-American War in 1848 brought an additional conundrum for the Tejano population as the Treaty of Guadalupe Hidalgo induced the repatriation of thousands of Mexican-born Texans living in the newly defined borders of the Lone Star State. The end of the war did not mean an end to the violence, however, as racial animosity continued the aggression along the Texas–Mexico border. As historian

Manuel Callahan notes, even though the violence on the border "was perpetrated by lawless elements, there was a great deal of military and paramilitary activity, much of it responding to subaltern resistance throughout the region."[20] The 1850s thus witnessed major conflicts such as the "Cart War" in South Texas and the "Cortina War" along the Rio Grande Valley. In the case of the Cart War, origins appeared to stem from longstanding racial animosity and resentment over Mexican oxcart freighters who transported goods more cheaply than their Anglo counterparts. Consequently, some Anglo freighters attacked their Tejano counterparts and used murder and violence to intimidate the Mexican Americans, who had been guaranteed citizenship rights by the Treaty of Guadalupe Hidalgo. Human rights was the issue that spurned the Cortina War in Brownsville. Juan Nepomuceno Cortina, a well-known Tejano leader in the region, intervened on behalf of a Mexican Texan against Texas law enforcement officials in September 1859. The ensuing quarrel led to a racial epithet directed at Cortina and resulted in the death of an Anglo lawman by the Tejano landowner, which in turn sparked a conflict that acerbated Anglo-Tejano relations along the Rio Grande for the next decade.[21] The general view of Tejanos, even those born in Texas, remained largely negative. In essence, Anglos saw Mexican Americans as lazy, corrupt, and irresponsible. Those feelings did not dissipate as the United States inched toward another war.[22]

The onset of the American Civil War in 1861 placed the Tejano in a difficult situation yet again. By that point, estimates of the Tejano population reached as high as 25,000 people, mostly concentrated along the border and Central Texas. But when Texas decided to cast its lot with the Confederacy and seceded from the Union, the call for troops placed the Tejano population in a quandary. On the one hand, Tejanos could aid Confederate Texas, the state that had regarded them as no better than the slaves the Anglo population fought to keep in the wake of Pres. Abraham Lincoln's election. In the years leading up to the war, Tejanos had been accused of aiding and harboring runaway slaves making their way to Mexico. On the other hand, they could join the Union forces and the nation seen as responsible for Manifest Destiny and the carving out the American Southwest from Mexico. They could, in essence, fight against Texas, and the people who had overseen the eclipse of Hispanic political and economic influence, by joining the Federals. Either way, the decision would not be easy. After all, they had fought on the winning side before and had lost. In the end the Mexican American population in Texas joined the ranks of both forces, enlisting more than 2,250 men in the Confederate Army, while approximately 958 Tejanos fought on the side of the Union.[23]

Historian Charles Grear has examined the motivations of Tejanos and maintains that the Mexican Texan population was split into two distinct groups at the onset of the war: those who had established favorable economic and political ties with Anglo

Texans and those who had remained isolated from the general nuances of party politics and conflict. Accordingly, a number of factors influenced the direction of Tejano volunteers as war came to their native land for the third time in a generation. The need to defend their homes and families marked their first motivating factor as Tejanos joined the various volunteer forces throughout the state. Others joined the ranks of the Union or Confederacy for the simple notion of viewing military service as an economic opportunity, similar to the motivating factors of any other Billy Yank or Johnny Reb. Others followed the path of their local political or economic leaders in hopes that their service would be rewarded following the war. Most of the Tejano population tried to avoid the conflict because they had no ideological or political motivation to fight on either side. This personal neutrality proved a challenge for Texas as Confederate forces attempted to rally support for their cause.[24]

Despite the fact that more Tejanos fought on behalf of the Confederacy than the Union, state officials recognized the perilous dynamics of recruiting Mexican Texans. The Mexican government noted as such in a Border Commission report of 1873, stating that the "majority" of Tejanos resisted the southern war effort "on account of their dislike for the Confederate cause, or on account of their living among its defenders, those very persons from whom they had received so many vexations."[25] Members of the Tejano elite who sympathized with the South curbed this hesitation as best they could. Along the upper Rio Grande, Santos Benavides, a descendant of Tomas Sanchez, who had founded Laredo in 1755, exemplified the efforts of wealthy Mexican Texans who fought on behalf of the Confederacy. Rising to the rank of colonel, the highest-ranking soldier of Mexican descent, Benavides recruited and led dozens of Tejanos for the sake of border defense. Commanding the Department of the Rio Grande, an area that stretched from Eagle Pass to Rio Grande City, he fought against Indian incursions, Mexican bandits, and Union forces. The relationships that Mexican Texans had cultivated during the 1850s reaped dividends by the Civil War as Benavides ultimately came to symbolize how some Tejanos could identify and accommodate themselves to the southern cause.[26]

Benavides, along with his brothers Refugio and Cristóbal, organized the 33rd Texas Cavalry and fought in various engagements while patrolling the upper Rio Grande.[27] His identification with Texas was not new to the Civil War, for the 1873 report noted that the Laredo landowner had already cast his lot with state forces in the previous decade. In 1850 Benavides led a Tejano force into Mexico under the guise of pursuing Indians but in reality to steal property. Accordingly, Benavides and his supporters viewed the war through the prism of local defense and individual loyalties, not as an ideological struggle for or against slavery. Other Tejanos who fought on behalf of the Confederacy made their way into the Army of Northern Virginia, the

8th Texas Infantry during the Red River Campaign, and in Brig. Gen. Henry Hopkins Sibley's New Mexico Campaign, among other actions. Unionist Mexican Americans fought in the 1st and 2nd Texas Cavalry and Adrian J. Vidal's Partisan Rangers, which interestingly had previously deserted as a unit from the Confederacy. Despite these numbers, problems with language, leadership, and resentment stemming from the Conscription Act of 1862 led to desertion or apathy among Tejanos serving in both the Confederate or Union armies.[28] Therefore, the support of the elite was more critical to the Confederate cause. As Jerry Thompson notes, "had Benavides refused to serve the Confederacy and remained neutral or joined the Federals, the war on the Rio Grande would have taken a much different course." Ultimately, the Mexican Texan population viewed the war as a way to influence their political and economic future.[29]

Following the Civil War, the Indian wars of Texas and continued banditry along the US-Mexico border marked the world of Tejanos for the next thirty years. Nevertheless, economic modernization and population growth had changed the dynamics of the Mexican Texan citizenry. By 1890 the Tejano population reached upward of 105,193, a figure that would increase by more than 50 percent at the turn of the twentieth century. Like before, Tejanos joined the various instruments of

Tejano Confederate officers from Laredo, Texas. Left to right: Refugio Benavides, Atanacio Vidaurri, Cristobal Benavides, and John Z. Leyendecker. Courtesy St. Mary's University Archives, San Antonio, Tex.

citizen-soldiery available to them during the Gilded Age. Specifically, with the passage of the Militia Law of 1879, Tejanos—like their Anglo counterparts—joined the ranks of the state militia, or the Texas Volunteer Guard, in this case serving in the Frontier Battalion. Men like Pvts. Miguel Martinez of Alice, Pedro Lopez of San Elizario, and Diego Rodriguez of San Antonio served in Texas' frontier forces during the latter part of the nineteenth century.[30]

With the onset of Spanish-American War in 1898, segments of the Tejano population scrambled to demonstrate their newfound loyalty to the United States and distance themselves from any accusations of harboring Spanish sympathies. Some Tejanos volunteered to fight in one of the four infantry and one cavalry regiments authorized by the federal government, the 1st, 2nd, 3rd, and 4th Regiments, Texas Volunteer Infantry (US Volunteers); and the 1st Regiment, Texas Volunteer Cavalry (US Volunteers). In San Antonio Agustin De Zavala, a descendant of Texas Revolutionary figure Lorenzo De Zavala, epitomized this sense of patriotic fervor as he enlisted for a period of two years as a corporal in the 1st Infantry. Even though his family demonstrated consternation that the eighteen-year-old St. Mary's College student would find danger in Cuba, De Zavala reassured them about his decision. "I will tell you the same as I told Momma yesterday," he wrote to his sister, Adina Emilia, "there is no use to worry about me, I am all right and this will do me a great deal of good and I will get to see something [in the war]."[31]

While De Zavala stood out as a wealthier Mexican American volunteer, the Spanish-American War did not spur a massive mobilization of Tejanos into the US armed forces. In fact, as historian David F. Trask notes in his study of that conflict, the average volunteer in 1898 was "white, youthful, unmarried, native-born, and of working class background." In essence, the US volunteers did not represent the "overall population as would be the conscripts" of the wars of the twentieth century.[32] For Texas this meant that out of the approximately 4,000 soldiers the Lone Star State provided to support the war, less than 1 percent were of Mexican descent. But Tejanos did join the various regiments; men like Eleno Castillo, George Chavez, Eugene Hernandez, and Henry Perez enlisted with the 1st Texas out of San Antonio. Others like Jesus Romo and E. L. Magnón volunteered for Troop K, 1st Texas Cavalry out of Laredo.[33]

Some Tejanos displayed an ambivalence in joining the ranks of the US military, likely because of a number of factors. Namely, the population influx of Mexican immigrants into Texas had made the Tejano population numerically stronger as they moved into new regions and began to participate more freely in the state's economic and political activities. At the turn of the twentieth century, the enhanced Tejano community straddled two cultures: that of the place of their birth and that of Anglo-American institutions.[34] The fact that Anglo-Texans still viewed Tejanos with suspicion was only heightened by the events that led the United States into war with Spain. These feelings were exacerbated by elements of the Spanish-language press that demonstrated sympathies with the old colonial power. For instance, residents of Piedras Negras, across the Rio Grande from Eagle Pass, raised $4,500 to send to Spain during the war.[35] In the border town of El Paso, school principal W. H. T. Lopez was harshly criticized by his fellow citizens for having sympathies for Spain and Mexico, based on his displaying the flags of Spain, Mexico, and Texas in his classroom. The incident prompted the educator to write to the *El Paso International Daily Times* to profess his loyalty to the United States: "The people of El Paso have treated me very kindly and I do not want them to think for one moment that they have been giving their confidence to a traitor to the country of his birth."[36] The heightened suspicions likely kept some Mexican Americans in El Paso from volunteering for military service. In April 1898 twelve El Pasoans volunteered to join Teddy Roosevelt's "Rough Riders"—all Anglo surnamed. In contrast, only two Tejanos joined the El Paso Home Guards during that time.[37]

Despite the growing affinity for state and national influences, the Tejano population remained fragmented as a large percentage of newer Mexican Texans still retained a loyalty to their native land. Tejanos also had to deal with the reality that even their elite had seen their influence wane at the end of the nineteenth century as the modernization of railroads and economic progress bound Texas closer to the rest of the nation. In the same period, Anglo-Tejano marriages declined, and harsh reminders of a racial caste system persisted as de jure and de facto segregation placed Tejanos in a separate category. Moreover, violence and intimidation continued as anti-Mexican sentiments persisted at the turn of the twentieth century. The diminished influence of the elite in state affairs at the end of the 1800s saw concerted efforts for change in the first two decades of the twentieth century as some Mexican Texans embraced Anglo-American culture, symbols, and values in the wake of newly arrived immigrants displaced by Mexico's revolution. At the same time, attempts to demonstrate Tejano loyalty to Texas and the United States came amid further anti-Mexican sentiment sparked by the lawless raids and subversive activities of Mexican revolutionaries into the United States, especially in Texas.[38]

The onset of World War I and the US entry into the conflict in April 1917 once again thrust Mexican Texans into the maelstrom of an American war with implications for them. The Tejano community, in the words of historian José A. Ramírez, thus "demonstrated patriotism, but also disloyalty." Some Tejanos fled the state to avoid military service, while others were quick to enlist for service, eager to demonstrate their loyalty to the United States. In Kingsville, about forty miles southwest of Corpus

Christi, more than one hundred Tejanos volunteered for military service in April 1917. Other Mexican Texans wrote the authorities in Washington to inquire about the possibility of organizing Spanish-speaking companies for the military.[39] But in contrast to the volunteer-laden army of the Spanish-American War, the First World War employed conscription through the Selective Service Act of May 1917 that integrated new recruits into the existing regular army. Three registration efforts netted a total of 24 million citizens and noncitizens for the draft. In Texas 5,000 of the 197,000 men who served in the armed forces had Spanish surnames. The advent of federal supervision of the draft and recruiting also allowed Tejanos other avenues in which to support the war. Throughout the Lone Star State, for instance, they made their way to serve as members of draft boards, as clerks, and as interpreters for US forces. Other middle-class Tejanos sponsored fundraisers and challenged the citizenry that had excluded them from politics and society to contribute to the war effort. This was a major turning point, for the burgeoning Mexican American population now sought to support the very system that had excluded them for generations. As historian Carole Christian notes, World War I gave Tejanos the first opportunity to consider themselves as Americans rather than continuing to remain on the margins of society.[40]

Tejanos of all classes answered the nation's call to arms during the Great War. Individual reasons may have varied, but they generally revolved around similar motivations: patriotism and support for the United States, a desire to escape the economic morass of poverty, ethnic pride indicative of demonstrating the worthiness of the "Mexicano" people, and the aspiration to seek adventure overseas.[41] In Laredo, Benjamin Ramos of El Democrata Fronterizo urged his readers to support the war effort "for honor, for patriotism, for gratitude, [and] for our own best interests" because as residents of the United States, "we have benefitted from her liberties."[42] This sense of patriotism was not absolute. While thousands rallied to the Stars and Stripes, many others simply fled to Mexico to avoid conscription, uncertain about supporting a state and nation that had disfranchised them politically and socially. Consequently, Tejano enlistment for the First World War could have been higher.[43]

Those who served largely demonstrated a discernable martial spirit that echoed that of most soldiers in the American Expeditionary Force. In addition to Marcelino Serna, who received the Distinguished Service Cross for his bravery in the Meusse-Argonne, other Tejanos also received awards for their actions on the battlefield. Pvt. Graviel García of Somerville, located about sixty miles east of Austin, earned the Distinguished Service Cross for his actions on October 16, 1918. Fighting as part of Company C, 325th Infantry Regiment, 82nd Division near St. Juvin, France, García voluntarily went out into no-man's-land under heavy enemy fire and administered first aid to a wounded comrade. While making his way back with the injured man, García was himself wounded.[44]

While García's actions proved heroic, the Central Texas native did not receive the highest honors of any Mexican American in the Great War. That distinction went to Pvt. David Bennes Barkley (David Barkley Cantú) of the 356th Infantry for his bravery in infiltrating German lines to obtain information about the enemy's dispositions. Barkley, born to a Mexican American mother and Anglo-American father in Laredo and reared in San Antonio, had volunteered to fight in 1917. Wary that he might be placed in a segregated unit, Barkley enlisted using his father's surname; he was living with his mother and had taken her surname as his own to this time. On November 9, 1918, he and a comrade succeeded in obtaining the necessary information on their mission. As the two men returned to their unit, Barkley drowned while trying to swim across the Meuse River. His companion made it back successfully, and their reconnaissance contributed to one of the final Allied offensives prior to the Armistice. For his actions, Barkley received the French Croix de Guerre, the Italian Croce al Merito di Guerra, and the Medal of Honor, the highest award for valor in the US armed forces. Later, when his ethnic origins were disclosed in 1989, he became recognized as the first Hispanic Medal of Honor recipient.[45]

In some cases acts of bravery from Tejano soldiers came from anger or resentment. Such was the case with Simon González, a day laborer from the small Central Texas town of Martindale, about ten miles east of San Marcos. González was drafted into the 360th Infantry Regiment despite the fact that his blind father, Maximiliano, protested the conscription due to his dependency on his son and the hardships his absence would cause. Protests to the local draft board and army officials went unheeded, and González soon left for Europe. He then transferred his hatred for the German American–led draft board in his hometown to the German soldiers in France. "I am here because of the Germans in Martindale!" he often exclaimed. González was killed in action in 1918.[46]

The end of the Great War did not signify an end to discrimination, however. The postwar elation and the federal government's awareness of the Mexican American presence in Texas soon gave way to old-fashioned stereotypes and prejudices.[47] Nevertheless, the war served as a turning point as Tejanos sought to stake a claim to the full promise of US citizenship. Fortunately for them, during the years following World War I, the burgeoning middle class had led to the creation of the League of United Latin American Citizens (LULAC), which emphasized attention on the civil rights of all Mexican Americans. LULAC saw that through military service, the gap between the American creed and practice could be exploited and closed. Accordingly, the organization published a volume entitled *Los México-Americanos y La Gran Guerra y Su Contingente en Pro de la Democracia, la Humanidad y la Justicia: Mi Diario Particular.* Written years earlier by José de la Luz Sáenz, it was the only chronicle of a Mexican American serviceman who fought in World War I. The book recounted the exploits of the thirty-year-old soldier of Mexican descent as he fought on behalf of democracy, humanity, and justice. Throughout his diary, Saenz maintained that the ideals of democracy could be applied to his fellow Mexican Americans in Texas in their struggle for social and economic equality. LULAC, for its part, continued to emphasize the essential credentials that Mexican Americans brought to the table. These feelings manifested themselves within the Tejano community with a burgeoning sense of American identity as more Texans of Mexican descent accommodated themselves to American traditions and values. As the 1930s drew to a close, Mexican Americans in Texas held a stronger sense of belonging to the United States than ever before.[48]

The nation's entry into World War II after the Japanese attack on Pearl Harbor on December 7, 1941, once again thrust the Tejano population into conflict. But unlike past wars, the Tejano community responded with the patriotic fervor of their Anglo-American neighbors. This was evident in the fact that as many as 750,000 Texans served in the armed forces during the war, a proportionally larger percentage than any other state; of that number, it is estimated that more than 100,000 were Tejanos.[49] Historians often refer to the Second World War as the watershed moment for Mexican Americans and their quest for social and political equality.[50] Yet as Arnoldo De León argues, Tejanos found themselves in a new place. The generation of the 1920s and 1930s "became increasingly insistent on their right to enjoy the privileges guaranteed them under the United States Constitution."[51] As such, Tejanos sought to become "genuine Americans," each striving to prove himself in battle while his family sacrificed for the war effort at home.[52] Like the previous world war, Tejanos viewed service in the military as a means to achievement and recognition that they were unable to attain in everyday life. These feelings were exemplified by Luis Leyva, born in Mexico but a resident of Laredo, who was an undocumented citizen and was not drafted. Nevertheless, Leyva volunteered. "I know no other country," he explained. "This is my country; this is where I live."[53]

Large numbers of Mexican Americans answered the country's call to arms, and their stories and anecdotes of military service or supporting those in combat held rich meaning to the Tejano community.[54] With the language barrier less of an issue than in previous wars, all Mexican Americans saw service in integrated units. Yet Company E, 141st Regiment, 36th (Texas) Division out of El Paso traveled to the European theater in a unit comprised mostly of Mexican Americans. In a fitting

Manuel Daniel Martinez (pictured as tech sergeant) of the 359th Infantry Regiment served honorably in the European theater during World War II. He received the Bronze Star for his heroism in battle and later the Jubilee of Liberty Medal from the French government in recognition of his participation in the D-Day invasion of Normandy. Courtesy Magda Martinez.

sense of irony, the men of Company E adopted the slogan "Remember the Alamo" as they campaigned and reminisced about their experiences of the Texas barrios.[55]

As in previous conflicts, Tejanos performed bravely on the battlefield. Of the thirty-three Texans to receive the Medal of Honor in the Second World War, five were of Mexican descent: Lucian Adams of Port Arthur, Macario García of Sugar Land, José M. López of Brownsville, Silvestre S. Herrera of El Paso, and Cleto L. Rodríguez of San Antonio. The figure was especially notable considering that out of the thirteen medals awarded to Hispanics in World War II, almost half came from Texas.[56] Formal recognition and honors for their service meant a great deal to these

Tejanos, particularly in the postwar era. For instance, Pfc. Manuel D. Martinez, a member of the 359th Infantry Regiment from Laredo, participated in the D-Day invasion, receiving the Bronze Star for his "heroic" actions in taking over an assault after his squad leader had been wounded. Fifty years after the war, Martinez received another honor, the Jubilee of Liberty Medal from the French government in recognition for his participation in the liberation of France. He appeared with that medal in his hometown newspaper, proudly displaying his honor on behalf of the nation's veterans.[57]

Amid the heroism and bravery, the notion of patriotism stood out. San Antonio native Manuel C. Vara, who served in the Pacific, exemplified this concept: "I was eager to get in to the war. I may not have understood it, but I saw it as someone attacking our country, and our response was that the proper thing to do was to fight back. We understood that [joining the military] was the patriotic thing to do, and for me at least, it was not a question of trying to get revenge against Japan, but simply that they needed to be stopped or else who knows where it would end if [the Japanese were] not stopped on their side of the Pacific."[58] These feelings epitomized how many Tejanos now felt.[59] And while others enlisted for the sake of romantic adventurism, to get out of jail, or to seek financial opportunities, most Mexican Texans were much like their Anglo-American comrades, joining the military for honor and country.[60] At the same time, unlike their Anglo brethren, Tejanos' ties to their ancestral land remained intact. Medal of Honor recipient José M. López of Brownsville, for instance, was also awarded the Aztec Eagle, the highest honor given to a foreign-born citizen by Mexico.[61]

The Second World War's military experience had a profound effect on Tejanos. While not as articulate as the "Double V" campaign that marked the African American war effort, Mexican Texans were keenly aware that the war against totalitarian dictatorships would serve to bolster their struggle for social and political equality at home. But first, many emboldened themselves to abandon the racial stereotypes of the past. Robstown native Cpl. Raymond Muníz noted that military officials disapproved of Mexican American soldiers speaking Spanish. In one instance, Muníz recollected, he and several other men were reprimanded for speaking Spanish among themselves. Laredoan Virgilio Roel, a private in the 84th US Infantry, noticed the discrimination right away. "I found a lot of prejudice, mainly resentment from white soldiers, especially if a Mexican American soldier got a better assignment because of his intellect. There was also crude discrimination by both commissioned officers and high-rank enlisted men in cases where the Mexican Americans were of a darker complexion," Roel recalled. Rio Grande Valley native

Pvt. Juan Martínez, 1st Cavalry Division, also noted the racial friction within the ranks, noting that one Anglo soldier in his own squad wanted nothing to do with him. "He hated me and didn't want to take orders from me," Martinez remembered. In some cases Tejanos simply had to overcome the harsh stereotypes their fellow servicemen held. "One guy was reading a cartoon and asked me if Mexicans really live with chickens," noted Pvt. Guadalupe Hernandez, a native of McAllen. Despite proving themselves on the field of battle, discrimination could still haunt Tejanos. In one outlandish case, Fort Bend County native Macario García, who had received the Medal of Honor along with twenty-seven other soldiers at a White House ceremony in August 1945, was denied service at a Richmond, Texas, restaurant the following month. An outraged García argued with the owner only to be arrested by police soon thereafter. LULAC and private groups rallied to his defense. After a trial, García was acquitted of all charges.[62]

The postwar world demonstrated that World War II was indeed a watershed moment for Tejanos, whose military service opened opportunities for education and financial security previously unavailable to them. Organizations like LULAC and the American GI Forum, organized in Corpus Christi in 1948 by Hector P. García, galvanized support for Mexican Americans in Texas and across the country. Yet negative feelings persisted, such as in the case of Pvt. Felix Longoria of Three Rivers, approximately seventy miles west of Corpus Christi. Longoria had been killed in action in the Pacific, his body buried in Luzon. In 1949 his remains were supposed to be sent to his family for burial in Three Rivers. Yet the local mortician

Tejano GIs in North Africa, World War II. American troops in North Africa sample the wares of a fruit vendor. Left to right: Sgt. Hardy Patillo of Austin; Capt. Louis Dubcak of Lexington; Sgt. Adan Garza of Laredo; and Pfc. Herbert Lipsey of Dade City, Florida. During the Second World War, Tejano soldiers found themselves fighting alongside fellow Americans who might have once discriminated against them in society. Courtesy Prints and Photographs Division, Library of Congress, Washington, DC (LC-USW33-000797-ZC).

refused to have a wake for a "Mexican" in his place of business despite Longoria's honorable service record, which included commendations for bravery and a Purple Heart. The resulting imbroglio, which harkened racial injustices of the past, led to the American GI Forum's involvement and the ultimate burial of Longoria's body at Arlington National Cemetery.[63] The Longoria case and other incidents notwithstanding, Tejanos refused to acquiesce to the social, economic, and racial subjugation of past generations. The war and the resulting GI Bill, which expanded educational and economic opportunities for Mexican American veterans, gave many Tejano servicemen hope that racial discrimination would remain in the past, viewing themselves now as fully Americans rather than partially Mexicans.[64]

The Tejanos' postwar world might have been changing amid the massive demobilization of the nation's military, but the onset of the Korean Conflict in June 1950 thrust US armed forces into another war, this time to contain Communism. Texans once more answered the nation's call to arms, with more than 289,000 servicemen from the Lone Star State making their way to East Asia; of these, an estimated 50,000 were of Mexican descent.[65] While the Selective Service Extension Act of June 30, 1950, focused on the National Guard and other reserve units as the first to go to Korea, more than 200,000 draftees were called to arms by the end of the year. The United States did not enter the war alone, American forces participating alongside those of seventeen other countries that were part of the United Nations peacekeeping force.[66] Accordingly, some Tejanos found themselves in positions of leadership. Sgt. Arnoldo Gutierrez, from Laredo, was part of the 500-man American Korean Military Advisory Group, a unit responsible for training the South Korean Army with modern weapons. In a fitting sense of irony, considering the status of Mexican-born Texans a generation earlier, Gutierrez and his unit, which included several other Tejanos, were charged with "Americanizing" the South Koreans. "We worked under the 8th Army and we were there to train the South Koreans . . . and instruct them on the American way of life, including the responsibilities of freedom and democracy," he noted.[67]

In some respects, the patriotic fervor that had marked enlistment in World War II was absent for the Korean War despite the fact that nearly 148,000 Hispanics served in the military during the conflict. Veteran Ernesto Gonzalez recalled: "We didn't have much knowledge in Duval County about the Korean War. The only reason I went was because my brother had been drafted . . . and my family would cry every night . . . and so I told my father 'As soon as I'm old enough I'm going to join the army so I can help my brother win the war, so that he can come back.'"[68] The need for more soldiers was partly fulfilled by earlier amendments to US

A native of Yorktown, Texas, Horacio Vela epitomized the new-found complexities for Tejanos in the armed forces during the post–World War II era. Vela served in the Sixth Army during the Korean War, earning the Korean Service Medal. He later joined the 7th Armored Division, "the Lucky Seventh." Courtesy Ricardo "Rick" Vela.

naturalization laws. In 1918 Congress modified the laws to make it easier for immigrants serving in the military to become citizens. In the 1940s the federal government had continued to support the streamlined naturalization process for foreign-born soldiers.[69] In the Korean War this process now included many Mexican immigrants who had made their way into the United States in search of a better life during the postwar economic boom. Pvt. Raúl M. Chavarría, a native of Tamaluipas, Mexico, found himself thrust into the military by the events around him. Originally arriving in Texas to search for work, the twenty-year-old laborer eventually made his way to Chicago, where he received a summons to report to Laredo for military service. After training in El Paso, Chavarría left the Lone Star State bound for New York, then to Germany, much to his chagrin. *"Yo pedí ir a Korea, pero me mandarin a Alemania* [I asked to go to Korea, but they sent me to Germany]," he recalled. Chavarría became a citizen in 1954, one year after the United States and North Korea signed an armistice. He later appreciated the opportunity that military service gave him for citizenship.[70]

Despite the heavier reliance on foreign-born soldiers, especially those from Mexico, the United States armed forces ultimately saw nine Hispanic soldiers receive the Medal of Honor for their acts of bravery on the battlefield during the Korean War. Of these, two medals went to Tejanos, US Marine Corps sergeant Ambrosio Guillen of El Paso, and US Army corporal Benito Martinez of Fort Hancock, about forty miles southeast of El Paso. Guillen distinguished himself for the military honors by helping fend off an enemy assault near Songuch-on and forcing the enemy to retreat; Guillen was mortally wounded in the fight. Martinez also received the Medal of Honor for fending off an enemy assault; he, too was mortally wounded.[71]

In the decade after the Korean War, the United States found itself embroiled in another Asian country as American military forces poured into Vietnam, again to prevent that nation from falling to Communism. Texas once again answered the

Cpl. Raúl M. Chavarría, a native of Tamaulipas, Mexico, ended up using his service in the US Army during the Korean War era to gain citizenship in the United States. Chavarría served in the US Army's Fifth Division. Courtesy Raúl M. Chavarría

call. More than 500,000 Texans served in the military during the 1960s and 1970s; of these, approximately 25,000 saw service in Vietnam. During that period, Tejanos found themselves in an improved social, political, and economic climate. Their foremost civil rights organizations, LULAC and the American GI Forum, had rallied against the remaining vestiges of discrimination and segregation during the 1950s and 1960s. Even so, the Tejano community continued to view military service as a way out poverty and as a demonstration of national pride and bravery.[72]

Perhaps no one exemplified the notion of bravery and pride like Raul "Roy" Perez Benavidez of El Campo, a town about fifty miles southwest of Houston. Born in Cuero, Benavidez hailed from Mexican and Yaqui Indian descent. His parents died at an early age, so he moved to El Campo to live with relatives. Like many Tejanos of that era, Benavidez dropped out of school in his teen years and worked a variety of labor-intensive jobs until he joined the army in 1955. Stung by the racial discrimination prevalent in the 1940s, he vowed to master English, changed his name from Raul to Roy, and strived toward obtaining an education and improving his lot in life.[73] Master Sergeant Benavidez left for Vietnam in 1965 to serve as an advisor for the Army of the Republic of Vietnam. He was wounded shortly thereafter when he stepped on a landmine. Three years later his actions during a firefight near Loch Ninh would earn him the Distinguished Service Cross for bravery. Benavidez exposed himself to enemy fire while rescuing comrades and retrieving vital documents left behind in a chopper that ferried US troops to action. He received thirty-seven wounds and fought off enemy soldiers in hand-to-hand combat. Army doctors originally thought that he was dead until the sergeant spit blood in their faces to show them that he was still alive. Surviving his wounds, in his later years Benavidez toured the country, giving speeches on honor, bravery, and patriotism. He became arguably the most celebrated Tejano war veteran, receiving the Medal of Honor years after his Vietnam service ended. In addition, his likeness was used for a GI Joe action figure and his name used to honor various schools and US naval vessels—he even had a commemorative US Postal Service stamp in his honor. Benavidez also published two autobiographies, describing his rise from poverty to war hero.[74]

Benavidez may have been the most popular Tejano to serve in Vietnam, but he was not the only one who distinguished himself for bravery. US Marine Corps sergeant Alfredo Gonzalez of Edinburg and Cpl. Miguel Keith of San Antonio each earned the Medal of Honor for their actions in Vietnam. In the both cases, the men received mortal wounds while in battle, their medals awarded posthumously. Both received additional honors, including the naming of schools, buildings, and in the case of Gonzalez, a US Navy destroyer. Tejanos thus earned three of the seventeen Medals of Honor awarded during the conflict.[75] Others, like Sergeant 1st Class Isaac "Ike" Camacho, earned additional service medals for acts of heroism and bravery. Camacho, a native of El Paso, was captured by the Vietcong in November 1963 after a skirmish and remained a prisoner for twenty months until he escaped in July 1965, for which he received the Silver Star and the Bronze Star.[76]

A final tally reveals more than 2.7 million Americans who served in Vietnam. Of those, 47,364 were killed in action; Texas claimed 3,450 of its own dead. A 1969 study revealed that 8,167 soldiers from Texas, Arizona, New Mexico, and California had suffered casualties since 1961. Of those, 19 percent were recorded as being of Hispanic descent, a figure seen as markedly high considering that the Hispanic population represented 11.8 percent of the total population in those five states.[77] In Texas, out of the 3,415 killed, 777 had Spanish surnames, a figure that represents 22 percent of the total figure and slightly higher than the Tejano representation in the state's population.[78]

The high casualty counts had little influence on the leading Mexican American civil rights organizations in Texas as LULAC and the American GI Forum rallied behind the American war effort in Vietnam. For instance, World War II veteran and LULAC activist John J. Herrera, a native of Houston, approved of the war to stop Communism. Hector P. García, the founder of the American GI Forum, concurred, contending that "the majority if not the total Mexican-American people approve of the present course of action in Vietnam." As historian Lorena Oropeza demonstrates, the forum kept a tally of the Mexican American casualties as a means of highlighting the "ethnic group's sacrifices on behalf of the war effort." In 1968 the organization even sponsored a tour to demonstrate the vitality of the conflict to Mexican American families. Garcia collected letters from soldiers in Vietnam supporting the commitment of what the troops were fighting for. In one letter Texan S. B. Sanchez pointed out the need to be a "good citizen" and that the war was America's responsibility as a "great country." He maintained that it was necessary to go to war "to defend our freedom and heritage." The feelings Sanchez expressed echoed those of Benavidez, who later said that he fought as a proud American.[79]

Yet by the late 1960s, the growing Chicano movement in the Southwest threatened the notion that a loyal and faithful population of Mexican Americans would remain docile to the interests of the United States. In fact, the new wave of Chicano leaders rallied behind a variety of different agendas, including education and the war.[80] Among one of the criticisms in Texas was the disproportionate number of Tejanos who died in Vietnam. In one case study, figures revealed that 66 percent of San Antonio's casualties in 1966 had Spanish surnames, even though the city's total Mexican American population stood at 41 percent. Critics also pointed out that no Mexican Americans sat on draft boards despite the fact that they composed more than 50 percent of the population in some areas along the Rio Grande Valley. Unlike other civil-rights-era protestors, the Mexican American movement did not actively criticize the soldiers. As Oropeza points out, unlike the white antiwar movement, Chicano protestors emphasized that Mexican Americans should fight for social justice at home and not in a foreign war for a government they considered the enemy. And while this movement may not have altered the rich tradition of Hispanic participation in the nation's wars, an opinion different from the mantra of assimilation and Americanization that had marked the Mexican American community in the wake of the Second World War was now evident.[81]

In the post-Vietnam era, Tejanos retained the strong elements that marked the longstanding cornerstones of military service: patriotism, bravery, and the concept of Americanism. Memorials, documentaries, monuments, and veterans groups are just some of the means by which the military service of Mexican Texans can lay claim to the most significant element of all, the importance of citizenship. In 2002 business and city leaders in Laredo succeeded in building the "nation's first monument honoring the 40 or so Hispanic soldiers who have received the country's highest award for military valor, the Medal of Honor."[82] The centerpiece for the downtown memorial was native son, David Cantu Barkley. Barkley also serves as a focal point of *Veteranos: A Legacy of Valor*, a play that combines theater, music, dance, and Department of Defense footage to tell the story of four soldiers in four wars. *Veteranos* creator and director Enrique Castillo has argued that his play had deep implications for the Mexican American community. He maintains: "The reason all people need to see this is that we [Latinos] didn't start with the Alamo, and we're still here, and we have always been here. If you are a good American, it's important to know the history of this country, which includes the culture of our young men."[83]

In 2008 Maj. Gen. Freddie Valenzuela, commander of the US Army South, published *No Greater Love: The Lives and Times of Hispanic Soldiers*, a book that explores "the legacy of Hispanic Americans in the military." In his introduction Valenzuela, who was born in Refugio but raised in San Antonio's West Side, minces no words, describing himself as "an American first, and foremost." And while his purpose was to honor the legacy of Hispanic soldiers, he hoped that his work could serve as a stepping stone for other Hispanics interested in military service. The general argues that all Hispanics, not just Mexican Texans, are special to the US armed forces because they have always been confronted with questions about their "loyalty to this country and willingness to contribute to American progress." Valenzuela maintains that Hispanic soldiers undoubtedly love and cherish their country. As such, they by and large join the armed forces not for the educational and economic opportunities military service affords, but because they represent the very embodiment of American values: sacrifice, selflessness, and hard work. "Hispanic soldiers by and large do not join for self-aggrandizement or personal gain. . . . [M]ost of these soldiers want to be among comrades, getting to get the job done. We learned to be workhorses, not show horses."[84]

While General Valenzuela's views on Hispanic soldiers are grounded in the experience of a rich military career that spanned more than thirty years, the history of Tejanos' military service offers an interesting paradox. To be sure, honor and the need to defend one's nation was (and remains) a predominant sentiment among the Mexican Texan population. But as George Mariscal notes, the need to assimilate was also a strong driving force behind the disproportionate number of high enlistments of the twentieth century. Mariscal argues that Hispanic views on bravery and courage, or as he calls it, "Warrior patriotism," draws from Mexican culture, which inherently supports bravery and the "readiness to die for la patria [the homeland]."[85] That concept was not always prevalent in the Tejano population, however. In the wars of the nineteenth century, the loyalty and allegiance of Tejanos was predicated more on local circumstances than any overriding feelings of patriotism and national identity, concepts that are more fluid, more gray than black or white. It was not

In 2003 the City of Laredo awarded the building of a memorial to honor all Hispanic Medal of Honor recipients to local artist Armando Hinojosa. Perched atop the monument is a statue of local Tejano World War I veteran David Bennes Barkley (Cantu), who posthumously received the Medal of Honor for his actions in the Great War. The names of all Hispanic Medal of Honor recipients are engraved in a plaque on the base of the memorial. Courtesy Alex Mendoza.

until World War II that Mexican Texans began to truly identify themselves with the concept of the American dream.

The ambivalence shown in the century since the Texas Revolution does not diminish the bravery and honor of those who fought in the various conflicts in the United States during those years. Yet the rationale behind Tejano motivation and support for each conflict was far more complex. Tejanos were always willing to risk their lives to defend their homes, but after the Texas Revolution, feelings of local loyalties and self-preservation usurped nationalistic sentiment, especially considering the racial discrimination and the political marginalization of the antebellum era. And while service in the Frontier Battalion was available to Tejanos in the late 1800s, most still shied away from service in the Old Army until the First World War. By World War II, Tejanos clearly recognized the benefits that military service could provide. Those extrinsic factors tied into longstanding notions of patriotism as more Tejanos were born in the United States and identified themselves as Americans rather than Mexicans in America. Accordingly, by the latter part of the twentieth century, Tejanos recognized that to overcome the doubts some expressed about their courage or loyalty, they had to emphasize their willingness to fight and die in battle.

Notes

1. Elena Gomez, "Marcelino Serna Became World War I Hero," *Borderlands* 23 (2004–2005): 10; US Government, *Hispanics in America's Defense* (Washington, DC: Neale, 1989), 25; Byron Farwell, *Over There: The United States in the Great War, 1917–1918* (New York: W. W. Norton, 1999), 212–17; Edward Coffman, *The War to End All Wars: The American Military Experience in World War I* (Lexington: University of Kentucky Press, 1998), 275–84; John S. D. Eisenhower, *Yanks: The Epic Story of the American Army in World War I* (New York: Free Press, 2001), 191–95.

2. Gomez, "Marcelino Serna," 10; US Government, *Hispanics in America's Defense,* 25; *El Paso Times,* May 4, 2009. Ralph A. Wooster highlights the honors earned by Texas soldiers during the First World War in *Texas and Texans in the Great War* (Buffalo Gap, TX: State House, 2010), 117–45. According to Laurence Stallings, the 89th Division "called itself the 'Middle Wests' and was filled with men from the Canadian border to the Rio Grande, mountain men and trappers, cowboys from the plains, farm lads from the prairies and cornfields, and sundry characters from the ranches and deserts." *The Doughboys: The Story of the AEF, 1917–1918* (New York: Harper and Row, 1963), 348.

3. The term "Tejano" (and in turn, "Tejana") is used to identify ethnic Mexicans who remained in Texas after the revolution. In many cases these Texans of Mexican origin would later claim, to varying degrees, a distinct identity as Tejanos.

4. Andrés Tijerina, *Tejanos and Texas under the Mexican Flag, 1821–1836* (College Station: Texas A&M Press, 1994), 79, 83–84; 88–90.

5. Frank Salinas, "Placido Benavides Narrative, 'The Texas Paul Revere,'" Dolph Briscoe Center for American History, The University of Texas at Austin (hereafter CAH).

6. Stephen L. Hardin, *Texian Iliad: A Military History of the Texas Revolution* (Austin: University of Texas Press, 1994), 16, 28, 83 (quote). A detailed examination of Tejanos' roles in the Texas Revolution is found in Raúl Ramos, *Beyond the Alamo: Forging Mexican Ethnicity in San Antonio, 1821–1861* (Chapel Hill: University of North Carolina Press, 2008), 133–65.

7. Ramos, *Beyond the Alamo*, 157; Arnoldo De León, *Mexican Americans in Texas: A Brief History* (New York: Harlan Davidson, 2009), 33.

8. One out of every ten Tejanos were executed in 1813, while Texas was under the Spanish flag, following the Battle of Medina. Thus enthusiasm for any uprising would have been mixed. See De León, *Mexican Americans in Texas*, 25–26.

9. Ruben R. Lozano, *Viva Tejas: The Story of the Mexican-born Patriots of the Republic of Texas* (San Antonio: Southern Literary Institute, 1936), 34–35.

10. Hardin, *Texian Iliad*, 209–13 (quote); Lozano, *Viva Tejas*, 36–37.

11. Ramos, *Beyond the Alamo*, 150.

12. Hardin, *Texian Iliad*, 271n. In many cases the language barrier served as an impediment to recognizing the veterans' efforts. For instance, see Cayetano Castillo to Texas Veterans Association, Apr. 22, 1880, Texas War Veteran Papers, CAH. Castillo was a veteran of the siege of San Antonio in 1835 under the command of Capt. Manuel Leal. Yet he had to be recommended by Thaddeus W. Smith, who served as a witness to Castillo's signature by mark. Smith also served as witness for Ygnacio Espinosa. Raúl Ramos's *Beyond the Alamo* devotes a chapter to examining the Anglo mistrust of Tejanos evident in the postwar period.

13. David Montejano, *Anglos and Mexicans in the Making of Texas, 1836–1986* (Austin: University of Texas Press, 1987), 25–26.

14. Andrés Reséndez, *Changing National Identities at the Frontier: Texas and New Mexico, 1800–1850* (New York: Cambridge University Press, 2006), 146–70; Ramos, *Beyond the Alamo*, 167–91; Montejano, *Anglos and Mexicans*, 26.

15. Montejano, *Anglos and Mexicans*, 28–29; Paul Horgan, *Great River: The Rio Grande in North American History* (New York: Rinehart, 1954), 569–85; Noel M. Loomis, *Texan–Santa Fe Pioneers* (Norman: University of Oklahoma Press, 1958). Even Seguin, a former mayor of San Antonio, was forced to flee. In later years he explained what happened: "The rumor, that I was a traitor, was seized with avidity, by my enemies in San Antonio. Some envied my position, as held by a Mexican; others found in me an obstacle to the accomplishment of their villainous plans. The number of land suits which still encumbers the docket of Bexar County would indicate the nature of plans, and any one, who has listened to the evidence elicited in cases of this description, will readily discover the base means adopted to deprive rightful owners of their property." Juan Seguin Memoirs, CAH.

16. A. Brooke Caruso, *The Mexican Spy Company: United States Covert Operations in Mexico, 1845–1848* (Jefferson, NC: McFarland, 1991), 83; Jerry D. Thompson, *Vaqueros in Blue and Gray* (Austin, TX: State House, 2000), 12. Ramos argues that US forces in the war with Mexico did "not include any Spanish-surnamed soldiers." *Beyond the Alamo*, 199. See also Charles D. Spurlin, *Texas Volunteers in the Mexican War* (Austin, TX: Eakin, 1999), 158, 166.

17. Armando C. Alonzo, *Tejano Legacy: Rancheros and Settlers in South Texas, 1734–1900* (Albuquerque: University of New Mexico Press, 1998), 132.

18. Michael L. Collins, *Texas Devils: Rangers and Regulars on the Lower Rio Grande, 1846–1861* (Norman: University of Oklahoma Press, 2008), 7; James W. Mills, "Irregulars: Guerrilla and Ranchero Warfare in South Texas and Northern Mexico during the Mexican-American War," *Journal of South Texas* 22, no. 1 (Spring 2009): 1–20.

19. Douglas W. Richmond, "A View of the Periphery: Regional Factors and Collaboration during the U.S.-Mexico Conflict, 1845–1848," in *Dueling Eagles: Reinterpreting the U.S.-Mexican War, 1846–1848*, ed. Richard V. Francaviglia and Douglas W. Richmond (Fort Worth: Texas Christian University Press, 2000), 141. See also Brian DeLay, *War of a Thousand Deserts: Indian Raids and the U.S.-Mexican War* (New Haven, CT: Yale University Press, 2008), 203–204.

20. Manuel Callahan, "Mexican Border Troubles: Social War, Settler Colonialism, and the Production of Frontier Discourses, 1848–1880" (PhD diss., The University of Texas at Austin, 2003), 2.

21. Arnoldo De León, *They Called Them Greasers: Anglo Attitudes toward Mexicans in Texas, 1821–1900* (Austin: University of Texas Press, 1983), 82–83; De León, Mexican Americans in Texas, 42; Jerry D. Thompson, *Cortina: Defending the Mexican Name in Texas* (College Station: Texas A&M University Press, 2007); David Urbano, "'When the Smoke Cleared': The 1857–1858 Cart Wars of South Texas" (PhD diss., University of Houston, 2009). For the legacy of the Cortina War, see Thompson, *Cortina*, 249–52.

22. De León, *They Called Them Greaser*, 38–39.

23. Thompson, *Vaqueros in Blue and Gray*, 81.

24. Charles D. Grear, *Why Texans Fought in the Civil War* (College Station: Texas A&M University, 2010), 156–61; Miguel Gonzalez Quiroga, "Mexicanos in Texas during the Civil War," in *Mexican Americans in Texas History*: Selected Essays, ed. Emilio Zamora, Cynthia Orozco, and Rodolfo Rocha (Austin: Texas State Historical Association Press, 2000), 51–62.

25. "Report of the Mexican Commission on the Northern Frontier Question," reprinted in *The Mexican Experience in Texas*, ed. Carlos E. Cortés (New York: Arno, 1976), 66.

26. Ramos, *Beyond the Alamo*, 229–30; Patrick J. Kelly, "'Is He a Mexican or a Texan?': Santos Benavides, Tejano Confederate," paper delivered at the Texas State Historical Association Conference, 2007; Hector Farias Jr., "Col. Santos Benavides: The Emergence of a Dynamic Military and Political Leader," in *LareDOS* 15, no. 10 (Oct. 2010), 50; Montejano, *Anglos and Mexicans*, 72–73.

27. Grear, *Why Texans Fought*, 159.

28. In 1864 a Benavides-led force of 42 men repulsed a 200-man Union contingent advancing from Brownville in the Battle of Laredo, securing the passage of more than 200 bales of cotton into Mexico. Kelly, "Is He a Mexican or a Texan?"; John Denny Riley, "Santos Benavides: His Influence on the Lower Rio Grande, 1823–1891" (PhD diss., Texas Christian University, 1976); Jerry D. Thompson, "Santos Benavides and the Battle of Laredo," *Civil War Times Illustrated* 19, no. 8 (Aug. 1980): 15–21; Grear, *Why Texans Fought*, 241–43; Thompson, *Vaqueros in Blue and Gray*, 107–10.

29. Thompson, *Vaqueros in Blue and Gray*, 23.

30. See the respective records in Texas Adjutant General Service Records, 1836–1935, Texas State Library and Archives, Austin.

31. Agustin De Zavala to Dear Sister, May 27, 1898, Adina De Zavala Papers, CAH. For the next several months, De Zavala's letters echoed the typical travails of boredom and

monotony of a soldier's life until his discharge in March 1899. See Agustin De Zavala to Dear Sister, May 17, 24, 27, June 1, 14, Aug. [?], 1898, ibid. For Texas' martial spirit, see James McCaffrey, "Texans in the Spanish American War," *Southwestern Historical Quarterly* 106, no. 2 (Oct. 2002): 259–60.

32. David F. Trask, *The War with Spain in 1898* (Lincoln: University of Nebraska Press, 1981), 157.

33. McCaffrey, "Texans in the Spanish American War," 257. See also the respective records in the Texas Adjutant General Service Records, Texas State Library. The figure of Tejanos in the Spanish-American War is derived from examining the pension rolls of over 4,300 veterans. Of these, only a dozen indicate their origins as "Mexican." This does not take into account soldiers of mixed ancestry.

34. De León, *Mexican Americans in Texas*, 58–59.

35. McCaffrey, "Texans in the Spanish American War," 268.

36. *El Paso International Daily Times*, May 24, 1898.

37. Ibid., Apr. 30, May 10, May 27, 1898. See also Christine Nelson, "Texas Militia in the Spanish-American War," *Texas Military History* 2 (Aug. 1962): 194.

38. José A. Ramírez, *To the Line of Fire: Mexican Texans and World War I* (College Station: Texas A&M University Press, 2009), 1–3, 6–7, 8–11, 15–18; De León, *Mexican Americans in Texas*, 65; Montejano, *Anglos and Mexicans*, 82–92; Elliott Young, "Red Men, Princess Pocahontas, and George Washington: Harmonizing Race Relations in Laredo at the Turn of the Century," *Western Historical Quarterly* 29 (Spring 1998): 50–51; Young, "Deconstructing *La Raza*: Identifying the *Gente Decente de Laredo*, 1904–1911," *Southwestern Historical Quarterly* 98, no. 2 (Oct. 1994): 228.

39. Ramírez, *To the Line of Fire*, 19 (quote), 20.

40. Ibid., 22–23; De León, *Mexican Americans in Texas*, 91, 93; Carole Christian, "Joining the American Mainstream: Texas' Mexican Americans during World War I," *Southwestern Historical Quarterly* 92 (Apr. 1989): 572–77, 592–94.

41. Ramírez, *To the Line of Fire*, 27–30. Ramírez examines the rich and disparate complexities of Tejanos' mobilization efforts in chapter 2.

42. *El Democrata Fronterizo* (Laredo, TX), Oct. 5, 1918 (translation mine). The editorial reads: "por honor, por patriotismo, por gratitude, por nuestro propio interes . . . por que residemos en los Estados Unidos y hemos gozado de sus libertades."

43. Ramírez, *To the Line of Fire*, 31–33.

44. Jose de la Paz Saenz, *Los México-Americanos y La Gran Guerra y Su Contingente en Pro de la Democracia, la Humanidad y la Justicia: Mi Diario Particular* [The Mexican Americans and the Great War and Their People in Favor of Democracy, Humanity, and Justice: My Particular Journal] (San Antonio: Artes Graficas, 1933), 174–75; Ramírez, *To the Line of Fire*, 102.

45. "Laredo's Only Medal of Honor Winner Remembered," *Laredo Morning Times*, Nov. 9, 2002; De León, *Mexican Americans in Texas*, 94.

46. Ramírez, *To the Line of Fire*, 26, 102.

47. Nancy Gentile Ford, *Americans All! Foreign-born Soldiers in World War I* (College Station: Texas A&M University Press, 2001), chap. 2, 144–45.

48. Alex Mendoza, "The Warrior Tradition," *LareDOS* 14, no. 4 (Apr. 2008): 65; De León, *Mexican Americans in Texas*, 108–109.

49. Robert A. Calvert et al., *The History of Texas*, 4th ed. (New York: Harland Davidson,

2007), 347. There is difficulty in providing a precise number of Tejanos due to the fact that under the race categorization on enlistment and discharge papers, Mexican Americans and other Hispanics were often described as "White," "Mexican," or simply "NA." Beyond Puerto Ricans, this figure is imprecise. See US Government, *Hispanics in American Defense*, 27. For a study on the American GI, see Lee Kennett, *G.I.: The American Soldier in World War II* (Norman: Oklahoma University Press, 1987).

50. Lorena Oropeza, *¡Raza Sí! ¡Guerra No! Chicano Protest and Patriotism during the Viet Nam War Era* (Berkeley: University of California Press, 2005), 12–13; George J. Sánchez, *Becoming Mexican American: Ethnicity, Culture, and Identity in Chicano Los Angeles, 1900–1945* (New York: Oxford University Press, 1993), 256.

51. Arnoldo De León, "Mexican Americans in Texas," in *The Texas Heritage*, ed. Ben Proctor and Archie McDonald, 4th ed. (Wheeling, IL: Harlan Davidson, 2003), 215.

52. Richard Griswold del Castillo, "The War and Changing Identities: Personal Transformations," in *World War II and Mexican American Civil Rights* (Austin: University of Texas Press, 2008), 51; Mario T. Garcia, *Mexican Americans: Leadership, Ideology, and Identity, 1930–1960* (New Haven, CT: Yale University Press, 1989), 114.

53. Griswold del Castillo, "War and Changing Identities," 56.

54. See David Zimmerman, "Mexican-American Texans," in *1941: Texas Goes to War*, ed. James Ward Lee et al. (Denton: University of North Texas Press, 1991), 128–43.

55. *Albuquerque Journal*, July 26, 1981; *Houston Chronicle*, Apr. 5, 1999.

56. De León, *Mexican Americans in Texas*, 117; Ralph A. Wooster, "World War II, Texans in," *Handbook of Texas Online*, accessed Sept. 26, 2009, http://www.tshaonline.org/handbook/online/articles/qdw02.

57. *Laredo Times*, undated clipping, in author's possession; "Manuel D. Martinez, Enlisted Record and Report of Separation," ibid. (courtesy Magda M. Martinez); "General Orders No. 394," Apr. 30, 1945, ibid. (courtesy Magda M. Martinez).

58. Manuel C. Vara Interview, US Latino & Latina WWII Oral History Project, Nettie Lee Benson Latin American Collection, University of Texas at Austin (hereafter cited as OHP, UT).

59. See, for instance, the Gonzalo Garza, Oscar Torres, Bob Sanchez, and Luis Leyva Interviews, ibid.

60. Reynaldo B. Rendon (Corpus Christi) joined the military to get out of jail for a previous transgression, Bob Sanchez (Laredo) thought service would be a "bit romantic," and Ramon M. Rivas (Eagle Pass) joined the army to make a little more money than he was earning with the Works Progress Administration. See Rendon and Rivas Interviews, OHP, UT. Other Tejanos shirked duty, to be sure. For instance, in 1942 the Falfurrias newspaper *Falfurrias Facts* reported that the local draft board was seeking information on Luis García and Gilberto Alcántar, two Mexican Texans who were believed to have fled to Mexico to avoid service. *Falfurrias Facts*, June 19, 1942.

61. Matt S. Meier and Feliciano Ribera, *Mexican Americans—American Mexicans: From Conquistadores to Chicanos* (New York: Hill and Wang, 1993), 161.

62. Raymond Muníz Interview, OHP, UT; Virgilio Roel Interview, ibid.; Juan Martinez Interview, ibid.; Guadalupe "Lupe" Hernandez Interview, ibid.; María-Cristina Garcia, "Garcia, Macario," *Handbook of Texas Online*, accessed July 29, 2010, http://www.tshaonline.org/handbook/online/articles/fga76.

63. Patrick J. Carroll, *Felix Longoria's Wake: Bereavement, Racism, and the Rise of Mexican American Activism* (Austin: University of Texas Press, 2003), 55–56; De León, *Mexican Americans in Texas*, 120–21; Carl Allsup, *The American G.I. Forum: Origins and Evolution* (Austin: University of Texas Press, 1982), 39–40; Ignacio M. García, *Hector P. García: In Relentless Pursuit of Justice* (Houston: Arte Publico, 2002), 115–23, 125–39.

64. See the Quirino Longoria, Luis Leyva, Julius V. Joseph, Joe Jasso, Rafael Hernandez, Jose Garza, and Gonzalo Garza Interviews, OHP, UT; and De León, *Mexican Americans in Texas*, 127–28, 134.

65. The figure is a rough estimate derived from examining the 1,719 casualty reports in Korean Conflict Casualty File, 1950–57 (Machine-Readable Record), Records of the Office of the Secretary of Defense, RG 330, National Archives, Washington, DC. Of the 1,700 casualties, 302 were of servicemen with Spanish surnames, a rough aggregate of 17.5 percent. That same percentage was used to calculate how many Mexican Americans could have been part of the 289,000 Texans who served in the Korean Conflict. It is difficult to surmise because at the time there were no racial/ethnic classifications, and many Hispanics were simply labeled as "White" or "NA." There is also the possibility that several, if not many, of the Spanish-surnamed servicemen were Puerto Rican or from some other nation. Further study is clearly needed in this area.

66. Terrence Gough, *U.S. Army Mobilization and Logistics in the Korean War* (Washington, DC: Center of Military History, US Army, 1987).

67. John Andrew Snyder, "Overdue Remembrance: Korean War Ceasefire and Veterans Finally Recognized by Congress," *LareDOS* 15, no. 9 (Oct. 2009): 31.

68. Quote in Julie Leininger Pycior, *LBJ and Mexican Americans: The Paradox of Power* (Austin: University of Texas Press, 1997), 79.

69. Ford, *Americans All!*, 63–64; Lucy E. Salyer, "Baptism by Fire: Race, Military Service, and U.S. Citizenship Policy, 1918–1935," *Journal of American History* 91, no. 3 (2001): 847–76.

70. Raúl M. Chavarría, interview by author, Aug. 1, 2009 (translation mine). Chavarría was eventually part of the US Army's 5th Division, which saw service in Europe during the 1950s. "Armed Forces of the United States Report of Transfer or Discharge, October 6, 1956," copy in author's possession.

71. US Government, *Hispanics in America's Defense*, 34, 59, 60.

72. For the numbers of Texans in Vietnam, see chap. 13; and De León, *Mexican Americans in Texas*, 128–32.

73. Undated newspaper clipping, Roy Benavidez Papers, CAH; *San Antonio Express News*, Nov. 8, 1998.

74. Roy Benavidez Biographical Sketch, Benavidez Papers; El Campo News Leader, Apr. 16, 1980, Feb. 21, Mar. 28, 1981, July 28, 2001; *Triad: Published in the Interest of Fort McCoy Personnel* 6, no. 6 (Mar. 24, 1989); Roy P. Benavidez, with Oscar Griffin, *The Three Wars of Roy Benavidez* (New York: Ballantine, 1986); Roy Benavidez, with John R. Craig, *Medal of Honor: One Man's Journey from Poverty and Prejudice* (Washington, DC: Potomac, 1995). For an in-depth look at the information on Benavidez, see the Benavidez Papers.

75. See John Flores, *When the River Dreams: The Life of Marine Sgt. Freddy Gonzalez* (Bloomington, IN : Author House, 2006); Oropeza, *¡Raza Si! ¡Guerra No!*, 189; Art Leatherwood, "Keith, Miguel," *Handbook of Texas Online*, accessed Sept. 21, 2009, http://

www.tshaonline.org/handbook/online/articles/fkeyj; and Art Leatherwood and Alicia A. Garza, "Gonzalez, Alfredo Cantu," ibid., accessed Sept. 21, 2009, http://www.tshaonline.org/handbook/online/articles/fgoqp.

76. US Government, *Hispanics in America's Defense*, 37.

77. Ibid., 38–39. Brady Foust and Howard Botts offered a lower estimate in "Age, Ethnicity, and Class in the Vietnam War," a conference paper presented in the 1980s–1990s, copy in author's possession. See also Oropeza, *¡Raza Sí! ¡Guerra No!*, 216n85.

78. [Southeast Asia] Combat Area Casualties Current File (electronic record), Records of the Office of the Secretary of Defense, RG 330, National Archives. Arnoldo De León, places Texas' Tejano population at 1.4 million in 1960 (14 percent of total) and 2 million in 1970 (20 percent of total). *Mexican Americans in Texas*, 122, 136.

79. Oropeza, *¡Raza Sí! ¡Guerra No!*, 62, 63; *San Antonio Express News*, Nov. 8, 1998. For views of Vietnam veterans, see Lea Ybarra, *Vietnam Veteranos: Chicanos Recall the War* (Austin: University of Texas Press, 2004).

80. Meier and Ribera, Mexican Americans, 218–20.

81. Oropeza, *¡Raza Sí! ¡Guerra No!*, 7–8, 67, 68, 191–93.

82. *Laredo Morning Times*, May 5, 2003.

83. Ibid., Oct. 16, 2002.

84. Freddie Valenzuela, with Jason Lemons, *No Greater Love: The Lives and Times of Hispanic Soldiers* (Austin, TX: Ovation, 2008), xiii, xvii, 4.

85. George Mariscal, "Mexican Americans and the Viet Nam War," in *A Companion to the Vietnam War*, ed. Marilyn B. Young and Robert Buzzanco (Malden, MA: Blackwell, 2002), 348–49.

3

Texas Women at War

Melanie A. Kirkland

FROM THE STRUGGLE for independence from Mexico to the war in Iraq, Texas women continue to contribute to war efforts with their time, money, and occasionally their lives. In the legendary Battle of the Alamo, Susanna Dickenson survived to tell the tale of what happened within the walls of the fortified mission. When war tore apart the Union, Texas women worked feverishly in munitions factories to support the Confederacy. As American soldiers suffered through the nightmare of trench warfare during the First World War, 449 women volunteered as nurses serving with the military. Many more joined women's clubs promoting the war effort and patriotism, while others rolled bandages, entertained troops, joined the Red Cross, or participated in a wide range of wartime activities. In World War II the nation's transformation, from its economy to the unprecedented expansion of its military establishment, witnessed an outpouring of participation from Texas women. When the Defense Department announced in 1942 that Texas contributed a larger percentage of its people to the war effort than any other state, over 12,000 women were included in their calculations, including Oveta Culp Hobby, director of the Women's Auxiliary Army Corps. Texas women also assumed roles in industry, replacing men who were serving as combat soldiers. Others joined scrap drives, bought and sold war bonds, and joined civil-defense efforts. During the Korean and Vietnam conflicts, Texas women assumed similar roles, joining the military and supporting the war effort. Others joined protest movements, harshly criticizing the war in Vietnam in particular. As American tanks rolled into the Persian Gulf in 1991, Texas women fought alongside their fellow servicemen in driving Iraqi forces from Kuwait. Lt. Kara Hultgreen served as the US Navy's first female fighter pilot to fly the F-14 Tomcat aboard an aircraft carrier. Currently, American forces in Afghanistan and Iraq include Monica Lin

Brown, an army medic from Texas who received the Silver Star in March 2008 for saving the lives of fellow soldiers after a roadside bomb tore through their convoy. Brown serves as one of many Texas women serving their country in wartime.[1]

Popular lore conjures images of women on the Texas prairie stalwartly defending the homestead against marauding Indians or nefarious outlaws while their husbands are away. Capable and independent, they serve as fitting companions for stereotypical Texas males. Despite this iconic image, any comprehensive study of the contributions of women in Texas during periods of conflict remains necessarily limited by a dearth of primary-source material. Within the context of the nineteenth century, women remained overwhelmingly subordinate to men. As a result, few instances of individual or collective initiatives by women in support of war efforts made headline news, perhaps due to contemporary ideals regarding acceptable female behavior. Letters, diaries, autobiographies, and secondhand accounts by relatives, while scarce, present the most common form of primary sources. Army wives often wrote letters home or kept journals documenting their struggles at military installations in early Texas. Since they were overwhelmingly married to officers, their experiences with military operations was minimal, and journal entries often focus on the challenges of maintaining a "civilized" household on the frontier. Twentieth-century accounts of women supporting war efforts are more abundant. Newspapers and periodicals reported on rallies, parades, and private-interest groups supporting war efforts. Texas women joined their sisters across the nation rolling bandages, conserving resources, and nursing sick and wounded soldiers during World War I. When the nation retooled for war after the attack on Pearl Harbor in 1941, Lone Star women bought war bonds, worked in war industries, and joined military establishments. Accounts of their contributions are among the most prolific for historians interested in Texas' contributions to World War II. Subsequent conflicts, from the Korean War to the fighting in Afghanistan, have witnessed the direct involvement of Texas women as many joined the military. As these intrepid women struggle to defend the nation alongside their male counterparts, accounts of their service grace the headlines of the state's leading newspapers. These sources reveal that Texas women play an increasingly significant and inclusive role while serving the nation in times of war.

As Texans fought for independence from Mexico, men and women supported the revolutionary movement while struggling to defend their families. In early 1836 Gen. Antonio López de Santa Anna defeated Col. William Travis's beleaguered band at the Alamo, killing virtually all defenders within the embattled mission. Of those inside, only Susanna Wilkerson Dickinson and her child survived to give an account of the battle. Her description of the action serves as one of the most enduring memoirs of the revolution. As Dickinson left the Alamo behind, many families had already begun to flee the advance of the Mexican Army, most making their way to Louisiana or Galveston Island. Known as the "Runaway Scrape," the flight of thousands of Texans escalated with Sam Houston's withdrawal to the Colorado River and his order that all sympathetic residents follow suit. Fleeing the Mexican advance, women led donkeys, oxen, and horses laden with their children and a few precious possessions. Women like Harriet Ames, a young mother left alone with her children when her husband joined the ranks, and Dilue Rose Harris, a young girl when the exodus began, set out with their families on a desperate trip to safety. Ames, Harris, and other refugees walked great distances, slept outdoors, and joined the massive throng of people hoping to escape the Mexican Army. While able-bodied Anglo males joined the army, women assumed responsibility for the welfare of their families. With the defeat of Santa Anna at San Jacinto in April 1836, refugees returned to their homes. The independence of Texas seemed safely within reach, and women overwhelmingly resumed their normal lives. The historiographical record, while scant, reveals that throughout the conflict, women remained overwhelmingly true to contemporary standards of female conduct and played an unofficial and limited role in the independence efforts.[2]

Some supported the revolution through donations of currency and supplies. Women also helped provide livestock and crops to feed the troops. Others offered to mortgage their land to fund the cause. Less-affluent women donated their time, sewing clothing for soldiers and making cartridges. These efforts, although arguably performed on a limited scale, provided relief for the desperate struggle against Mexico.[3]

Just more than a decade later, the Civil War deeply divided Texans, presenting them with challenges not encountered in many Confederate states. Approximately 90,000 able-bodied men not only chose sides during the war, fighting for the Confederacy or the Union, but also struggled to protect Texans from attacks by American Indians on the state's western frontier. Although Texas escaped much of the physical devastation experienced in many southern states due to its geographical position, most Texans were deeply committed to the Confederate cause. Women across the state demonstrated their support for the war effort by engaging in a wide range of activities. Some publically endorsed the Confederacy. In one Austin parade, women rode in a public demonstration of support for secession, carrying flags of the states in rebellion. Others attended to the logistical needs of the Rebel army. The demands of the war required Texans to supply their soldiers with uniforms, food, and munitions. Consequently, women often worked to fill the labor shortage by working on farms to bring in the crops, toiling in munitions factories, and sewing uniforms. Historian Angela Boswell, in her study of women in Colorado County during the war, has documented activities in support of the war effort. Colorado County's female residents raised funds through the Ladies Military Association to outfit a company of men. Mildred Satterwhite Littlefield, a wealthy Texan who supported the Confederate cause, turned her home into a small production facility manufacturing cloth for the troops. She installed spinning jennies and looms in her home, inviting local women to join her in supplying Texas' troops. Using cotton and wool from her property, she and the women of Guadalupe sewed countless uniforms. The wives and daughters of businessmen serving in the armies assumed responsibility for legal and day-to-day operations of private enterprise in Texas, despite the tenuous legality of such activities. They entered into contracts, sold property, and managed their husbands' affairs. As her husband and son served in the Confederate Army, Rebecca Adams, managing the family plantation near Fairfield, wrote often to her husband, describing her efforts to maintain the crops, manage their slaves, and care for the family. Despite her many duties, she sent clothing, gloves, and food to her husband and son during the war. Adams frequently alluded to the pride she felt in her accomplishments during their absence. As Boswell notes, many women found that they enjoyed such independence and resisted forfeiting their newfound freedom after the war. Their participation in the war effort demonstrates that women took a more public role in support for this struggle than they had in the Texas Revolution. Although women were prevented from participating in an official capacity in the military, their contributions aided the logistical demands of the Confederate Army.[4]

Despite the bitterness that lingered in the South after the Civil War, Texans joined their countrymen in the US military after the American entry into World War I. Approximately 197,789 Texas men joined the army, navy, or Marine Corps. In addition, 449 women from the Lone Star State served as military nurses. Thousands of other women engaged in community service and war industries across the state. In August 1917 the *San Antonio Light* ran an article by Isaac F. Marcosson reminding readers that national service was the key to victory. Marcosson noted that the war effort would require men *and* women to contribute to preparedness and to support the troops. In the *Brownsville Daily Herald* of May 8, 1918, an article also declared that women must help win the war through service: "In the army of Democracy, some must go 'over the top'—some must engage in the prosaic work of mule driving—some making ammunition—others again must provide the money.

All are necessary. Do your part and you will share equally in the glorious triumph which must one day be ours. Women of the Southwest, we look to our men to subscribe the Liberty Loan quota. We look to you to double it."[5]

Such challenges were enthusiastically accepted by the women of Texas. The *Denton Record-Chronicle* proudly proclaimed in June 1918 that women across the state had contributed to the war effort through every available venue. A short paragraph in the *Brownsville Daily Herald* earlier in May had called into question the patriotism of Texans unwilling to buy war bonds or stamps. According to that paper, a five-year-old Ellis County girl believed that her "Mamie" supported the Germans because she failed to buy a war stamp. It further reminded Texas men that any who failed to subscribe to a Liberty Loan could expect criticism—even from little children. On a more elaborate scale, the Texas Woman's Fair of 1917 focused a portion of its resources on issues relating to war work and patriotism. According to the *Brookshire Times,* the event promised to teach women how to "do their bit" for the nation. Representatives from across the country attended the Houston fair. Pres. Woodrow Wilson's daughter, Margaret, supported the women's efforts and demonstrated her support of the event, singing at a fundraiser aimed at war-relief aid. On June 24, 1918, women from around the state met in Austin for the War College for Women. This gathering focused on coordinating the diverse efforts of women on the home front. These events garnered statewide media attention and led thousands of women to consider making a personal commitment to the war effort.[6]

The army refused to enlist women in any capacity other than nursing during World War I. Although some served as "volunteers" working with the Signal Corps and the Medical Corps in Europe, they received no official status or military benefits for this service. Many women served near the front lines in France as ambulance drivers and volunteers for the Red Cross. As historian Ralph E. Wooster notes in *Texas and Texans in the Great War,* San Antonio resident Katherine Stinson volunteered as a pilot for the US Army Air Service but was rejected. Like many American women, Stinson instead became a volunteer ambulance driver in France.[7]

While the army refused to allow women to enlist, Secretary of the Navy Josephus Daniels anticipated a critical manpower shortage in the event of US involvement in a large-scale conflict. Daniels instructed aides to search regulations regarding the enlistment of naval personnel for any stipulations involving female recruits. His aides reported that the regulations contained ambiguous language calling for enlistment of "persons," which could allow enrolling women without additional congressional debate or presidential authorization. Daniels seized the opportunity, controversially instructing his aides to begin the process of enlisting female "yeomen." Representing the Lone Star State, Teresa Lake joined approximately 329 other American women in joining the Marine Corps. Ultimately, almost 13,000 women enlisted as yeomen in the navy and Marine Corps, becoming the first women to earn full military status in American history. When hostilities ended in 1918, female yeomen were placed on "inactive status."[8]

Countless other women joined local efforts to support the war. County and community councils sold war bonds, organized Red Cross benefit drives, knitted sweaters for soldiers, rolled bandages, entertained troops, participated in propaganda campaigns, encouraged conservation, and planted home gardens to provide food. Kate Harrison Friend of Waco organized local clubwomen and was selected as one of four Americans in charge of a women's recreational canteen in war-torn France. The women of Brownwood joined together to discuss such topics as the purchase of war bonds, increased savings, and community efforts to conserve resources. Led by chairwoman of the Thrift Stamp Committee, Mrs. W. M. Knowd, church societies and women's clubs in Brownwood joined together to support the war effort. In addition, Brownwood hosted a patriotic parade to demonstrate support for the troops on April 6, 1918. Members of Red Cross auxiliaries in the region enthusiastically participated. In addition, several Texas women served in the Smith College Unit of the Red Cross. May Agness Hopkins, a physician and native of Austin, served with the Red Cross in France, where she led an evacuation of wounded servicemen and hospital staff after the Battle of Chateau-Thierry. Hopkins served as the only female physician from Texas with the military. Her presence in France proved not only essential to wounded servicemen abroad but also demonstrated the efficacy of employing female physicians—a controversial practice at best at that time. Community efforts and Red Cross benefits represented the most accessible venues for women in Texas to participate in the war effort.[9]

Texas women joined others across the nation as members of the domestic workforce. Although female members of the lower classes already worked in factories or in clerical fields out of necessity, American leaders promoted further female participation in the workforce as an act of patriotism. Business owners aggressively pursued applicants as employment opportunities previously closed to women opened. Grace Parker, national commandant of the National League for Women's Service, crossed the state extolling the service of Allied women in Europe and imploring women in Texas to follow their example. The Manufacturer's Association of San Antonio met at the Gunter Hotel on May 14, 1918, to discuss labor shortages and recommended the employment of men not eligible for military service and previously unemployed women. In October 1918 J. D. Dickson, examiner of the Brownwood district, urged women to band together in the Women's Working Reserve. He insisted that every able-bodied woman not already involved in war work or otherwise unable to serve "should be induced to take up war work." According to Dickson, such activities required organization, and he encouraged women to form branches of the reserve in their communities. In addition, he delivered a laundry list of activities these new branches should undertake, including delivering public speeches, producing patriotic publications, and cooperating with local churches to encourage congregants in their contributions to the war effort. Those working in the home were instructed to shoulder additional responsibilities to enable their male relatives to join the military or the industrial workforce. On October 28, 1918, the *Galveston Daily News* published an article calling on Texas women to serve as munitions workers in factories as far away as Tennessee. According to the paper, they were needed to work filling shells as well as other jobs not performed by machinery. The US government expected Texas to fill approximately 850 positions in munitions factories, with 200 coming from the Houston area alone. Prospective employees could expect $3.50 per eight-hour workday. Although no significant statewide promotion beckoning women to work on farms existed during the war years, those on family farms also accepted additional responsibilities for growing and harvesting crops. Others tended to herds across the state while able-bodied men left their ranches and went to war. Nevertheless, many Texas leaders believed that the mass employment of women for farm work, though widespread throughout Europe, was unnecessary in the United States. During the brief period of American involvement in the conflict, Texas women answered the call to public service and enthusiastically supported the war. Women assumed a prominent role in public affairs and assumed more unconventional roles in US industry during World War I. Industrial leaders in the state and across the nation came to accept that women might make significant labor contributions during wartime.[10]

Texas women contributed significantly to the Allied effort in World War II. They filled a plethora of invaluable roles to win the conflict. Some joined community efforts to conserve vital resources for the military, while others organized efforts to house the influx of new workers. Girl Scouts often led salvage drives for sources of metal and other war materials or engaged in other projects for local communities. Texas Christian University organized female volunteers for war-related agencies, such as the Red Cross and the USO. Local newspapers proudly extolled the contributions of women working in nontraditional jobs for the duration.

Dr. Pepper Bottling Company in Abilene promoted "WATCH" (Workers at the Civilian Homefront) groups in newspapers across the state, urging all Texans to join the war effort. Women joined the Red Cross and the USO as well as worked with ailing servicemen at Brook Army Hospital in San Antonio and at Harmon General Hospital in Longview. The War Housing Committee of the Homes Registration Bureau of Fort Worth, led by Sally Tillery, labored tirelessly to find lodging for workers. When the US government initiated a campaign to mobilize American women for war work, over six million responded. Working in various

Three Pilots at Avenger Field, Sweetwater, Texas. Courtesy Texas Woman's Collection, Texas Woman's University.

industries, women in Texas joined others across the nation in answering this call to service, many leaving small towns and moving to larger cities. Fort Worth hosted a "Women at War Week" to promote female participation and to attract mothers to employment by establishing daycare facilities for children of laborers. Women assembled aircraft at Consolidated Aircraft Corporation in Fort Worth, manufactured shirts for GIs at the Hawk and Buck Company, and performed other tasks essential to the military effort. In Galveston a parade encouraged women to support the war effort and adopted the theme "American Womanhood Serves." It preceded a war-bond auction offering over $2,000 in prizes to those who made purchases. At Kelly Air Force Base in San Antonio almost 40 percent of the 15,000-member civilian workforce needed for the repair, overhaul, and modification of planes and related equipment were women, who were known as "Kelly Katies." Representing the diverse ethnic backgrounds of Texans working together for a common cause, the activities of women in Fort Worth, Longview, San Antonio, and Galveston exemplify the efforts of women across the state to aid their nation.[11]

War industries and their accompanying training programs sprang up across the state. With price controls in place and wages high, many women experienced a newfound independence. They worked building aircraft at defense manufacturers in Fort Worth and in the shipyards of Orange. Consolidated Aircraft Corporation trained women in a small facility in the Fort Worth Stockyards before they began building bombers at the assembly plant. Ultimately, these workers turned out more B-24 Liberator bombers than any other production line in the United States. Consolidated riveter Vera Conwell Cluck later recalled that she found pride in her work, even as her young husband fought in the Pacific theater. The Industrial Department of the Fort Worth Chamber of Commerce joined other cities in establishing training programs for engineering, technical, and mechanical jobs. According to the Fort Worth chamber, an estimated 4,000 men and women received training through its programs. Other women across the state worked in unconventional jobs as pipe fitters, assembly line operators, and railroad employees, replacing men then serving in the military. The mobilization of the female workforce in the United States reached unprecedented levels and proved that women could perform admirably in positions previously reserved for men. Women across the Lone Star State demonstrated not only their competence and skill but also their patriotism on assembly lines from Fort Worth to Houston.[12]

Grassroots efforts to guard the home front often found a receptive audience in Texas. Sponsored by Company D, 19th Battalion, Texas Defense Guard, women took up arms in Texas Defense Guardettes units across the state. Members received instruction in administration, first aid, handguns, rifles, chemicals, and riot control. Baytown established a women's ambulance corps to train volunteers to care and transport the injured in emergencies. Units of the Women's Motor Corps for Home Defense sprang up across the state. Local women formed and dedicated themselves to serving as a "nucleus for aid to home defense." Supported in part by the American Legion and the Red Cross, the motor-corps members received training in first aid, mechanics, radio operation, and map reading. They also practiced procedures for transferring troops between airfields and ships waiting at docks and often competed against each other in rifle proficiency contests. Many communities across Texas supported these grassroots civil-defense efforts.[13]

Many Texas women enthusiastically joined the military establishment. Estimates place their numbers at approximately 12,000 during World War II. The military already allowed women to serve as nurses in the army and navy. In fact, a nursing shortage plagued the military throughout the conflict. At the West Texas Hospital School of Nursing, a government-sponsored program offered young women an education in exchange for a commitment to serve for the duration of the war in a military, federal, or essential civilian post. Uniforms and a monthly stipend were added enticements to the program, which included the option of graduate training. Other facilities across the state prepared women to become military nurses. Army nurse Regina Hawkins, a native of White Deer, joined others in promoting service in the military to women's groups in Texas. While many nurses served in military installations across the state, others were stationed overseas. After taking her service oath in Dallas, H. R. Brantley entered the Army Nurse Corps in 1939, which would soon place her in the Philippines and into enemy hands. After the capture of the islands by the Japanese, the Jefferson native followed the army as it struggled to resist the invaders. After the US surrender on Corregidor, Brantley spent the next three years in the Santo Tomas Internment Camp before she was freed. In the European theater, Texan Dolly Vinsant was killed when the medical-evacuation plane she was working in crashed. Brantley and Vinsant represent dedicated nurses from the Lone Star State who risked their lives to aid wounded American servicemen.[14]

When the army established the Women's Army Auxiliary Corps in 1943, Oveta Culp Hobby received an appointment as director of the program. Congressional legislation later changed the status of the auxiliary corps from an organization working *with* the army to a component *of* the army. In so doing, the army renamed it the Women's Army Corps (WAC). As director and subsequently colonel, the Killeen native guided the corps through its developmental stages while dodging mudslinging by a public often critical of women in the military. Known for her diplomacy and organizational skills, as well as for her professional and political expertise, Hobby successfully maneuvered the labyrinthine military bureaucracy to ensure that the WAC contributed effectively to army operations. Though hardly without her critics, who lambasted the Texan for attending too many parties and notoriously accused the colonel of secretly encouraging women to meet the personal "needs" of male personnel, Hobby effectively managed the largest women's corps of any military branch. She steadfastly defended the WAC against salacious rumors and enlisted the aid of political leaders across the nation. To her credit, women serving in the WAC served in conventional and unconventional roles, both at home and abroad.[15]

Colonel Hobby received the support of a number of Texas women who joined the army and provided essential services. By September 1943, newspapers were reporting that the state ranked third in numbers of women volunteering to serve in the army, with 3,441 recruits. Statewide recruitment drives encouraged Texans to join the WAC. In fact, women trained and worked at army installations across the state. Over 270 WACs worked at Harmon General Hospital in Longview. In addition, the army established the WAC's Army Administration School at Nacogdoches in 1943 on the campus of Stephen F. Austin College. Ultimately, over 2,000 women received their training at the Nacogdoches school. Texans also held important positions within the WAC. Houston native Mattie Treadwell, postwar author of the definitive account of the organization, served as an aide to Colonel Hobby. Although she remembered feelings of trepidation during basic training, Treadwell took solace in the knowledge that she could serve her country proudly. In her first assignment as a member of the WAC, Patsy Bruner Palmquist of Houston served as a chaplain's assistant at Camp Fannin in Tyler. Her duties included conversations with men whose wartime experiences in Italy often resulted in severe physical and psychological trauma. Palmquist later served at the 8th Corps Area Service Command Headquarters in Dallas and at the War Department Personnel Center in San Antonio. Lois Jones served as one of many Texas women stationed overseas during the war. After extensive training in survival skills, her unit had the distinction of being the first WAC battalion to serve abroad when it transferred to the European theater. Patricia Hutchinson of New Braunfels served in the Philippines and Manila, working to return property stolen by the Japanese to its Filipino owners. Teresa Campbell, also a resident of New Braunfels, was stationed on Leyte as a member of the WAC. She served as head dietician at the army hospital on Leyte. Responding to negative gossip concerning the WAC, Amelia Arizpe of Laredo, serving in New Guinea in 1944, wrote of the resentment many servicewomen felt for such gossip and insisted that she was proud of the valuable service the WAC provided during the war. When the Japanese surrendered, Texans in the WAC could boast that they contributed extensively to the US victory, both in their home state and across the globe.[16]

The US Navy also enlisted women into the Women Accepted for Volunteer Emergency Service (WAVES). While the navy enlisted fewer women than the army, it nevertheless utilized their services extensively. In Texas many WAVES served at naval installations along the Gulf Coast, while others served at inland posts. Future San Antonio mayor Lila Cockrell was among the volunteers serving in Washington, DC. Like many other young women, Ruth Dunnam decided it was time to serve her country in 1943, her husband and brothers already active in the navy. Dunnam quit her job as a bookkeeper for a Houston bank and traveled to Hunter College in New York. She and twenty-one other navy recruits from Texas traveled aboard a coach set aside for WAVES and connected with a train bound for New York. Once at Hunter, Dunnam joined approximately five thousand women for basic training, rising at 5:00 A.M. for a day of drills, inspection, and courses that prepared cadets for naval service. Transferring to Yeomen's School at A&M College in Stillwater, Oklahoma, after basic training, Dunnam received an additional two months of training before her assignment to Naval Air Station (NAS) Kingsville, Texas. There she served as a captain's yeoman at the station's aircraft hanger, taking notes as the captain inspected the planes. Later Dunnam transferred to NAS Corpus Christi, where she served in the Housing Office, locating housing for navy officers and their families. Consolidated employee Pearle Crisler also joined the navy, serving in the WAVES until July 1945. Crisler worked as an aviation machinist mate. After attending training courses at the Naval Air Technical Training School in Norman, Oklahoma, her assignments included working the flight line training new cadets, maintaining aircraft, guiding planes to and from the runway, and securing aircraft when not in use. Mary King of Dallas also served in the WAVES, becoming an aerographer's mate and working at the US Weather Bureau in Washington, DC, during the war. After the Japanese surrender, she pursued a career at a television station in Waco, Texas. Dunnam, Crisler, and King represent only a fraction of the Texas women who joined the navy during World War II.[17]

A few intrepid Texans joined the comparatively smaller female contingent of the Marine Corps. Delaying the implementation of a female presence in the corps as long as possible, marine leadership ultimately agreed to enlist women. The corps opted not to attach an acronym to their female reserve and simply called their personnel "marines." Women from across the nation, including Texans, accepted the challenge of joining the elite branch. Midlothian native Janie Sheppard left a lucrative position at the Consolidated assembly plant in Fort Worth and began a thirty-seven-year career with the Marine Corps in April 1943. After training at the Corps School of Electronics at Camp LeJeune, North Carolina, Sheppard received orders to report to Arlington, Virginia, where she screened and edited combat footage for commercial newsreels. Like many Americans, Texas women in the corps saw service throughout the nation.[18]

The Coast Guard stationed female reservists at its Texas installations during World War II. Women in this oldest US service branch proudly answered to the acronym SPARS, an amalgamation of the first letters of the guard's longstanding motto, "*Semper Paratus*—Always Ready." Doris Baker Howard, a Texan from Gonzales, later recalled that she felt compelled to carry on her family's tradition of military service when the nation went to war. The Coast Guard offered her the opportunity to serve. Howard also believed that duty in the SPARS lacked the negative connotation sometimes attached to the WAC. At Coast Guard stations in Corpus Christi and Galveston, women helped ensure that Texas coasts remained secure.[19]

Before the attack on Pearl Harbor, experienced pilot Nancy Harkness Love led a force of distinguished female aviators known as the Women's Auxiliary Ferrying Squadron (WAFS). These pilots ferried aircraft to military bases and transport facilities across the nation. When the US Army Air Force began recruiting male aviators for combat, the WAFS expanded. Although the organization remained a civilian institution and qualification requirements were daunting for fliers of either sex, the government required WAFS pilots to undergo additional training in military procedures and regulations. The *Amarillo Daily News* proudly spread the news in October 1942 that Delphine Bohn, an experienced flight instructor with over one thousand hours in the cockpit, had joined the WAFS. Bohn had previously been an instructor for male cadets in the army and navy. In January 1943 the WAFS split into four divisions, with Dallas serving as the organizational headquarters as well as home base for one squadron. Ultimately, WAFS pilots flew virtually every type of aircraft the army possessed during the war.[20]

As Nancy Harkness Love organized the WAFS, Army Air Force general Henry "Hap" Arnold approved a plan by famed flier Jacqueline Cochran that not only employed female pilots to ferry planes across the nation but also would, if successful, eventually allow them to conduct all military flights within the continental United States. Arnold, though skeptical regarding the efficiency of female pilots, recognized that this program would allow the air force to assign all male aviators to overseas or training duty. On September 15, 1942, the general appointed Cochran director of the trial program, known as the Women's Flying Training Department (WFTD). Cochran's fledgling organization found temporary quarters at Howard Hughes Field in Houston, Texas, with classes beginning on November 15, 1942. Hughes Field, a municipal airport, before the war housed a civilian aviation school, Aviation Enterprises, which provided additional instruction to WFTD volunteers during their stay. Army oversight ensured that the women received the training necessary to pilot military aircraft and familiarized them with regulations. Dubbed the "Fifinellas" because of their official Disney-designed insignia, these women spent their time in flight training and ground-school instruction. In ground school they learned everything from meteorology to engine repair and disassembly. On April 24, 1943, the first WFTD class graduated with ceremonies at Ellington Field. The department moved to new quarters at Avenger Field in Sweetwater, Texas, in May 1943.[21]

After the move to Avenger Field, Cochran began to lobby for the integration of the WAFS and WFTD programs. As a result the two were merged in the summer of 1943. Soon thereafter, the War Department announced that the new organization, serving with the Army Air Forces, would be known as the Women Air Force Service Pilots (WASP). The air force organized the program without congressional approval, instead utilizing the War Department's authorization to use civilian pilots for domestic missions. Historian Molly Merryman argues that accounts of a fierce rivalry between Love and Cochran have been exaggerated and lack substantial documentation. Both women initiated proposals through official channels before the war and had achieved fame as experienced pilots. Significantly, both were representative of strong, powerful women throughout the United States determined to aid their country during the war against the Axis. Cochran became director of women pilots, while Love served as the WASP executive assigned to the Air Transport Command's ferrying division.[22]

Women from across Texas joined others from across the country to train as military pilots at Avenger Field in Sweetwater, Texas. The WASPs filled many roles in the Army Air Force, including ferrying aircraft across the nation, towing targets for servicemen in gunnery practice, testing experimental aircraft, and putting repaired planes through their paces. Located in the arid climate of West Texas, the heat, spiders, and dust hardly fazed Madge Moore, a spunky Texan with a passion for adventure. Moore spent the duration of the war in-state, working at Perrin Field in Sherman, where she tested repaired planes and taught airmen to fly with instruments. Other female aviators worked in more obscure, though equally important, work. Col. Oscar A. Heinlein of the 3rd Weather Region in Texas, when asked to evaluate the work WASPs performed in his unit, stated that "WASPs have displayed untiring energy, sound professional judgment, and a keen devotion to duty. They have willingly and cheerfully dispatched their duties without regard for personal convenience or the difficulty of the assignment." In addition, he noted that WASPs in his unit, though "required to meet physical standards higher than those set for aviation cadets. . . possessed the physical stamina necessary for the performance of the flying duties to which they were assigned. The thirty weeks training course they received at Avenger Field, Sweetwater, Texas made the WASPs as well qualified as any male pilots to fly primary, basic, and advanced type training planes in the United States."[23] Along with other WASPs, Texas women proved that they could contribute significantly to the service and fly wingtip to wingtip with their male counterparts.[24]

After World War II, women gained a firm foothold in the regular military establishment with the passage of the Women's Armed Services Integration Act in 1948. Subsequently, all military branches, however reluctantly, enlisted women as regular members of the service. The Coast Guard proved an exception. The act had failed to specify the Coast Guard, an omission resulting from that branch's transfer back to its original jurisdiction as a part of the Department of the Treasury. Separate legislation later resolved the discrepancy, allowing the Coast Guard to reestablish the Women's Reserve in 1949 for female enlistees. Yet despite their service and official status, women across the nation as well as those in Texas found that veterans' associations frequently denied them membership. In 1955 legislation formally declared ex-servicewomen "veterans" and instructed such groups to inform them of their rights and benefits. Female veterans soon began to take active roles in these organizations. Marine Corps veteran Janie Sheppard represented just one Texan who assumed a leadership position in her local veteran's group, eventually becoming commander of Post 569.[25]

Texas women were also among those nationwide volunteering for service during the Korean Conflict. Hostilities began on June 27, 1950, and came to an inconclusive end on July 27, 1953, when the warring nations declared an armistice but no formal peace treaty resulted from negotiations. During the fighting, approximately 6.8 million American men and women served in the military. Of these, 54,200 lost their lives. Within days after UN troops landed at Inchon, US Army nurses were on the ground, tending to wounded soldiers and preparing seriously wounded personnel for transport to hospitals. Army nurses also followed the troops into the war zone, joining Mobile Army Surgical Hospital (MASH) units. Navy nurses also received orders to Korea, serving in naval hospitals onshore and aboard hospital ships. Other female members of the military served far from the front lines, with some stationed in Japan, Okinawa, and the Philippines. In Texas, promotional efforts focused on acquiring new recruits. WAC officers encouraged women to join the army or air force. Capt. Gertrude Stevens traveled across the state informing young Texans of the advantages offered women through military service. Many responded to this call, serving their country during the Korean War. At this time a fundamental change took place in the military, American culture, and the nation's women. No longer simply serving in a crisis, the war demonstrated that American women now served as regular members of the US military machine.[26]

At home, women in Texas aided the war effort through a wide range of volunteer services. Red Cross officials in the state worked diligently, its members participating in national efforts to support the troops and prepare local areas for civil defense. The executive director of the Galveston chapter of the Red Cross, Gertrude Girardeau, assured Texans that her staff stood "prepared to take an active part in the development of a local civilian defense organization." In San Antonio, air-force wives volunteered to sew hospital garments and worked with the Red Cross. Donors across the state answered calls from Red Cross officials and donated blood for wounded military personnel. Although support for the war in Korea operated at a much smaller scale on the home front than that during World War II, this new generation of Texas women proved their commitment to the nation and to its troops.[27]

Historians exploring the role of women in the military during the Vietnam War are confronted with a surprising lack of official documentation. Although estimates claim that between 4,000 and 15,000 American women served as military personnel in Vietnam, no records exist to determine their exact numbers. As a result, little data is available to determine how many women from the Lone Star State went to Vietnam. Military nurses and Red Cross workers are widely considered the two largest groups of women to serve in Southeast Asia. Nevertheless, many joined the military for a variety of reasons: some out of patriotism, others out of a desire for adventure. Twenty-one-year-old Specialist 5 Varina Albers of Houston served in Vietnam and claimed that boredom, as well as a desire to "see what was happening," led to her enlistment. Unlike those who served during World War II, women deployed to Vietnam found themselves part of an unpopular war and confronted by an often hostile public at home.[28]

Nurses comprised approximately 90 percent of servicewomen in Vietnam, serving aboard the hospital ships USS *Repose* and USS *Sanctuary,* in evacuation hospitals and aircraft, or in MASH units. Their contributions to the war effort and their dedication to their patients earned them the gratitude and respect of their fellow servicemen. Charlotte Capozoli Miller, after attending officer training in San Antonio, left immediately for Vietnam. She soon found herself surrounded by wounded servicemen and civilians. Texas nurse Cissy Shellabarger returned to the United States with painful memories of her service overseas—her mind filled with visions of wounded and dying patients. The experiences of these two brave nurses mirrored that of thousands of women who volunteered to serve their nation during one of its darkest periods. These Texans brought honor to their home state.[29]

Young women across the Lone Star State participated in rallies denouncing American participation in Vietnam. Students at Lamar College in Beaumont, Texas Tech in Lubbock, Southern Methodist University in Dallas, Baylor University in Waco, and Rice University in Houston joined demonstrators at other institutions across the state in staging protests against the war. On April 15, 1970, delegates to the twenty-fifth annual convention of the Young Women's Christian Association expressed their opposition to the war by ending their session with a silent protest. Walking in a candlelit procession from the convention, the women showed their support of an earlier resolution urging the president of the United States to negotiate an end to hostilities and support a coalition government for South Vietnam.[30]

While some joined demonstrations against the conflict in Vietnam, others joined rallies supporting the war and American servicemen in Southeast Asia. Women displayed American flags, attended parades, supported a military review at Texas A&M University, and joined political rallies. In San Marcos a large group of students from Southwest Texas State University participated in a march that espoused a "stand up for America" theme. Other Texans joined organizations that supported the war effort by attempting to improve the morale of military personnel overseas. Women volunteering for the Red Cross packaged Christmas gifts for US troops in Vietnam. According to Moree Sawtelle, executive secretary of the Big Spring chapter of the Red Cross, the gift bags served as a reminder to American servicemen that "we care about our troops in Vietnam." Whatever their stance regarding the war, Texas women joined the political debate and proclaimed their patriotism, with many striving to support their fellow Texans overseas.[31]

In Operation Desert Storm, approximately 33,000 servicewomen were deployed to the Middle East. Thirteen women lost their lives in the line of duty, and two were held as POWs. Texas women's clubs, teachers, and special-interest groups demonstrated their support for the troops by sending care packages and letters. Del Rio educator Dorothy Chamber led student efforts to bedeck that city in yellow ribbons in honor of American troops. Red Cross chapters offered twenty-four-hour service to military personnel and their families. The Paris unit joined other chapters in notifying military personnel and their families of deaths, births, illnesses, and injuries. According to one staff member, Ruth Mazy, hundreds of military personnel received assistance in acquiring or gaining an extension of official leaves. In Deer Park, residents established "National Desert Storm Reservist Day" to demonstrate their gratitude to men and women who served in the Middle East operation. Such demonstrations took place in several cities across the state.[32]

Many women joined Texas' own military forces after 1956. Reporting to the Texas adjutant general, these organizations include the Texas State Guard, the Texas Army National Guard, and the Texas Air National Guard. In 1956, lawmakers in Washington passed Public Law 845, permitting women to serve in the National Guard as officers. Throughout the 1960s, most women with Texas military units were medical personnel. Nurses entered the guard as officers. Lt. Col. Melanie Truesdell, a nurse practitioner currently in the Air National Guard's 149th Fighter Wing, has served aboard the USNS *Comfort* in deployments from Belize to Haiti. In the 1970s the military began to open more positions to women and by the 1980s allowed them to assume combat-support roles. Ultimately, revised legislation prohibited women only from direct service as combat personnel. Senior Airman Elizabeth Gonzalez and Staff Sergeant Vida Reveles of the Texas Air National Guard's 447th Expeditionary Security Forces Squadron deployed to Sather Air Base in Iraq in 2009 to work as heavy weapons operators, manning .50-caliber machine guns. Logistical Specialist Tiffany Frenchwood, of Apache Troop, 1st Squadron, 124th Cavalry Regiment, currently works as a logistical specialist in Baghdad and is one of many women from Texas now stationed in Iraq. In February 2006 the Department of Defense honored eleven African Americans for their service in Iraq and Afghanistan, among them Texas Army National Guard first lieutenant Nicole L. Robertson, who was recognized for her service as a rail load officer, effectively managing the logistics of transferring service personnel and equipment from Fort Hood to Baghdad. As skilled members of the National Guard, Robertson and the others consistently prove that Texas women continue to contribute significantly to the prosecution of America's war efforts.[33]

Women comprise an increasingly larger number of Texas recruits, and a select few enroll in the nation's elite military academies. Female army enlistees from Texas account for approximately 19 percent of the present total, while those for the navy total 14.7 percent. Plano native Maj. Katie Matthew serves as a logistics officer in the army and is an instructor at West Point, while Cadet Christina Tamayo of Humble is a member of the academy's 2011 class. The *Kerrville Daily Times* proudly announced the graduation of Kylie C. Adams from the US Air Force Academy in Colorado Springs. Two years later Lauren A. Carr of Fredericksburg graduated from the US Naval Academy in Annapolis. In May 2010 the naval academy announced that Peggy LeGrand of Amarillo would serve as one of eleven graduating midshipmen to be assigned to serve on submarines. LeGrand and her fellow midshipmen will be the first American women to enter the "silent service."[34]

Currently, Texas women not only fill military positions within the state but also some in Iraq and Afghanistan. Unlike their predecessors, servicewomen deploy to war zones where the boundaries between combat and noncombat positions frequently blur. Civilians, security forces, and military personnel risk their lives guarding office buildings, traveling to outposts, or patrolling marketplaces and other public areas. Texas women share these dangers, while some forfeit their lives in the line of duty. West Point graduate Emily J. T. Perez, stationed out of Fort Hood, died on September 12, 2006, at the age of twenty-three when a roadside bomb exploded under the Humvee in which she was riding while on patrol in southern Iraq. Texans Tina M. Priest (Smithville), Isela Rubacava (El Paso), Analaura Esparza Gutierrez (Houston), Melissa Valles (Eagle Pass), Adriana Alvarez (San Benito), Kamisha J. Block (Vidor), and Amy A. Duerksen (Copperas Cove) also have made the ultimate sacrifice while serving their nation in Iraq and Afganistan. The town of Clute honored servicewoman Vanessa Gee-Miller as a hometown hero and declared December 17, 2004, as "Sgt. Vannessa Gee-Miller Day." Gee-Miller served six months in Kandahar, Afghanistan, and one year in Mosul, Iraq. Navy lieutenant Estella Salinas, a dedicated nurse working in a military hospital, and marine corporal Priscilla Kispetik of Houston, a combat-support specialist who has volunteered to perform the delicate process of searching women for explosives, also serve in Iraq. In response to the efforts of dedicated servicewomen abroad, civilian women in Texas continue to support the troops, regardless of their stance on the wars in Iraq and Afghanistan. Women such as Mary Moreno, founder of Military Moms and Wives, send care packages to troops overseas. Others engage in letter-writing campaigns to boost the morale of American troops deployed far from home.[35]

The roles Texas women have played during periods of war continue to evolve based on contemporary standards of gender roles. Nineteenth-century women were strictly limited in opportunities to support their nation in wartime. Those volunteering for service during the first half of the twentieth century labored with the understanding that they merely filled vital, but temporary positions. Female Texans joining the military today face a different scenario. While women supporting the war effort during the Texas Revolution, the Civil War, or the World Wars rarely considered taking up arms against the enemy, today's Texans willingly join the fray, whether by contributing their time or money or by risking their lives. Currently, Texas boasts the third-largest population of female veterans, with approximately 84,000 living in the Lone Star State. Clearly, these Texans have demonstrated that while the iconic image of eighteenth-century women as fearless and independent might stretch the bounds of historical fact, women from the modern Lone Star State continue to meet the challenges of defending their homeland.[36]

Notes

1. Lt. Kara Hultgreen's death on October 25, 1994, resulted from an accident that occurred during a training exercise as she attempted to land the F-14 Tomcat on the deck of the USS *Abraham Lincoln.* Controversy immediately ensued. While the navy cited an engine malfunction as responsible for the crash, speculation regarding pilot error and the place of women at the controls of combat aircraft persisted. Robert A. Calvert and Arnoldo De León, *The History of Texas,* 2nd ed. (Wheeling, IL: Harlan Davidson, 1996), 137, 340; "Presumed Dead," *Indiana (PA) Gazette,* Oct. 27, 1994, 1; "Female Navy Pilot Killed in Accident," *Santa Fe New Mexican,* Oct. 27, 1994, 2; "Female Pilot Rated above Average," *Indiana (PA) Gazette,* Nov. 21, 1994, 6; "Body of Female Pilot Found," *Garden City (KS) Telegram,* Nov. 15, 1994, 6; "Pilots' Death Renews Debate over Women in Combat," *Indiana (PA) Gazette,* Oct. 30, 1994, 3; "Navy Recovers Body of Woman Fighter Pilot," *The Capital* (Annapolis, MD), Nov. 15, 1994, 2; "Woman Fighter Pilot Buried with Honors at Arlington National Cemetery," *Brazosport Facts* (Paris, TX), Nov. 22, 1994, 2; "Woman Fighter Pilot Was Rated above Average," *Paris (TX) News,* Nov. 21, 1994, 8A; "Pioneer Woman Fighter Pilot Buried in Arlington Cemetery," *Altoona (PA) Mirror,* Nov. 22, 1994, 14.

2. Willard Griffith Nitschke, "Susanna Wilkerson Dickinson (1814–1883)," in *Women in Early Texas,* ed. Evelyn M. Carrington (Austin: Texas State Historical Association, 1994), 74–75; Andrew Hutton, "The Alamo as Icon," in *The Texas Military Experience,* ed. Joseph G. Dawson III (College Station: Texas A&M University Press, 1995), 23; Carolyn Callaway Covington, "Runaway Scrape," *Handbook of Texas Online,* accessed Feb. 30, 2009, http://www.tshaonline.org/handbook/online/articles/pfr01; "The Battle of San Jacinto," Texas State Library & Archives Commission, accessed Feb. 30, 2009, http://www.tsl.state.tx.us/treasures/republic/san-jacinto.html; Calvert and De Leon, *History of Texas,* 78; Ann Fears Crawford and Crystal Sasse Ragsdale, *Texas Women:*

Frontier to Future (Austin, TX: Austin State Press, 1998), 26–27; Dilue Rose Harris, "The Runaway Scrape: The Non-Combatants in the Texas Revolution," Texas A&M University, accessed Feb. 30, 2009, http://www.tamu.edu/faculty/ccbn/dewitt/roseharris.htm; Rupert N. Richardson, Adrian Anderson, Cary D. Wintz, and Ernest Wallace, *Texas: The Lone Star State*, 8th ed. (Upper Saddle River, NJ: Prentice Hall, 2001), 119.

3. Richardson et al., *Texas*, 124.

4. Calvert and De Leon, *History of Texas*, 137; Ralph A. Wooster, "Civil War," *Handbook of Texas Online*, accessed Jan. 13, 2009, http://www.tshaonline.org/handbook/online/articles/qdc02; Angela Boswell, "The Civil War and the Lives of Texas Women," in *The Fate of Texas: The Civil War and the Lone Star State*, ed. Charles D. Grear (Fayetteville: University of Arkansas Press, 2008), 69–81; Crawford and Ragsdale, *Texas Women*, 76; David B. Gracy II, "Mildred Satterwhite Littlefield (1811–1880)," in Carrington, *Women in Early Texas*, 165–66; Gary Doyle Woods, "Rebecca Ann Patillo Bass Adams," in *Texas Tears and Texas Sunshine*, ed. Jo Ella Powell Exley (College Station: Texas A&M University Press, 1985), 130–34, 139; "Endora Inez Moore," in ibid., 143; Richardson et al., *Texas*, 228.

5. "Women of America Must Help Win War," *Brownsville Daily Herald*, May 8, 1918.

6. Calvert and De León, *History of Texas*, 291–93; Isaac F. Marcossan, "Full National Service the One Guarantee of Victory in the War," *San Antonio Light*, Aug. 10, 1917, 21; "Buy W S S," *Denton (TX) Record-Chronicle*, June 5, 1918, 2; Poldi Tschirch and Eleanor L. M. Crowder, "Nursing," *Handbook of Texas Online*, accessed Mar. 29, 2009, http://www.tshaonline.org/handbook/online/articles/shn02; Ralph W. Steen, "World War I," ibid., accessed Mar. 30, 2009, http://www.tshaonline.org/handbook/online/articles/qdw01; "Of Interest to Women," *Brownwood (TX) Daily Bulletin*, Apr. 5, 1918, 6; "Auxiliaries to Enter Parade," ibid., Apr. 5, 1918, 6; untitled article, *Brownsville Daily Herald*, May 8, 1918; "Society," ibid., Mar. 22, 1918, 3; Margaret Swett Henson, "Texas Woman's Fair," *Handbook of Texas Online*, accessed Mar. 30, 2009, http://www.tshaonline.org/handbook/online/articles/lkt09; "War College for Women," *Brownwood (TX) Bulletin*, June 11, 1918, 2; "Washington County Delegate to Attend War College Meet," *Galveston Daily News*, June 22, 1918, 8.

7. Ralph E. Wooster, *Texas and Texans in the Great War* (Buffalo Gap, TX: State House, 2009), 101–103; "Of Interest to Women," *Laredo Times*, Mar. 10, 1918, 11; "Five San Antonio Women as Canteen Workers Overseas," *San Antonio Light*, Sept. 25, 1918, 7.

8. Linda L. Hewitt, *Women Marines in World War I* (Washington, DC: History and Museums Division Headquarters, US Marine Corps, 1974), 40–41; Gina DiNicolo, "Marching into the Corps," *Military Officer* 1, no. 11 (Nov. 2003): 62–64; Linda Grant De Pauw, *Battle Cries and Lullabies: Women in War from Prehistory to the Present* (Norman: University of Oklahoma Press, 1998), 225; Wooster, *Texas and Texans in the Great War*, 102–103; "Women Are Wanted for the U.S. Navy," *Victoria (TX) Daily Advocate*, Oct. 19, 1918, 1; Kathleen Winters, "Women in the U.S. Armed Forces," *Air Force Journal of Logistics* 16, no. 2 (Spring 1992): 1.

9. May Agness Hopkins also established children's hospitals in France and provided medical treatment for repatriated children after the conflict ended. Debbie Mauldin Cottrell, "May Agness Hopkins," *Handbook of Texas Online,* accessed Feb. 12, 2009, http://www.tshaonline.org/handbook/online/articles/fholn; Henson, "Texas Woman's Fair"; "Woman's Fair to be Purely Educational: Women Taught How to do Their Bit for Country by Exhibits and Lectures," *Brookshire (TX) Times,* Nov. 2, 1917, 6; "Annual Texas Woman's Fair Will Be Opened with Parade," *Galveston Daily News,* Nov. 5, 1917, 3; "No War Tax Assessed against Woman's Fair: Judges Will View Exhibits and Make Awards Today," ibid., Nov. 7, 1917, 8; "Outdoor Sports Will Be Many and Varied: Amusements Galore during Texas Woman's Fair at Houston in November," *Kerrville (TX) Mountain Sun,* Nov. 2, 1917, 8; Untitled article, *Brownsville Daily Herald,* May 8, 1918; "Society," ibid., Mar. 22, 1918, 3; "Drive for Red Cross Fund Is to Be Delayed," *San Antonio Light,* Feb. 17, 1918, 7; "Behind the Firing Line in America," *Denton Record-Chronicle,* June 12, 1918, 2; "Future of Red Cross Rests on Roll Call," *The Galveston Daily News,* Dec. 17, 1918, 7.

10. Calvert and De Leon, *History of Texas,* 293; Wooster, *Texas and Texans in the Great War,* 103; "Work of Officers in Arresting the Idlers Is Indorsed: Manufacturers Call Attention to Need for Laborers. Other Matters Discussed," *San Antonio Light,* May 15, 1918, 3; "Women on the Farms," ibid., Mar. 10, 1918, 6; J. D. Dickson, "U.S. Employment Service Greatly Assists Laborers," *Brownwood (TX) Bulletin,* Oct. 1, 1918, 5; "War Work of Women Is Told of by Service President," *Galveston Daily News,* Apr. 13, 1918, 8; "Women to Have Opportunity to Enlist in Branch War Work," ibid., Oct. 28, 1918, 7; "Women in Industry Are Now Important," *Laredo Times,* Jan. 13, 1918, 3; "Various Fields Open to Women in War Work," *San Antonio Light,* May 26, 1918, 6; "To Solve Farm Labor Problem," *Hearne (TX) Democrat,* Nov. 27, 1918, 2.

11. Women across Texas joined campaigns to sell war bonds, as evidenced by numerous articles in local newspapers promoting bond drives. See "Women Launch City War Bond Canvass," *Abilene Reporter-News,* Apr. 21, 1943, 11; "Nolan County Rates A-Plus on War Activities," ibid., June 25, 1943, 4; "Miss Latham in War Work," *Port Arthur News,* Feb. 16, 1943, 6; "Salvage Drive Helped along by Girls," *Big Spring (TX) Daily Herald,* Mar. 14, 1943, 8; "Community War Projects Find Girl Scouts Working," ibid.; "Be a Loyal WATCH," *Abilene Reporter-News,* Feb. 14, 1943, 9; "Volunteers Asked to Fill Service Kits," *Paris (TX) News,* Nov. 19, 1942, 1; David Castevens, "'You Wanted to Do Anything You Could,'" *Fort Worth Star Telegram,* Aug. 10, 2008, 4B; "Red Cross Director of Volunteer Services Lauds Woman Power," *Del Rio (TX) News-Herald,* Nov. 26, 1942, 3; "Visit to USO Replaces B-PW Social Meeting," *Pampa (TX) News,* Nov. 25, 1942, 2; "Stenographers, Typists Wanted," *Weimar (TX) Mercury,* Oct. 9, 1942, 7; "Quarterly Meetings to Be Held by City Federation of Women's Clubs because of War Work," *Del Rio (TX) News-Herald,* Sept. 29, 1942, 3; "1942 Annual Report Edition of the Fort Worth Chamber of Commerce," 4, 9; Cindy Weigand, *Texas Women in World War II* (Lanham, MD: Republic of Texas Press, 2003), 225; Ty Cashion, *The New Frontier: A Contemporary History of Fort Worth & Tarrant County* (San Antonio: Historical Publishing

Network, 2006), 87–88; Ken Durham, "Harmon General Hospital," *Handbook of Texas Online,* accessed 13 Feb. 2009, http://www.tshaonline.org/handbook/online/articles/qnh11; "The Return of Kelly Field," *Air Force Magazine,* July 2001, 49; "A Brief History of Kelly Air Force Base" (San Antonio: Office of History, San Antonio Air Logistics Center, Kelly Air Force Base, Oct. 1995), online at Proft's Website, accessed July 24, 2010, http://proft.50megs.com/kelly.html#ww2; "A Tribute to Kelly Air Force Base," *Congressional Record,* n.d., ibid., accessed July 23, 2010, http://proft.50megs.com/kafb-cr.html; "Kelly Field Historic District," *Aviation: From Sand Dunes to Sonic Booms,* National Park Service, accessed July 23, 2010, http://www.nps.gov/nr/travel/aviation/kel.htm; "Kelly Katies," *Airman* (Sept. 2001), BNet.com, accessed July 23, 2010, http://findarticles.com/p/articles/mi_m0IBP/is_9_45/ai_79352618/?tag=content;c011; Stanley Babb, "Looking Backward: Fighting Pieces Add Color to 'Women at War' Parade," *Galveston Daily News,* May 5, 1970, 4; and "Women's Role in WWII Focus of Nimitz Exhibit," *Kerrville (TX) Daily Times,* Nov. 10, 1992, 1–2.

12. Castevens, "You Wanted to Do Anything You Could," 4B; "1942 Annual Report Edition of the Fort Worth Chamber of Commerce," 5; Lee Bennett, "Fort D. A. Russell," *Handbook of Texas Online,* accessed Feb. 13, 2009, http://www.tshaonline.org/handbook/online/articles/qbf14; Cashion, *New Frontier,* 87–88; Calvert and De Leon, *History of Texas,* 341–42.

13. "First Texas Defense Guardettes Formed," *Laredo Times,* Feb. 19, 1942, 1; "Defense Guardettes Are Now Organized," *Corsicana (TX) Daily Sun,* Feb. 19, 1942, 2; "Defense Guard," *Laredo Times,* Nov. 11, 1942, 10; "Texas State Guard," *Port Arthur Times,* Nov. 15, 1944, 2; "Guardettes on Program for Service Party," *Port Arthur News,* Dec. 17, 1944, 9; "Open Letters from Arthur Port: To the Guardettes," ibid., Jan. 13, 1945, 6; "Guardettes Will Camp for Weekend," ibid., Mar. 26, 1945, 2; "Texas Guard Formed in Time of Need," *Galveston Daily News,* Feb. 23, 1986, 170; "Proposed Women's Defense Unit Gets Pledges of Cooperation," *Big Spring (TX) Herald,* Sept. 7, 1941, 5. "Remembering World War II, Our Sacrifices," *Baytown (TX) Sun,* May 29, 2005, 2A; "Calendar: Tuesday," *Laredo Times,* Aug. 30, 1942, 5; "B & P W Club to Have Called Meeting Monday to Discuss New Unit," *Big Spring (TX) Daily Herald,* Sept. 7, 1941, 9; "Mexican Dinner Enjoyed by Women's Motor Corps When Losers Entertain Winners," *Del Rio (TX) News-Herald,* Oct. 27, 1942, 3; "Personal," *Del Rio (TX) News,* Aug. 4, 1941, 2; "Calendar: Tuesday," *Laredo Times,* Aug. 24, 1942, 2; "Women's Motor Corps Met Tuesday," ibid., Oct. 7, 1942, 3; "Letters Tell of Doings of Laredoans," ibid., Oct. 1, 1944, 2.

14. Weigand, *Texas Women in World War II,* 112–21; Tschirch and Crowder, "Nursing"; Margaret Edmonson, "A Tribute to Women Veterans," *Kerrville (TX) Daily Times,* Nov. 11, 1994, 1; "Volunteer Nurses Finish One Course," *Brownsville Herald,* Dec. 4, 1942, 1; "U.S. Nurse Corps Training Offered by Local Hospital," *Lubbock Morning Avalanche,* Nov. 22, 1943, 14; "Venado Blanco Club Studies Women, War," *Pampa (TX) News,* Feb. 8, 1943, 2; "Nurses Wanted to Train for Service in Armed Forces," *Galveston Daily News,* Feb. 8, 1943, 10; Richardson et al., *Texas,* 408.

15. Mattie Treadwell, *The Women's Army Corps* (Washington, DC: Office of the Chief of Military History, Department of the Army, 1953), 21–22, 28–29, 50; "Mrs. Hobby's Wacks: New Women' Auxiliary Will Girdle 25,000 for War," *Newsweek*, Mar. 30, 1942, 32; "'Major' Hobby's WAACs," *Time*, May 25, 1942, 47; Weigand, *Texas Women in World War II*, 4–16; "WAACS Fight Back: Sinister Rumors, Aimed at Destroying Their Reputation Are Denounced," *New York Times*, June 27, 1943, X9.

16. Weigand, *Texas Women in World War II*, 8–9, 34–39, 40–45; "Area Asked to Replace WACs," *Morning Avalanche*, Nov. 22, 1943, 14; "Army Administration School: Women's Army Corps," collection information, Ralph W. Steen Library, Stephen F. Austin State University, accessed May 11, 2009, http://libweb.sfasu.edu/proser/etrc/collections/manuscript/corporate/armyadminschool/index.html; "Pfc. Amelia Arizpe in New Guinea," *Laredo Times*, Oct. 1, 1944, 2; Durham, "Harmon General Hospital"; Susan Flint England, "They Answered the Call," *New Braunfels Herald-Zeitung*, Aug. 27, 1995, 13.

17. Pearle C. Crisler, written survey conducted by author, June 15, 2005; Ruth B. Dunnam, written survey conducted by author, June 8, 2005; Mary Francis King, written survey conducted by author, Aug. 1, 2005; Judith Zaffirini, "Especially Important to Recognize Efforts of Women Veterans," *Sequin (TX) Gazette Enterprise*, Nov. 9, 1989, 9; "Women's Role in WWII Focus of Nimitz Exhibit," 1–2.

18. Weigand, *Texas Women in World War II*, 167–69; Frank Perkins, "She Remains a Marine at Heart," *Fort Worth Star Telegram*, n.d.; Janie M. Sheppard, written survey conducted by author, Aug. 2005.

19. Weigand, *Texas Women in World War II*, 162–65; Robin J. Thomson, *The Coast Guard Women's Reserve in World War II* (Washington, DC: Coast Guard Historian's Office 1992), 4; Jeanne M. Holm, *In Defense of a Nation: Servicewomen in World War II* (Arlington, VA: Vandamere, 1998), 97–98.

20. The first casualty of the WAFS was Cornelia Fort, whose plane crashed on March 21, 1943, near Merkel, Texas. "Plane Crash at Merkel Takes Life of WAF Flier," *Abilene Reporter-News*, Mar. 23, 1943, 8; "Women Ferry Pilots Get Ready to Take Full Jobs," ibid., Sept. 21, 1943, 6; "Commander Gets First WAFS," ibid., Sept. 25, 1942, 5; "Miss Dephine Bohn of Amarillo Accepted as Ferry Service Pilot," ibid., Oct. 23, 1942, 10; "Army Recognized Need of Women's Flying Auxiliary Squadron," *Pampa (TX) News*, Nov. 25, 1942, 2; "Dallas Is Center for Lady Pilots," *Morning Avalanche*, Jan. 8, 1943, 13; "WAFS Director," *Corpus Christi Times*, Feb. 4, 1943, 14; "Want to Join Up?," *Corsicana (TX) Daily Sun*, Feb. 3, 1943, 7; "Women's Airforce Service Pilots (WASP)," TWU Libraries, Texas Woman's University, accessed July 30, 2007, http://www.twu.edu/library/wasp.asp; Molly Merryman, *Clipped Wings: The Rise and Fall of the Women Air Force Service Pilots (WASPs) of World War II* (New York: New York University Press, 1998), 7, 11–12; Valarie Moolman, *The Epic of Flight: Women Aloft* (Alexandria, VA: Time-Life, 1981), 143–47. Karen Donnelly, *American Women Pilots of World War II* (New York: Rosen Group, 2004), 14; "WASP Statistics," WASP on the Web, accessed July 30, 2007, http://www.wingsacrossamerica.us/wasp/stats.htm; Cornelia Fort, "At the Twilight's Last Gleaming," *Eyes of the Eagle: Magazine for the 552nd Air Control Wing* 26, no. 3 (Mar. 2004): 8–9 (printed posthumously as a firsthand account of why Fort joined the WAFS;

Fort wrote the article two weeks before her death in 1943); Ernestine Evans, "The Sky Is No Limit," *Independent Woman* 21, no. 11 (Nov. 1942), Folder "1942—November," MSS 250, Texas Woman's Collection, Texas Woman's University, Denton (hereafter cited as TWC), 326–28, 346; Rowland Carter, "The Ladies Join the Air Forces," *Flying* 31, no. 6 (Dec. 1942), Folder "1942—December," ibid., 67, 88, 96; "The WAFS," *Look,* Feb. 9, 1943, Folder "1943—February," ibid., 17–21; Memorandum Regarding Hiring Civilian Women Pilots, Sept. 15, 1942, Jacqueline Cochran and the Women's Airforce Service Pilots (WASPs) Papers, Digital Documents Project, Eisenhower Presidential Library and Museum, accessed Feb. 11, 2008, http://www.eisenhower.archives.gov/Research/Digital_Documents/Jacqueline_Cochran/BinderD.pdf; Letter and Survey to All Women Holders of Licenses, July 29, 1941, ibid., accessed Feb. 11, 2008, http://eisenhower.archives.gov/Research/Digital_Documents/Jacqueline_Cochran/BinderA.pdf; "Our Women Pilots," *Air Force: The Official Journal of the U.S. Army Air Forces,* Sept. 1943, Folder "1943—September," MSS 250, TWC, 10. Texas Woman's University in Denton currently houses the national repository for WASP archives.

21. Merryman, *Clipped Wings,* 6–7, 11–14, 17–18, 29, 31, 45, 566–57; Moolman, *Epic of Flight,* 13, 147, 149, 151, 153; Donnelly, *American Women Pilots of World War II,* 7, 15, 33–39; Letter from H. H. Arnold to Members of the WASP, Oct. 1, 1944, File "Deactivation, 20 Dec. 1944," Box Historical Subject Files Ba–Fi, MSS 250, TWC; "U.S. Hints at Forming a Flying Corps of Women to Ferry Planes to Airfield," n.d., Folder "1942," ibid.; "Miss Cochran Ready to Organize 1500 Women Pilots," n.d., ibid.; "Aviatrix Calls for Women's Air Corps Unit," n.d., ibid.; "Women's Place in Air Defense," n.d., ibid.; "Women Aviators Praised as Teachers," n.d., ibid.; "Women Fliers Eager to Give Talents to U.S," n.d., ibid.; Carter, "Ladies Join the Air Forces," 96; Barbara Selby, "The Fifinellas," *Flying* 34, no. 1 (July 1943), Folder "1943—February," MSS 250, TWC, 76–77, 166–67; Press Release Regarding Jacqueline Cochran's Appointment as Director of Women's Flying Training, Sept. 14, 1942, Jacqueline Cochran and the Women's Airforce Service Pilots (WASPs) Papers, Digital Documents Project, Eisenhower Presidential Library and Museum, accessed Feb. 11, 2008, http://eisenhower.archives.gov/Research/Digital_Documents/Jacqueline_Cochran/BinderD.pdf; Memorandum from General H. H. Arnold Appointing Jacqueline Cochran Director of the Office of Special Assistant for Women Pilots, June 21, 1943, ibid., accessed Feb. 11, 2008, http://eisenhower.archives.gov/Research/Digital_Documents/Jacqueline_Cochran/BinderHH.pdf; "Girl Pilots," *Life,* July 19, 1943, 76; John Stuart, "The WASP," *Flying,* Jan. 1944, Folder "1944—January," MSS 250, TWC, 163; "The Girls Make Good: Women Pilots Overcome Both Masculine Tradition and a Tough Flying Chore," n.d., Folder "1943—February," ibid.; Douglas Hinton, "The Right Stuff," *General Aviation News,* Dec. 6, 2002, Folder "Leonora 'Nonie' Anderson," Box BioFiles A–BA, ibid.; Charlotte Knight, "Women as Service Pilots," *Skyways,* Feb. 1944, Folder "1944—February," ibid., 74.

22. Merryman, *Clipped Wings,* 6–7, 11, 14, 17, 31, 56–57; Moolman, *Epic of Flight,* 151, 153; Donnelly, *American Women Pilots of World War II,* 7, 34; Hinton, "The Right Stuff"; Knight, "Women as Service Pilots," 74; "WASP Statistics"; Richard N. Cowell, "St. Louis Wasps—They've a Sting All Their Own," n.d., Folder "1943—February," MSS

250, TWC; Headquarters, Army Air Forces, Director of Women Pilots, "A Handbook for Women Student Pilot Trainees," online archival collection, Texas Woman's University, accessed July 30, 2007, http://www.twu.edu/downloads/library/hdbk_print.pdf; AAF Regulation 40–9, "Personnel, Civilian: Wearing of the WASP Uniform," Feb. 14, 1944, ibid., accessed July 30, 2007, http://www.twu.edu/downloads/library/uniform.pdf.

    23. *History of the AAF Weather Service: Utilization of WASP in AAF Weather Service,* Special Study 2 (Asheville, NC: Headquarters, AAF Weather Wing, Feb. 1945), 4, App. 4, pp. 9, 11, Texas Woman's University, http://www.twu.edu/downloads/library/weather.pdf (accessed 20 May 2008).

    24. Weigand, *Texas Women in World War II,* 204–10; Moolman, *Epic of Flight,* 141–43, 151–52; Merryman, *Clipped Wings,* 6–7, 11–13, 20, 23–24; Donnelly, *American Women Pilots of World War II,* 8, 28, 32–33; Leslie Haynesworth and David Toomey, *Amelia Earhart's Daughters: The Wild and Glorious Story of American Women Aviators from World War II to the Dawn of the Space Age* (New York: Morrow, 1998), 5–7, 16; Elizabeth R. Valentine, "No 1 Woman Flier," *New York Times Magazine,* July 12, 1941, Folder "1941—July," MSS 250, TWC; Letter from H. H. Arnold to Members of the WASP, Oct. 1, 1944; "The Girls Make Good," TWC; Stuart, "The WASP," 74; Charlotte Knight, "She Wears a Pair of Silver Wings," *Air Force: The Official Journal of the U.S. Army Air Forces* (Jan. 1944), Folder "1944—January," MSS 250, TWC, 49–50; Alice Rogers Hager, "Women as Service Pilots," *Skyways,* Feb. 1944, Folder "1944—February," ibid., 28, 67; "WASP Are Flying B-26 'Marauders,'" n.d., Box Newsclippings 1939–71, ibid.; "Avenger Field Due Expansion," *Abilene Reporter-News,* Apr. 29, 1943, 6; "Women Ferry Pilots Given Silver Wings," ibid., July 4, 1943, 16; "Sweetwater-Trained WASPS Deliver Planes to 11th Armored Division Here," ibid., Nov. 13, 1943, 9; "Girls Are 'Sad and Mad' as WASPS Quit Flying for AAF," ibid., Dec. 21, 1944, 10.

    25. Most histories of the Marine Corps acknowledge that the majority of contemporary officers believed that the acceptance of women into the corps as regular members was a situation forced upon the military by a liberal Congress. Allan R. Millett, *Semper Fidelis: The History of the United States Marine Corps* (New York: Macmillan, 1980), 468; Zaffirini, "Especially Important to Recognize Efforts of Women Veterans," 9; Weigand, *Texas Women in World War II,* 166–70.

    26. De Pauw, *Battle Cries and Lullabies,* 266–67; US Department of Veterans Affairs, "Data on Veterans of the Korean War," June 2000, http://www.va.gov/VETDATA/docs/SpecialReports/KW2000.pdf; "WAC-WAF Recruit Officers to Be Here July 26," *Paris (TX) News,* July 22, 1951, 14; Jean Ebbert and Marie-Beth Hall, *Crossed Currents: Navy Women in a Century of Change* (Washington, DC: Batsford Bassey, 1999), 140–45.

    27. "Red Cross Ready for War Effort," *Galveston Daily News,* July 1, 1950, 1 (quote); Eve Bartlett, "Air Force Wives Work Together," *San Antonio Express,* Aug. 23, 1953, 54; "Sizable Increase in Blood Donors Noted; Total Is 157," *Big Spring (TX) Daily Herald,* Nov. 14, 1952, 1.

    28. "Sign of the Times: Women in Fatigues," *Corpus Christi Caller-Times,* July 21, 1968, 28; "Fort Military Women: Service in Vietnam Is Far from 'Ball,'" *Port Arthur News,* July 21, 1968, 10; Tom Tiede, "WAC's Back to War: The Girls Seem Eager for Vietnam,"

Victoria (TX) Advocate, Oct. 30, 1967, 4; Jurate Kazickas, "U.S. Women in War Zone Way Ahead in Dating Game," ibid., July 21, 1968, 6; Kathryn Marshall, *In the Combat Zone: An Oral History of American Women in Vietnam* (Boston: Little, Brown, 1987), 4–5. Sculptor Glenna Goodacre, a resident of Texas during the Vietnam War, designed the statue dedicated to female veterans of Vietnam in Washington, DC. "Statue of Vietnam War Women Is Traveling across the Nation," *Paris (TX) News*, Aug. 8, 1993, 5B.

29. "Not Just Pretty Faces: The Women of the Vietnam War," The Vietnam Center and Archive, Texas Tech University, http://www.vietnam.ttu.edu/exhibits/whm/; Marshall, *In the Combat Zone*, 4–5; "The Women of the Vietnam War: Nurses," Vietnam Center and Archive, Texas Tech University, accessed June 11, 2009, http://www.vietnam.ttu.edu/exhibits/whm/nurses.htm; Georgia Dullea, "Viet Vet's Horror Stories Continue—But Now Women Are Telling Them," *The Ledger*, May 3, 1981, 16A; Keith Walker, *A Piece of My Heart: The Stories of Twenty-Six American Women Who Served in Vietnam* (New York: Ballantine, 1985), 262.

30. Demonstrations against the war took place at virtually every university across the state. William Lee Coltrane, "Higher Education and Anti-Vietnam War Demonstrations: Comparing Occurrences and Administrative Responses" (PhD diss., Texas Tech University, May 1992), available online, http://etd.lib.ttu.edu/theses/available/etd-02262009-31295007020232/unrestricted/31295007020232.pdf, accessed July 31, 2010; "Reaction," *Corpus Christi Times*, Oct. 14, 1969, 13; "Moratorium Called Ironic Peace Attack," *Denton Record-Chronicle*, Oct. 10, 1969, 1; "NTSU Plans Own Session," ibid., Oct. 10, 1969, 1; "Silent Protest of Viet War by YWCA Delegates," *Big Spring (TX) Daily Herald*, Apr. 16, 1970, 2-A; "Parade," *Corpus Christi Times*, Oct. 15, 1969, 13.

31. "300 Show Support of Vietnam," *San Antonio Express and News*, May 21, 1967, 16; "Silent Majority Heard throughout Texas," *Odessa American*, Nov. 12, 1969, 4-A; "Red Cross Readies Gifts for Soldiers," *San Jacinto News-Times*, Sept. 26, 1968, 5; "Volunteers Prep Vietnam Gifts," *Paris (TX) News*, July 21, 1968, 14; "Ditty Bags for Christmas: GI's Need 'You' to Help in Making Gifts," *Big Spring (TX) Herald*, May 19, 1968, 3-C.

32. Linda Wertheimer, "Wounded in War: The Women Serving in Iraq," National Public Radio, accessed June 11, 2009, http://www.npr.org/templates/story/story.php?storyId=4534450; "Why There's No Mail at Mail Call," *Syracuse (NY) Herald-Journal*, Feb. 4, 1991, B3; Sen. Lloyd Benson, "Honoring Reserve Soldiers," *Deer Park (TX) Progress*, May 26, 1991, 4; "Local American Red Cross Unit Stayed Busy during Past Year," *Paris (TX) News*, May 26, 1991, 5; "Troop Support," *Del Rio (TX) News Herald*, Nov. 4, 1991, 1; Diane Gonzales, "Yellow Ribbons Everywhere Show Troops We Care," ibid., Feb. 10, 1991, 4A.

33. Tim Beckham, "Texas Airmen Provide Show of Force," Mar. 31, 2009, 149th Fighter Wing Air National Guard, accessed June 11, 2009, http://www.149fw.ang.af.mil/news/story.asp?id=123142123; Gregory Ripps, "149th Fighter Wing Nurse Treats Patients from Ship," Apr. 17, 2008, ibid., accessed June 11, 2009, http://www.149fw.ang.af.mil/news/story.asp?id=123094803; John W. Listman, "Women in the Army National Guard," National Guard Educational Foundation, accessed June 11, 2009, http://www.ngef.org/index.asp?bid=31; Mark Burrell, "Just One of the Guys: 1–124th Cav Women Warriors

Stand Guard in Iraq," May 17, 2009, US Army, accessed June 11, 2009, http://www.army
.mil/-news/2009/05/17/21221-just-one-of-the-guys-1–124th-cav-women-warriors-stand-
guard-in-Iraq/index.html; Kia Riddley-Colbert, "Women Soldiers Contribute to 36th
Infantry Division Mission," Aug. 25, 2005, US Department of Defense, accessed June 11.
2009, http://www.defenselink.mil/news/newsarticle.aspx?id=16807; Rudi Williams, "DoD
Honors 11 African-American Servicemembers," Feb. 28, 2006, ibid., accessed June 11,
2009, http://www.defenselink.mil/news/newsarticle.aspx?id=14729; William C. Wilkes
and Mary M. Standifer, "Texas State Guard," *Handbook of Texas Online,* accessed Feb. 11,
2009, http://www.tshaonline.org/handbook/online/articles/qqt01; "Brief History of the
Texas State Guard," Texas State Guard Association Trust, accessed June 11, 2009, http://
www.txusa.com/tsga/briefhist.html.

34. Joshua Partlow and Lonnae O'Neal Parker, "West Point Mourns a Font of
Energy, Laid to Rest by War," *Washington Post,* Sept. 27, 2006, accessed Aug. 12, 2010,
http://www.washingtonpost.com/wp-dyn/content/article/2006/09/26/AR2006092601765.
html; Kirsten Holmstedt, *Band of Sisters: American Women at War in Iraq* (Mechanicsburg,
PA: Stackpole, 2007), 1–25, 253–81, 310–11, 317–20; "Soldier Deserving of Honor," *The
Facts* (Clute, TX), Dec. 20, 2004, 6A; Nathaniel Lukefahr, "Marathoner Running for U.S.
Troops," ibid., May 26, 2008, 1B. 3B; "Brazos Mall Raking Letters for Soldiers," ibid., Apr.
11, 2003, 5A; Earl Kelly, "Naval Academy Introduces First Women to Serve on Subs," *The
Capital,* May 7, 2010, accessed Aug. 11, 2010, http://www.hometownannapolis.com/news/
nav/2010/05/07–14/Naval-Academy-introduces-first-women-to-serve-on-subs.html; "The
Grey Zone: West Point on Leadership," *Washington Post,* Mar. 22, 2010, accessed Aug. 11,
2010, http://views.washingtonpost.com/leadership/panelists/2010/03/cadets-bios.html.

35. Partlow and Parker, "West Point Mourns a Font of Energy"; Fernando Del
Valle, "Pfc. Adriana Alvarez," *Brownsville Herald,* Feb. 12, 2010, accessed Aug. 12, 2010,
http://www.brownsvilleherald.com/common/printer/view.php?db=brownsville&id=108545;
Liz F. Kay, "A Consoler's Consolation: Aberdeen Chaplain's Faith Helps Him Cope with
Daughter's Death in Iraq," *Baltimore Sun,* Apr. 9, 2006, accessed Aug. 12, 2010, http://
www.baltimoresun.com/news/maryland/harford/bal-id.chaplain09apr09,0,5446677.story;
"Texas Military Stats," StateMaster.com, accessed May 11, 2010, http://www.statemas-
ter.com/red/state/TX-texas/mil-military&b_cite=1&all=1; "Army Spc. Isela Rubalcava,"
Honor the Fallen, accessed Aug. 12, 2010, http://militarytimes.com/valor/army-spc-isela-
rubalcava/257303/; "Hispanics Overrepresented among War Casualties," *The Facts* (Clute,
TX), Nov. 13, 2004, 7; Juan A. Lozano, "Soldier Killed in Iraq Remembered," *Texas
City Sun,* Oct. 9, 2003, 8; Paul Garwood, "U.S. Forces Swoop through Tikrit, Detaining
30 Iraqis Suspected of Attacks on Coalition Forces," *Paris (TX) News,* Jan. 9, 2004, 14;
"Fallen," *Kerrville (TX) Daily Times,* May 7, 2005, 60; "Mother Seeks Answers about
Army Soldier's Death," *Paris (TX) News,* July 25, 2003, 7; "In the Service," *Kerrville (TX)
Daily Times,* Sept. 25, 2002, 8C; "In the Service," ibid., July 10–11, 2004, 7A.

36. 'Women Veterans Have Earned Our Appreciation," *Kerrville (TX) Daily Times,*
Mar. 1, 2000, 4A; "Salute to Women Vets Set for Today at Cailloux Theater," ibid., Feb.
24–25, 2007, 9A.

4

The Influence
of War and Military Service
on African Texans

Alwyn Barr

WAR AND MILITARY service confronted African Texans with a variety of challenges and opportunities at different times from the Spanish colonial period through the twentieth century. In the years of slavery, that institution might be strengthened or weakened by conflict, with mixed results for African Americans. For those who had achieved freedom, war could require efforts to protect that status. Following emancipation, military service took on both symbolic and practical meanings: participation in the responsibilities of citizenship, an opportunity to overcome images of inferiority that denied manhood, and an opportunity for improved economic status. Struggles to gain equality within the military proved most successful during new conflicts, while degrees of discrimination lingered for over a century. War crises might also expand job possibilities for African Texan civilians, but at the same time they could increase social tensions.

African slaves entered Texas as part of Spanish military expeditions that explored the region in the sixteenth century. The first, Esteban, came ashore on the coast in 1528 with Alvar Nunez Cabeza de Vaca and other survivors of the Panfilo de Narvaez expedition. Esteban's ability to speak with American Indians expanded his role as the men searched for Spanish settlements. Africans labored for Francisco Vazquez de Coronado during his military explorations in the Southwest, including West Texas, in the 1540s. Some of them escaped Spanish control along with Indian workers on the expedition. In the same decade, Hernando de Soto brought African slaves with his military march from Florida to the Mississippi River, where he died. Luis de Moscoso then led an expedition into East Texas. Three of the

Africans accompanying him escaped to seek greater freedom by joining American Indian communities.[1]

Spanish settlements in Texas did not develop until the late seventeenth and early eighteenth centuries in response to the failed French colony of Rene-Robert Cavalier, sieur de La Salle on the Texas coast in the 1680s. To establish a claim to the region, Spanish expeditions sought to develop missions and a military presidio in East Texas.

By that period, persons of African ancestry often had gained their freedom and some had intermarried with Indians, although others remained slaves. When the expedition of Domingo de Teran faced a severe winter in 1691, a black bugler joined other soldiers who deserted, perhaps to find shelter with the Caddo Indians. Afro-Hispanics played roles in later military expeditions from 1716 to 1718, with duties such as herder and cook. The garrisons at presidios on the Texas frontier came to include Afro-Tejanos, who improved their status through military service, with some of them becoming landowners. African American roles in the Spanish military ranged from early escapes out of slavery to later upward mobility as a result of service.[2]

African Americans played complex roles in the Texas Revolution of 1835–36, in part because their status varied. Most had been brought to Texas from the United States as slaves, while smaller groups lived there as free people. Further complexity existed since some free blacks lived as part of the Spanish-Mexican society and culture, while others came from the United States and lived in the Anglo-American settlements and society. In the 1790s, censuses listed about 15 percent of the population in Spanish Texas as black or mulatto. In 1835 an Anglo-Texan described the Mexican troops at San Antonio as including Afro-Hispanics, with one serving as a sergeant.[3]

Free African Americans entered Texas from the United States in the 1820s and 1830s. Historian George Woolfolk suggests that they appear to fit the image of people escaping problems in more settled areas by using the frontier as a "safety valve," as described by Frederick Jackson Turner. They sought greater opportunity there and freedom from discrimination in the United States. Some came to escape ostracism because they had married white men or women at a time when many states declared interracial marriage illegal.[4]

When the Texas Revolution began in 1835, about 150 free African Americans lived in the Anglo settlements. The conflict forced them to make a choice. They had found less discrimination in Mexican Texas, but they lived among Anglo-Texans, whose acceptance of them would be crucial to their future. Generally, those free black men either joined the Texan Army or offered other aid to the independence movement. Their motives involved a mixture of concerns about undemocratic actions by the Mexican government and the need to protect their free status among Anglo-Texans.

When the Texans captured Goliad in October 1835, Samuel McCullough, an African American from Matagorda, suffered the first wound of the war, which left him partially disabled. Greenbury Logan, a blacksmith from Brazoria, joined the attack by the Texas Army that led to the capture of San Antonio in December 1835. He became one of the Texas wounded, with a permanent injury.[5]

Among the volunteers who came to Texas from the United States, Peter Allen, an African American out of Pennsylvania, served with James Fannin at Goliad and died there during the execution of Texan prisoners in March 1836. Another free black, known as Dick the Drummer, helped provide the marching music for Sam Houston's men as they launched their successful assault at San Jacinto in April 1836. Dick fought again in the war between the United States and Mexico in the 1840s.[6]

William Goyens, a blacksmith, also kept an inn, operated freight wagons, and owned land near Nacogdoches in East Texas. During the revolution, he acted as an interpreter for General Houston in negotiations to maintain peace with East Texas Indians. Several interracial Ashworth families had moved from Louisiana to raise cattle in the area near Beaumont. They joined with another free African American rancher and horse raiser, Robert Thompson, to provide supplies for the Texan Army.[7]

One of the most intriguing and debated stories concerns Emily West. A free African American, she served as a housekeeper for Lorenzo de Zavala and his wife, who were staying at the home of James Morgan on Buffalo Bayou near the San Jacinto battlefield. Mexican soldiers captured West before the battle. One account suggests that she helped send information to Houston and, as an attractive woman, distracted Mexican general Antonio Lopez de Santa Anna at the time of the Texan attack. Another account claims that she inspired the song "Yellow Rose of Texas." She clearly escaped to the Texas Army during the fighting at San Jacinto.[8]

A larger group of about 5,000 African American slaves lived in Texas by 1835. Many of them also participated in the revolution in diverse roles. Some aided the Texas cause, either with the hope of earning their freedom or because they remained under the control of their owners. Other slaves served behind the battle lines. Peter and Sam, bondsmen of Josiah Bell, helped protect his family and others against possible raids. Cary, a slave of Thomas F. McKinney, and Peter, a bondsman of Wyly Martin, delivered messages and supplies for the Texas Army. Texas slaveholders required other slaves to aid the revolution by using over one hundred of them to fortify Galveston. Owners directed other slaves to provide wood for the steamboats that connected Galveston Island to the mainland.[9]

Other bondsmen joined the fighting. Thomas Stephens helped in the capture of San Antonio in 1835. At the Alamo, Joe, the slave of William B. Travis, and Sam, a bondsman of Jim Bowie, fired on the Mexican attackers who captured the mission fortress. Joe suffered a wound, yet he and Sam convinced Mexican officers that they were only slaves and should be allowed to leave to take the news of the battle to other Texans. Two slaves served at San Jacinto. Mark Smith entered the fighting, while James Robinson helped guard the Texas camp and supplies. Before the battle, slaves in the area seem to have passed information to Houston about the Mexican Army.[10]

Still other slaves recognized the chaos of conflict as an opportunity for freedom in different ways. After its independence in the 1820s, Mexico had taken steps toward abolishing slavery but allowed Anglo-Texans to retain slaves with some limitations. When the war began in 1835, slaveowners feared that the Mexican government would declare the bondsmen free or encourage them to revolt.[11]

In October 1835 some slaves along the Brazos River tried to organize an uprising for freedom and land. The better-armed slaveholders defeated them, capturing about one hundred, some of whom received whippings while Anglos executed the leaders by hanging. As Mexican forces advanced into Texas in the spring of 1836, slaves near the Trinity River tried to gain their freedom by cooperating with East Texas Indians. They apparently hoped to then escape to the Mexican lines. Texas slaveholders and soldiers broke up the plan, killed one leader, and whipped a second, while a third escaped.[12]

The Mexican Army had no plan about bondsmen until the spring of 1836, when the government ordered the seizure of rebel property, including slaves. Dozens of bondsmen near the Gulf Coast escaped on their own to the Mexican Army in search of freedom. After victory at San Jacinto, Texans included the return of slaves in the treaty they required Santa Anna to sign while a prisoner of war. Some Mexican officers denied the presence of slaves with their troops as they withdrew to the Rio Grande, which allowed the runaways to reach the protection of the newly proclaimed boundary between Texas and Mexico. Several others escaped without aid from the army and probably reached a growing settlement of free blacks at Matamoros.

After achieving independence, Anglo-Texans created a republic in which free blacks retained their liberty but faced greater legal and political discrimination. The republic strengthened protection for slavery, which grew rapidly to include 38,000 bondsmen by 1847. Of the slaves who had hoped for emancipation through service in the Texan cause, only two clearly gained that status: Peter Martin and Cary McKinney. Texas slaves continued to run away to Mexico, however, with slaveholders claiming 3,000 escapees up to 1851. The most ironic case involved Joe, the slave of Travis, who despite his service at the Alamo, continued life as a slave. As historian Paul Lack has explained, Joe "created his own method of celebrating the first anniversary of San Jacinto" by escaping in April 1837 to find freedom.[14]

For the Texas slaves who accounted for 30 percent of the people in the state by 1860, the Civil War became an epic moment in their lives. Anglo-Texans attempted secession, panicked that Abraham Lincoln, recently elected president of the United States, would begin to limit the expansion of slavery and undermine its future. The battles that followed occurred primarily in the eastern border states and the Mississippi Valley, with slavery in Texas less disrupted than in most other parts of the Confederacy. Yet slaves there did face changes in their lives.

Bondsmen from neighboring states joined them as slaveholders moved them to Texas to avoid advancing Union forces and raids. State and Confederate officials hired slaves from their owners or impressed them to create earthwork defenses for gulf ports such as Galveston. Others received new duties loading and moving goods necessary for the army. Elsie Reece and other slaves found themselves required to sew uniforms or assist in military hospitals.[15]

After young white males left for military service and Anglo women or elderly men took over direction of slaves' work, bondsmen increased their efforts to control life under slavery. Lizzie Neblett's slaves Will, Joe, and Tom reduced their labor, avoided corrections, and traded away plantation animals. Secretly many slaves offered prayers for Union success that would end their bondage. Texas slaveholders feared revolt by bondsmen and reacted strongly to rumors of such a plan near Tyler. Escape efforts continued, with Mexico or Union-held areas in the Indian Territory as the goal. Matt Gaines, later a Reconstruction legislator, fled slavery in East Texas only to be intercepted in the Hill Country by frontier soldiers. Dave, an urban slave in Galveston, ran away to Houston on two occasions to avoid rural labor.[16] Because the Union Army did not invade East Texas, most slaves remained too far away to join Federal military units, unlike their counterparts in other Confederate states.

In some instances, Texas slaveholders who had fathered sons with slave mothers freed the children and paid for their education outside the South, as in the case of Milton, William, and James Holland. Milton then enlisted in a black Union regiment and rose to sergeant. In 1864 he earned the Medal of Honor for ably directing his men in action near Richmond, Virginia. His brother William also served in the Union Army and fought at the Battle of Nashville in 1864. After the war William studied at Oberlin College, then came back to Texas as a teacher. Later he served in the state legislature, where he urged the creation of Prairie View College as well as a school for blind and deaf African Americans, which he then guided as superintendent.[17]

The Civil War ended slavery in Texas, with confirmation coming in a proclamation on June 19, 1865, the beginning of "Juneteenth" emancipation celebrations. Despite continued discrimination toward African Texans after the conflict, emancipation had opened the way not only to military service and education but also to greater potential for economic opportunity and control over family life and social activities.

Following the Civil War, the US government for the first time recruited African Americans for the regular army serving in the West, including Texas. Black soldiers found their duty attractive for several reasons. The military offered pay that compared favorably to what was available for most African American civilians and also provided economic stability. The men also gained skills working with horses and firearms. An opportunity for soldiers who had been slaves to become literate existed through the efforts of African American chaplains who offered classes for the men. Limitations remained, however, for African Americans served in segregated regiments, the 9th and 10th Cavalry as well as the 24th and 25th Infantry. Their

Buffalo Soldiers, 9th US Cavalry. From Century Magazine, *October 1891.*

officers included only one African American, Henry Flipper, who was dismissed under debatable circumstances. Despite the protection they provided for frontier towns, black soldiers often met discrimination in such communities.[18]

Enlisted men in the black regiments developed records of fewer desertions and drinking problems than those in most other units. Over twenty individuals added to that positive image by earning the Medal of Honor, five during service in Texas. Sgt. Emanuel Stance of the 9th Cavalry at Fort McKavett became the first to achieve that recognition for his success in leading a patrol that seized a number of horses taken by Apaches and freed one of two boys held prisoner by the Indians. A second Medal of Honor went to Adam Paine, a member of the Seminole Negro Indian Scouts. The scouts descended from escaped slaves who had joined the Seminoles in Florida and moved with them to the Indian Territory, then Mexico, and finally Texas after the Civil War. Paine and three fellow scouts defended themselves against more than twenty Comanches in the Red River War during the 1870s. A few months later thirty Comanches attacked an Anglo lieutenant and three scouts along the Pecos River. When the lieutenant lost his horse, Pvt. Pompey Factor and bugler Isaac Payne held off the attack with rifles while Sgt. John Ward rode to rescue the officer. All of the scouts earned Medals of Honor.[19]

During Reconstruction, Republican legislators in Texas created state militia units, including some composed of African Americans. Although the black units seldom served on active duty, white Democrats opposed their existence. One company of black militia did protect Republican governor Edmund J. Davis in January 1874, while he unsuccessfully contested his defeat in the election of 1873.[20]

Once Democrats resumed political leadership after Reconstruction, worries about armed African Texans declined to the extent of allowing them to form a limited number of militia units. After the remaining companies had diminished to three in 1879, Capt. A. M. Gregory of the Waco unit, a preacher and educator, gained acceptance from the state adjutant general for organizing more companies. Success led to his appointment as colonel of an African American regiment in 1880. The following year Gregory held a camp for his units that allowed them to parade at the Juneteenth festival in Houston. Companies also gathered money to create a home for black orphans in 1881.

A new adjutant general began to show reluctance about Gregory's continued recruiting efforts. When he tried to form a company during 1883 at Marshall in an area of a large African American population, local Democrats opposed the idea, fearing black opposition to recent lynchings in the region. White vigilantes forced the colonel to leave town, which led to a brief skirmish. The adjutant general then removed Gregory from command despite his protest of innocence. This burst of paranoia slowly subsided by the end of the year.[21]

The black militia survived the crisis as a battalion, with four companies in larger towns. Jacob Lyons from San Antonio became the major in command. The battalion held a drill competition during the Negro State Fair at Fort Worth. The Ireland Rifles from Seguin received orders in 1889 to cooperate with an Anglo company to maintain order in the face of threats that a mob might lynch a Mexican American. The African American militiamen no doubt recognized the irony of that service in a period when several black men died at the hands of white mobs. With state and federal support, battalion encampments that focused on training and drills followed in the years from 1889 to 1892 in San Antonio and Austin. Games and dances added a lighter side on these occasions. The drills as well as the name "Camp Attucks" and a talk on the "History of the Negro Soldier" promoted self-respect for each soldier and "pride in his military organization."

The Panic of 1893 led to a recession and an end to encampments in that decade. Black militia officers offered their companies for service in the Spanish-American War in 1898, but none received the call. Two new volunteer companies formed in Texas for federal duty under officers with prior service in the militia. Under the leadership of Maj. James P. Bratton of Austin, the battalion held new encampments in 1902 and 1903. Despite praise for their drills, the units received orders to disband in 1905 as the militia reorganized into the National Guard. That decision at the state level fit the pattern of disfranchisement and increased segregation spanning two decades from 1890 to 1910. Disappointment among African Americans reflected a sense of loss.[22]

The African Texan militia units had served as social organizations, supported economic events such as black state fairs, and helped raise funds for an orphans' home. The companies provided social status and self-respect for enlisted men and leadership experience for officers. Disbanding the units denied the men a chance to serve their country and prove they deserved respect and equal treatment in society. Following the dismissal of the militia units, several fraternal groups in the black community formed uniform-rank companies that held drill competitions and thus replaced some of the militia roles.[23]

While black Texans lost their opportunity to serve in the National Guard, African Americans in the US Army's 9th and 10th Cavalry and 24th and 25th Infantry continued to be stationed in Texas during the early twentieth century. They served primarily along the Rio Grande border with Mexico to control smuggling and cattle rustling. Many of the African American units had participated with good records in the Spanish-American War and the Philippine resistance to US control as well as under Gen. John J. Pershing's command in pursuit of Pancho Villa during the Mexican Revolution. In that period, however, several clashes occurred between black soldiers and Anglo or Hispanic citizens in Texas. The incidents began at Texarkana, involving soldiers returning from service in Cuba. Most clashes happened because of civilian discrimination and frustrated responses by soldiers. Some resulted in greater racial tension but no injuries. Other conflicts at Laredo and Rio Grande City in 1899, El Paso in 1900, and Del Rio in 1916 led to beatings, shooting incidents, and prison sentences for a few soldiers but no civilians.[24]

The most significant incident involving African American soldiers along the border also became the most controversial. During one summer night of 1906, someone fired shots in Brownsville that killed one civilian. Some Anglos blamed black troops from Fort Brown for responding to discrimination in the town. By presidential order, three companies faced dismissal when the troops denied involvement. Yet a Senate investigation found the evidence against the servicemen unreliable. Alternate possibilities appeared to be an effort at framing the soldiers to open the way for illegal trade activity or to bring in Anglo troops to replace the African Americans.[25]

When the United States entered World War I, Pres. Woodrow Wilson proclaimed it a war to protect democracy. Such a goal raised hopes among African Americans for a "Double Victory" for democracy abroad and at home, as some black newspaper editors declared. African Texans pursued that goal through military service and civilian support for the war. Black civilians attended patriotic parades or rallies in thirteen towns or cities, contributed to Liberty Bonds and the Red Cross, and supported efforts to conserve food. African American newspapers and new NAACP chapters urged that blacks should have opportunities for service and expressed concern about discrimination in the army and around military camps in Texas. As the war stimulated some industries and reduced immigration into the United States, numbers of African Americans in the South and Texas migrated to northern cities in search of new jobs in areas with less discrimination. Other black Texans and southerners moved into Texas cities to find greater economic opportunities. This population growth in turn stimulated the development of new African American businesses and labor organizations. Yet the migration also led to crowded housing and black-white tensions resulting from competition for jobs and housing. In the South and Texas, fears of change led to a revival of the Ku Klux Klan and anti-black riots such as the one in Longview, Texas.[26]

The US Army recruited 367,000 African Americans, including 31,000

African Texans. Fewer deferments meant that black soldiers formed a higher percentage in the army than in the civilian population. Over 12,000 black Texans served in Europe among the 200,000 African American soldiers there. About 20 percent served in combat units, with the others in supply and service units. Among the 5,000 blacks killed and wounded were 240 Texans.

Black leaders across the nation lobbied successfully for the training of African Americans with college degrees or some college education to become army officers. Other black officers received that status after prior service as enlisted men in regular units. As a result, more than a thousand black men earned commissions as captains or lieutenants, including perhaps sixty-five to seventy Texans. Despite this significant increase, African Americans still composed less than 1 percent of all army officers. One of those officers, Carter Wesley, later became the prominent editor and owner of the *Houston Informer,* a newspaper that strongly advocated equality for African Americans.[27]

Problems remained, however, for African Americans interested in military service. The US Navy accepted black recruits only as messmen who worked in food services. The US Marine Corps and the new US Army Air Corps did not accept any black enlistments. And the army continued to place all black soldiers in separate units. Discrimination existed also in the services offered around many military camps in Texas and across the nation. Black officers reported reasonable treatment at Camp Travis near San Antonio. Yet barbed wire segregated African Americans at Camp Bowie near Fort Worth. Violent harassment of black soldiers by Houston police led to a riot by some soldiers, who believed that they had been attacked. Nineteen people died in the chaos. Military courts sentenced nineteen soldiers to be executed and sent over eighty to prison. Minor clashes occurred in San Antonio and Waco. For African Americans the war offered mixed results, ranging from frustrations to pride in service and limited gains.[28]

When the United States entered World War II, Pres. Franklin Roosevelt also spoke of defending democracy, which again stirred hope among African Americans in Texas and across the country. The conflict produced some similarities with the First World War. Blacks again migrated from the South and Texas to northern and western industrial cities, seeking jobs and less discrimination. Rural black Texans again increased their movement into the cities, which offered a greater range of employment. Those movements produced positive results, but competition for jobs and housing again led to tensions. Anglos in Dallas resorted to arson and bombings to limit the expansion of black neighborhoods in 1941. In Beaumont a false accusation that a black man had raped a white woman stirred white shipyard workers to riot, attacking African American workers, businesses, and homes in 1943. When black labor leader A. Phillip Randolph proposed a march on Washington in 1941 to express concern over job discrimination, Roosevelt created the Fair Employment Practices Commission to investigate and reduce the problem. Other advances followed. In a case brought by Lonnie Smith of Houston, the US Supreme Court ruled the "white primary" unconstitutional in 1944. A new civil rights organization, the Congress of Racial Equality, formed to oppose segregation. James Farmer of Texas, a Wiley College graduate, became its leader by the 1960s.[29]

In the longer Second World War, more than a million African Americans joined the military, including 84,000 Texans; about half of them served overseas. Officer training became desegregated for the first time and graduated 7,700 black lieutenants, still below the percentage of whole black population. For the first time, African Americans served in the marines, the Women's Auxiliary Army Corps, and the Army Air Force. A class of thirty-six black women that graduated from WAAC training included four Texans. At Pearl Harbor Doris Miller, a young black man from Waco, came onto the deck of his battleship to aid wounded, then manned an antiaircraft gun to shoot down Japanese planes, which earned him the Navy Cross. His actions may have helped convince the navy to allow black sailors duty in roles other than as messmen. Perhaps the most important new development came with the training of black pilots, who became known as the Tuskegee Airmen. They flew fighter planes that protected US bombers attacking German targets in Europe. Several Texans served in that unit, including four who lost their lives. Two others, Capt. Leonard M. Jackson and Lt. Norman W. Scales, received the Distinguished Flying Cross for their exceptional successes.[30]

African American soldiers still faced segregation and discrimination in facilities at many camps. Fewer recreation options existed at Camp Barkeley near Abilene. At Camp Howze near Gainesville, black soldiers could not read African American newspapers. A black soldier at Camp Swift near Bastrop explained: "The camp bus went through our area last, so by the time it got to us it was usually full. I was three hours late getting to my wedding, waiting for a place on the bus." White military police used the term "nigger" and pushed black soldiers around at Camp Bowie near Brownwood, with similar events at Pampa Army Air Field, San Marcos, Fort Clark (near the Rio Grande), and Fort Hood (in Central Texas).[31] Perhaps the most compelling comment came from a black soldier who observed at the prisoner of war camp for Germans "a sign in the latrine, actually segregating a section . . . for Negro soldiers, the other being used by the German prisoners and the white soldiers. Seeing this was honestly disheartening. It made me feel, here, the tyrant is actually placed over the liberator."[32]

In the most notable incident in Texas, Lt. Jackie Robinson refused to sit in the back of a bus at Fort Hood. Robinson faced a court-martial but won acquittal and went on to integrate major league baseball in 1947.[33] The fight against Nazi racism did cause an increasing number of white Americans to rethink their own racial views and favor equality. Thus the advances in World War II foreshadowed desegregation of the military in 1948 and the civil rights movement of the 1950s and 1960s.

Pres. Harry Truman ordered the desegregation of the US armed forces in 1948, encouraged by growing black-voter participation. At first the process moved slowly, especially in the army. The Korean War (1950–53) speeded the pace of integration, which proved generally successful. Decorated African Americans in Korea included two Texans, Lt. Chester J. Lenon and M.Sgt. Levy Hollis, who earned the Distinguished Service Cross.[34]

Some problems lingered. Most officers remained white at that point, with varied attitudes toward black soldiers. As more frequent and stiffer punishments for African Americans seemed to follow, the NAACP raised legal questions that led to reductions in some of the more extensive punishments. National Guard units in ten southern states still excluded African Americans as late as the 1960s. In Texas, by 1965 only 177 black soldiers served in National Guard units that included more than 17,000 members.[35]

As US involvement in the Vietnam War expanded during the 1960s, draft boards with few black members continued to assign deferments to a smaller percentage of African Americans, which led to controversy. In 1968 the numerous draft boards in Texas counted just twenty-six black members. During the 1970s that number increased. African American reenlistment levels remained above average early in the Vietnam conflict, however, because the military still represented economic opportunities for many in the black working class. Since a higher percentage of African Americans served in combat units, they suffered over 20 percent of the casualties in some years. That led to rumors among new black draftees that the purpose of the war was "to get rid of us," which caused the African American reenlistment rate to decline. Black soldiers developed mixed views of the war that reflected in part the growing divisions in the black community over the conflict as well as in overall public opinion.[36]

Tensions within the desegregated military persisted between black and white enlisted men, which paralleled the struggles of the civil rights movement in the United States. A growing focus on black culture and pride sustained black enlisted men while worrying some white officers. Although African Americans formed only

2 percent of military officers, more did advance into higher levels of command, including the first black admiral and the first black general in the air force. Higher-ranking African American officers who served in Vietnam included at least four Texans. Brig. Gen. George M. Shuffer and Col. Herbert Brewer had entered the military during World War II. Brewer became the first black colonel in the Marine Reserve Corps. Col. Clarence A. Miller Jr. served as a deputy brigade commander in the 101st Airborne Division. Lt. Col. Clarence L. Davis, who attended Texas Southern University, led a section of the 1st Marine Aircraft Wing.[37]

For enlisted men, survival became the immediate goal in combat and empha-sized cooperation and concern for fellow soldiers. Black Texans provided clear examples. After Pvt. Oscar P. Austin died in action trying to save wounded marines of his unit, he was honored with the Medal of Honor. Specialist Clarence E. Sasser survived his wounds to receive the Medal of Honor for aiding other wounded men. For his leadership and ability in combat, Stanley Goff, who "had grown up in Tyler, Texas," earned the Distinguished Service Cross.[38]

In the years after Vietnam, the new volunteer army made further progress toward equality as the percentage of black officers increased from 2.5 percent in 1973 to 6.7 percent in 1989. The establishment of Navy ROTC units at histori-cally black colleges, with the first at Prairie View A&M, provided one of the rea-sons as well as more black cadets at the US armed-forces academies. Two Texas officers also reflected the trend toward greater opportunity for promotion as John Q. T. King rose to major general in the US Army Reserve and Lester L. McIntyre advanced to the rank of colonel in the Texas Air National Guard.[39] Discrimination around military bases declined in this period too as a result of new laws supporting desegregation and civil rights, although subtle forms lingered in some locations.

Progress toward desegregation of the military had taken place in the period from 1948 to 1990, with black Texans participating in a variety of roles for com-plex reasons. Some served as draftees with reservations about the Vietnam War and about the racial attitudes of some white soldiers. Others continued to volunteer for economic reasons as well as the traditional hope of advancing the cause of equality in the service and in society.

Wars changed the status of African Texans, although the alterations could be negative or positive and the amount of change varied considerably. Mexico's war for independence expanded ideas of individual rights and led toward the end of slavery in that nation. Before emancipation reached Texas, however, the Texas War for Independence placed African Americans in an ironic situation, with sev-eral free blacks aiding the revolt to protect their status, while many slaves sought to escape in a search for freedom. When the revolution succeeded, it strengthened the institution of slavery in Texas and allowed its rapid growth. The Civil War, won with the aid of black Union troops, reversed the trend by abolishing slavery in Texas and the nation. That opened the way for new African American opportunities, including service in the US Army on the Texas frontier and in the state militia. This provided stable jobs for some African Americans and opportunities to serve their country while achieving self-respect and a sense of manhood in a society that reflected white assumptions of superiority. A peak period of racial discrimination in the 1890s and early 1900s, however, allowed Texas and other southern states to dissolve their black militia units.

With the US entry into World War I, African Americans, including Texans, began to make advances again in the military, with an increase in the number of black army officers. That trend took another step forward in World War II with increased opportunities for African American pilots and sailors, including black Texans, as well as their entry into the Marine Corps and the Women's Army Corps. Both world wars also created new job possibilities for black Texans and other African Americans. Desegregation of the US armed forces and service in the Korean and Vietnam Wars opened even more opportunities for advancement by black Texans, despite struggles that paralleled those of the civil rights movement.

Notes

1. Rolena Adorno and Patrick Charles Pautz, *Alvar Nunez Cabeza de Vaca: His Account, His Life, and the Expedition of Panfilo de Narvaez*, 3 vols. (Lincoln: University of Nebraska Press, 1999), 2:414–22; Quintard Taylor, *In Search of the Racial Frontier: African Americans in the American West, 1528–1990* (New York: Norton, 1998), 29; Lawrence A. Clayton, Vernon James Knight Jr., and Edward A. Moore, eds., *The De Soto Chronicles: The Expedition of Hernando de Soto to North America in 1539–1543*, 2 vols. (Tuscaloosa: University of Alabama Press, 1993), 1:198–99, 201, 2:315, 326.

2. William C. Foster, *Spanish Expeditions into Texas, 1689–1768* (Austin: University of Texas Press, 1995), 69–70; David J. Weber, *The Spanish Frontier in North America* (New Haven, CT: Yale University Press, 1992), 328.

3. Alwyn Barr, *Black Texans: A History of African Americans in Texas, 1528–1995* (Norman: University of Oklahoma Press, 1996), 3; Barr, *Texans in Revolt: The Battle for San Antonio, 1835* (Austin: University of Texas Press, 1990), 14.

4. George R. Woolfolk, *The Free Negro in Texas, 1800–1860: A Study in Cultural Compromise* (Ann Arbor: University Microfilms, 1976), 9, 20, 22.

5. Harold Schoen, "The Free Negro in the Republic of Texas, II," *Southwestern Historical Quarterly* 40 (July 1936): 26–27.

6. Ibid., 30–34.

7. Ibid., 30–32; Victor H. Treat, "William Goyens: Free Negro Entrepreneur," in *Black Leaders: Texans for Their Times*, ed. Alwyn Barr and Robert A. Calvert (Austin: Texas State Historical Assoc., 1981), 31–34; Andrew Forest Muir, "The Free Negro in Jefferson and Orange Counties, Texas," *Journal of Negro History* 35 (Apr. 1950): 185–87.

8. Margaret Henson, "She's the Real Thing," *Texas Highways* 33 (Apr. 1986): 60–61; Martha Ann Turner, "Legend of the Yellow Rose," ibid., 58–61.

9. Schoen, "Free Negro in the Republic of Texas," 32; Paul D. Lack, *The Texas Revolutionary Experience: A Political and Social History, 1835–1836* (College Station: Texas A&M University Press, 1992), 247–49.

10. Schoen, "Free Negro in the Republic of Texas," 32–33; Lack, *Texas Revolutionary Experience,* 244, 247.

11. Lack, *Texas Revolutionary Experience,* 238–41.

12. Ibid., 242–43.

13. Ibid., 244–46.

14. Ibid., 247–48; Schoen, "Free Negro in the Republic of Texas," 32; Randolph B. Campbell, *An Empire for Slavery: The Peculiar Institution in Texas* (Baton Rouge: Louisiana State University Press, 1989), 55, 63.

15. Alwyn Barr, "Black Texans during the Civil War" in *Invisible Texas Women and Minorities in Texas History*, ed. Donald Willett and Stephen Curley (Boston: McGraw-Hill, 2005); 88–89.

16. Ibid., 89–91.

17. "Milton M. Holland" and "William H. Holland," in *The New Handbook of Texas*, ed. Ron Tyler et al., 6 vols. (Austin: Texas State Historical Association, 1996), 3:663–64.

18. Alwyn Barr, *The African Texans* (College Station: Texas A&M University Press, 2004), 40–43; Barr, *Black Texans,* 87–88.

19. Frank N. Schubert, *Black Valor: Buffalo Soldiers and the Medal of Honor, 1870–1898* (Wilmington, DE.: Scholarly Resources, 1997), 20–21, 32–37; Kevin Mulroy, *Freedom on the Border: The Seminole Maroons in Florida, the Indian Territory, Coahuila, and Texas* (Lubbock: Texas Tech University Press, 1993), 117, 122–25.

20. Otis Singletary, "The Texas Militia during Reconstruction," *Southwestern Historical Quarterly* 60 (July 1956): 23–35.

21. Alwyn Barr, "The Black Militia of the New South: Texas as a Case Study," *Journal of Negro History* 63 (1978): 209–12.

22. Ibid., 212–15 (quotes on 213).

23. Ibid., 215–16.

24. Garna L. Christian, *Black Soldiers in Jim Crow Texas, 1899–1917* (College Station: Texas A&M University Press, 1995).

25. John D. Weaver, *The Brownsville Raid* (New York: W. W. Norton, 1970); Weaver, *The Senator and the Sharecropper's Son: Exoneration of the Brownsville Soldiers* (College Station: Texas A&M University Press, 1997).

26. Steven A. Reich, "Soldiers of Democracy: Black Texans and the Fight for Citizenship, 1917–1921," *Journal of American History* 82 (Mar. 1996): 1478–1504; Bruce A. Glasrud, "Black Texans, 1900–1930: A History" (PhD diss., Texas Tech University, 1969), 69–71.

27. Margaret Bourland Baker, "The Texas Negro and the World War" (MA thesis, University of Texas at Austin, 1939), 13–14, 23–24, 28–29, 43–66; Barr, *Black Texans*, 114–15, 138–39, 145–46.

28. Arthur E. Barbeau and Florette Henri, *The Unknown Soldiers: Black American Troops in World War I* (Philadelphia: Temple University Press, 1974), 48, 50, 75–77, 89; Robert V. Haynes, *A Night of Violence: The Houston Riot of 1917* (Baton Rouge: Louisiana State University Press, 1976); Glasrud, "Black Texans," 71.

29. Barr, *Black Texans*, 163, 174, 188–89, 197; Neil G. Sapper, "A Survey of the History of the Black People of Texas, 1930–1954" (PhD diss., Texas Tech University, 1972), 370–71, 388–90; James A. Burran, "Violence in an 'Arsenal of Democracy': The Beaumont Race Riot, 1943," *East Texas Historical Journal* 14 (Spring 1976): 39–52.

30. Jack D. Foner, *Blacks and the Military in American History* (New York: Praeger, 1974), 144, 150, 165; Charles E. Francis, *The Tuskegee Airmen: The Story of the Negro in the U.S. Air Force* (Boston: Bruce Humphries, 1955), 196, 200, 205, 207–209; Robert Ewell Greene, *Black Defenders of America, 1775–1973* (Chicago: Johnson, 1974), 389; Barr, *Black Texans*, 188.

31. Mary Penick Motley, ed., *The Invisible Soldier: The Experience of the Black Soldier, World War II* (Detroit: Wayne State University Press, 1975), 83; Phillip McGuire, *Taps for a Jim Crow Army: Letters from Black Soldiers in World War II* (Santa Barbara, CA: ABC-Clio, 1983), 13–15, 27, 67–69, 113–15, 173, 192–93.

32. McGuire, *Taps for a Jim Crow Army*, 51.

33. Maury Allen, *Jackie Robinson: A Life Remembered* (New York: Franklin Watts, 1987), 40–41; Jackie Robinson, *I Never Had It Made* (1972; repr., Hopewell, NJ: Ecco, 1995), 18–23; Arnold Rampersad, *Jackie Robinson: A Biography* (New York: Alfred A. Knopf, 1997), 102–109.

34. Greene, *Black Defenders of America*, 215.

35. Barr, *Black Texans*, 189.

36. Ibid.; Foner, *Blacks and the Military*, 204, 208; Stanley Goff and Robert Sanders, with Clark Smith, *Brothers: Black Soldiers in the Nam* (New York: Berkley, 1985), 12.

37. Foner, *Blacks and the Military*, 171, 207–208, 211, 217; Greene, *Black Defenders of America*, 231, 244, 277, 292.

38. Goff and Sanders, *Brothers*, xv, 138, 169, 215; Greene, *Black Defenders of America*, 224, 290.

39. Department of Defense, *Black Americans in Defense of Our Nation* (Washington, DC: US Government Printing Office, 1991), 192, 231, 281; Foner, *Blacks and the Military*, 217.

5

The Patriot-Warrior Mystique

JOHN S. BROOKS, WALTER P. LANE, SAMUEL H. WALKER, AND THE ADVENTUROUS QUEST FOR RENOWN

Jimmy L. Bryan Jr.

IN THE 1830S AND 1840S, Texas served as a beacon to a restless generation of American men who sought to quell an often uneasy longing for adventure. When they crossed the Sabine, young men like John S. Brooks, Walter P. Lane, and Samuel H. Walker followed adolescent daydreams fraught with images of masculine renown, patriotic sacrifice, martial glory, and meaningful deaths. They traveled to Texas with the expectation that adventurous experiences would transform them from inconspicuous and inconsequential boys into exceptional and memorable men.

Although observers often viewed them as quaint and capricious, adventurers represented an important cultural moment in the early nineteenth-century United States. As products of a pervasive romantic ethic, they sought risk for its authentic emotional experience. They imagined new archetypes of American manliness and succumbed to an intense yearning for the elsewhere.[2] Adventurism assumed several different guises, such as fur trappers, overland traders, and continental explorers, but Brooks, Lane, and Walker represented another sort—the patriot-warrior. To construct this ideal, adventurers conflated two powerful narratives that told the stories of Revolutionary patriots and frontier warriors.[2] Furthermore, as the United States expanded into new territories, it opened the physical spaces where adventurers could enact those new roles and thereby transform themselves into the heroes of their imagination. As both perpetrators and victims, they embraced the violence requisite for this martial persona, yet a deeply personal aspiration to find something meaningful in their own lives underlay their adventurous drive. They looked for the reassurance that the camaraderie of likeminded men could provide and craved the esteem of their peers, who could sanction their newfound manliness. Brooks, Lane, and Walker welcomed, but were not satisfied with, such limited acknowledgement. When they sought their fortunes in Texas, they hoped to achieve a wider fame— a lasting renown that would fix their names in perpetuity within the pantheon of American patriot-warriors.

Brooks, Lane, and Walker epitomized those adventurers who surrendered to this particular, martial allure. John S. Brooks, a native of Staunton, Virginia, was born on January 31, 1814, the son of a saddle maker. He served as a print-er's apprentice for the *Staunton Spectator* but soon realized that such menial work could not satisfy his yen for adventure. In March 1836 he confided to his sister, "[T]here is some thing, *I know not what,* which whispers [to] me," but he was feign-ing ignorance to elicit sympathy. In numerous letters written in the two years after he left home, Brooks knew precisely what propelled him into "a wayward and use-less" life—it was the chimera of martial acclaim. "*I am a soldier of fortune;* and all the premonitions of my child hood early told me that I should be one." The soldier's life, he further explained, "is the only pursuit in which I could feel a throb of interest," illustrating how his preoccupation was a product of his romantic disposition. His musings, "premonitions of my child hood," and "day dreams of my boyhood" were decidedly imaginary and fueled by an emotional reaction, describing his desidera-tum as "a throb of interest" or "my military ardor." The persistence of what he per-ceived as boyish caprice exemplified how the romantic elsewhere was part of a vac-illating quest to achieve an elusive manhood. Between July 1834 and July 1835, he traveled from Staunton to Baltimore, New York, Boston, and Newfoundland before joining the US Marines in September 1835. He crossed the Atlantic aboard an unnamed "man-of-war," but upon his return he promptly begged for and received his discharge. By October 1835 Brooks took a job as a bartender in Hoboken, New Jersey, resigned to endure the life of "a wretched, aimless, reckless wanderer."[3]

Although scarce examples of their writings survive from this period, Walter Lane and Samuel Walker matched Brooks in his avid pursuit of adventurous exploits. Born on February 18, 1817, in County Cork, Ireland, Lane came to the United States with his parents when he was but four years old. The voyage, dim in his memory, foreshadowed a life of persistent movement. His father, a farmer, settled along the National Road in southeastern Ohio, where Lane grew into young adulthood. He admired the tales of chivalry expressed in Walter Scott's popular novels. Through Wilfred Ivanhoe, one of his title characters, Scott explained that the knights of old sustained themselves upon the food of battle and that "the dust of the *melée* is the breath of our nostrils!" Lane dedicated his life to realize these ideals.[4]

Samuel H. Walker, a native of Prince George County, Maryland, was born on February 24, 1817, six days after Lane. He was the son of an aging mechanic who was also a veteran of the American Revolution. When he came of age, his father arranged for him to apprentice with a carpenter in Washington, DC, but Walker was more interested in becoming the hero he often read about in the histories of the Revolution. Like Brooks, he admitted to "being naturally fond of military glory" and chafed at the doldrums of the carpenter's life. He "determined to try my fortune on the field of battle on the first opportunity," and in May 1836 his first chance arrived. Benjamin L. Beall arrived in Washington and called on volunteers to march with him to Alabama and chastise the Creeks, who resisted Anglo-American encroachment upon their territory. Walker promptly enlisted. Unfortunately, he and the Washington City Volunteers did not find the battlefields they sought. Instead, they worked clearing campgrounds and enduring harsh treatment from their superiors.[5]

The fascination that Brooks, Lane, and Walker exhibited toward martial adventurism grew from two narratives that celebrated the heroism of the American Revolution and the exceptionalism of the American frontier. Walker, for example, grew up enthralled by the fables that romanticized revolutionary warfare and its participants. He revealed to his sister that "nothing so much interested me as to read of the chivalry and noble deeds of our forefathers in the wars with Great Britain." Furthermore, his father, Nathan; uncle Charles; and grandfather Isaac were veterans of the Revolution, and family events were likely rife with the tales they told, intimately reinforcing the notions of patriotic sacrifice.[6]

The narrative that emerged from family tradition and national literature created a potent mythos that gave rise to the patriot-warrior mystique. Indeed, martial adventurers viewed themselves as the heirs to the patriots of 1776. Walker believed that his veteran father had left him an important patrimony that girded him with a proper sense of Americanness and manliness. He explained that his father was "always a true friend to the cause of freedom and justice between man and man; and these principles he always endeavored to instill into the minds of his children." Brooks echoed the significance of this legacy as he contemplated joining the separatists in Texas, calling for his fellow adventurers who had "inherited enough of the spirit of their fore-fathers" to join him there.[7]

Lane's experience suggests that he identified more with the frontier narrative. He had no family history with the American Revolution, and his introduction to martial romance lay in his readings of Scott's knightly tales, but the Irish native grew up in a region where stories of warfare with American Indians dominated the local newspapers. The nearby *Guernsey Times,* for example, featured stories, both historical and fictional, like "Indian Battle," "The Dark and Bloody Ground," and "The Ghost Riders," which contributed to the stories of the bold frontiersman and Indian fighter, and these tales significantly shaped Lane's imagination. In the early spring of 1836, as he traveled aboard a steamboat plying for Texas, he experienced

Samuel H. Walker. In late 1846, after garnering renown in the early battles of the Mexican-American War, Walker traveled to the East Coast to visit family and to recruit for his new company of US dragoons. Crowds often greeted him as a returning hero. At New York he sat for this portrait in Matthew Brady's studio. Many observers have commented on how Walker's youthful appearance and slight build contrasted with his reputation as a fierce and intrepid Texas Ranger—that is, contrasted with the imagined persona of the patriot-warrior. Matthew Brady [?], Captain Samuel Hamilton Walker, half-length portrait, facing slightly right. Half-plate daguerreotype, ca. 1846. Courtesy Daguerreotype Collection, Library of Congress, Washington, DC.

a nightmare that inspired a violent bout of sleepwalking. He cried in the middle of the night, "*Murder!* Indians, kill them," and attacked one of his cabin mates. "He tried to shake me off," Lane remembered, "but I thought he was the 'Big Brave.'" The episode affirms how deeply the images of frontier violence consumed his thoughts.[8]

To fulfill their desires for a soldier's life, Brooks joined the US Marines, while Walker joined a company of volunteers bound for the Creek territories in Alabama and Florida. Both were disappointed in their choices, and for the same reasons. They both discovered that the servitude, discipline, and boredom in the military contradicted the stirring visions of action and distinction. Brooks described his stint with the marines as "galling bondage," and he desperately wanted out. After eleven months in the service, he succeeded in obtaining an early discharge. Walker, and perhaps Brooks as well, understood the necessity of discipline in the ranks "when conducted on proper principles," but his experience in Florida exposed him to officers who were "tyrannical, pitiful, cowardly, disgusting, and contemptible scamps." In 1840, after four years of service, he published a biting condemnation of the current state of the US military, warning his fellow middling-class Americans "that no man with purely patriotic feelings can content himself to remain long in the United States army."[9]

The toil, discipline, and arbitrary officers certainly compounded the disappointment that they felt, but what Brooks and Walker found most intolerable was the abject anonymity of the common soldier. As a member of the rank and file, they could not stand out. Who remembered the Isaac and Nathan Walkers of the American Revolution? The nation, however, remembered the commanders—the George Washingtons, the Ethan Allens, the Frances Marions. Upon their exploits adventurers base the idea of the patriot-warrior. Brooks realized this and informed one of his benefactors that he "cherished [his] most glowing ambition to attain a situation of respectability." To emphasize this point, he noted in the letter in which he described his desperation for a discharge from the marines that he desired a commission in the very same corps. Attaining rank, "an elevated station," as Brooks describes it, provided the necessary circumstances for acquiring the celebrity about which he dreamed.[10]

Lane and Walker also expressed how significantly this desire for recognition operated in their thoughts. In his memoirs, for example, Lane admitted to returning home from his adventures in Texas in order to "ventilate my laurels." During his career in the Mexican-American War and the Civil War, he persistently clamored for higher rank. Walker, however, expressed best how he and his fellow adventurers felt about their quest for renown. In a letter he wrote from Florida in January 1842, he explained how his brother had encouraged him to return home, but he refused because he had yet to achieve his ambitions: "The love of chivalric immortal fame still clings to my heart [and] . . . urges me on." He also reveals how he equated renown to manliness when he remarks: "Heaven forbids that I should ever mistake the path of true glory, forgetting the true and proper elements of a great man in his pursuit of that honourable distinction. . . . [T]o return without wealth or Fame it is too bad."[11]

The grand narrative of patriot and frontier heroes, furthermore, taught Brooks, Lane, and Walker that achieving renown required conspicuous acts of violence. At the core of the martial adventurer's daydreams and experience lay action and warfare, bloodshed and death. For Brooks, dying on the battlefield represented the ultimate expression of adventurous celebrity. He was eager, if not obsessive, about meeting a glorious death. In letters to family and friends, he consistently promised, "I will die like a soldier," or "I shall not murmur" when he faced his demise. He explained on several occasions that he had envisioned the moment that would come. "My prayer has been, since my earliest recollection, to die on the field of battle, with the shout of victory in my ears."[12] Like Walker and many of their comrades, Brooks was less concerned about how his actions benefited his nation than about how his nation rewarded his actions. This was not selfless patriotism. This was the self-indulgence of the romantic's pathetic egocentrism that led many patriot-warriors to their deaths.

Upon their first attempts, Brooks and Walker did not find the renown that they seemed to crave, but they were romantic adventurers, trusting in the hope that the ever-shifting elsewhere would open new arenas of adventure. As he served drinks in Hoboken, for example, Brooks simply bided his time, waiting for "the waves of mighty destiny," as he once described. Residing in the United States during the age of expansion, however, he did not have to wait long. By August 1835, reports from the far Southwest brought rumors of war. "What do you think of Texas?" he asked a friend. In that province Anglo-American and Tejano residents expressed dismay over the centralist policies of Mexican president Antonio López de Santa Anna, and brief outbreaks of violence heightened the tensions. Brooks considered the possibility of war in Texas and what it might mean for him. To his brother he noted, "There is then some hope, of my finding active employment in a military capacity there." By November, reports of the battles that opened the Texas Revolution reached Hoboken, confirming for him that "Texas opens a wide and variegated field to the ambition and enterprise of the soldier of fortune," perhaps vindicating his faith in the elsewhere.[13]

Those adventurers like Samuel Walker who missed the opportunity to fight in the Texas Revolution need not despair. The Texas rebels succeeded in establishing a republic, but it was a nation based upon a tenuous independence. Animosities persisted with Mexico, and numerous native groups resisted Anglo-American settlement. The Republic of Texas was a nation that suffered an interminable state of war—fertile fields for the martial adventurer. After five years of toilsome camp life and degrading discipline, Walker continued to look to other places. Writing from Tallahassee, Florida, in January 1842, he explained to his sister how his desire for adventure and renown continued to afflict him, alerting her, "be not surprised if my next communication to you should be written in Texas."[14]

Unlike Brooks and Walker, Lane did not endure the privations of the common soldier or try his fortune in less violent arenas. In the autumn of 1835, from his parents' home in Ohio, he left directly for Texas. Along with Brooks and hundreds of other volunteers, many of whom were likeminded adventurers, Lane responded to the calls for assistance from the embattled province. He arrived overland via the Red River, and when he reached the rustic village of San Augustine, he promptly found a company outfitting for war. A recruit decided that he did not want to join and hired Lane as a substitute. "[He] gave me a fine horse, double-barreled gun, and a brace of pistols. . . . I was alright, then." When he arrived at the port of Velasco, Brooks was no less satisfied, if not more enthusiastic. "The die is cast," he declared to his father, "I am over the Rubicon and my fate is now inseparably connected with that of Texas."[15]

For Brooks, the conflict in Texas fulfilled his longstanding dreams of assuming the role of his patriot heroes. The rhetoricians in Texas deliberately equated their struggle with the American Revolution, both as a means to define their causes as well as to peddle their promises of renown to adventurers in the United States. They had sold Brooks. "Its near similarity to the glorious struggle of our own ancestors in 'Seventy-six' must produce a sympathy for them in every part of the Union." The young men of the United States, he believed, had the opportunity to stake a claim to the manly heritage of their patriot grandfathers. "I hope and believe that there are many of the youths of our country who have inherited enough of the spirit of their fore-fathers to induce them to procure, like myself, a musket and a hundred rounds of ball cartridge, and join the holy crusade." As Lane had also suggested, in order to claim that inheritance, patriot-warriors must arm themselves and ultimately commit, or become victims of, bloodshed.[16]

Such renown that Brooks, Lane, and Walker sought was quite rare, but Texas, and the wars fought over it, provided opportunities for a few to rise above their middling stations through adventurous exploit. Samuel Walker was one such adventurer. After his arrival in the Republic of Texas in January 1842, he joined Alexander Somervell's expedition to the Rio Grande. When the command disbanded at Laredo, Walker continued with the other filibusters to Mier, where the Mexican Army defeated and captured the Texans. He remained a prisoner in Mexico for a eighteen months. During that time, he kept a journal that he probably intended to publish, but he made the mistake of turning it over to Thomas J. Green, one of the campaign's leaders, who used it as the basis of his own *Journal of the Texian Expedition to Mier* (1845). Although widely reviewed in the United States, Green's *Journal* only briefly mentions Walker, but at least it lauded him as "a daring and efficient spy."[17]

Walker's moment as a national hero, however, arrived in 1846 with the outbreak of the Mexican-American War. After the United States annexed the Republic of Texas, US president James K. Polk sent Brig. Gen. Zachary Taylor to the Rio Grande, hoping to touch off a war so that he might conclude his nation's expansionist destiny. Walker led a company of Texas Rangers in support of Taylor's effort to establish a supply depot at Point Isabel and a fort across the river from Matamoros. On April 8 Walker and his Rangers assisted in holding off a large Mexican force advancing toward Point Isabel and the next day carried dispatches through enemy lines.[18]

Correspondents of New Orleans newspapers reported Walker's actions, and other periodicals across the nation reprinted the exploits of "the valiant and undaunted WALKER, of the Texas Rangers." One obviously exaggerated account that circulated nationally credited Walker and twelve Rangers for fighting off 3,500 Mexicans in defense of Point Isabel.[19] The *New York Globe* ran a feature on Walker, testifying to his emerging renown. "His late unequalled conflict with the Mexicans . . . and his daring heroism . . . have excited in the public's mind a strong desire to know more of him."[20] Newspapers from Philadelphia to Tallahassee, from Hudson, Ohio, to Raymond, Mississippi, reprinted stories extolling the adventures of Samuel H. Walker. He continued fighting with Taylor's forces at the opening battles of Palo Alto and Resaca de la Palma, and in recognition of his service, President Polk appointed him captain in a new regiment of mounted rifles. Before he took that position, Walker joined the regiment of Texas Rangers organized by John C. Hays. They were very active in the battle for Monterrey and received considerable press, but those accounts only mentioned Walker occasionally, overshadowed by his commander Hays, the martyred captain Robert A. Gillespie, and the growing lore surrounding the Texas Rangers.[21]

Nevertheless, after Taylor discharged the Rangers, Walker returned to the United States in order to visit his relatives in Maryland and recruit for his new company of mounted rifles. He received a hero's welcome. On November 12, 1846, when he arrived at New Orleans with Hays, the residents met them with cheers. The *Daily Picayune* noted, "The gallant deeds of both have rendered their names familiar throughout the land." As Walker traveled east, communities along the way organized fetes and greetings to the patriot-warrior from Texas. On the twenty-third he attended a reception in Washington, DC, in which a thousand people reportedly clamored to see him. As he passed through Philadelphia on the thirtieth, the *North American* touted him as the "renowned Texas Ranger, and hero of the Rio Grande and Monterey." Walker sojourned in New York City, where he offered suggestions to Samuel Colt for improving his revolvers and sat for a daguerreotype at Matthew Brady's studios. His tour continued as he returned to the scenes of battle with his new company.[22]

The Ranger's adventures also caught the attention of Charles Deas. Acclaimed for his works capturing mountain-man vitality and American Indian stoicism, the artist completed *The Last Shot or Captain Walker's Encounter with the Ranchero* by August 1846, when it appeared on exhibition in St Louis. For Deas, Walker embodied the same frontier heroism and violence that he celebrated in his earlier works like *Long Jakes* (1844) or *The Death Struggle* (1845), suggesting a fusion with the young man's martial persona and thereby constructing an image of the adventurous patriot-warrior. According to a critic who observed *The Last Shot,* Deas created a "scene wild and picturesque," depicting Walker lying upon the ground, unhorsed, as a ranchero approaches to finish him with a knife. Instead of falling victim, Walker, with a "firm, determined countenance," blasts away at his adversary with his pistol. The painting contributed to the national fascination with Walker. At St. Louis it "attracted the attention of hundreds." It may have been exhibited at Cincinnati before arriving at the American Art-Union in New York City.[23]

Walker left few clues about whether or not this celebrity gratified his yearning for "chivalric immortal fame," as he once termed his quest for renown. Publicly, such as when he attended the reception at Washington, he assumed a humble deportment. After rounds of laudatory speeches, he told the crowd that "he had done nothing more than his duty as an American soldier." Yet for Walker, who had so admired the patriot heroes of the past, the term "American soldier" was fraught with personal significance, and the admiration of the throng was a manifest expression that he had realized his dreams.[24]

By the time Walker returned to Mexico in May 1847, the focus of US war efforts had shifted from the Monterrey theater in the northeast to the campaign against Mexico City. US commanders attached Walker and his mounted rifles to units patrolling the long route between the invading force and its supply depot at Vera Cruz, clashing sporadically with local partisans. On October 9 he and his riflemen charged into a large force of Mexican lancers, chasing them through the small town of Huamantla. In the subsequent Mexican counterattack, Walker fell. Upon hearing the news, a correspondent who had conversed with the captain at Washington claimed that Walker, like John S. Brooks, had anticipated his violent demise. "He was, of course, always expecting death, and not surprised when it came."[25]

Laments of the captain's death and celebrations of his adventurous life appeared in newspapers across the United States. The details differed, but each account added to what the *Scotio Gazette* of Chillicothe, Ohio, termed the "Romantic Death of Capt. Walker." He died leading his mounted rifles in a charge, or was the victim of a superhumanly enraged father, avenging his son's death. American mythmakers created different versions of his dying words, but all agreed that in his final breath, Walker urged his men forward, to never surrender. Seemingly, Walker fulfilled Brooks's, if not his own, dreams of dying on the battle-field with cries of victory around him.[26]

At least for his time, Walker also achieved his stated ambition of acquiring patriotic fame. Newspaper editors and correspondents confirmed his nationwide esteem. In an editorial titled "The Brave Ranger," for example, the *New Orleans Delta* noted how his career had "become part of our national glory and of our national records." These commentators further illustrated the central role that violence played in defining national heroes. The *Commercial Times* of New Orleans stated that the captain "was one of those spirits that seem designated by fate to acquire renown in their tasking of their physical energies in the heat of a hand to hand fray; in the crowded melee," and the *Delta* emphasized Walker's skill with the Rangers' instruments of bloodshed—"the deadly rifle, the sure revolver, or the irre-sistible bowie-knife."[27]

Such renown that Walker achieved, however, was quite rare. The experiences of Brooks and Lane, who arrived in Texas a decade earlier, exemplify the more common results of adventurous careers and further testify to the elusive quality of "immortal fame." Most men survived and remained inconspicuous, and those who gave their lives often found empty, forgotten deaths.

Brooks numbered among the latter. On the morning of Palm Sunday, March 27, 1836, the twenty-two-year-old found himself writhing in pain, lying in a makeshift hospital just outside the fortifications at Goliad. He lay with several dozen other wounded—Texas rebels and Mexican soldiers. A week before, a Mexican musket ball had shattered his thigh during the Battle of Coleto, where Mexican general José de Urrea forced the Texans under Col. James W. Fannin to surrender. Urrea imprisoned the Texans at Goliad. There Brooks could not endure the pain. The muscle around his wound cramped so severely that he begged the attending surgeon to end his life. Dr. Joseph E. Field did the best he could to relieve the volunteer's discomfort but refused his request for death. Earlier on that Palm Sunday, Mexican officers had awakened Fannin and over three hundred Texas prisoners of war. Their captors marched those who could walk in squads under the pretense of gathering wood or herding cattle. After reaching a safe distance from the town, the soldiers drew their arms and shot down their prisoners. Another group of soldiers came into the hospital, picked Brooks up, carried him outside, and beat him. Doctor Field could only listen as Brooks "gave his last shriek" and wait until one of the Mexican soldiers returned and informed him, "Your friend is dead."[28]

Perhaps in some way Brooks achieved part of his adolescent dreams. He did not acquire individual renown, but Anglo-Texans have immortalized the 342 victims of the Goliad Massacre, though overshadowed by the fall of the Alamo. Perhaps Brooks would have been satisfied that the deaths at Goliad and the Alamo served as rallying cries for Walter Lane and his comrades during the Texan victory at San Jacinto. If his professions to patriotism were sincere, he would have been pleased that his sacrifice, however anonymous, assisted in the creation of the Republic of Texas. In the Anglo-American imagination, that nation advanced the cause of liberty for which Brooks claimed to have fought, and it certainly served as a conspicuous example of US expansion.

Several newspapers noted Brooks's sacrifice when two survivors of Goliad published accounts of their ordeals. Joseph Field's version appeared in New Hampshire, New York, and Washington but only mentioned "Captain Brooks," noting how the wounded, would-be hero "extended his arms toward me, imploring my assistance"—perhaps not the last image for which Brooks wanted his admirers to remember him. Jack Shackelford recalled Brooks as a "highly gifted young [man]" who "shared the fate of many other gallant spirits." His account appeared in Tuscumbia, Alabama; Washington, DC; and in Brooks's hometown of Staunton. But even his former employer expressed dismay over the manner of his death: "Had he died on the battle-field, the death which the soldier covets, our feelings would be different."[29]

Walter P. Lane. This photograph depicts Lane at about sixty years old. He had survived an adventurous career but did not achieve the renown for which he longed. In 1890 he sent this likeness to Henry A. McArdle to assist the artist's completion of his painting The Battle of San Jacinto *(1898). Lane, however, would not figure prominently in the work, which depicts a whirling melee of a hundred other, mostly anonymous soldiers. Unknown,* Walter P. Lane, McArdle San Jacinto Companion Notebook, [photostat?], *ca. 1876. Courtesy Texas State Library and Archives Commission, Austin.*

Perhaps in the end, Brooks was disappointed in his adventurous career. He was, after all, an egocentric romantic who espoused an equally egocentric patriotism. His daydreams did not celebrate American greatness so much as they celebrated the greatness of himself. Brooks had envisioned a glorious death on the battlefield with "the shout of victory in my ears," but his experience in Texas quashed his romantic indulgences. His one battle resulted in an inglorious surrender, and when his final moment arrived, Brooks did not hear the shout of victory but his own shrieks as his captors beat him to death. Imagination compelled Brooks to Texas, and the transformation of his empty death into a meaningful sacrifice also required a leap of imagination.

Unlike Walker and Brooks, Walter Lane survived his adventurous career but never achieved the wide acclaim for which he longed. He was only one of several hundred San Jacinto veterans. During the Mexican-American War, he fought alongside Walker at Monterrey, but the many accounts of Texas Rangers' daring and ferocity failed to mention him. He later commanded a battalion, but by that time the scenes of violence, requisite for attainting adventurous celebrity, had moved to the Vera Cruz–Mexico City theater, where John C. Hays expanded his reputation and Samuel Walker achieved his martyrdom. Lane clashed with Comanches near Saltillo, and a letter he wrote detailing that event received moderate circulation in US newspapers. At war's end the citizens of Rio Grande City, Texas, invited Lane and his Rangers to a dinner to honor their service. He thanked them, explaining that "nothing can give more pleasure to the soldier . . . [than] the approbation of his fellow citizens." Although grateful for those expressions, Lane did not enjoy a statewide, much less a national, tour of fete and acclaim similar to that Walker had experienced.[30]

After the Mexican-American War, Lane participated in the rush to the California gold fields but failed to find wealth or fame. When the Civil War opened, he joined the Confederate Army as a regimental officer. Although he enjoyed active tours, promotion and wide renown eluded him. In January 1864 he considered leaving the service when his superiors placed a junior officer in command of his brigade. When he finally receive his elusive brigadier wreaths, his emblem of renown, they came on the last day the Confederate Congress met—two months before General Robert E. Lee's surrender at Appomattox Court House. During the war, Lane did not make the ultimate sacrifice or lead decisive charges that would generate the recognition he sought. Later in retirement, he experienced disappointments with both business and political failures.[31]

By surviving his adventures, however, Lane enjoyed an advantage over Brooks and Walker in that he had the opportunity to contribute to the construction of an enduring patriot-warrior mythos. He served as president of the Texas Veteran Association and corresponded with early Texas historians like John Henry Brown, James T. DeShields, and Victor M. Rose as well as artists William H. Huddle and Henry McArdle, all of whom helped construct the Texas warrior mystique. Lane also capitalized upon imperfect recollections with the erroneous reports that he had been responsible for the recovery of the remains of those Mier prisoners executed at Salado, Mexico. This reclamation took place in May 1848 at the close of the Mexican-American War. His only role in the affair was giving his consent to ten Rangers of his battalion to retrieve the bodies and transport them back to Fayette County, Texas, for reburial at Monument Hill. Thirty years later in 1878, however, a story began to circulate that claimed that Lane had personally performed this deed.[32]

Despite the opportunities to correct it, Lane allowed the misunderstanding to persist. When he wrote his memoirs in 1887, he not only declined the opportunity to correct the myth, he embellished it. In this fabrication he emphasized how Capt. John Pope of the Topographical Engineers, who accompanied Lane, balked

Memorial plaque at Monument Hill. Placed upon the shell-stone shaft erected at Monument Hill, this plaque immortalizes the fiction that Walter P. Lane was directly responsible for the return of the remains of the Mier prisoners from Mexico. Whether deemed an error, an exaggeration, or an untruth, it nevertheless exemplifies how the quest for, and the achievement of, renown is fundamentally imaginary. Courtesy Jimmy L. Bryan Jr., 2007.

Monument Hill, Fayette County, Texas. In 1936 the Texas Centennial Commission erected the forty-eight-foot frescoed shaft over the crypt that holds the remains of those killed at the Dawson Massacre and the Mier prisoners executed at Salado, Mexico. Many of these men likely desired the same adventurous renown that had captivated John S. Brooks, Walter P. Lane, and Samuel H. Walker. Courtesy Jimmy L. Bryan Jr., 2007.

at his insistence of making a detour to Salado, the site of the prisoners' mass grave. Lane reportedly admonished the captain: "I told him it could not be expected that he would have the same feeling on the subject as I had—as a Texan—but those bones I was going to have, all the same."[33] It was the only moment in his memoirs in which Lane expresses a sense of Texas exceptionalism that reinforced the image of the patriot-warrior to which Brooks and Walker had contributed.

Lane apparently co-opted this honor because the exhumation of the Mier prisoners offered him an opportunity to lay claim to a renown that had long eluded him. It was a dramatic story of chivalry in the deliverance of martyrs from the clutches of the enemy. His friend and historian John Henry Brown confirmed this point when he wrote that it was the "[o]ne episode" that would "embalm his memory forever in the hearts of Texans." When Lane died in 1892 at the age of seventy-four, the Texas legislature and many statewide newspapers marked the moment and specifically mentioned his invented role in the reclamation of the Mier prisoners. In the 1930s, as part of Texas centennial celebrations, the state erected a forty-eight-foot shaft over the mass grave at Monument Hill and included a plaque that affixed Lane's fiction to the enduring Texas shell stone. Its persistence, however, did not translate into national renown. Like Brooks, Lane never achieved the heroic status that Walker had.[34]

Renown, as the experiences of Brooks, Lane, and Walker illustrate, was an ambition that was intricately associated with the idea of adventurous manhood because it served as the ultimate form of group sanction. It transcended the recognition an adventurer might attain from his comrades and represented the validation from a nation of peers. In attaining it, adventurers could lay claim to a more permanent masculinity—one that would endure over time—after they made the ultimate sacrifice or even as they aged and became less vital.

The patriot-warrior archetype was central to this quest for acclaim because it conflated the popular images of revolutionary heroism with frontier ruggedness, which not only redefined measures of manliness but also convinced many Americans of their exceptionalism. As patriot-warriors, adventurers incorporated the ideas of duty, sacrifice, and renown with violence and aggression to fulfill their mission as the vanguard of expansion. Individuals like Brooks, Lane, and Walker exemplified these experiences and illustrated success and failure, fulfillment and emptiness. They imagined themselves as steadfast patriots and backwoods warriors, eager agents of violence and conquest, because for Brooks, Lane, Walker, and many of their adventurous comrades, only the crucible of bloodshed and death could reify their daydreams of becoming renowned American men.

Notes

1. Rollin G. Osterweis used the term "elsewhere" to describe this important aspect of romanticism. *Romanticism and Nationalism in the Old South* (New Haven, CT: Yale University Press, 1949), 8–9. For the many definitions of romanticism, see Morse Peckham, *The Triumphs of Romanticism* (Columbia: University of South Carolina Press, 1970), 3–35; and Colin Campbell, *The Romantic Ethic and the Spirit of Modern Consumerism* (New York: Basil Blackwell, 1987), 72–76, 179–81, 201–203. For literary explorations of adventure, see Paul Zweig, *The Adventurer: The Fate of Adventure in the Western World* (Princeton, NJ: Princeton University Press, 1974); and Martin Green, *Dreams of Adventure, Dreams of Empire* (New York: Basic Books, 1979). Robert W. Johannsen notes the important role that romanticism played in the motivation of volunteers for the Mexican-American War in *To the Halls of the Montezumas: The Mexican War in the American Imagination* (New York: Oxford University Press, 1985), 68–86. Amy S. Greenberg examines the cultural expressions of US expansionism through the travelogues and literature that advocated filibuster campaigns in Latin America during the 1850s. Like the adventurers of the 1830s and 1840s, "aggressive expansionists" capitalized upon the nation's approbation of "martial manhood" to generate support for their territorial ambitions. *Manifest Manhood and the Antebellum American Empire* (New York: Cambridge University Press, 2005), 1–17.

2. For example, Richard Slotkin shows how American culture makers of the early nineteenth century grafted together the notions of Daniel Boone's frontier exceptionalism and George Washington's patriot heroism to fashion the idea of an American "natural aristocracy." *The Fatal Environment: The Myth of the Frontier in the Age of Industrialism, 1800–1900* (1985; repr., New York: Harper Perennial, 1994), 77–78.

3. Brooks to Mary Ann Brooks, Brooklyn, July 4, 1835, John Sowers Brooks Papers, Center for American History, University of Texas Austin (hereafter cited as JSBP); Brooks to Absalom H. Brooks, Brooklyn, July 30, 1835, ibid.; Brooks to Absalom H. Brooks, Hoboken, Oct. 1, 1835, ibid.; Brooks to Absalom H. Brooks, New York, Nov. 4, 1835, ibid.; Brooks to Mary Ann Brooks, Goliad, Mar. 4, 1836, ibid.; Ron C. Tyler et al., eds., *The New Handbook of Texas*, 6 vols. (Austin: Texas State Historical Association, 1996), 1:750–51; Jos. A. Waddell, *Annals of Augusta County, Virginia, from 1726 to 1871* (Staunton, VA: C. Russell Caldwell, 1902), 428; Muster Rolls of the US Marine Corps, 1798–1892, Records of the US Marine Corps, RG 127, National Archives, Washington, DC, Microfilm Publication T1118. Original emphasis in all quotations. Brooks obtained his early discharge by pointing out that he had been a minor when he enlisted, making his contract invalid. A select number of Brooks's correspondence appear in John E. Roller, ed., "Capt. John Sowers Brooks," *Texas Historical Association Quarterly*, 9 (Jan. 1906): 157–209.

4. Walter P. Lane, *The Adventures and Recollections of Gen. Walter P. Lane, a San Jacinto Veteran, Containing Sketches of the Texian, Mexican, and Late Wars with Several Indian Fights Thrown In* (Marshall, TX: Tri-Weekly Herald Job Print, 1887), 36, 71, 73; Walter Scott, *Ivanhoe* (1819; repr., New York: Penguin, 1994), 317; Jimmy L. Bryan Jr., *More Zeal Than Discretion: The Westward Adventures of Walter P. Lane* (College Station: Texas A&M University Press, 2008), 9–11; Tyler, *New Handbook*, 4:62–63.

5. S. H. Walker, "Florida and Seminole Wars" (Washington, DC: S. H. Walker, 1840), 1–2; Tyler, *New Handbook*, 6:797–98.

6. Walker, "Florida and Seminole Wars," 1–2; Henry C. Peden Jr., *Revolutionary Patriots of Prince George's County Maryland, 1775–1783* (Westminster, MD: Heritage, 2006), 312, 313, 314.

7. Walker, "Florida and Seminole Wars," 1–2; Brooks to Absalom H. Brooks, New York, Nov. 4, 1835, JSBP; Edward Tang, "Writing the American Revolution: War Veterans in the Nineteenth-Century Cultural Memory," *Journal of American Studies* 32 (Apr. 1998): 63–80.

8. *Guernsey Times* (Cambridge, OH), July 20, 1833, Sept. 20, Oct. 18, 1834; *Guernsey Times, and Farmers' and Mechanics' Advocate* (Cambridge, OH), Apr. 11, 1835; Lane, *Adventures and Recollections*, 5; Bryan, *More Zeal*, 10–11.

9. Brooks to James Hagarty, Brooklyn, July 30, 1835, JSBP; Brooks to Norborne C. Brooks, Brooklyn, Aug. 12, 1835, ibid., Brooks to Absalom H. Brooks, New York, Nov. 4, 1835, ibid.; Walker, "Florida and Seminole Wars," 10–11.

10. Brooks to Hagarty, Brooklyn, July 20, 1835, JSBP; Brooks to Norborne C. Brooks, Brooklyn, Aug. 12, 1835, ibid.; Brooks to Hagarty, Brooklyn, Aug. 19, 1835, ibid.

11. Lane, *Adventures and Recollections*, 16; Walker to Ann Walker, Tallahassee, Jan. 22, 1842, Samuel Hamilton Walker Papers, Archives Division, Texas State Library, Austin.

12. Brooks to Mary Ann Brooks, Goliad, Feb. 25, 1836, JSBP; Brooks to Hagarty, Goliad, Mar. 9, 1836, ibid.; Brooks to Mary Ann Brooks, Goliad, Mar. 4, 1836, ibid. Other examples include Brooks to Mary Ann Brooks, Velasco, Jan. 8, 1836, ibid.; and Brooks to Absalom H. Brooks, Velasco, Jan. 20, 1836, ibid.

13. Brooks to Norborne C. Brooks, Brooklyn, Aug. 12, 1835, ibid.; Brooks to Hagarty, Brooklyn, Aug. 19, 1835, ibid.; Brooks to Absalom H. Brooks, New York, Nov. 4, 1835, ibid.; Brooks to Mary Ann Brooks, Goliad, Mar. 4, 1836, ibid.

14. Walker to Ann Walker, Tallahassee, Jan. 22, 1842, Walker Papers.

15. Lane, *Adventures and Recollections*, 6; Brooks to Absalom H. Brooks, Velasco, Dec. 23, 1835, JSBP. Almost a thousand volunteers from the United States arrived before the Battle of San Jacinto, representing over 40 percent of the Texas force. They created severe discipline problems, suggesting that many came with ambitions of individual renown similar to Brooks and Lane. Paul D. Lack, *The Texas Revolutionary Experience: A Political and Social History, 1835–1836* (College Station: Texas A&M University Press, 1992), 118–36; Stephen L. Hardin, *Texian Iliad: A Military History of the Texas Revolution, 1835–1836* (Austin: University of Texas Press, 1994), 180–82, 203–206.

16. Brooks to Absalom Brooks, New York, Nov. 4, 1835, JSBP; Brooks to Mary Ann Brooks, Velasco, Jan. 8, 1836, ibid.

17. Thomas J. Green, *Journal of the Texian Expedition against Mier*, ed. Sam W. Haynes (1845; repr., Austin: W. Thomas Taylor, 1993), xvii, xix–xx, 32, 33, 3–40, 70. After he returned from imprisonment, Walker also participated in several fights with Comanches, including the Pedernales, the first action in which combatants used revolvers, but he received little notice from those actions at the time. Tyler, *New Handbook*, 6:197–98.

18. K. Jack Bauer, *The Mexican War, 1846–1848* (New York: Macmillan, 1974), 48–49.

19. *Columbia South Carolina Temperance Advocate and Register of Agriculture and General Literature*, May 21, 1846; *Jackson Mississippian*, May 13, 1846. Other versions included *New Orleans Bulletin Extra*, May 9, 1846; and *Philadelphia North American*, May 18, 1846.

20. As reprinted in the *Tallahassee Floridian*, June 6, 1846; *Nashville Union*, June 10, 1846; and *Barre (PA) Gazette*, June 5, 1846.

THE PATRIOT-WARRIOR MYSTIQUE 131

21. Other notices of Walker in the early days of the Mexican-American War include *Washington (DC) Daily National Intelligencer*, May 19, 1846; *Mississippi Free Trader and Natchez Gazette*, May 14, 1846; and *Hudson Ohio Observer*, May 27, 1846. So moved were some leading men at New Orleans that they purchased a "fine blooded steed for Capt. Walker." *New Orleans Daily Picayune*, May 14, 1846. Such was the interest in Walker that the *Vicksburg Sentinel* felt it necessary to clarify his family history. *Sentinel* as reprinted in *Jackson Mississippian*, July 15, 1846.

22. *New Orleans Daily Picayune*, Nov. 13, 1846; *Washington (DC) Daily National Intelligencer*, Nov. 25, 1846; *North American*, Dec. 2, 1846; *Scotio Gazette* (Chillicothe, OH), Mar. 24, 1847; *Captain Samuel Hamilton Walker*, half-length portrait, facing slightly right, Dag. No. 199, Daguerreotype Collection, Library of Congress, Washington, DC; Tyler, *New Handbook*, 6:197–98.

23. *The Last Shot* has not survived. Carol Clark, *Charles Deas and 1840s America* (Norman: University of Oklahoma Press, 2009), 105, 201–202; *St. Louis Weekly Reveille*, Aug. 31, 1846, quoted in ibid., 201.

24. Walker to Ann Walker, Tallahassee, Jan. 22, 1842, Walker Papers; *Washington (DC) Daily National Intelligencer*, Nov. 25, 1846.

25. Bauer, *Mexican War*, 331; *New York Commercial Advertiser*, as reprinted in *New York Emancipator*, Dec. 1, 1847.

26. *Scotio Gazette* (Chillicothe, OH), Nov. 17, 1847; *Jackson Mississippian*, Nov. 12, 1847; *New Orleans Daily Picayune*, Nov. 6, 1847; *Greenville (SC) Mountaineer*, Nov. 9, 1847.

27. *New Orleans Daily Delta*, Nov. 7, 1847; *Hartford (CT) Daily Times*, as reprinted in *Mississippi Free Trader and Natchez Gazette*, Dec. 11, 1847; *New Orleans Commercial Times*, as reprinted in *Raleigh Register and North-Carolina Gazette*, Nov. 20, 1847.

28. Jack Shackelford to Norborne C. Brooks, Courttako, AL, Aug. 5, 1836, and Joseph E. Field to Norborne C. Brooks, Charlemont, MA, Sept. 6, 1836, quoted in Roller, "Capt. John Sowers Brooks," 196–98; Tyler, *New Handbook*, 3:218–21.

29. Field's account originally appeared in the *Greenfield (NH) Mercury*, as reprinted in *New-York Spectator*, Sept. 1, 1836. Shackelford's first appeared in the *Tuscumbia North Alabamian*, as reprinted in *Washington (DC) Globe*, Aug. 3, 1836; *Staunton (VA) Spectator*, Aug. 11, 1836, quoted in Roller, "Capt. John Sowers Brooks," 205–209.

30. *American Flag* (Matamoros, Mex.), July 22, 1848; Bryan, *More Zeal*, 59–76.

31. J. D. McAdoo to [Pendleton] Murrah, Houston, Jan. 4, 1864, Pendleton Murrah Papers, Office of the Governor, Archives Division, Texas State Library, Austin; Bryan, *More Zeal*, 128–29, 133, 136–37, 140–42. For Lane's Civil War service, see Anne Bailey, "Walter Paye Lane," in *The Confederate General*, ed. William C. Davis, 6 vols. (n.p.: National Historical Society, 1991), 4:20–21; and Ralph A. Wooster, *Lone Star Generals in Gray* (Austin, TX: Eakin Press, 2000), 142–45, 237.

32. For details regarding the evolution of this myth, see Bryan, *More Zeal*, 172–78; and James M. Day, *Black Beans and Goose Quills: Literature of the Texan Mier Expedition* (Waco: Texian, 1970), 146–47.

33. Lane, *Adventures and Recollections*, 59

34. William S. Speer and John Henry Brown, eds., *Encyclopedia of the New West* (1881; repr., Easley, SC: Southern Historical Press, 1978), 311; Bryan, *More Zeal*, 178.

Civil War Soldier Monument, New Braunfels, Texas. Courtesy Charles D. Grear.

6

"All Eyes of Texas Are on Comal County"

German Texans' Loyalty during the Civil War and World War I

Charles David Grear

NEW BRAUNFELS, TEXAS, the seat of Comal County, has a notable history of German culture and heritage. German settlers established the city in 1845 near the eastern edge of the Hill Country along the banks of the Comal and Guadalupe Rivers and on the major transportation route between San Antonio and Austin. Until the mid-twentieth century, the city was largely composed of German immigrants and their descendants. Despite a significant non-German population boom and the decrease of its Teutonic ties, Deutsche names still dot local businesses; restaurants; annual celebrations such as Wurstfest, Saengerfest, and Wassailfest; and the world-famous Schlitterbahn Waterpark. Other remnants from the past are two statues solemnly standing in the historic square: one depicting a Civil War soldier, neither Confederate nor Union, and the other an American "doughboy" from World War I. No other conflicts are memorialized there except these two—the most controversial for German Texans. These symbols inspire questions: How did New Braunfelsers react to the Civil War and the First World War, which tested their loyalties to their adopted country? Particularly, how did residents respond to questions over ethnic origins and national loyalty?

During both wars, the surrounding region questioned the loyalty of the German population of New Braunfels. Residents also raised the ire of the Anglo-Texan population because of their resistance to cultural assimilation, fiercely maintaining their language, architecture, political ideas, and culture. Additionally German Texans thrived economically, especially the people of New Braunfels because of their proximity to San

World War I Soldier Monument, New Braunfels, Texas. Courtesy Charles D. Grear

Antonio and Austin. Texans tolerated these annoyances during peacetime, but wars created distrust of anybody outside of the conventional culture. During the Civil War, neighbors questioned the loyalty of the recently arrived immigrants and their views toward the institution of slavery and their support for and defense of the southern cause. World War I produced similar sentiment, except that the Anglo population suspected

New Braunfelsers' devotion to Germany since they maintained its culture and their connections to the country. In both conflicts the citizenry of New Braunfels asked themselves, Do we fight for our views and homeland, or do we compromise to maintain our livelihood in Texas?

Questions of loyalty are never easy to answer, especially in situations where one's loyalty is split between two factions (proslavery or antislavery) or two localities. New Braunfelsers and German Texans as a whole had multiple local attachments: to their ideals, to their current home, and to their ancestral lands. When Germans immigrated to Texas, they did not simply forget who they were, their connections to their home-land, and their culture. In their lifetimes they amassed attachments involving issues that concerned them the most, including families—both immediate and extended (even those still in Germany)—and friends; localities, where they were born and their current homestead; and a way of life, ranging from their European culture to antislavery beliefs. All of these attachments had a direct bearing on New Braunfelsers' decisions during the Civil War and the Great War.

Regardless of how one analyzes the Civil War, it was a conflict over the future of the institution of slavery. The first German immigrants, commonly called "Greys" and arriving during the 1820s through the 1840s for economic opportunities, composed the majority of the New Braunfels population. Greys viewed slavery differently from their Anglo counterparts in Texas. Most were more apathetic, not openly hostile, to the institution because of their assimilation to southern and Texas culture. An editorial in the town's newspaper, the *Neu Braunfelser Zeitung,* stated: "the majority of the Germans are not against the institution of slave labor and will support this institution in every political struggle. The Republicans, of course, have maintained that the Germans own no slaves, because it is not morally right. This is not true."[1] Complicating matters was another Grey, Dr. Hermann Nagel, who wrote to his mother in Germany describing his abhorrence toward the existence of slavery in the Lone Star State. In one letter he declared, "I will never be able to reconcile myself with the belief that slavery is the actual foundation of the state, that the continued existence of slavery is not merely a temporary necessity but the true essence and basic principle of the state." Later he expressed his ignorance by penning: "I am not particularly afraid of Negro uprisings; . . . in general, the blacks have had it too good. I do hope, at least, that I am right about this, although I must admit that I cannot form an opinion based on my own experience, since I live far away from the plantations and don't really know much myself about the blacks and their condition."[2] Years of living in Texas did not force the Germans to forget their culture, but their connection to Texas allowed them to accept the practices that thrived in the state.[3]

The prospect of war and the issue of slavery influenced the Greys when the question of secession heated up in 1861. Early German immigrants reluctantly embraced the Anglo population's desire for Texas to separate from the Union and join the Confederacy. Before the secession crisis, Dr. Adolph Doulai, editor of the *San Antonio Zeitung,* expressed antislavery opinions in his newspaper. The local proslavery community reacted quickly by withdrawing their advertisements, almost bankrupting the press. Most New Braunfelsers remembered events like this and the plight of their German neighbors. When secession appeared inevitable, Ferdinand Jacob Lindheimer, the editor of the local German-language newspaper, *Neu-Braunfelser Zeitung,* championed secession to protect his interests—his press. He argued that New Braunfels would benefit if the citizens voted for secession. Lindheimer began his campaign in the December 14, 1860, edition when he wrote that the German citizens of Comal County believed that "the institutions of the Southern States, up to now so gloriously a part in the Union, to be endangered." He further described how it was the duty of Texans to fight for states' rights. The following month Lindheimer continued by printing, "if Comal and Gillespie counties at this time would show no signs of participation in the Southern movement, their inaction would bring on serious consequences." A few days later he refined his points: "Since it is undeniably foreseeable that Texas will secede from the Union . . . all questions cease as to whether it would be to the advantage of Germans here, if Texas secedes or stays in the Union. The only practical question remaining is: How shall the Germans at [the] secession of our State conduct themselves." His arguments did not fall on deaf ears since many Germans in New Braunfels agreed by electing Walter F. Preston and Dr. Theodore Koester as pro-secessionist delegates from Comal County to attend the state secession convention. Before the elections, Lindheimer published on January 11, 1861, a campaign statement written by these two men. The candidates described their ambitions to defend the Union and protect their southern institutions—slavery—unless secession proved inevitable. If dissolution prevailed, then the men would work to join the fledgling Confederacy to assure Texans' "rights."[4] Koester and Preston clearly expressed the ideas of the town by siding with the secessionists, the prevailing position in Texas, to better protect their locality. In other words, though this German population in New Braunfels did not completely agree with disunion, they had assimilated enough to southern culture to realize the benefits of supporting the position, and thus they did not experience any persecutions during the war—they made a business decision.

New Braunfelsers supported secession because they knew that even if the South lost the war, their towns, property, and lives would remain protected until the northern army reached Texas. Yet more-recent German settlers, commonly referred to as

"Greens," were more isolated in frontier settlements such as Fredericksburg, which opposed secession. A majority of these immigrants escaped from the fatherland to sparsely populated Gillespie County to avoid compulsorily military service and persecution for their support of the European revolutions of 1848. With strong ideological beliefs of unionism and republicanism, practical grounds of their reliance on US Army posts for protection and business, and their relative isolation on the frontier, these German Texans never realized that upholding their beliefs would produce retaliation by the Anglos in their community.

The election of 1860 accentuated the differences between these differing factions. At the time, most Germans belonged to the Democratic Party because of its white egalitarian beliefs and the nativist tendencies of its opponents. The crisis that developed during this election influenced the German Texans to switch from the Democrats because of the potential split from the Union. The threat of disunion and the lack of any favorable candidates influenced many of them to remain at home instead of voting. Their lack of participation in the general election and their later vote against secession made the proslavery population of Texas suspicious of the Germans throughout the war. Those who did vote showed the split of opinion between the Greys and Greens. The vote for secession in Comal and Gillespie Counties demonstrates a major difference between the two regions. In Comal the vote was 239 to 86 in favor of secession, while in Gillespie the polls reported 398 to 16 against leaving the Union. The split between the two regions is also evident in the men's decision to join the Confederacy.[5]

Germans in Texas were divided on the issues but not enough to organize themselves to defend their interests and homes. Germans in Central Texas tended to fight, though reluctantly, for the Confederacy because of their attachments to the region. Originally, many of them organized local militia and state units for the sole purpose of protecting their towns. Comal County formed three local companies during the war that the Confederate Army eventually absorbed. Gustav Hoffmann raised the first company from Comal County, which eventually served in the 7th Mounted Rifles, Sibley's Brigade. Hoffman was a Grey, and many men in the ranks belonged to the founding families of New Braunfels, upholding their connection to their locality. Another unit raised in New Braunfels was Julius von Bose's infantry company, which he organized, according to his announcement in the *Neu Braunfelser Zeitung*, "to serve our adopted Fatherland." This unit became Company K, 3rd Texas Infantry. Finally, late in the war Theodore Podewils raised the Comal Horse Guard to protect New Braunfels. It shared the same fate as the other local units, becoming Company F, 36th Texas Cavalry.[6]

Many other German Texans formed Confederate companies in several units, including Company E, 1st Texas Cavalry; three companies in Waul's Texas Legion;

Company F, 2nd Texas Cavalry; Company G, 4th Texas Cavalry; Company E, 5th Texas Cavalry; one and half companies in the 6th Texas Infantry; Company B, 8th Texas Infantry; and the 32nd Texas Cavalry. Many of these men reluctantly joined the ranks, most after conscription. They fought for many reasons, the greatest motivation being to defend their homes from the Union Army and their Anglo neighbors. Lindheimer articulated this idea when he wrote in his newspaper in March 1862, before the April deadline of conscription, "all eyes of Texas were on Comal County during this time of preparation for the war and that the conduct of Comal County would be a guide to the forming of judgments on the Germans in Texas. It would be of the greatest importance for the Germans in Texas whether Comal County furnished its contingent with volunteers or by conscription."[7] Loyalties to New Braunfels and Texas influenced these men to fight, not for a cause, but for the security of their homes from the enemy, both northern and southern.

Central Texas Germans to a lesser extent tended to fight for adventure or loyalty to their adopted state. They expressed this influence in their letters and memoirs. Arriving with his family in New Braunfels at the age of nine in 1846, twenty-four-year-old Carl Coreth wrote to his younger brother Rudolf: "Father writes [that] you want to present yourself if the militia is called up. I will do it too if necessary. There are people here who say they would not leave, they had not started the things etc. I feel duty bound to go through." A few months later Rudolf enlisted in a company "made up of farmers who, like ourselves, only want to defend the coast of Texas." His desire to protect Texas and New Braunfels continued throughout the war. In January 1862 he advised Carl, "If the militia is called up now . . . you would probably be able to stay up there on the Indian frontier, and so you wouldn't be so far from home." When rumors of transferring from the coast or to Arkansas began to permeate through camp, Rudolf reacted only as a man with the desire to defend his locality would—he complained. "I won't be going voluntarily yet," was his response to the rumor of receiving orders to move to the St. Bernard River or Velasco. When confronted with the prospect of fighting in Arkansas, he responded: "we have to decide whether we want to enlist for the duration of the war in order to march to Arkansas directly, or whether we want to be released and expose ourselves to being drafted from the militia. We—Munzenberger and I—decided for the above reasons to do the later." Essentially, he would rather stay in Texas and risk the Confederate Army possibly drafting him than remain in his unit and certainly march to Arkansas. His motivation to fight for Texas was the defense of his hometown, New Braunfels, because "I cannot get enthusiastic about our cause."[8] Germans from Comal County, most of whom had moved to Texas in the first wave of immigration, fought for the defense of their adopted state and the way of life they developed in the years before the war.

Some of the Germans who arrived after 1848 and settled in the region also joined the ranks of Confederate units. Joseph Faust, born in Hambach, Prussia, in 1844, moved to Texas with his parents in 1855 because of the revolutions in Europe. His family left Prussia so that Joseph would not have to serve in the army when he turned eighteen and settled in New Braunfels because relatives and friends lived there. Though having lived in Texas for such a short period of time, New Braunfels became the only attachment Faust developed in the United States. When he turned seventeen at the start of the war, Faust enlisted in Capt. Gustave Hoffman's company in the 7th Texas Mounted Volunteers serving in Sibley's Brigade, later called Green's Brigade. John Henry Brown, a Texas historian and newspaperman in Missouri, noted in a letter how a German he knew adopted the United States as his new homeland but feared once again that he would live under a totalitarian government. This German sided with the South because he was "convinced that the people of the United States do not enjoy the liberties guaranteed to them by the constitution."[9] He sided with Texas and the South to escape the perceived tyranny of the US government.

New Braunfels's demonstration of loyalty to the Confederacy proved successful throughout the war. Though their neighbors remained suspicious, no major atrocities or harassment occurred in the town. The most notable occurrence there did not involve Confederates; instead, a small unionist mob broke into Lindheimer's house in 1862 and threw his press and type into the Comal River. Lindheimer raised the press and recovered most of his type the next day without missing an issue. Unfortunately, the Greens in Fredericksburg made no overt expressions of devotion to the South and suffered the wrath of Rebel soldiers. Frontier Germans created tension by not joining the Confederate Army and forming the Union Loyal League, their own home guard, but the boiling point came when they ignored the Conscription Act in 1862. Upset about this blatant disregard of state authority, the Texas government sent Capt. James Duff and a contingent of Texans to the Hill Country to break up the Union Loyal League, enforce the oath of allegiance, and conduct lawful conscription. Fearing punishment, many Germans fled Texas for safety in Mexico and possibly the North. Their flight out of the state led to one of the deadliest events in German Texan history. Duff overtook a group of fleeing German unionists on August 10, 1862, near Fort Clark on the banks of the Nueces River, leading to what became known as the Battle of the Nueces or the Nueces Massacre, depending on one's perspective. In this action Confederate Texans killed the majority of the immigrants, approximately sixty, then executing the captured,

even the wounded. Killings of frontier Germans continued for the rest of the year—
clearly, the Confederacy did not tolerate defiance.[10]

When the war ended, the German population displayed its loyalty to the
United States. The first Fourth of July after the Confederacy's demise was not
widely celebrated across the Lone Star State, except by two groups: African
American freedmen and Germans. Citizens of New Braunfels held a parade with a
marching band, along with numerous dances around the city, while flying the Stars
and Stripes from the highest hill in celebration of the renewed independence of
their adopted country. Additionally, on August 20, 1865, Hill Country Germans
erected the Treue der Union monument in Comfort, the only shrine to the Union
erected by inhabitants on former Confederate soil. At the site locals interred the
bones of the men killed in the Battle of the Nueces. These actions demonstrate
that Lone Star Germans held more loyalty to the state of Texas than to the institution of slavery and southern culture. Monuments to Confederate soldiers are
ubiquitous on courthouse squares across the South, but New Braunfels only erected
theirs in 1935—with a difference. Even today, New Braunfels has a statue in the
town square dedicated to Civil War soldiers from Comal County—both Union
and Confederate—and in 1926 named an elementary school named for Union
general and Republican cabinet member Carl Schurz, despite a wave of Ku Klux
Klan activities against Germans at the time. Instead of mourning the loss of slavery
(the cause of the South), German Texans celebrated the changes in their state and
expressed their loyalty to the United States, the bearer of their true interests—a
good life in Texas.[11]

In the years after the Civil War, German culture dominated New Braunfels
through continual immigration from the fatherland. Similar to the differences
between the Greys and Greens, these new immigrants diverged from the previous
groups because they were a product of imperialism. Unlike their predecessors, they
came from a Germany united by Otto von Bismarck through the Franco-Prussian
War in 1870–71. The rise of the German Empire produced stronger nationalistic and patriotic feelings toward their homeland among German Texans since
kingdoms no longer divided it. Combined with the eventual dying off of original
settlers and older generations, residents in New Braunfels were a different breed.
Demographic changes gave further relevance to this generation. By 1910, only 37.6
percent of the Comal County population were foreign born, demonstrating that
second- and third-generation German Texans dominated New Braunfels. Despite
this major shift in the population, residents had similar reactions to the stressful
situation of war being thrust upon them.[12]

When World War I began, slavery was no longer an issue that plagued German Texans, but new circumstances created new tension within the community. Even before the threat of war loomed over Europe and the United States, surrounding Anglo-Texans knew that the loyalties of New Braunfelsers were divided. Many in the town had varying connections to Germany, either directly as an immigrant or the descendent of one. In many cases they corresponded regularly with relatives in Europe, and more publicly the local newspaper, the *New Braunfels Herald* (an English-language edition of the *Neu Braunfelser Zeitung*), ran a regular column, "In the Fatherland," summarizing major occurrences in Germany. This connection to the homeland amplified by the resistance to cultural assimilation continued to annoy neighboring communities. Germans in New Braunfels as well as in the rest of the United States made an earnest effort to maintain their traditional language, customs, and culture. Just as with the Civil War, when clouds of war gathered toward the United States, Texans became suspicious of their German neighbors. The same principles of making a business decision applied to New Braunfelsers in World War I, but this conflict was more personal since their country declared war against their ancestral homeland and the reactions of other Americans threatened their heritage.[13]

Initially most Americans, including German Texans, thought the war would be isolated to Europe. Even as the fighting escalated and most European countries entered the fray, the United States remained relatively detached from the events. New Braunfelsers, though, expressed favorable views of Germany and the Central Powers. Even at the first declarations of war, before Germany entered the conflict, a local citizen predicted that Germany would be dragged into the fighting but would be victorious. This trend continued, with several published letters and editorials all predicting a German victory. One such letter, written by New Braunfels attorney Adolph Seidemann, was truly prophetic if one reverses the named countries. Seidemeann predicted a victorious Germany that would receive part of France, would force England to pay $5 billion in reparations and forfeit the Royal Navy, and would annex Belgium. Despite the confidence held for Germany, words were not enough for Victoria's German Texans, who organized a regiment to fight for Germany, which the US government prevented from leaving the country. In a *New Braunfels Herald* issue soon afterward, warnings appeared discouraging the people of New Braunfels from engaging in such activities that threatened the neutrality of the United States.[14]

Regardless of US neutrality, New Braunfelsers expressed their pride in Germany. Richard Walter, a native-born Texan of German descent, felt "enthused over Germany's advances over the enemy, that every time the Germans report of new successes, I feel like turning a handspring in the air." He additionally displayed loyalty by criticizing people of Teutonic descent who "speak with contempt of Germany or Austria." George Schnabel also expressed his pride in Germany while visiting Europe. His correspondence depicted a positive picture of Germany and the men of its army by boldly stating, "they [the Allies] can't get into Germany because she is too strong." Pride also extended to non-Germans such as Artemio V. Medel, a Tejano living in New Braunfels, who expressed his devotion to the town and his adoration toward his Teutonic neighbors.[15]

Such activities early in the war did not raise the ire of the local population. Opinions changed quickly once the naval conflict heated up between England and Germany in August 1914. England employed its traditional wartime strategy by establishing a naval and communication blockade. From that point on, the Allies controlled most routes of information and news from Europe. Stories soon emerged telling of German atrocities in Belgium, collectively know as the "Rape of Belgium," which persuaded the general American population to side with the Allies. Ever loyal to Germany, the citizens of New Braunfels protested this influence in numerous articles and letters. Some people questioned, "Is U.S. Friend or Foe of Germany?"[16] When news from Belgium arrived, Walter Mittendorf declared that these were "'doctored' reports." He lamented, "It is really wonderful to see how a very hostile press is concerned in the vain effort to arouse the world's sentiment against a hemmed-in nation when she is fighting single-handed, so to speak against what might be called the combined military and naval strength of Europe."[17] Fred Tausch, a descendent of an original settler, the editor of the *Herald,* and deeply committed to his German heritage, asserted that the American press mirrored "England's interest that the two protagonists of the Teutonic race—Germany and Austrian-Hungary—should be represented to the world as bloodthirsty nations. . . . Now the truth of the matter is Germany and Austria-Hungary are acting on the defensive."[18] New Braunfels's resistance to the common views of Americans brought unwanted attention and stirred some negative attitudes toward the community.

Adding to the strain was New Braunfelsers justifying Germany's actions as the war escalated, especially unrestricted naval warfare. Germany, which had the smaller navy, liberally planted mines in the North Sea to keep British warships from bombarding its coast. Many criticized the German Empire for this act since many countries, namely the Allies, considered the use of mines illegal under the Second Hague Convention of 1907. Despite these views, the citizens of New Braunfels justified this since the English blockade prevented food shipments from reaching

Germany, creating shortages for civilians. Additionally, they defended Germany's unrestricted submarine warfare by criticizing the Allies for ramming German subs and treating their crews like "pirates" by not rescuing the sailors. The greatest controversy emerged when a U-boat sank the British liner *Lusitania.* Citizens of New Braunfels quickly defended the German Navy, arguing that the ship was part of the Royal Navy: "In spite of great outcries by a section of the press, Germany—after a cool consideration of all facts—had a right to sink the ship regardless of passengers, all of whom had been warned."[19] Despite their best efforts, New Braunfelsers and other German Americans were unable to sway Americans.

If surrounding Texans doubted New Braunfels's devotion early in the Great War after reading the *Herald,* the residents' actions clearly demonstrated their continued loyalty to their original homeland. Within the first months of the war, New Braunfels started a Red Cross drive to collect money to aid wounded German soldiers. As the war progressed, residents also established a "Gold for Iron" program. Based on the Prussian government's actions during the Napoleonic Wars, when the French emperor invaded Central Europe, citizens received iron rings for their gold, which then was donated to the German Red Cross. Even in June 1916, when Americans first began hearing the dogs of war, New Braunfelsers still displayed their support for the fatherland with the "Kaiser Wilhelm Skat Turnier," a card-game tournament in honor of the German emperor. Within the same week, a play written in Germany, aptly named *Germany Fighting the Allies,* debuted at the Seekatz Opera House in downtown New Braunfels. Only when America's entry into the war on the side of the Allies appeared inevitable did the town finally change its tone toward Germany. Charity organizations no longer raised money for German soldiers but to "Aid War Sufferers in Germany and her Allied Countries." Leading this movement was the Texas Bazaar Association in San Antonio, which sold American flags, a display of loyalty to the adopted country, to raise money for the suffering citizens of Germany and Austria-Hungary. New Braunfels women raised $233.10 for the association and proudly displayed the flag they received for their effort. Taking their stance of neutrality further, the Red Cross in New Braunfels now emphasized that they served "friend and foe alike."[20]

As American attitudes continued to side ever stronger with the Allies, it forced New Braunfelsers to decide which of their loyalties was strongest: those for the United States, or those toward Germany. Not yet willing to neither betray their ancestral home nor be disloyal to the adopted country, these German Texans beseeched state and national leaders to avoid war. The citizens took a unique approach to their protests, using arguments and rationalizations in petitions and newspapers rather than organizing rallies in the streets such as San Antonians did. New Braunfelsers were proud of the fact that they, "so far as we know have not gone on record as yet protesting their unanimous sentiment against the pro-English and anti-German tendencies of the Washington administration, particularly as to recent threatening developments in our controversy with Germany."[21]

Resistance to America's entering the war began in the summer of 1915. An editorial in the *Herald* favored Pres. Woodrow Wilson's idea of arbitration to end the fighting without the United States entering the conflict and put forth its concern over relations with Germany. Less than a year later, New Braunfelsers submitted a petition to Wilson warning US citizens "from traveling on an armed ship of any of the warring powers" so the country could maintain its neutrality and avoid warfare. As the national debate continued, Seidemann submitted a letter to Rep. John Nance Garner arguing that the United States should not go to war; instead, it should appropriate money to fortifying the country's borders and coasts. He further questioned: "Can President Wilson not understand that the Central Powers are fighting the battle of the world? Can he not see that England's navalism is a menace to the progress of humanity and is also a menace to our commerce?" Joining the call for neutrality, H. Wertheim submitted a column outlining why the United States should circumvent the European conflict. His argument evolved around the idea that it would not benefit the nation because it was not prepared since the course of the war was already determined (an inevitable German victory), Japan would defeat America and take all of the Pacific islands acquired during the Spanish-American War, and England, when defeated, would abandon its allies. Resistance increased further when the president announced his peacetime preparations. Though it contradicted their arguments, New Braunfelsers dubbed his policy "preparationist hysteria" and deemed it "[m]ore dangerous than any foreign menace." Not surprisingly, one issue of preparedness that struck a raw nerve was prohibition, a direct threat to the *bier gartens;* a major staple in German culture and the town's social fabric.[22]

By early March 1917, when America's entrance into the war with the Allies appeared certain, another op-ed piece appeared pleading for peace with Germany: "The difference between the points of view of the United States and Germany are, in my opinion, not too far apart for an agreement, so that the state of war between the two countries may be avoided, especially as the two nations have absolutely no other disagreement whatever, and have never had any."[23] Despite its futility, one last argument emerged, "Another Reason against Wars," which rationalized the notorious Zimmerman Telegraph and once again stated that the war was almost over—why should the country get involved now? These spirited arguments failed to dissuade the United States from declaring war against Germany. Now the German Texan population of New Braunfels had to decide where their loyalties lay—with their current and future country, or with the land of their ancestors and culture.[24]

The dual nature of German Texan loyalty clearly emerged when the United States declared war against Germany and the Central Powers. Up to this point there were no real repercussions for their defense of the fatherland, but once the United States joined the Allies, they had to be careful of their actions since the eyes of Texas were on them. Opposing their current homeland would spell doom for their lives socially, politically, and most noticeably economically. Concurrently, they also did not want to turn their backs on their ancestral homeland. Their solution was to be outwardly loyal to the United States while maintaining their German heritage privately. Just like the Civil War generation before them, German Texans expressed their opinions against the conflict, but once the country crossed the threshold of war, New Braunfelsers did what needed to be done to avoid conflicts with their neighbors and maintain their livelihoods.[25]

New Braunfels did not herald the announcement of war on April 13, 1917. There were no large headlines, just a small article conveying the news. Receiving more coverage was the concern over the status of German nationals and the limitations placed on them by the government. The following week the greatest change in peoples' attitude appeared. Loyalty to the United States and democratic ideas was the theme. Initializing the change was a letter published in the *Herald,* titled "Oath of Allegiance not Empty Form to German-Americans," explaining that German Texans were loyal to the United States and the war did not change anything. Once again words were not enough, so the city planned a Loyalty Parade that included every group in the city: the military, local neighborhoods, Hispanics, African Americans, and Confederate veterans. City leaders organized the event to demonstrate "the undoubtable loyalty of the good people of New Braunfels" since "in this emergency we must prove ourselves to be one and undivided in the loyalty and devotion to our country, no matter how sadly we may regret the entrance of our beloved country in this world conflict."[26]

Additionally, New Braunfels charity events changed dramatically. Though initially Red Cross donations in the city went to aid the German soldiers and citizens, they now supported US troops. Community leaders published numerous letters encouraging citizens to help the American cause. Despite their efforts, there was a small group of New Braunfelsers that opposed this change, blaming the organization for prolonging the war and helping the government reserve more money for manufacturing cannons and guns. The most noticeable fundraising difference after the declaration of war was Liberty Bonds. Citizens used Liberty Bond drives to demonstrate their unquestionable patriotism. Leading the drive was prominent businessman Harry Landa, who published a letter appealing to the population to purchase bonds and support the war effort. Other local businesses and German American organizations like the Hermannsoehne, commonly called "Sons of Hermann," advertised their contributions. So many advertisements of Liberty Bonds appeared in the newspaper that one historian called New Braunfels's effort and constant publication of charitable contributions "obnoxious."[27]

Even with such public displays of loyalty, German New Braunfelsers had no intention of betraying the culture of their ancestral homes. Prior to the war, the community had maintained its culture through its food, language, German-language newspapers, and plays. Though these activities annoyed their Anglo neighbors during the nationalistic period of the early twentieth century, there were no repercussions. Even during America's period of neutrality, German Texans enjoyed the freedom to practice their culture, such as the German plays performed at the Seekatz Opera House, where they could hear the true German accent and language without the "American easy speech." As tension mounted over the accusations of atrocities in Belgium, New Braunfelsers began to defend their culture by discussing its contributions to American society. But when the United States declared war, the German community immediately reduced all public displays of their heritage. Jacob F. Walters published a letter in the *Herald* suggesting to his fellow German Texans how to behave during the war. Some of his suggestions included learning English and to speak it in public: every "citizen of German extraction must make it their personal duty to see that . . . acts of disloyalty . . . will not be permitted. . . . In America there is but one flag. It is the stars and stripes, and it symbolizes all of the ideals of America: Respect it." Also it was their duty to expose any German agents and explain to people that the colors used by the Hermannsoehne in ceremonies (old gold, black, and red) were those of the Revolutions of 1848, not of Imperial Germany.[28]

With nativism and intolerance, under the guise of 100 percent Americanism, rampant across the country, the government's and public's reaction to German culture changed from being a tolerated annoyance to being banned anti-American activities. In the spring of 1918, Texas' Thirty-Fifth Legislature passed the "Loyalty Laws," with the purpose of prohibiting public expression of German culture, such as speaking a language in public other than English or exhibiting a symbol of any other country, upon penalty of arrest. Even though these laws forbade the German language from public life, the citizens of New Braunfels fought against its exclusion from the schools. Among their arguments were: "That Germany is our present political enemy should not depreciate the value of the German language in this country."[29] Others urged that knowledge of German would aid in collecting military intelligence of the enemy. As the ban on language persisted, more and more German Texans protested the laws as a factor in Americanization and the stripping of the peoples' culture. Suppression of their culture and potential harassment made life difficult for New Braunfelsers, but they made the conscious decision to do what was necessary to maintain their livelihood while defending their culture.[35]

Communities around New Braunfels quickly enforced the Loyalty Laws. The Verein Frohsinn Society, a German fraternity in Weimar, banned beer and the German language during their meetings, and T. E. Suttles Furniture Store in San Marcos forbid speaking "Deutsch" in his building. Enforcing these laws were the Texas Rangers, who regularly forced German Texans to act as informants on any potential enemy spies. Instances of public outrage toward German Texans occurred throughout the state, from Abilene, where three men raided a sympathizer's home to tear down a German flag and picture of the Kaiser, to East Texas, where assailants flogged six men for refusing to join the Red Cross and shot another for telling his mother to avoid purchasing Liberty Bonds. In New Braunfels "Sheriff Adams . . . entered the home of one of New Braunfels' prominent and highly respected citizens, who was suspected of disloyalty namely, of displaying or having recently displayed in his house a German flag." Fortunately, the sheriff discovered a French flag, which was legal under the Loyalty Laws since France was an ally, and thus the man was not arrested.

As the war progressed, anti-German sentiments continued to plague New Braunfels. By early 1918, a subscriber to the *Herald* suggested that it "should 'boost' by continually abusing and vilifying the enemy [Germany] in every manner possible." Editor Tausch gave a simple reply: "the editor of the *Herald* is too true and proud an American for that." Despite his claim of patriotism, Tausch realized his predicament, and within a couple of months, opinion editorials of the war decreased significantly. The *Herald* continued to cover the fighting but expressed no opinions because Tausch's divided loyalty prevented him from portraying his German countrymen poorly, nor did he display anything that could further anger his non-German readers. In the same edition that the opinions began to decrease, Tausch's father-in-law published an article examining loyalty. He argued: "No man's loyalty should be measured by his nativity or his ancestry, but every man's loyalty should be judged by his obedience to the law, by his allegiance to the law, by his adherence to the enforcement of the law, by his continuous efforts to secure the honest administration of the law."[32] Respecting a country's laws is a form of loyalty greater than flags and posters.

Despite overt displays of loyalty, Comal County citizens continued to criticize the war and military conscription. Notwithstanding, James L. Slayden, representative for the state's 14th Congressional District, which included Comal County, justified their dissention as similar to "the sentiments and convictions of thousands of his [President Wilson's] constituents, and thousands [of] others, good loyal [and] opposed against [*sic*] the Country's entrance in this horrible war . . . because they are true, loyal, patriotic Americans." Essentially, German Texans inferred that the democratic process of expressing one's opinion spawned their actions.[33]

Unlike the Civil War, military service posed a greater threat since New Braunfelsers not only risked losing their lives but also were fighting against their ancestral people. Fighting in the US Army was a true test of German Texans' loyalty. During the war, five hundred men from Comal County served in some capacity in the American military. Unlike other communities, the departure of these men was a solemn event given no pageantry. Unlike the Civil War, there were no home guards to protect New Braunfels because no threat existed, but a large number of men were drafted into the army. Those with the strongest connection to Germany did not express resentment toward the young men who went to fight the fatherland. Some soldiers like Hellmuth C. Ludwig did not express any connection to Germany in a letter home but avoided active fighting by joining the 141th Infantry Band. As is common with immigration in various ethnic communities, the younger generations did not have as strong a connection to their ancestral lands. In a letter home, Sgt. Emil O. Haas declared that the Americans were "Beating the Huns" and "somebody has to pay dearly for us coming over here, but don't worry, it won't be long."[34] As in the Civil War, others avoided service. Charles Rogan, agricultural advisor to the Western District Draft Board, actually provided information to New Braunfelsers on how to "claim deferred classification" as an industrial or agricultural worker to circumvent the draft. Unfortunately, it is impossible to judge if German Texans had legitimate concerns to evade service or if they used the deferment legitimately. The surrounding region used this issue and German Texans' desire to avoid service to carp on the population generally. An anonymous author responded to such critics, charging that they demonstrate "how little one understands the significance and meaning of American history." Despite the controversies of German Texans fighting against the fatherland, the people of New Braunfels supported "our loved ones in the army and navy." Those on the home front even prayed "for victory for the cause of liberty and humanity; for those, whose homes and families and hearts are torn asunder by the war etc."[35] Although the population was torn by the conflict, it supported its adopted country, despite some reservations, while encouraging its young men who fought and those who found ways to remain home.

Overall the town focused less on military support as a display of their loyalty, instead using the more public monetary contributions to negate their detractors.

As the guns in Europe fell silent—after five years of war—the church bells of New Braunfels rang loudly through the streets at seven o'clock the morning of November 11, 1918. Once news spread of the Armistice, a large celebration began. "The screeching of steam whistles, the tolling of church and fire bells, and the popping cannon-crackers, brought hundreds, and during the day thousands of people gathered at the plaza and the streets." People gave speeches, spoke sermons, sang songs, and organized an impromptu parade celebrating the end of the conflict, all of which lasted until 2 A.M. Even with the conclusion of the war and the adversity the people of the town had endured because of their ethnicity, German Texans continued defending their dual loyalties: "Make No Mistake. . . . If anyone doubts that the great mass of naturalized or native born Germans in America were not faithful to the land of their adoption, he either makes a cruel mistake, or is blinded by a prejudice unbecoming a brave and fair minded man. . . . [T]he wholesale charge of disloyalty is false." On the same day, Tausch defended Germany by condemning a group of "non–Comal County men" that joined the parade and hanged the Kaiser in effigy, ultimately shooting it. He commented that their actions deeply offended the people of New Braunfels, especially him.[36] Essentially, the town was excited about America's victory but at the same time would not tolerate any denigration toward Germany.

Years after the war, the people of New Braunfels celebrated Armistice Day (now Veterans Day) with elaborate parades around the town square and a moment of silence at 11 A.M. to honor "the heroic dead of the World War."[37] Adding to the festivities in 1935 was the addition of a monument dedicated "To the Memory of Our Fallen Soldiers" from the Civil War. Donating this statue of a Civil War soldier—neither Confederate nor Union—to the city was Ernest A. Clausnitzer, a local businessman who owned the Citizen Ice and Ice Cream Company. Clausnitzer bought the monument from the city of Jacksonville, Texas, which commissioned it but was unable to pay for it. Two years later he unveiled a statue of a World War I soldier, the Spirit of the American Doughboy monument, on the town square during Armistice Day celebrations.[38]

The statues stand on the plaza today as the only monuments to New Braunfels men who fought in war. Both conflicts tested the loyalties of the German town and its people, who compromised to maintain their lifestyles while avoiding conflict with surrounding communities. They had viewed the Civil War as a conflict over slavery. Not having any strong attachment to that institution, they did not see the war as that important to their community. But realizing that inaction would create resentment with their neighbors, they did enough to avoid any hostilities, thus protecting their homes and enabling them to maintain their livelihood during and after the war. Fifty years later in the twilight of the Civil War generation, New Braunfels followed this same path during a more personal war. With Germany as an enemy, residents had to decide what was most important, defending their homeland and ostracizing themselves from their neighbors or turning their back on the fatherland and displaying complete devotion to the United States. The people devoted themselves to the simple solution of honoring Germany until the United States entered the war and avoid hostilities afterward by exhibiting complete loyalty to their current land while maintaining their ancestral culture in private. Overall, the citizens of New Braunfels made difficult decisions during these wars, with the eyes of Anglo-Texans watching them, choosing wisely to preserve themselves and to protect the future of their children.

Notes

1. *Neu Braunfelser Zeitung,* Mar. 11, 1859; Walter L. Buenger, "Secession and the Texas German Community: Editor Lindheimer vs. Editor Flake," *Southwestern Historical Quarterly* 82 (1979): 384. The editor of the *Neu Braunfelser Zeitung* was Ferdinand Jacob Lindheimer. He is discussed in further detail later in the chapter.

2. Walter Kamphoefner and Wolfgang Helbich, eds., *Germans in the American Civil War: Letters from the Front and Farm, 1861–1865* (Chapel Hill: University of North Carolina Press, 2006), 396–97.

3. Walter Struve, *Germans & Texans: Commerce, Migration, and Culture in the Days of the Lone Star Republic* (Austin: University of Texas Press, 1996), 75.

4. Clement Eaton, *The Freedom-of-Thought Struggle in the Old South* (New York: Harper and Row, 1946), 247; Dale Baum, *The Shattering of Texas Unionism: Politics in the Lone Star State during the Civil War Era* (Baton Rouge: Louisiana State University Press, 1998), 71; Ella Lonn, *Foreigners in the Confederacy* (Chapel Hill: University of North Carolina Press, 1940), 51; Buenger, "Secession and the Texas German Community," 379, 382; *Neu Braunfelser Zeitung,* Dec. 14, 1860, Jan. 4, 11, 14, 1861; *New Braunfels Herald Zeitung,* Feb. 28, Mar. 7, 21, 28, Apr. 4, 1961.

5. Baum, *Shattering of Texas Unionism,* 53; Walter L. Buenger, *Secession and the Union in Texas* (Austin: University of Texas Press, 1984), 102; Melvin C. Johnson, "A New Perspective of the Antebellum and Civil War Texas German Community" (MA thesis, Stephen F. Austin State University, 1993), 57, 58; Lonn, *Foreigners in the Confederacy,* 417; Buenger, "Secession and the Texas German Community," 399; Anne J. Bailey, "Defiant Unionists: Militant Germans in Confederate Texas," in *Enemies of the Country: New Perspectives on Unionists in the Civil War South,* ed. John C. Inscoe and Robert C. Kenzer (Athens: University of Georgia Press, 2001), 209; Stanley S. McGowen, *Horse Sweat and Powder Smoke: The First Texas Cavalry in the Civil War* (College Station: Texas A&M University Press, 1999), 79.

6. Greg Woodall, "German Confederates from Comal County," *Columbiad* 2 (1999): 50, 51, 52, 53; *Neu Braunfelser Zeitung,* Mar. 26, 1862; *New Braunfels Herald Zeitung,* July 11, 1961, Mar. 20, 1962. Lindheimer also listed the number of Germans from New Braunfels that joined the different Texas units. "Our county has furnished the Captain Hoffman Company with 81 men; the Captain Podewils company, 79 men; Captain Bose company, 60; the 1st and 2nd Regiments of Sibley's Brigade, 29; the McCulloch Frontier Regiment, 16 men; Captains Wood & Benton Companies, 20; the companies on the coast with 18; Col. Sweet's Regiment, 4; serving in Virginia, Missouri, Tennessee are 8 men; in a number of other companies and hauling supplies for the government, 9, a total of 314. . . . Plus 110 men enrolled in the seven Comal County State Troops . . . and others the *Zeitung* may not have known, would bring the total to over 500." *Neu Braunfelser Zeitung,* Apr. 25, 1862.

7. Carl L. Duaine, *The Dead Men Wore Boots: An Account of the Thirty-second Texas Volunteer Cavalry, CSA, 1862–1865* (Austin, TX: San Felipe, 1966), 21; McGowen, *Horse Sweat and Powder Smoke,* 167; Lonn, *Foreigners in the Confederacy,* 124, 126; Walter D. Kamphoefner, "New Perspective on Texas Germans and the Confederacy," *Southwestern Historical Quarterly* 102 (1999): 449, 450; Kamphoefner, "German Texans: In the Mainstream or Backwaters of Lone Star Society?" *Yearbook of German-American Studies* 38 (2003): 122; Diary of Julius Giesecke, Sophienburg Museum and Archives, New Braunfels, TX; *Neu Braunfelser Zeitung,* Mar. 14, 1862. The 6th Texas Infantry further demonstrates the reluctance of Germans to fight for the Confederacy. After the regiment's capture at Arkansas Post, 152 men from the ranks, mostly Germans and Poles, took an oath of allegiance to the United States to avoid any further military service for the Confederacy and returned home.

8. Minetta Altgelt Goyne, *Lone Star and Double Eagle: Civil War Letters of a German-Texas Family* (Fort Worth: Texas Christian University Press, 1982), 8, 10, 17, 22–23, 37, 46, 48, 49.

9. Oscar Hass Papers, 1844–1955, Hermann Seele Letters, Center for American History, Austin, TX (hereafter cited as CAH); John Henry Brown to Unknown, n.d., John Henry Brown Papers, Texas State Library and Archives, Austin. See also McGowen, *Horse Sweat and Powder Smoke,* 168; Erma Baker, "Brown, John Henry," in *The Handbook of Texas,* ed. Ron Tyler et al., vol. 1 (Austin: Texas State Historical Association, 1996), 765; and L. E. Daniell, *Types of Successful Men of Texas* (Austin, TX: Von Boeckmann, 1890), 508.

10. Desmond Puloski Hopkins Diary, Apr. 24, 1862, CAH; *New Braunfels Herald-Zeitung,* Nov. 7, 2007; Stanley S. McGowen, "Battle or Massacre? The Incident on the Nueces, August 10, 1862," *Southwestern Historical Quarterly* 104 (2000): 69, 75–80; Wyatt to Unknown, Aug. 25, 1862, Telemechus Scott Wyatt, Thirty-fifth Texas Cavalry (Liken's) File, Texas Heritage Museum, Hillsboro; Lonn, *Foreigners in the Confederacy,* 426, 428, 431; Claude Elliott, "Union Sentiment in Texas. 1861–1865," in *Lone Star Blue and Gray: Essays on Texas in the Civil War,* ed. Ralph A. Wooster (Austin: Texas State Historical Association, 1995), 96, 97; Bailey, "Defiant Unionists," 216, 217; James Marten, *Texas Divided: Loyalty and Dissent in the Lone Star State, 1856–1874* (Lexington:

University Press of Kentucky, 1990), 77, 120, 221; Kamphoefner, "German Texans," 122; Kamphoefner, "New Perspective on Texas Germans," 449; Bobby D. Weaver, *Castro's Colony: Empresario Development in Texas, 1842–1865* (College Station: Texas A&M University Press, 1985), 135; R. H. Williams, *With the Border Ruffians: Memories of the Far West, 1852–1868* (Lincoln: University of Nebraska Press, 1982), 248, 249, 266–67. See also Richard Selcer and William Paul Berrier, "What Really Happened on the Nueces: James Duff, a Good Soldier or 'The Butcher of Fredericksburg,'" *North and South* 2 (1998): 57–60. The best firsthand account of the Nueces incident is by Ernest Cramer, one of the German unionists who survived the fight. Ernst Cramer to parents, Oct. 30, 1862, Treue der Union Monument File, Primary Documents, Comfort Heritage Foundation Archives, Comfort, TX. Excerpts of Cramer's letter are found in Kamphoefner and Helbich, *Germans in the American Civil War,* 428–35.

11. Kamphoefner, "New Perspective on Texas Germans," 451; Kamphoefner, "German Texans," 123; Buenger, "Secession and the Texas German Community," 379–80.

12. Edward Crankshaw, *Bismarck* (New York: Viking, 1981), 294–95; A. J. P. Taylor, *Bismarck: The Man and the Statesman* (New York: Alfred A Knopf, 1969), 126; Frederick C. Luebke, *Bonds of Loyalty: German Americans and World War I* (De Kalb: Northern Illinois University Press, 1974), 29–30, 33; Judith Lynn Dykes-Hoffmann, "On the Edge of the Balcones Escarpment: The Urban and Cultural Development of New Braunfels and San Marcos, Texas, 1845–1880" (PhD diss., University of Texas, 2003), 73–74; Nancy Gentile Ford, *Americans All!: Foreign-born Soldiers in World War I* (College Station: Texas A&M University Press, 2001), 17; Benjamin Paul Hegi, "'Old Time Good Germans': German-Americans in Cooke County, Texas, during World War I," *Southwestern Historical Quarterly* 109 (2005): 243.

13. Hegi, "Old Time Good Germans," 239; Mark Sonntag, "Hyphenated Texans: World War I and the German-Americans of Texas" (MA thesis, University of Texas at Austin, 1990), 17; Luebke, *Bonds of Loyalty,* 45; *New Braunfels Herald,* Oct. 2, 9, 1914; *New Braunfels Herald-Zeitung,* July 27, 2009. The editor during this period was Fred Tausch, a second-generation German Texan born in 1871 who took over the press in early 1914. His views will be expressed throughout the rest of the chapter.

14. Lubke, *Bonds of Loyalty,* 83; *New Braunfels Herald,* July 31, Aug. 7, 1914, Feb. 26, 1915; Matthew D. Tippens, "Turning Germans into Texans: World War I and the Assimilation and Survival of German Culture in Texas, 1900–1930" (PhD diss., Texas Tech University, 2006), 87–88.

15. *New Braunfels Herald,* Sept. 18, Nov. 13, 1914, Aug. 30, 1915.

16. Lubke, *Bonds of Loyalty,* 85, 89; Larry Zuckerman, *The Rape of Belgium: The Untold Story of World War I* (New York: New York University Press, 2004); *New Braunfels Herald,* Aug. 7, 1914, Apr. 23, 1915.

17. *New Braunfels Herald,* Aug. 28, 1914.

18. Tausch Family Folder, Sophienburg Museum and Archives; Glen E. Lich, *The German Texans* (San Antonio: Institute of Texan Culture, 1996), 166; *New Braunfels Herald,* Aug. 21, 1914. Tausch's attachment to his German heritage is evident in his asso-

ciation and membership in Echo Hall, Echo Singing Society, and Sons of Hermann, all promoting the German language and culture.

19. Lubke, *Bonds of Loyalty*, 87, 133; Martin Gilbert, *The First World War: A Complete History* (New York: Holt Paperbacks, 2004), 102; *New Braunfels Herald*, Mar. 5, 12, May 14, 21, June 18, 1915.

20. Ford, *Americans All!*, 17; *New Braunfels Herald*, Sept. 18, 1914, Mar. 15, 1915, June 16, July 21, Sept. 15, 22, Oct. 20, 1916.

21. *New Braunfels Herald*, Apr. 28, 1916.

22. Ibid., July 16, 1915, Jan. 14, 21, 28, Feb. 4, Mar. 3, 10, 31, 1916, Jan. 19, 1917.

23. Ibid., Mar. 2, 1917.

24. Ibid., Mar. 23, 1917.

25. Lubke, *Bonds of Loyalty*, 47.

26. Ibid., 50; *New Braunfels Herald*, Apr. 13, 20, 27, May 4, 1917.

27. Lubke, *Bonds of Loyalty*, 237; Sonntag, "Hyphenated Texans," 71; *New Braunfels Herald*, June 22, 1917, Jan. [?], Mar. 1, Apr. 12, 26, 1918.

28. William J. Breen, *Uncle Sam at Home: Civilian Mobilization, Wartime Federalism, and the Council of National Defense, 1917–1919* (Westport, CT: Greenwood, 1984), 79–80; *New Braunfels Herald*, May 7, June 4, 1915, Apr. 20, 1917.

29. David M. Kennedy, *Over Here: The First World War and American Society* (New York: Oxford University Press, 1980), 67–68; *New Braunfels Herald*, Jan. 18, 1918.

30. *New Braunfels Herald*, Aug. 9, 1918; Tippens, "Turning Germans into Texans," 183.

31. Walter Prescott Webb, *The Texas Rangers: A Century of Frontier Defense* (Austin: University of Texas Press, 1965), 504; Hegi, "Old Time Good Germans," 242; Sonntag, "Hyphenated Texans," 8; Unknown newspaper article, Apr. 22, 1918, Germans in Texas Scrapbook, CAH; *New Braunfels Herald*, Mar. 15, 22, Aug. 2, Sept. 20, 1918.

32. *New Braunfels Herald*, Feb. 15, Apr. 12, 1918.

33. Ibid., Jan. 19, May 11, June 1, 15, Nov. 9, 16, 1917.

34. World War I Folder, Sophienburg Museum and Archives; Oscar Haas, *History of New Braunfels and Comal County, Texas, 1844–1940* (San Antonio: Burke, 1968), 217; *New Braunfels Herald*, Nov. 23, Dec. 14, 30, 1917, Feb. 22, Mar. 1, Oct. 18, Nov. 1, 1918.

35. *New Braunfels Herald*, Aug. 16, Nov. 8, 1918.

36. Lottie Kronkosky and Howard Hufft, interviewed by J. C. Reagan, June 12, 1994, "Reflections" Oral History, no. 776, Sophienburg Archives and Museum of History; *New Braunfels Herald*, June 8, 1917, Nov. 15, Dec. 13, 1918.

37. *New Braunfels Herald*, June 3, Nov. 4, 1932.

38. Kelly McMichael, *Sacred Memories: The Civil War Monument Movement in Texas* (Denton: Texas State Historical Assoc., 2009), 80–81; *New Braunfels Herald*, Mar. 15, 1935, Nov. 12, 1937; "1930 U.S. Federal Census—Population," Footnote.com, accessed Oct. 2009, http://www.footnote.com (digital copy of original records in the National Archives, Washington, DC).

PART II

Wars in Texas History

Chronological Conflicts

7

Between Imperial Warfare

Crossing of the Smuggling Frontier and Transatlantic Commerce on the Louisiana-Texas Borderlands, 1754–1785

Francis X. Galán

N THE FALL of 1762, French officials at Natchitoches learned that a German deserter named Christophe Haische sold stolen goods to soldiers at the nearby Spanish fort of Los Adaes. Haische bartered twenty-five pounds of gunpowder and thirty-four pounds of ammunition with Antonio Gil Ybarbo in exchange for fifteen cowhides as well as three hundred flints for three piasters (French currency).[1] With formal conclusion of the Seven Years'/French and Indian War (1754–63) only a stroke of the pen away from eliminating French sovereignty in North America, the region between Texas and Louisiana increasingly attracted the movement of peoples and goods from completely opposite directions and cultures. English traders soon appeared along the upper gulf coast of Texas, while Comanches began their own expansion eastward following their victory over the Spanish at San Sabá. The Mexican silver trade that Spain denied its European and indigenous rivals unintentionally placed the British and Comanches on a collision course in Texas, but for the American Revolution. What these emerging powerful nations least expected was strong local resistance from Spanish, French, and Caddo regional elites, who jockeyed for control of smuggling routes through the Louisiana-Texas borderlands as transatlantic commerce clashed against mercantilism.

Apparently, Haische followed in the footsteps of others seeking similar opportunities in the borderlands. In 1757, as the French and their Algonquian allies held off the British in the Ohio Valley, an English deserter named Chomure made his own residence in Natchitoches and engaged in smuggling with Los Adaes through the assistance of African slaves. Under interrogation, a slave named

Etienne, who belonged to Cesar De Blanc, commandant of the Natchitoches post, divulged to French officials that a female slave named Marion, owned by the commandant's wife, had sent stolen goods from another slaveholder to Los Adaes in exchange for silver pesos. Among the contraband items were cloth, a bottle of "wild cherry," and a box of undisclosed contents. But unable to obtain the silver, Marion deposited the items with Chomure, who paid her with a horse "until the arrival of the Spanish army."[2] These seemingly isolated instances of desertion at the Louisiana-Texas border were byproducts of warfare and contraband trade on a wider scale in North America.

The Louisiana-Texas borderlands remains in the shadows of the US-Mexican border, yet the origins of the latter began with the Franco-Spanish rivalry of the late seventeenth century following French claims to the vast wilderness west of the Mississippi River to the Rio Grande. In response, Spain dotted the Texas landscape with forts to prevent foreign encroachment upon its silver mines in Mexico as well as with missions to convert *indios bábaros* into Christians as justification for expansion. Los Adaes, established in 1721 with the expedition of the Marqués de Aguayo, stood for half a century at *la frontera* ("the border") of Texas and Louisiana, approximately fifteen miles west of present Natchitoches in northwestern Louisiana. The terminus of the Camino Real that stretched from Mexico City, Los Adaes was designated the capital of Texas.[3] During the middle decades of the eighteenth century, the Spanish, French, Caddo, and African inhabitants of the region had learned to live in peaceful coexistence following a disastrous start.[4] Yet troubles loomed on both sides of the border whenever Spain attempted to enforce its imperial boundaries and as warfare raged across the North American continent.[5]

The mid-eighteenth century witnessed the phenomenon whereby the smuggling frontier intersected with the rise of transatlantic trade, propelling new empires and the steady decline of others shortly after the Louisiana-Texas borderlands debuted. Scholars have recently identified this forgotten borderland in North American history, a region that shaped the boundaries of both the American and Texas republics.[6] Smuggling blended into two competing economic systems, one mercantile and the other "free trade." Both economies helped define as much as confound national boundaries, which could quickly erupt into warfare as nations pursued the flow of commerce. The overlap of smuggling in Texas with transatlantic trade and the appearance of the borderlands occurred precisely within the period that the horse frontier crossed with the gun frontier in North America.[7] Yet as historian Pekka Hämäläinen argues, Comanche political economy makes their

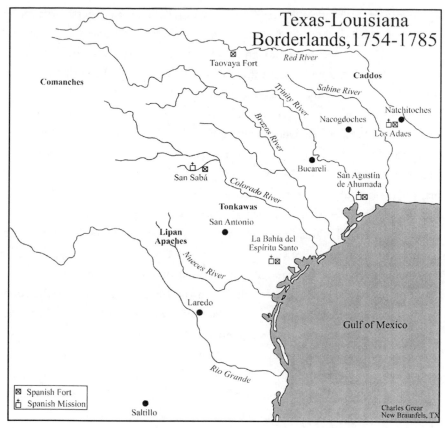

Texas–Louisiana Borderlands, 1754–1785. Courtesy Charles D. Grear.

empire difficult to define and recognize, smugglers and deserters in the borderlands are also virtually invisible.[8]

During the 1750s, the Spanish governor at Los Adaes profited tremendously off smuggling with French Natchitoches and Caddos during the Seven Years' War. Gov. Jacinto de Barrios y Jáuregui, who doubled as commandant of the post, utilized his officer corps and personal servants to import many goods from the French, including gunpowder, ammunition, guns, vermilion, knives, beads, tobacco, combs, and other small items. According to the testimony of Juan Antonio Maldonado, who was a muleteer and cargo loader, he "returned with buffalo hides, deerskins, and horses, which were distributed among the company [Los Adaes]." Maldonado added that many times he arrived from Natchitoches with such goods loaded upon twelve mules. Lt. Joseph Gonzalez, who had served at Los Adaes since the late 1720s and was in charge of the company store, testified that Spanish soldiers also transported anywhere from 800 to 1,500 buffalo hides and deerskins from the Indians to Natchitoches.[9] Smuggling on the borderlands became a two-way corridor that funneled resources through Natchitoches into the French war against the English in the Ohio Valley and through Los Adaes into the Spanish war against the Indians on the southern plains.

Spain attempted to reenforce its borders in Texas as anxious officials in Madrid and Mexico City worried about French naval maneuvers and settlement along the Mississippi. In late 1754, Spanish soldiers from Los Adaes arrested a French trader from New Orleans named Joseph Blancpain, his brother, and two black males in southeast Texas for illicit commerce among the Bidai and Orcoquisa Indians. One of the French prisoners informed interrogators that the group had expected the arrival of fifty families from New Orleans at the mouth of the Trinity River under the direction of Capt. Monsieur de Sacreu. Spanish officials feared an imminent attack upon Texas despite the fact that the French were more concerned about preparing for an English assault east of the Mississippi.[10] Among the goods that Blancpain trafficked were shirts for men and women, cotton linen, hats, axes, rifles, pistols, gunpowder, and other goods. Although he had no formal trade agreement with these particular Indians, Blancpain declared that he held a license from Governor Kerlerec of New Orleans and that he had traded with the Attakapa Indians of the Gulf Coast region on both sides of the Louisiana-Texas border for twenty-five years.[11] Evidently, Governor Barrios disliked this French competition and oversaw Spanish expansion on the lower Trinity River valley with another presidio-mission complex, San Agustín de Ahumada, to reduce the Bidais and Orcoquisas.

Imperial Spain and imperial France averted war over trade at the Louisiana-Texas border only because Caddos played off both sides while greater threats loomed elsewhere. In the early 1740s, Spanish officials made an investigation of its boundaries in Texas and determined that La Gran Montana and Arroyo Hondo defined the border with Louisiana, approximately halfway between French Natchitoches and Spanish Los Adaes.[12] For Spain, there were grave concerns about fighting two wars, one against ever stronger and bolder insurgent Indians in Texas and the other against Britain in the Caribbean, where the English made their smuggling stronghold on the island of Jamaica and retaliated against Spain's enforcement against contraband trade. For the French, they held commercial, political, and kinship motivations for backing Spain against Britain. France's principal interest was in the Cadiz trade since anywhere from half to seven-ninths of all goods aboard galleons and flotas shipped to Spanish America were made in France.[13] For Caddo

Indians, they wanted to defend their native ground and their benefits as gatekeepers of commerce between southeastern woodland cultures and the southern plains.[14] The separate spheres of plains and transatlantic commerce from the Gulf of Mexico moved ever closer on the Louisiana-Texas borderlands.

Whatever reservations Spanish officials held against their French Bourbon cousins over the limits of Louisiana and Texas were ultimately outweighed by seemingly unrelated warfare in Texas and Canada. In September 1759, while Britain achieved victory over France at the Battle of Quebec on the St. Lawrence River, Col. Diego Oritz Parrilla arrived in the Texas Hill Country from San Antonio to launch retaliatory strikes against the Comanches for their destruction of Mission San Sabá the previous year. From Madrid, this new Comanche menace played in the background as the wife of Carlos III (1759–88) expressed her husband's sentiments that Britain "can become the owners of Mexico with the settlements they have made."[15] In 1761 Spain entered into the third, and last, "Family Compact" with France after the fall of Montreal to Britain. The English victory in the Seven Years' War not only eliminated French claims west of the Mississippi but also meant the loss of lucrative trade with New Spain in favor of British-made manufactures. France secretly transferred Louisiana to Spain, however, just prior to the Treaty of Paris (1763) with the intention of blocking Britain's path overland to Mexico and hopefully regain some of its lost possessions in the future. Carlos III in turn wished to draw the eastern boundary of Louisiana as far north as possible to prevent the English from acquiring New Orleans and other gulf ports that could be used to support pirate raids upon Spanish shipping.[16] Europeans and Indians in North America moved along parallel paths, as historian Daniel Richter describes, into "a single, ever more consolidated, transatlantic imperial world."[17] The British *and* the Comanches were on course for such a march through Texas from different directions.

Spain bled slowly at the edges of its empire in the Americas, and not even the Bourbon reforms could prevent smuggling in the borderlands. In fact, two-thirds of all of its commerce was illicit. Smuggling only became more pronounced in the eighteenth century as the numbers of French and English traders increased.[18] In Texas smuggling spanned an arc from New Orleans to Natchitoches, Los Adaes, San Antonio, La Bahía (Goliad), and Saltillo. One major reason for the illicit trade was the lack of a manufacturing sector in Spain, where even the smuggling of tobacco, salt, and raw silk became institutionalized.[19] According to historian David Weber, foreign-made goods from Louisiana at Los Adaes far surpassed those manufactured in Spain. Los Adaes and East Texas hence became incorporated into the Louisiana trade in deerskins, bear oil, buffalo robes, tobacco, indigo, horses, and captives. Although King Carlos III considered smuggling an obstacle to growth, there was very little he could do overall except to loosen the reigns of mercantilism, permitting free trade and greater immigration on the frontier, where independent Indians continued to hold the upper hand against Spanish settlements.[20]

Meanwhile, the enlightened monarch became aware of the call for economic and military reform throughout the Spanish Empire. Spanish scholar Manuel Antonio de Gándara's *Notes on the Strength and Ills of Spain* (1759) argues that the root cause of Spanish troubles was smuggling and the lack of support for local manufacturing. Madrid's colonial policy had been to isolate Mexico from Jamaica, which the British utilized as a base for smuggling goods throughout Spanish possessions in the Americas, from Venezuela, Honduras, Guatemala, and Yucatan to Florida and soon Louisiana, Texas, and California. The engine behind all this was the early Industrial Revolution, with the sudden preference of consumers for relatively cheaper cotton fabrics instead of linens. England increasingly became a manufacturing, rather than an agricultural, nation and interested in new markets, while its population and trade in the Caribbean and mainland colonies boomed.[21] In his *Defense of the Spanish Nation* (1771), the intellectual writer José Cadalso expressed the view that Castilian honor and manliness was not at fault, but Spain's decline was due rather to luxury that arose from commerce and the decadent Francophile character of the Bourbon dynasty in Madrid. To open up Spain and its overseas territories meant growing possibilities for heresy, so Spanish officials, including Carlos III, clung to the belief that the empire's survival required political and social control beyond any reforms, even though observers had argued that removal of trade restrictions could end smuggling.[22]

The British threat was very real to officials in Mexico City and Texas. In June 1771 the viceroy of New Spain, Marqués de Croix, forewarned Gov. Baron de Ripperdá of Texas to prepare for the defense of his province and the interior of New Spain in case war is declared against England. This included quelling rebellion on the southern plains and preventing the English from allying with Indians. The following year Governor Ripperdá informed the viceroy that Spain needed "not only to keep those nations quiet, subjugate the Comancha [sic], castigate the Apache, but also to prevent the invasions which are to be expected from the nations protected by the English and in time of war from the English themselves."[23] But this came too late, for seventeen loads of British guns had already reached the Comanches by 1768 through third parties. The Taovayas on the upper Red River, who formed part of the Caddoan-speaking Wichita tribes, obtained English arms just as they had received guns from French traders. By 1772, British traders in Texas had boasted that they traded wherever they pleased. To Spanish officials it must have appeared that the new boundary between Spain and Britain in North America at the Mississippi had moved farther west.[24]

Spanish officials were obsessed with discovering exactly where in Texas English traders appeared. Perhaps they wandered far beyond the infamous Proclamation Line of 1763 that Britain drew to keep its subjects from moving west across the Appalachian Mountains. Maybe deserters like Haische and Chomure moved onto the southern plains from other French posts in the West. Although one can only speculate where the smugglers' trail disappeared into the wilderness, an unexpected shipwreck off the Texas coast brought the attention of Spanish officials to the likeliest places along the gulf coast.

On August 23, 1771, the English schooner *Two Friends* apparently crashed ashore at the mouth of the Nueces River near the Spanish presidio-mission settlement of La Bahía. According to Spanish records, the captain of the vessel, Hector McAllester, of Scottish nationality, and his pilot, also Scottish, had a crew of three white mariners and a free black. The latter individual was the only one who spoke Spanish, having been born in Curacao, while the others only knew English. They also had a merchant named Charment aboard, along with two free blacks and two black slaves, who planned "to sell a ten-pound cargo of cane liquor or rum and five barrels of inferior sugar with which they left New Savana [*sic*] for Jamaica . . . but were blown off course toward the Florida coast and then to this province [Texas] in whose islands they were stuck." The Nueces River was labeled in an English letter as the "Flores," some thirty leagues or more (approximately seventy-five miles) from La Bahía, where Captain McAllester allegedly succumbed to an illness two weeks later. A Franciscan priest from the nearby mission discovered the deceased captain and his shipmates "by chance while searching for Indians" with assistance from mission Indians and three soldiers from the presidio. Among the inventory of the goods taken from the wreck were a candle, two axes, two chisels, two pipes *mollenas*, clothing, three books, and one broom. The Scottish pilot claimed for himself the black slave, named Jerman, and a black female slave named María, along with three barrels of sugar. He also requested passage to San Antonio, while the other survivors wished to remain at La Bahía.[25]

Evidently, the survivors did not stay long in Texas. Spanish officials allowed them to return to their English colony along the Camino Real through Los Adaes and into Louisiana, taking with them the livestock they were provided. But the viceroy in Mexico City urged Governor Ripperdá to remain cautious of this accident and its possible consequences.[26] Were these foreigners truly shipwrecked as they indicated to Spanish investigators, or had they already spent their time smuggling at the beach? Regardless, he notified the governor in November 1772 about securing the Texas coast in view of rumored aggressions by the British "just as the French in Louisiana had done before procuring establishments in our conquered territories, particularly these same precise locations." The viceroy then ordered Capt. Luis Cazorla from Presidio La Bahía to reconnoiter the spot where the English dared to introduce themselves. If the captain found any other foreigners, they must be apprehended, imprisoned in the presidio, and then transferred to Mexico City for further interrogation.[27] Whether Governor Ripperdá had taken the prerogative of setting Captain McAllester's crew free is uncertain, but the viceroy reminded him about similar occurrences in the future.

Meanwhile, Southern Plains Indians hammered northern Mexico and Texas as Spanish officials considered means of rooting out the smuggling of tobacco and guns from Louisiana. As early as 1766, Mexico City officials feared that prohibition against the harvesting and "free trade" in tobacco actually undermined warfare against the "barbarous" Indians and unsettled the nations who were friendly as well as mission Indians. Spanish officials wanted to know not only the quality, size, and price of tobacco in Texas but also where it was traded in "coins."[28] They soon discovered from Don Hugo O'Conor's investigation into smuggling at Los Adaes that apostate Indians from Mission La Bahía found French tobacco "most desirable." Spanish authorities prosecuted Friar Francisco Zedano from the mission for having smuggled French tobacco from Louisiana with the hope of luring the Indians back to mission life.[29] By 1772 the viceroy learned from Governor Ripperdá that "arms, gunpowder, and ammunition" were also trafficked from Louisiana in the alliance of Texas Caddo and Bidai Indians with the Lipan Apaches.[30] Mexico City officials feared this mixing of independent Indians and smuggling among mission Indians that only made pacification of the frontier much more difficult.

Officials initially rested their hope for a truce with the Indians in Texas upon an agreement with the governor of Louisiana in New Orleans through the French commandant at Natchitoches, Athanese De Mezieres, who remained in his post after the transfer of Louisiana to Spain. De Mezieres had strong ties to the powerful Saint Denis family of Natchitoches and with the Indians in the region. Marqués de Croix had forewarned Governor Ripperdá to maintain peaceful relations with friendly Indians with De Mezieres's assistance. The viceroy added that they should also give much consideration to waging "war against the Apaches who infest the province of Coahuila" and could spill over the border into Texas.[31] Essentially, Spanish officials began implementing a new Indian policy based upon the French model in Louisiana of trade, treaties, and toleration with friendly nations and warfare against the Apaches. Carlos III's Royal Regulations of 1772 were based largely upon the recommendations of Marqués de Rubí's inspection of military defenses in northern Mexico in the aftermath of the Seven Years' War and the Louisiana transfer.[32] Yet the specter of both British activities on the upper gulf coast of Texas and Comanche uprisings near San Antonio and Laredo convinced the viceroy to condemn both Indian depredations and the French policy of arming "Nations of Gentile Indians."[33] With the appearance of this dual threat in Texas during 1773–74 came his order to Ripperdá to cease all correspondence with Commandant De Mezieres.[34]

The concerns of Mexico City officials about suspicious English traders in Texas were not without merit. In May 1775 de Croix wrote to Governor Ripperdá that he had learned the previous month from Don O'Conor, who became commandant inspector general of presidios, that a "French trader named Monsieur La Mee had information about some Englishmen engaged in commerce among the Bidais and Orcoquisa Indians near the lower Trinity River and supplying them with guns and munitions." The Bidai Indians had grown accustomed over the years to goods they obtained from the Spanish governor at Los Adaes. Since Carlos III had ordered the abandonment of Los Adaes, San Agustín, and their accompanying missions, the Bidais and their allies looked to other suppliers. The viceroy affirmed O'Conor's order to the governor that he find and apprehend those Englishmen "soliciting" against the laws of the Spanish government and that they be sent to Mexico City. Lastly, he reminded the governor that in his service to the king, and in the interest of his dominions, the entry of foreigners must be stopped.[35] The last thing officials wanted, as did regional Spanish and French traders, was competition from British traders for control of smuggling in the Louisiana-Texas borderlands.

The viceroy was also displeased upon learning that a resident from Natchitoches smuggled two bundles of tobacco into Texas. He reminded Governor Ripperdá about the order ceasing communication with Commandant De Mezeries and with residents of New Orleans, even though they were all now considered subjects of Spain. De Croix subsequently ordered the return of goods to Louisiana that were sent by the lieutenant governor of that province via the captain of militias, a sergeant, and three soldiers from other former French posts because they ignored the prohibition against commerce in Texas.[36] Evidently, Ripperdá had prosecuted contraband cases against residents from both San Antonio and the abandoned fort of Los Adaes involving tobacco from Natchitoches, but there remained other serious problems.[37]

De Croix remained adamant against opening commerce with Louisiana in the belief that smuggling was the root cause of Indian rebellion as Apache hostilities spilled over into Texas. According to Governor Ripperdá's own correspondence, the Lipan nation for several years had been "forcefully entering the homes of that town [San Antonio] and bartering without being able to resist or prevent the commerce in guns and munitions." In light of the prohibition against commerce and communication with Louisiana, the viceroy thought it strange that the governor continued to insist that he be allowed to permit Commandant De Mezieres from Natchitoches to raise friendly Indians against the Bidais "without a doubt [that] this would destroy the peace they pretend to have with the *Lipanes*," who had been successfully double-dealing Spaniards in Texas against Comanche and Norteño enemies. He also warned Ripperdá to obey the laws and "have less confidence in the Barbarous Nations: stop entirely their entry into the presidio" and all illicit trade.[38] Essentially, the governor needed to prosecute gun-smuggling cases in Texas, not just those involving tobacco.

Above all, the fear of English traders and Indian troubles in Texas had to be resolved in order to ease border tensions from Mexico to Louisiana. In February 1777 Commandant General Teodoro de Croix warned Ripperdá about the incursions of Capt. James Cook on the California coast, which could also happen in Texas. In May his subordinate officer wanted information from the governor about an English innkeeper whom mission Indians picked up near the mouth of the Nueces River after he was left on the beach and wished to be transported to the Mississippi. Ripperdá was reminded again to be vigilant against "illicit commerce." Yet if he determined that the Englishman was not at fault under the circumstances, then the innkeeper was to be sent to the requested destination. Apparently, this lone survivor was no Captain Cook. Later that year, however, Croix wrote concerning two English landings on the coast near the mouth of the Trinity River. He told the governor to use the most efficient measures possible to prevent "the introduction of contraband trade of the English with the Gentiles" and keep him informed through presidio lines of communications. The following spring an Englishman named Bautista Miller was found near the lower Trinity River claiming that he came from Jamaica headed to the Mississippi with Capt. José David, who had left him behind intent to steal his cargo of coffee, whiskey, and five blacks. The commandant general also had instructed the governor to maintain vigilance over sworn enemy Indians while being careful to preserve peace with "friendly nations." Ripperdá had informed him earlier that a lieutenant and twenty-eight soldiers from San Antonio visited with the Taguacanas and Yscanis Indians and that he was gathering intelligence on the Norteños and Lipan Apaches.[39] Spanish officials feared that English traders on the coast along with unlicensed traders from Louisiana would provide a volatile combination of guns, tobacco, and liquor to rebellious Indians and subjects.[40]

By then Spanish officials were just as concerned about rebellion within their own dominions as Britain was attempting to quell its own subjects in North America. In February 1778 Commandant De Mezieres reported that the English attempted to enter Louisiana from the Mississippi with "the intention of raising the natives in revolt." He also suggested that in case of war between Spain and England, the Spanish should enter into an alliance with the Comanches, destroy the Apaches, and help the resistance against English-allied Osages, who launched raids upon Louisiana, especially Natchitoches, from the Arkansas River to the north. This meant arming Comanches and Norteños as no better time existed for seeking improved relations and for placing Spanish merchants among the Indian pueblos, including the veritable Indian fortress at Taovaya on the upper Red River, which Col. Diego Parrilla had been unable to penetrate. Despite a past history of relentless Comanche attacks upon the presidios and haciendas of Spanish subjects, the fact remained that the Comanches also pursued "incessant war" against the Apaches. From De Mezieres's perspective, why not join forces with them and make the Apaches the common enemy? After all, he reasoned, it was no different than what the Romans did on their frontiers. Furthermore, Spanish inhabitants of Louisiana were already engaged in commerce with the Indians of Texas, supplying them with guns, ammunition, powder, blankets, handkerchiefs, axes, knives, and vermillion in exchange for "chamois, hides of deer, bear, buffalo, tallow and lard from cattle."[41] By the late 1770s, the Comanches established hegemony over the southern plains and overtook the Wichitas' trade niche between the Texas plains and the Mississippi Valley. Indeed, Commandant General Croix organized war councils that declared a general war against the Apaches with support from Comanches and Wichitas.[42]

But Croix remained fearful over the activities of British traders, "who lose no opportunity to introduce themselves among the Indians" of the Texas plains while the latter managed to use guns so efficiently.[43] The presence of these traders, the rise of the Comanche empire, the spillover of warfare into Louisiana from the American Revolution, and the Indian revolt in Coahuila made it seem like the world was closing in upon Texas. By September 1778 Croix wrote Governor Ripperdá discussing plans for the control of the Karankawa, Orcoquisa, and Coco Indians on the Texas gulf coast who continued to resist the missions. He also called for the reinforcement of La Bahía, San Antonio, and the recently established town of Bucareli on the lower Trinity River, founded by Antonio Gil Ybarbo and his fellow settlers from Los Adaes. Croix backed Ripperdá's assignment to Ybarbo, as captain of the militia at Bucareli, with finding a fugitive Indian from Coahuila named Yujuan and the capture of all apostate mission Indians among the Tonkawas. Croix then learned of the death of Cayetano Travieso by the Comanches, following word from De Mezieres, and ordered the governor to punish Comanche hostility. He also instructed Ripperdá to prevent the gathering of Apaches, Texas Caddo, and Bidai Indians and to send troops and munitions to Bucareli, where the Adaeseños (former soldier-settlers from Los Adaes) became engaged in skirmishes with Comanches over control of the tobacco trade with the French from Louisiana and the Norteños in Texas.[44] Evidently, the situation was now so out of control that the following month Croix stressed to Ripperdá's successor as governor about the importance of seeking aid from De Mezieres.[45] Imperial warfare and domestic unrest together caused an abrupt shift in Spanish economic policy over the limited commerce between Texas and Louisiana beyond Enlightenment ideas.

Meanwhile, Spanish officials in Mexico awaited the official position of Madrid in the war between France and Britain during the American Revolution. France entered the patriot cause in 1778, following the British surrender at Saratoga the previous year. Spain in turn officially joined their Bourbon cousins by declaring war against England in June 1779. Yet for several years leading up to its declaration, the Spanish smuggled guns and ammunition to the Anglo-Americans and sent subsidies and loans through agents. Texas vaqueros also drove cattle to Louisiana, which supplied the beef Gov. Bernardo de Galvez used to help support the American rebels.[46] In August 1779 Commandant General Croix instructed Gov. Domingo Cabello of Texas to assist Francisco Garcia with securing the 1,500 or 2,000 cattle that Governor Galvez requested, along with the support from the settlers of San Antonio and Friar Pedro Ramirez, father president of the Texas missions. Croix had even approved the request of María Saint Denis, the daughter of the famed French commandant at Natchitoches, to bring 300 cattle from Texas to that post with the assistance from Don Felix Menchaca of San Antonio.[47]

Few Spanish officials could have ever imagined that the fate of Texas against British encroachment and Comanches hinged upon the survival not only of Anglo-American rebels on the eastern coast of North America but also upon a small group of settlers from Bucareli and Texas Caddo Indians in the Louisiana borderlands. At their former settlement of Los Adaes, Plains Indians did not "molest" Spanish soldiers and settlers, historian Juliana Barr notes, because they "enjoyed the alliance and protection of Caddo warriors." Historians H. Sophie Burton and F. Todd Smith state that Natchitoches had close economic and social ties with Los Adaes for over half a century.[48] The abandonment of Los Adaes in 1773 by royal order only served to remind Spanish, French, Caddo, and African inhabitants in the region of their close ties with one another, especially given the threat of Comanche expansion into East Texas. De Mezieres reported in early 1778 that the Caddos, specifically the Hasinai, Nacogdoches, Nacacoges, and Navedachos, were inter-related by language and blood, applied themselves to agriculture, and showed "love for the Spaniards." They also shared a history of close alliance dating back to 1731, when Natchez Indians rose in revolt against the French on the lower Mississippi and attacked Natchitoches, where Spanish troops from Los Adaes came to the defense of their French and Caddo neighbors.[49]

The only matter that remained in the late 1770s was who would emerge as the regional powerbroker to fill the vacuum of the Spanish governor commandants at Los Adaes and control commerce through the Louisiana-Texas borderlands. De Mezieres stood to benefit from peace with Comanches through his position as commandant at Natchitoches and his mastery of Indian relations much like his predecessors. So too did Antonio Gil Ybarbo, who was born at Los Adaes and served in the military with his father in Texas and had a penchant for smuggling in the borderlands that he parlayed into a lucrative ranching career. Then there was the Texas Caddo chief whom Governor Cabello called "El Texito" ("Little Texan"), who cast his people's lot against the Comanches in defense of Ybarbo and other Adaeseños at Bucareli.

There were conflicting reports about which group attacked the other first. According to De Mezieres's report, based upon Comanche testimony, the son of Comanche chief Evea was on his way to Bucareli to meet with De Mezieres after not finding him at Taovaya. Suddenly, settlers from the town attacked him on the outskirts and killed several warriors. The Comanches in turn laid siege upon Bucareli in 1778. De Mezieres was exasperated over the Spaniards' actions because he was brokering a peace with the Indians.[50]

According to Ybarbo, however, Comanches raided Bucareli first, stealing cattle from the town's herd and killing his sergeant, Juan de Mora, while another soldier, Pedro Gonzalez, suffered a broken leg. Both Mora and Gonzalez were comrades of Ybarbo from Los Adaes with intimate relations among the Caddos. Gonzalez also served as Caddo interpreter for Govenor Cabello because he spoke the "Texas language . . . with a perfect accent and is well known by all of them."[51] The Texas Caddos even rode to Bucareli to warn its settlers that the Comanches were coming. Father Juan García Botello, who arrived from Mission Espada in San Antonio to tend the spiritual needs at Bucareli, had informed the governor about the impoverishment of the town and the need for troop reinforcements against such a strong Comanches presence. Ybarbo himself had requested arms and ammunition not only to stave off Comanches but also to prevent English trade with coastal Indians. The government acted with too little too late to support Ybarbo, who decided to move the residents to the former mission site at Nacogdoches for better protection by Texas Caddos. He also yearned to move near his own Ranch Lobanillo farther east on the Camino Real, where he had left behind his ailing mother and other Adaeseños in 1773 with the intent to return to East Texas from San Antonio.[52] Ybarbo felt that he had no other choice but to protect his people from further Comanche attack, even if he did so with a personal stake in future ranching and commerce in the borderlands.

Neither De Mezieres nor any Spanish officials bothered to ask Chief Texito his perspective, but he hoped that Ybarbo and the Spanish settlement at Nacogdoches could serve as a barrier to Comanche expansion into the Piney Woods that had been the Caddoan homeland for centuries. While Texas Caddos knew how to play off the Spaniards and French, they were not so sure about the Comanches, whom historian Ned Blackhawk argues were becoming at that time "imperialists on their own account," seeking to monopolize trade between New Mexico and Louisiana. In the process the Comanches broke down Euro-American frontiers into its component parts with their own Indian cores and peripheries.[53] In essence, the Louisiana-Texas borderlands became a stronghold of Caddo resistance to the world outside, allowing room in that region only for those like Adaeseño, French, and African inhabitants who abided by native customs.

Whether Ybarbo was unaware of De Mezieres's unfolding peace process or intent to sabotage it, several events occurred that delayed any truce with the Comanches for another six years. Pekka Hämäläinen explains that King Carlos III rejected the local war council's proposed campaign against the Apaches as genocidal and contrary to Enlightenment thinking. By mid-December 1779, word of Spain's entry into the American Revolution reached Texas in the form of orders to reduce spending. Lastly, the death of De Mezieres in that same month left the Spanish government without its most skillful diplomat to the Comanches.[54] The commandant had accidentally fallen off his horse in East Texas, suffering a head injury, but managed to visit Governor Cabello at San Antonio and present him with many goods for distribution among the Indians in the effort to regulate trade with those nations who remained at peace with Spain. In return, he received a subsidy of 450 pesos from the governor of Texas for the militia at Natchitoches.[55] De Mezieres set in motion the process of legitimizing the gun and tobacco trade between Louisiana and Texas as smuggling increasingly gave way to Indian gifts from the Texas governors. Liquor remained a wholly different matter and unresolved. Meanwhile, Commandant

General Croix appointed Ybarbo as lieutenant governor of Nacogdoches, with an annual salary of 500 pesos, in the effort to maintain the loyalties of both Ybarbo and De Mezieres. While the latter succumbed to his injury, Ybarbo went on to become captain, judge, and undisputed leader at Nacogdoches from his Old Stone Fort, which became the official trading post for the Indians of Texas.[56]

Spanish officials in Texas concluded a peace treaty with the Comanches in 1785 (as did their counterparts in New Mexico the following year) upon the heels of Britain's removal as a threat from North America when the Treaty of Paris (1783) concluded the American Revolution, leaving the Ohio Valley to a new nation and returning Florida to Spain. Imperial warfare and the merging of the smuggling frontier with transatlantic commerce left Antonio Gil Ybarbo as the undisputed Spanish powerbroker in East Texas along with Chief Texito and the Caddos. Together these forces blocked Comanche expansion into the region and continued to dominate the borderlands until another Louisiana transfer brought the western boundary of the vibrant young American Republic into touch with Texas.[57] By then there were too many deserters, smugglers, and slaves infiltrating the region, even though the Spanish government grew more intent than ever upon sealing off the Louisiana-Texas border as Captain Ybarbo prepared his final resting place in a land he could never fully claim as his own domain.

In essence, the crossing of the smuggling frontier with transatlantic commerce on the Louisiana-Texas borderlands during the mid-eighteenth century drew attention to the region from imperial powers engaged in warfare elsewhere in North America. The resulting clash between mercantilist and "free trade" policies established a fault line upon which political boundaries emerged at this edge of empires.[58] For the borderlands, the transnational and transcultural interaction of European, African, and American Indian people defied all constraints. No one could fully comprehend that their world would be pulled in different directions at Los Adaes, the spot where the southeastern and southwestern borderlands blended before, and after, the Louisiana Purchase.

Notes

1. Interrogation, Christophe Haische, Sept. 20, 1762, Natchitoches, LA, *Natchitoches Parish Legal Records*, trans. Elizabeth A. Rubino, vol. 1 (Natchitoches, LA: Natchitoches Genealogical and Historical Association, 2003), 125 (hereafter cited as NPLR). According to historians H. Sophie Burton and F. Todd Smith, "piaster" was the French term for one Spanish peso and the equivalent of an American dollar during most

Francis X. Galán

of the eighteenth century. Burton and Smith, *Colonial Natchitoches: A Creole Community on the Louisiana-Texas Frontier* (College Station: Texas A&M University Press, 2008), 172–73n14. The author would like to thank George Avery, archeologist with the Center for Regional Heritage Research at Stephen F. Austin State University in Nacogdoches, for bringing the NPLR to my attention in 2006.

2. Interrogation, Etienne, July 13, 1757, Natchitoches, NPLR, 68–69. In her own interrogation, Marion claimed that she did not know that the goods had been stolen in the first place. Ibid., 73–74.

3. Robert S. Weddle, *Wilderness Manhunt: The Spanish Search for La Salle* (College Station: Texas A&M University Press, 1999); David J. Weber, *The Spanish Frontier in North America* (New Haven, CT: Yale University Press, 1992); Henry Folmer, *Franco-Spanish Rivalry in North America, 1524–1763* (Glendale, CA: Arthur H. Clark, 1953).

4. Francis X. Galán, "Presidio Los Adaes: Worship, Kinship, and Commerce with French Natchitoches on the Spanish-Franco-Caddo Borderlands, 1721–1773," *Louisiana History* 49, no. 2 (Spring 2008): 191–208; Juliana Barr, *Peace Came in the Form of a Woman: Indians and Spaniards in the Texas Borderlands* (Chapel Hill: University of North Carolina Press, 2007); Elizabeth A. H. John, *Storms Brewed in Other Men's Worlds: The Confrontation of Indians, Spanish, and French in the Southwest, 1540–1795* (Lincoln: University of Nebraska Press, 1975), xiii, 343.

5. Pekka Hämäläinen, *The Comanche Empire* (New Haven, CT: Yale University Press, 2008); Ned Blackhawk, *Violence over the Land: Indians and Empires in the Early American West* (Cambridge, MA: Harvard University Press, 2006); Fred Anderson, *Crucible of War: The Seven Years' War and the Fate of Empire in British North America, 1754–1766* (New York: Alfred A. Knopf, 2000).

6. David Weber refers to the "borderlands between Texas and Louisiana" as one of many "strategic frontiers" in his latest masterpiece. *Bárbaros: Spaniards and Their Savages in the Age of Enlightenment* (New Haven, CT: Yale University Press, 2005), 85–86. Ned Blackhawk describes the region as an "imperial borderlands" that helped the rise of the Comanche. *Violence over the Land*, 61.

7. Frank Raymond Secoy, *Changing Military Patterns of the Great Plains Indians* (1953; repr., Lincoln: University of Nebraska Press, 1992), 105.

8. Hämäläinen, *Comanche Empire*, 4.

9. Declaration, Juan Antonio Maldonado, muleteer and loader, Jan. 31, 1761, Presidio Los Adaes, appearing before Gov. Angel Martos y Navarrete in the *residencia* proceeding against former Governor Barrios, Bexar Archives, University of Texas at San Antonio (hereafter cited as BA), reel 9, frames 0952–53; Declaration, Lt. Joseph Gonzalez, Feb. 10, 1761, Presidio Los Adaes, ibid., 9:0961–62 (author's translation). All quotations from original documents are the author's translations unless otherwise indicated.

10. Opinion, Don Antonio Gallardo, royal advisor, concerning establishment of four Frenchmen with arms and ammunition at the mouth of the Trinity River, Feb. 11, 1755, Mexico City, Archivo San Francisco el Grande, box 2Q249, Center for American History, University of Texas at Austin, 6:19–20, photostat copy; Herbert E. Bolton, *Texas in the*

Middle Eighteenth Century: Studies in Spanish Colonial History and Administration (1915; repr., Austin: University of Texas Press, 1970), 325–74.

11. Interrogation, Joseph Blancpain, Feb. 19, 1755, Royal Prison of the Court and Hall of Confessions, Mexico City, BA, 9:0574–80; 9:0758.

12. Burton and Smith, *Colonial Natchitoches*, 13.

13. Walter L. Dorn, *Competition for Empire, 1740–1763* (New York: Harper and Row, 1940), 122, 124–25, 129. The rise of Prussia on the European continent in the mid-eighteenth century presents tantalizing comparisons with the rise of the Comanche nation on the North American continent.

14. Kathleen DuVal, *The Native Ground: Indians and Colonists in the Heart of Continent* (Philadelphia: University of Pennsylvania Press, 2006). On the Caddos, see David La Vere, *The Caddo Chiefdoms: Caddo Economies and Politics, 700–1835* (Lincoln: University of Nebraska Press, 1998); and F. Todd Smith, *The Caddo Indians: Tribes at the Convergence of Empires, 1542–1854* (College Station: Texas A&M University Press, 1995).

15. Stanley J. Stein and Barbara H. Stein, *Apogee of Empire: Spain and New Spain in the Age of Charles III, 1759–1789* (Baltimore: Johns Hopkins University Press, 2003), 359n27 (quotes, author's translation); Anderson, *Crucible of War*, 348–62; Robert S. Weddle, *After the Massacre: The Violent Legacy of the San Sabá Mission* (Lubbock: Texas Tech University Press, 2007), 1–13.

16. Stein and Stein, *Apogee of Empire*, 11–13, 315–16. English woolens were already less costly as French woolens to Spain, and its colonies peaked during the 1750s. By the 1770s, English woolens comprised 50 percent of total sales to Spanish markets. See also J. H. Elliott, *Empires of the Atlantic World: Britain and Spain in America, 1492–1830* (New Haven, CT: Yale University Press, 2006), 293. Britain preemptively declared war on Spain in January 1762. On the secret transfer of Louisiana from France to Spain, see Arthur S. Aiton, "The Diplomacy of the Louisiana Cession," in *The Louisiana Purchase Bicentennial Series in Louisiana History, Vol. II: The Spanish Presence in Louisiana, 1763–1803*, ed. Gilbert C. Din (LaFayette: University of Southwestern Louisiana, 1996), 13, 22. In the subsequent Treaty of Paris, Spain gave up Florida to Britain for the return of Havana, Cuba, which the English had captured in 1762. Spanish officials considered Florida as less harmful than English acquisition of Louisiana, with the consequent danger of smuggling into Mexico and their advance into the silver mines.

17. Daniel K. Richter, *Facing East from Indian Country: A Native History of Early America* (Cambridge, MA: Harvard University Press, 2001), 151.

18. Weber, *Spanish Frontier in North America*, 176.

19. Stein and Stein, *Apogee of Empire*, 4–5. The Steins explain that institutionalization of smuggling in Spain occurred at five levels by the 1730s: large landlords, merchant bankers in foreign ports, the church, underpaid petty officials, and powerless bureaucrats. See also Francis X. Galán, "The Chirino Boys: Spanish Soldier-Pioneers from Los Adaes on the Louisiana-Texas Borderlands, 1735–1792," *East Texas Historical Journal* 46, no. 2 (Fall 2008): 43–44.

20. Weber, *Spanish Frontier in North America*, 173, 176; Burton and Smith, *Colonial Natchitoches*, 110; Stein and Stein, *Apogee of Empire*, 6; Weber, *Bárbaros*, 173. For a discus-

sion of barter exchange on the frontier, see Daniel H. Usner Jr., *Indians, Settlers, & Slaves in a Frontier Exchange Economy: The Lower Mississippi Valley before 1783* (Chapel Hill: University of North Carolina Press, 1992).

21. Jorge Canizares-Esguerra, *Nature, Empire, and Nation: Explorations of the History of Science in the Iberian World* (Stanford, CA: Stanford University Press, 2006), 104; Stein and Stein, *Apogee of Empire*, 59, 319, 352; Paul Mapp, "British Culture and the Changing Character of the Mid-Eighteenth Century British Empire," in *Cultures in Conflict: The Seven Years' War in North America*, ed. Warren R. Hofstra (Lanham, MD: Rowman and Littlefield, 2007), 49.

22. Canizares-Esguerra, *Nature, Empire, and Nation*, 100–102; Anthony Pagden, *Lords of All the World: Ideologies of Empire in Spain, Britain, and France, c.1500–1800* (New Haven, CT: Yale University Press, 1995), 118, 123. The War for Spanish Succession ended in 1713 with the ascension of King Louis XIV's grandson to the Spanish throne.

23. Viceroy Marqués de Croix to Gov. Baron de Ripperdá of Texas, June 22, 1771, Mexico City, BA, 11:0019–20; Colin G. Calloway, *One Vast Winter Count: The Native American West before Lewis and Clark* (Lincoln: University of Nebraska Press, 2003), 362 (quote).

24. Calloway, *One Vast Winter Count*, 358, 362–63. Meanwhile, Spanish officials also fretted over the appearance of the Osages, who built their own trade empire in the Arkansas Valley to the north after migrating westward from the Ohio Valley during the French and Indian War. The Osage had secured guns in the East from French traders and then in the West trained them against Wichitas, Pawnees, and Caddos, having raided for horses, furs, and captives as well as hunting their buffalo. See DuVal, *Native Ground*, 8. See also Gilbert C. Din and Abraham P. Nasatir, *The Imperial Osages: Spanish-Indian Diplomacy in the Mississippi Valley* (Norman: University of Oklahoma Press, 1983).

25. Paper concerning the English schooner *Two Friends*, Oct. 22, 1771–May 16, 1772, La Bahía, box 2S31, Center for American History, University of Texas at Austin, 1a, 2, 7a, 8, 8a, 9a, 10, 10a. Capt. Francisco Tovar of Presidio La Bahía apparently treated the survivors well. For background on the links between the West Indies and Savannah as one importance source of settlers, slaves, and commerce, see Betty Wood, *Slavery in Colonial Georgia, 1730–1775* (Athens: University of Georgia Press, 1984), 89, 93, 98, 108.

26. Viceroy Antonio María de Bucareli to Governor Ripperdá, June 30, 1772, Mexico City, BA, 11:0231–32.

27. Viceroy Bucareli to Governor Ripperdá, Nov. 10, 1772, Mexico City, BA, 11:0280–81.

28. Viceroy Marqués de Criox to Gov. Martos y Navarrete, Dec. 1, 1766, Mexico City, BA, 10:0454.

29. Testimony, Fr. Francisco Xaxier de la Concepción, Dec. 4, 1776, Los Adaes, BA, 10:0452.

30. Viceory Bucareli to Governor Ripperdá, Oct. 7, 1772, Mexico City, BA, 11:0260–62. The viceroy also ordered that the places where the enemies entered Spanish territories be found.

31. Viceroy Bucareli to Governor Ripperdá, Oct. 12, 1771, Mexico City, BA, 11:0055–56; Viceroy Bucareli to Governor Ripperdá, June 30, 1772, Mexico City, BA, 11:0235–36.

32. For discussion of Rubí's military inspection and shifting Indian policy, see Weber, *Spanish Frontier in North America,* 204–30.

33. Viceroy Bucareli to Governor Ripperdá, Jan. 6, 1773, Mexico City, BA, 11:0304–0306. The viceroy added that while Apaches still maintained good relations with the Spanish in Texas, they wrecked havoc upon Spanish settlements in the neighboring province of Coahuila as well as Nueva Vizcaya (present Chihuahua). Buacreli to Ripperdá, Feb. 9, 1774, Mexico City, BA, 11:0388–89; Bucareli to Ripperdá, Mar. 1, 1774, Mexico City, BA, 11:0390–91; Bucareli to Ripperdá, May 8, 1774, Mexico City, BA, 11:0407–10.

34. Viceroy Bucareli to Governor Ripperdá, Dec. 21, 1774, Mexico City, BA, 11:0516–17. The viceroy also disapproved correspondence with Saint Denis on a pacification project with the Indians.

35. Viceroy Bucareli to Governor Ripperdá, May 24, 1775, Mexico City, BA, 11:0609–10. King Carols III subsequently approved the measures that Viceroy Bucareli and Commandant General O'Conor had taken. Viceroy Bucareli to Arriaga, *sobre armas Ingles a los Indios de Texas,* Nov. 26, 1775, Mexico City, Archivo General de Indias—Mexico City, microfilm, reel 23, doc. 18, 1–2, Our Lady of the Lake University. On the reorganization of presidial defense, see Max L. Moorhead, *The Presidio: Bastion of the Spanish Borderlands* (Norman: University of Oklahoma Press, 1975).

36. Viceroy Bucareli to Governor Ripperdá, July 26, 1775, Mexico City, BA, 11:0636; Bucareli to Ripperdá, Jan. 17, 1776, Mexico City, BA, 11:0684–86.

37. Certified copy of proceedings, Gov. Ripperdá va. Joaquín Benitez, Nepomuceno Travieso, and Juan Antonio Cuevas, charged with smuggling, Aug. 1–Sept. 28, 1774, San Antonio de Béxar, BA, 11:0430–44; Certified copy of proceedings, Governor Ripperdá va. Juan Antonio Diaz and José Manuel Diaz, accused of contraband, Oct. 3, 1774–Feb. 4, 1775, San Antonio de Béxar, BA, 11:0456–64; *Diligencias,* Governor Ripperdá vs. Jacinto de Mora and Marcos Hernandez, charged with contraband, Apr. 9–July 2, 1775, San Antonio de Béxar, BA, 11:0570–90; Vicroy Bucareli to Governor Ripperdá, Sept. 13, 1775, Mexico City, BA, 11:0651–52.

38. Viceroy Bucareli to Governor Ripperdá, Feb. 28, 1776, Mexico City, BA, 11:0698.

39. Commandant General Teodoro de Croix to Governor Ripperdá, Feb. 22, 1777, Mexico City, BA, 11:0829–30; Josef Rubio to Governor Ripperdá, May 17, 1777, Chihuahua, BA, 11:0955–56; Croix to Ripperdá, Sept. 11, 1777, Zacatecas, BA, 12:0022–23; Bolton, *Texas in the Middle Eighteenth Century,* 435–26. Spanish officials also instructed Captain Ybarbo to reconnoiter the lower Sabine River against other English landings.

40. As late as the fall of 1778, Spanish officials still debated opening up trade with Louisiana and establishing a policy on Louisianans trading with Indians in Texas. See Commandant General Croix to Governor Ripperdá, May 16, 1778, Chihuahua, BA, 12:0287–88; and Croix to Ripperdá, Sept. 11, 1778, Chihuahua, 12:0398–99.

41. Commandant Athanese DeMezieres, Report, Feb. 20, 1778, San Antonio de
Béxar, Biblioteca Nacional Mexico, microfilm, in Old Spanish Mission Records, Our Lady
of the Lake University, reel 33, doc. 62, 2a, 3,3a, 4, 4a. A copy of De Mezeries's report also
appears in box 10, folder 4, Archivo General de Indias de Guadalajara, Catholic Archives
of Texas, Austin, 118–30, Spanish transcription (hereafter cited as CAT).

42. Hämäläinen, *Comanche Empire*, 90, 98; Barr, *Peace Came in the Form of a
Woman*, 231.

43. Hämäläinen, *Comanche Empire*, 97 (quote).

44. Commandant General Croix to Governor Ripperdá, Sept. 12, 1778, Chihuahua,
BA, 12:0401–0402; Croix to Ripperdá, Sept. 15, 1778, Chihuahua, BA, 12: 0412–14;
Croix to Ripperdá, Sept. 15, 1778, Chihuahua, BA, 12: 0415–16. For several years,
Viceroy Bucareli disliked the fact that the Adaesenos had traded tobacco freely (libre-
mente) with the French and Norteños since their reestablishment in East Texas, but all he
could do was admonish the governor. See Viceroy Bucareli to Governor Ripperdá, July 26,
1775, Mexico City, BA, 11:0630–31.

45. Commandant General Croix to Gov. Domingo Cabello, Oct. 4, 1778, BA,
12:0570–71.

46. Elliot, *Empires of the Atlantic World*, 352; Weber, *Spanish Frontier in North
America*, 266–67; Governor Cabello to Commandant Croix, June 20, 1779, San Antonio,
BA, 13:0087–89. Domingo Cabello, who succeeded Ripperdá as governor of Texas,
made sure to post a royal order in the presidio of San Antonio instructing the burning of
all French and English copies of the work entitled *Año Dos Mil Cuatrocientos Cuarenta*
(The Year 2440), which promoted the liberty and independence of the subjects of Spain.
Cabello, Royal Order, Mar. 1, 1779, Royal Presidio of San Antonio de Béxar, BA,
12:0255–57. See also Croix to Ripperdá, July 26, 1778, BA, 12:0317–18. In this letter
Croix ordered the governor to observe English movements and prevent their landing in
Texas and provided news that France had ordered reprisals against English ships that went
to their ports. The contents of this letter were to be kept secret. For a general discussion
of Spain and the American Revolution, see Light T. Cummins, *Spanish Observers and the
American Revolution, 1775–1783* (Baton Rouge: Louisiana State University Press, 1991).

47. Commandant Croix to Governor Cabello, Aug. 16, 1779, Chihuahua, BA,
13:0294–96; Croix to Cabello, Aug. 17, 1779, Chihuahua, BA, 13:0299; Cabello to Croix,
Sept. 15, 1779, San Antonio, BA, 13:0427–28.

48. Barr, *Peace Came in the Form of a Woman*, 211; Burton and Smith, *Colonial
Natchitoches*, 17.

49. Commandant De Mezieres, Report, Feb. 20, 1778, 33:62, 2.

50. Barr, *Peace Came in the Form of a Woman*, 231–32.

51. Antonio Gil Ybarbo to Governor Cabello, June 13, 1779, Brazos de Dios,
Archivo General de Mexico—Historia, vol. 51, box 29, folder 6b, CAT, 544–46, transcription; Governor Cabello to Croix, Aug. 20, 1779, San Antonio de Béxar, BA, 13:0321–22.

52. Fr. Juan Garcia Botello, Dec. 23, 1778, Mission Espada, Archivo General
de Mexico—Historia, vol. 51, box 29, folder 6a, CAT, 481–84; Commandant Croix to

Governor Cabello, Jan. 12, 1779, Chihuahua, BA, 12:0765–66; Cabello to Croix, Apr. 3, 1779, San Antonio, BA, 12:1016–20; Ybarbo to Commandant Croix, May 13, 1779, Nacogdoches, Archivo General de Mexico—Historia, vol. 51, box 29, folder 6a, CAT, 520–23, transcription.

53. Blackhawk, *Violence over the Land,* 53; Hämäläinen, *Comanche Empire,* 9; DuVal, *Native Ground,* 28. On Indians playing off Europeans against each other, see Richard White, *The Roots of Dependency: Subsistence, Environment, and Social Change among the Choctaws, Pawnees, and Navajos* (Lincoln: University of Nebraska Press, 1983).

54. Hämäläinen, *Comanche Empire,* 97–98; Burton and Smith, *Colonial Natchitoches,* 17.

55. Governor Cabello to Commandant General Croix, Oct. 12, 1779, San Antonio, BA, 13:0511–13; Cabello to Croix, Nov. 4, 1779, BA, 13:0592–94. Cabello's October 12 communication contains a list of the goods De Mezeries presented to him. Among the items were: 30 bundles of tobacco, 36 large axes, 18 medium axes, 18 hoes, 18 guns, 33 shirts, 18 pounds of vermillion, 16.5 dozen knives, 15 dozen combs, 43.5 *armas* of *pano de zembra* (54.67 blue cloth), 81 pounds of gunpowder, 172 pounds of ammunition, and 33 pounds of beads of all colors.

56. Bolton, *Texas in the Middle Eighteenth Century,* 437; Burton and Smith, *Colonial Natchitoches,* 17.

57. F. Todd Smith, *From Dominance to Disappearance: The Indians of Texas and the Near Southwest, 1786–1859* (Lincoln: University of Nebraska Press, 2005); Lance R. Blyth, "Fugitives from Servitude: American Deserters and Runaway Slaves in Spanish Nacogdoches, 1803–1808," *East Texas Historical Journal* 38 (Fall 2000): 3–14.

58. See Eric Hinderaker and Peter C. Mancall, *At the Edge of Empire: The Backcountry in British North America* (Baltimore: Johns Hopkins University Press, 2003), ix. Hinderaker and Mancall acknowledge historians Jack Greene and J. R. Pole for their challenge to conceptualize "early America along regional instead of topical lines," seeking to move the backcountry into the "center" of the American story.

8

The Mexican-American War

Reflections on an Overlooked Conflict

Kendall Milton

THE MEXICAN-AMERICAN WAR lasted from 1846 to 1848, and by the time it was over, Mexico had lost half its territory to the United States and gasped the final breaths of North American dominance. The annexation of Texas was a major contributing factor to this war, and the state served as one of the front lines of battle. Mexico at that point saw its territory and influence slipping into the grasp of a new US empire and forced to fight for its survival. But the Mexican-American War is often eclipsed by those conflicts that preceded and followed it, the Texas Revolution and the Civil War. So what are Texans' memory, or lack thereof, of the Mexican-American War, what recent changes have occurred to the state's collective memory, and what themes might public historians explore to present the war to a modern audience?

Despite being one of the most influential events for the Lone Star State, there are few memorials to the Mexican-American War in Texas. The state capitol in Austin has a plaque listing the names of US officers killed during the war. Fort Brown, formerly Fort Texas, in Brownsville has a flagpole memorializing the two soldiers who died in battle there, including Maj. Jacob Brown, after whom the fort was renamed. The Old Bayview Cemetery in Corpus Christi contains the unmarked graves of sixty-nine of Brig. Gen. Zachary Taylor's men who perished there in 1846 and 1847. As a memorial, a granite headstone sits on a random site, noting the names of the fallen and praising their patriotism. Other memorials exist in Maryland, South Carolina, California, Pennsylvania, Kentucky, and Tennessee, organized and sponsored by lineage societies, including the plaque on the Texas State Capitol grounds.

Staff at the Palo Alto Battlefield National Historical Site have recognized the void and are spearheading a new trend of recording and teaching the events that transpired on its grounds. Private citizens began the process in 1893 by erecting the first monument on the battlefield. In succeeding decades, the National Survey of Historic Sites and Buildings and the National Park Service (NPS) have recognized the site. The

NPS now administers the area under the authority of the Palo Alto Battlefield Historic Site Act of 1991. It is a relatively new park, and staff members are working diligently to develop permanent structures and offer activities that soon will make the battlefield a fitting, lasting, and overdue memorial to the Mexican-American War.[1]

In contrast, Mexico has long memorialized *los Niños Héroes*, the six young cadets of the Mexican Military Academy who defended Chapultepec to the very last on September 12, 1847. Over time they came to symbolize the virtues and dedication of soldiers and Mexican citizens as a whole. The monument has six columns surrounding the figure of a woman cradling a boy's body. Cadets from the military academy still conduct daily ceremonies at its base.[2]

Also, the National Cemetery in Mexico City includes a white stone shaft erected by the US government marking the mass grave of 750 American soldiers killed in Mexico during the war. It simply reads, "To the honored memory of 750 Americans known only to god whose bones collected by their country's order are here buried."[3] The soldiers actually can be identified—their names can be found on service records—but they are not named there. Notice that the war is not mentioned either. The inscription is vague, but still it is there. Only recently has the NPS begun making strides to develop national recognition of the mass burials at Palo Alto. Until that time, it fell to genealogical societies to erect monuments commemorating the American sacrifice.

Two separate and distinct lineage societies are trying to maintain the memories of the Mexican-American War, the Aztec Club and the National Association of Veterans of the Mexican War. The Aztec Club was founded on October 13, 1847, while the United States occupied Mexico City. Regular and volunteer officers wanted to establish a clubhouse for the entertainment of members and guests while in the city and for the promotion of good fellowship among US servicemen. It had 149 original members who met the eligibility requirements of being commissioned officers of the army, navy, or marines who served in any part of Mexico, including the coast, during the war. The club met at the former home of Señor Boca Negra, Mexico's former minister to the United States, and annual dues were twenty dollars. The founders knew their time in Mexico City was temporary, so they made provisions to preserve the organization in essence if not in location. In the years that followed, the club evolved from being purely social to military then to hereditary in membership.[4]

Meetings and reunions were sporadic at first and nonexistent during the Civil War, but these stabilized in the 1870s. The Aztec Club developed insignias and medals and started keeping better records of its members, including maintaining rolls of the deceased. Realizing their mortality, the founders gradually expanded the club's membership. New members at first included the eldest son of current members or the next

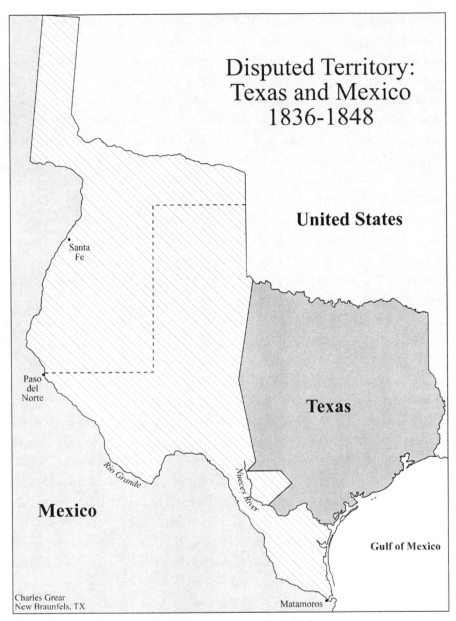

Disputed Territory: Texas and Mexico, 1836–1848. Courtesy Charles D. Grear.

blood relative. Later it expanded to any son, or all sons, as the club allowed more than one representative per family. It also grew to include the descendents of officers who served in the war but never joined the organization or who had died before given the opportunity. By the turn of the twenty-first century, the Aztec Club had entered 1,043 members to its rolls.[5]

While officers organized the Aztec Club purely for social reasons, another organization fought for veterans' benefits and compensation. Alexander Kenady started the National Association of Veterans of the Mexican War in California in 1866, and the organization opened nationally several years later, publishing a monthly newsletter, the *Vedette*. Between 1874 and 1910, the organization held annual reunions, and in 1901 Mrs. Moore Murdock created a women's auxiliary, the Dames of 1846. Besides the establishment of memorials, the lasting contribution of this organization was veterans' benefits, including a pension of eight dollars per month in 1887, which was raised to twelve dollars per month in 1912. The veterans group itself is no longer active, obviously, but has morphed into a lineage society called the Descendents of Mexican War Veterans. Membership in that group is not limited to descendents of officers but to those of all veterans regardless of rank.[6]

These organizations remember the Mexican-American War, and for good reason—their members had relatives who fought in it. For so many others, however, the conflict is merely a footnote in the Texas experience, if it is remembered at all.

Close to 13,000 Americans died in the war, more than 11,000 of them from disease. The hot and humid climate was a contributing factor, and the rate of disease was much higher among volunteers than regulars. In terms of deaths per participant, it was the costliest war in US history, with a casualty rate almost twice as high as that of the Civil War.[7]

Moreover, the Mexican-American War began in the Lone Star State. Granted, it moved its way south into Mexico quickly, but it started in Texas and largely because of Texas. The spilling of "American blood on American soil" was the rallying cry Pres. James K. Polk used to justify the war. Fort Texas was here, and so were the battlefields of Palo Alto and Resaca de la Palma, which are still intact today. These are battlefields of a war against a foreign country on which were fought the beginning battles of the nation's first invasion into a foreign country.[8] In a state that takes such pride in its history it is worth considering why this war is so often overlooked.

The mid-1800s were a dramatic time in Texas history. The territory went from barren frontier to populated state to independent republic. Nine years later it obtained US statehood. Fighting in two more wars made three major conflicts within thirty-five years, not counting the Somervell, Mier, and Santa Fe Expeditions; Adrian Woll's invasion of San Antonio; and the Indian campaigns of the Council House Fight and the Battle of Plum Creek. In a relatively short amount of time, Texas faced several climactic and historically significant events. The Mexican-American War was just one of these, and it had the misfortune of falling between the two most memorable conflicts in Texas history: the Texas Revolution and the Civil War.

The Texas Revolution had a direct link to the outbreak of war ten years later. It exposed the vulnerabilities of Mexico's northern provinces and the shortcomings of a centralist government. It exemplified how Anglos had come to populate and dominate Mexican territories in western North America. And even before Texas annexation, it expanded the control of the United States on the continent. Mexico was not ignorant of its vulnerabilities and fought to maintain control of the territories it had left, especially the western portion of Texas, which Mexico still claimed using the Nueces River as the border.[9] In fact, losing Texas created a deep national wound from which Mexico could not easily recover, and the nation never recognized Texas as having gained independence, at the Nueces River or otherwise. The Mexican-American War was a last stand against the spread of an imperialist nation that already had tendrils of influence on the western coast.

The Treaty of Guadalupe-Hidalgo (1848) settled the dispute over the southern border of Texas, officially making it the Rio Grande. In addition, Mexico ceded land to the United States that now comprises the states of California, Utah, and Nevada as well as parts of Arizona, New Mexico, Wyoming, and Colorado. But this vast expansion of territory rekindled sectional conflicts over slavery. More land meant new territories and renewed debates between Free-Soilers and slaveowners. The slavery issue, which had been held at bay by the Missouri Compromise of 1820, burst wide open again through the Compromise of 1850 and the Kansas-Nebraska Act of 1854. The latter essentially allowed new states the choice of entering the Union as slave or free. It also virtually ensured another war would be waged to determine the status of territories gained in the last one. Those legislative measures were temporary solutions to slavery—the Civil War was a more permanent one. In that conflict, officers who first met at West Point and saw combat in Mexico in the 1840s fought beside each other and against each other, using the skills and experiences gleaned from combat fifteen years earlier and applying their military training and experience in a new theater.

Despite the important link the Mexican-American War provides for these events, it is often overshadowed by these martial bookends. Historians can spout out as many statistics as they want about being the deadliest war by percentage, but they will never come anywhere close to obtaining the fervent following for the Mexican-American War that those other two events have among Texans. One reason is that the cause of this war arguably was less noble than the other two. The Mexican government was oppressive, and Texas wanted to be *free*. The Civil War was about *slavery* and *states' rights*. Simplistic statements, perhaps, but not altogether wrong. The Mexican-American War erupted not over trampled civil liberties but over something a little more mundane—land.

Historian Otis Singletary has suggested that the unpopularity of the war also helped relegate it to the sidelines of the history books.[10] Texans embraced the war wholeheartedly. They had the most vested interests, of course, that of settling the state's southern boundary and essentially "finishing" the Texas Revolution. But northerners feared that it would lead to the expansion of slavery. US congressmen, including Abraham Lincoln of Illinois, proposed the "Spot Resolution" to find the exact location of the initial Thornton incident and compare it with maps and other documentation to determine whether or not it indeed took place on Texas soil or if the Mexicans had a valid invasion claim. The excitement that first swept the nation at the outbreak of hostilities waned as the war persisted. A quick victory is typically the key to maintaining interest.[11] The conflict was essentially a large-scale version of a Texas border war. There were no other countries involved to take sides or serve as allies. The land in question was located on the southwestern frontier of the county, and the general public quickly lost interest despite a barrage of war correspondence from the front lines.

This was the first foreign war covered extensively by US correspondents. Not only did journalists write stories and sketch drawings about the war, but they also published them in record time. In the spring of 1846, Moses Yale Beach, the publisher of the *New York Sun*, established a pony express to deliver news of the fighting. His express used all methods of delivery at its disposal, including stagecoaches, railroads, steamships, and the newly developed telegraph. His efforts allowed him to deliver war dispatches almost a full day faster than the traditional mail routes used at the time. Beach sold interests in his express to other major New York City newspapers, forming a system of collaboration and organized dissemination of news from the front that became the basis for the Associated Press.[12] War correspondents like George Wilkins Kendall were able to submit stories and even eyewitness accounts with increasing speed. Most newspapermen supported the war effort, but like the rest of the country, interest declined as the story dragged.[13]

Singletary also has posited that the overtly aggressive nature of the war made Americans feel a little guilty. After all, the US Army invaded a foreign country, captured its capital, and occupied it for months, after which the United States sequestered half of its land. To some, these are not things to be proud of and thus were embarrassedly wiped from memory.

The prevailing trend among military historians of the early twentieth century was that the war was inevitable, unapologetically fought for the acquisition of land under the divine sanction of manifest destiny. Some revisionists of the 1950s and 1960s adopted the more cynical interpretation of a blatant land grab perpetrated by a strong nation upon a weaker neighbor.[14] Singletary said the United States waged war with no moral pretensions, only greed. He has also called the millions of dollars the United States paid for the Mexican Cession of land "conscience money" and indicated that popular opinion of the time echoed such sentiments. Citizens of the United States felt guilty that Mexico had lost so much territory so quickly and seemingly so easily. All of the major battles were clear US victories. Mexican casualties greatly outnumbered American. In New Mexico, Stephen Kearny took Santa Fe in a matter of weeks and without firing a shot. The combined naval and land forces captured the Pacific Coast and all of California before the Battle of Buena Vista. The offensive nature of the war is one of many reasons, in Singletary's opinion, why Americans might want to forget it.

More-contemporary military historians concede that expansionism was a huge factor. But they present a more nuanced explanation than an outright seizure of land from a weak nation. For one thing, Mexico was not completely helpless. It was almost as large as the United States with an army more than twice the size. In every battle, the United States faced a larger enemy force, an army often commanded by an aggressive and ambitious general in Antonio Lopez de Santa Anna.[15] Even when faced with the superior training and firepower of the US Army, and despite losing every significant battle, the Mexican government made no concessions, and the war continued. Only the taking and occupation of the capital convinced Mexican politicians to open negotiations, which then lasted months and nearly broke down.

Also, the dominant ruling faction in Mexico was fervently pro-war. Some saw it as an opportunity to retake Texas and put an end to the rampant border wars. Sentiment was so strong, in fact, that merely meeting with an American emissary caused the overthrow of the government by pro-war factions. When the United States sent John Slidell to negotiate a settlement of the Texas border before the war, the Mexican government refused even to acknowledge his presence for fear that it might instigate another coup.[16] This added to the instability of an already tenuous regime, which would continue to plague the nation for years to come.

Recently, more ethnically sensitive works on the Mexican-American War seem to focus less on the war itself and more on the social effects afterward. Some discussed the nomenclature of the conflict, if calling it the "Mexican War" was insensitive, the implication being that Mexico started it. *The United States and Mexico at War,* edited by Donald S. Frazier, is a good example of historians attempting to write an unbiased history of a still sensitive subject. The book is encyclopedic, almost six hundred pages of entries on relevant topics from before, during, and after the war. Entries are written by different authors from all over North America and Europe, many of which contain separate articles, usually dividing the topic into Mexican and American perspectives. Those on specific battles are relatively brief, while more-extended musings are offered on topics relating to the causes or the aftermaths of the war, such as those on "Class Structure in Mexico" and "Racism." The entries on the legacy of the war, again divided into Mexican and American, are particularly interesting.[17]

Of course, the most obvious legacy was the altered border, but Jesus Velasco-Marquez notes other less noticeable effects, such as new ambivalent attitudes in Mexico toward the United States. Some hesitated to believe that the United States was satisfied with the terms of the treaty and feared continued invasions seeking more land. That country remained a potential enemy of Mexico's interests and prosperity.[18] But US political stability was something Mexicans desperately wished to emulate in their own country, serving as a model for a unity their country had yet to obtain. Uncertainty and general dislike and mistrust of the United States gave all Mexicans a common enemy to rally around and spurred its own nationalist movement. Unfortunately, once again political disagreements proved insurmountable and resulted in civil war and the restoration of the monarchy. Still, events like the Punitive Expedition in 1916, which followed a brief occupation of Vera Cruz, kept the events of the Mexican-American War fresh in the consciousness of Mexican citizens.

According to Richard Griswold del Castillo, the US legacy of the war centers on land. For one, the addition of 500,000 square miles of territory is a pretty significant legacy, especially considering the vast natural resources soon found in those territories. But border disputes continued and eventually led to the Gadsden Purchase in 1853, which added the southern part of Arizona to the United States. Another consequence concerns the people living in those new territories, the close to 100,000 former Mexican citizens now considered residents of the United States.

This brings up one of the central themes confronting public historians: exploring and addressing how the Treaty of Guadalupe-Hidalgo shaped relations between Anglos and Mexican Americans. The Mexican-American War flipped the long-standing roles of majority and minority for many in the Southwest and thrust into the forefront of social and political discourse the conflicting paths of Anglos and Mexicans in Texas.

Americans migrated in droves to Mexican Texas in the 1820s and 1830s. The Mexican government offered cheap land and encouraged the settlement of some of the northern areas of the country in hopes of populating a seemingly desolate wasteland. Anglos were forced to pass citizenship standards that included conversion to Catholicism and repudiation of slavery—by that time already illegal in Mexico—in exchange for generous land grants. But the settlers only half-heartedly adopted the customs of their new country and instead clung much more tightly to the beliefs of their former one. This set Texas apart from interior Mexico from the very beginning of its existence. Its inhabitants identified with the United States more than it did the Mexican government. Conflicts arose over constitutions, method of government, representation, taxes, and tariffs. By 1835, Anglos outnumbered native Mexicans in Texas by a ratio of four to one despite immigration restrictions enacted in 1830. By then it was too late to stem the tide, and the rumblings of revolution soon sounded among like-minded Texians.[19]

In 1836, when Texas won independence, the new republic was predominantly Anglo but also significantly Tejano. Many Tejanos supported the revolution against Mexico's centralist government and actively participated in the Texas cause. After the war, political alliances of Texians and Tejanos unraveled as thoughts of revenge took control. Many Mexicans, even Texas loyalists, were expelled from the new republic, the most notable being Juan Seguin.[20] Consequently, few Anglo settlements existed south of San Antonio, especially on the disputed strip of land between the Rio Grande and the Nueces River, which became almost exclusively Hispanic. It would be several years, well after the Mexican-American War shone a spotlight on the region, before both Anglos and Hispanics developed significant communities there.

North of the Nueces, conflicts arose over three main issues: race, citizenship, and land. Original drafts of the Treaty of Guadalupe-Hidalgo spoke specifically to the latter two, but Articles IX and X, which granted those rights, did not make it past the US Senate floor, at least not intact. Many elected officials either shared the opinion of or cowed to pressure from their constituents' racist beliefs that Mexicans were inherently inferior and undeserving of the equal treatment afforded them in the treaty.

Stating that Americans of the 1840s and 1850s held negative attitudes toward Mexicans is an oversimplification of matters, but it holds some truth. Aside from the wealthy landowners who could pass as "Spanish" or "Castilian," most were regarded by US citizens as members of a mixed race, containing African and Indian blood.[21] Mexicans were associated with deficiency, incapacity, and general helplessness. It did not help matters that they were also Catholic. Many US journalists described the Mexican-American War as a battle between the civilized and the barbaric. Others expressed the opinion that it was a learning experience for the Mexican people, an exercise in recognizing their moral and intellectual superiors, or the fulfillment of manifest destiny.[22]

Therefore, the general opinion of the time was that Mexicans were not ready for an "equal union" with the United States, and some argued that they never would be. In response to this, elected officials rewrote Article IX of the treaty. Instead of becoming US citizens automatically, Mexicans living within the Mexican Cession would be incorporated into the United States "at the proper time," that instance being unspecified and at the complete discretion of Anglo lawmakers.[23] In addition, Mexican Americans legally had the right to vote, but rampant discrimination and sometimes active confrontation often prevented them from doing so.

The article in the Treaty of Guadalupe-Hidalgo that protected the land of Mexican Americans was removed from the final draft completely. Rather than recognize existing property claims outright, the federal government devised a land-grant adjudication process. Texas received an exemption from the federal process, citing that it retained control over all annexed lands. Therefore, the state developed its own system for land adjudication in the Bourland-Miller Commission, which was assigned the task of validating Tejano claims.

Although a majority of land claims were recognized, the commission faced opposition from Mexican landowners who distrusted Texans' motives and worried about their own rights. Indeed, even if the commission recognized the grants, some counties and municipalities developed legal but questionable means of confiscating property. David Montejano cites sheriffs' sales and auctions ordered by county clerks to settle taxes and outstanding debts. Though legal, the winning bids could be conspicuously low valuations of the property. For example, a Hidalgo County sheriff once sold 3,000 acres of the Hinojosa grant for a total cash price of fifteen dollars.[24]

Mexican Americans' failure or unwillingness to assimilate may have made them easier targets for discrimination. Del Castillo asserts that they developed a diverse culture distinct from traditional "Americanism." The first wave of Tejanos and their descendents spoke Spanish and maintained ties with Mexico. They lived in separate neighborhoods and barrios, sometimes having lost their land and having difficulty finding adequate work. This unified them as a people but isolated them from Anglo society.[25]

Mexican Americans were understandably frustrated. Rodolfo F. Acuña has expressed it thusly: those people did not cross the border, the border crossed them.[26] The treaty ultimately granted them US citizenship that, for all intents and purposes, they did not receive. Suffice to say, the legal system did not work in the Hispanics' favor. Mexican Americans were treated as outsiders and as immigrants, though many families had owned their property since before Texas was a republic, let alone a state. This perpetuated a distrust of the US government and its people and fostered a bitterness and moral outrage that somehow flowed in both directions.[27]

Arnoldo De León, in *They Called Them Greasers*, contends that Anglos treated

Mexican Americans badly out of fear. They anticipated an uprising, revolt, or retribution for lost land and respect because, had the situation been reversed, Anglos certainly would have stood up for their rights, with violence if necessary. The Texas Revolution had proven that much. After so many decades of contention and strife with Mexico, Texans had a hard time grappling with a newfound sense of peace. To ensure things stayed calm, they asserted physical and social dominance over Tejanos and the Mexican immigrants who continued to come.[28]

As seeming confirmation of this fear, the Mexican Revolution and the nationalistic sentiment fostered therein began to spill across the Texas border in 1915 in the form of the "Plan of San Diego." This called for Mexican nationals and Mexican Americans living in Texas, Arizona, and New Mexico to rise up against the prejudice and discrimination they confronted in the United States and establish a new republic they could eventually repatriate to Mexico. Officials uncovered the plan and at first took little notice, until border raids led by both Mexicans and American citizens connected to it occurred along the Rio Grande. During that summer, raiders used quasi-military and guerrilla tactics to kill Anglo-Americans and destroy their property in South Texas. Army units were eventually sent to the border, but anxious Anglos often sought their own retribution. "Lynchings [of Hispanics] became almost commonplace."[29] The raids petered out soon after the United States recognized the new Carranza government in Mexico, but hostility remained on both sides. A year later the Punitive Expedition into Mexico, which drew the US military into the hunt for Francisco "Pancho" Villa, once again exacerbated tensions on the border.[30]

The Mexican Revolution had another consequences for Texas, driving many immigrants from Mexico north of the Rio Grande. While 100,000 Mexicans may have joined the United States through the Mexican Cession, as many as 1 million more crossed the border between 1910 and 1930, many through El Paso. The new immigrant population overwhelmed the "original" Mexican Americans and erased any remaining class distinctions that might have separated the landholding elite from the common laborers. Perhaps as a result of this, the 1930 census was the first to classify Mexicans or Hispanics as a separate race.[31]

Discriminatory attitudes toward Mexican Americans by no means disappeared in the 1930s. One could argue that the Great Depression actually made things worse. When the labor market dried up, the United States embarked on large-scale repatriation and deportation programs. Only after World War II did veterans groups like the American GI Forum lead the charge for equal rights and better benefits for Mexican Americans. Organizations like the League of United Latin American Citizens and the Community Service Organization soon followed, and the Chicano movement was born. Early leaders such as Reies López Tijerena and Alianza Federal de Mercedes

Libres organized protests and lawsuits against the federal government with the hopes of drawing attention to the unfulfilled promises of the Treaty of Guadalupe-Hidalgo in much the same way that various American Indian tribes have sought reparations for treaty violations.[32] Essentially, they and others now argue that the treaty is not irrelevant just because it is "old."

Indeed, some historians still seek land-dispute settlements. Humberto Garza has analyzed the peace treaty and compared its notations to the current boundaries of California and Mexico, concluding that the border is several miles farther south than where it should be. He goes so far as to say that this issue needs to be resolved—by force if necessary. The veracity of these claims may be suspect, considering in his introduction Garza quotes selections from *Mein Kampf* as an illustration of Anglo "mass think," berates the educational system for indoctrinating American schoolchildren with "historical misrepresentations" and "patriotic fabrications," and accuses US authorities of committing "unlawful, blatant acts of thievery and genocide."[33] But who is to say? As recently as 1968, Texas and Mexico were settling claims over tracts of land in El Paso and Chamizal dating back to the 1840s.[34]

It is not only overt discrimination that affects Mexican Americans, however. Del Castillo mentions a unique consciousness left over from the experiences of 1840s Tejanos who felt more acutely the awareness of what might have been for Mexico.

Again, this circles back to the land. When the Mexican-American War concluded, Mexico had lost half of its territory and the United States had more than doubled in size. It was not only the amount of land that was significant but also its location and its resources. The cession gave the United States two western ports, access to trade in the Pacific, a moderate climate suited to agriculture, and abundant natural resources of both silver and gold. Therefore, the nation sat poised with nothing but potential, imminent physical and economic growth, and the status of a continental power. Meanwhile, Mexico faced loss: loss of land and resources, of status and esteem, and of North American dominance. Decades of political and social instability and economic underdevelopment afflicted the country, smothering any hopes of a return to its former glory. Del Castillo contends that, though they may not know it, Mexican Americans to this day carry with them a sense of lost pride dating back to the Texas Revolution and the Mexican-American War.[35]

The United States has made some strides in race relations since the 1850s, obviously, and Mexican Americans are now a celebrated part of American, and Texan, history and culture. In May 2009 the Texas legislature passed HB4114, authorizing the placement of a Tejano monument on the south grounds of the Texas State Capitol. Rep. Trey Martinez Fisher stated at the signing, "Tejanos have played a role in Texas history before there was a Texas, and contributed to the rich and diverse culture our state is known for."[36] But as the Mexican American population grows, so may the fears and concerns of a dwindling white majority.

But the fate of Mexican Americans is not the only theme from the Mexican-American War that continues to resonate in modern times. Issues concerning the politics of the conflict remain particularly relevant in today's society. Abiel Livermore's 1850 book, *The War with Mexico Reviewed,* won the American Peace Society award for the "best review of the Mexican-American War on the principles of Christianity."[37] The work had an obvious pacifist stance, as one might suspect, and never quite edged its way into mainstream historical discourse. But Livermore presented dissenting views that should strike a familiar chord with modern readers. He complained that the war was illegal, "unnecessarily and unconstitutionally begun," and then continued without an act of war from Congress. He had concerns that it was really fought to expand slavery and that other possible reasons (manifest destiny, among others) were merely pretext. He asserted that the war did "incalculable harm to the cause of liberty throughout the country and the world."[38] Finally, he bemoaned that the new worldview of the United States was now one stigmatized by aggression and perpetrated by fear. Personal political affiliations aside, similarities to the recent conflict in Iraq are undeniable—not similarities to the war itself necessarily, but certainly to public opinion about it.

Livermore may not have been mainstream media, but he was not alone in his opposition. In *Invading Mexico: America's Continental Dreams and the Mexican War,* Joseph Wheelan devotes a chapter to "Dissent, Patriotism, and the Press," which includes excerpts of several poems, news articles, and other print material against the war.[39] He also notes the fine line journalists had to toe between supporting the troops and criticizing the government. In Congress Whigs had a similar problem, decrying the conflict in Whig newspapers such as the *New York Tribune* and the *National Intelligencer* while remaining supportive of Whig generals Winfield Scott and Zachary Taylor. They denounced the war but approved funding for it so as not to seem antimilitary. Whigs attacked Polk for lying to draw the United States into war and using stampede tactics to hurriedly push legislation. The president countered by claiming that speaking out against him and the war effort gave "aid and comfort to the enemy."[40] Politicians felt pressure from their constituents and their own consciences to end the war, and midterm elections shifted the balance of power in Congress from pro-war Democrats to antiwar Whigs.

This was the first important antiwar movement in America, the other notables being Vietnam and Iraq. Each of these three wars began under questionable circumstances (Texas border, Gulf of Tonkin, weapons of mass destruction) and dragged on for years afterward. The saving grace of the Spanish-American War, in Wheelan's opinion, is that it ended before people could get worked up against it.[41]

Such similarities can bring dialogue of the Mexican-American War into the twenty-first century. Discussion need not devolve into a political debate. Rather, let it be a jumping-off point for analysis of the possible motives for the Mexican-American War much as newsroom pundits busy themselves analyzing contemporary events. The correlations between the antiwar movements show that the politics surrounding national events existed then much the way they do now. That is a connection contemporary historians can explore.

What public historians really look for in historical events are context and relationships. How does the past relate to the present? What can we learn about those experiences and how can we apply those lessons? How can we convey that information to new audiences? How do we engage? Relevance is the key; it is what makes people care. In the information-overload society we live in, historians have to fight for their place in the world, for their own sliver of attention. I feel the Mexican-American War has plenty of relevance in today's society, and others would believe it too if we could only get the chance to show them. But there are too few Palo Alto Battlefields and Aztec Clubs, not enough Fort Browns and Bayview Cemeteries. Historians need to take an active interest in the Mexican-American War before we can convince others to do so as well.

During the sesquicentennial of the Treaty of Guadalupe-Hidalgo, beginning in 1998, Miguel Breto of the Smithsonian Institution expressed regret that there were no plans for a major exhibition and concluded that an important opportunity had been lost. He was right. What he did not know at the time was that the Autry Museum of Western Heritage (now the Museum of the American West) in Los Angeles had developed such an exhibit. *Culture y Cultura: How the U.S. Mexican War Shaped the West* sought to "address the significant historical forces that have determined what it means to be Mexican American." It examined the struggle for equality and those ramifications on the Mexican American character. The museum offered traveling versions of the exhibit and published a book with a similar if not identical title and purpose.[42] The printed version is informative, interesting, and insightful. I suspect that the exhibit was also, but probably conspicuous in its singularity. It was indeed a lost opportunity to educate the public about the consequences of the Mexican-American War.

With the 150th anniversary of the Civil War beginning in 2011 will come untold numbers of articles, exhibits, reenactments, and other festivities commemorating the conflict. Historians no doubt will capitalize on the anniversary to further historical research and academic discourse. But as Julie Holcomb points out in her essay "Tell it Like it Was," public historians have had their share of problems interpreting that war as well and continue to struggle with the balance of accurate history and public sentiment. On the issue of slavery, Civil War sites have been accused of both glossing over it as a key element in the interpretation of events and straying too far from historical fact when addressing that aspect of the personal narrative. In short, they either address slavery too much or not enough. Holcomb states:

> Until the 1990s most public historians avoided any discussion of the causes and
> consequences of the war in their institution's exhibits and program. Yet there are
> signs that this attitude is beginning to shift. Change is being driven by the grow-
> ing body of scholarship about slavery and the Civil War, the growing number of
> African American history museums, the increasing emphasis on education and
> professionalism for public historians, and the continuing work of the American
> Association of Museums and other public and academic professional organiza-
> tions in addressing diversity issues at museums.[43]

Interpretation of the Mexican-American War stands to benefit from some of the
changes mentioned above: emphasis on education and professionalism and the efforts of
national organizations to address diversity issues. Certainly scholarship on that war has
flourished recently. But Holcomb cites the increased occurrence of African American
history museums as an important factor in shifting public perception about the Civil
War. Is there an increase in museums presenting Hispanic heritage and history? County
and general history museums in South and West Texas reflect their demographics and
include more Hispanics in their local histories. But does Texas have any dedicated
Mexican American museums to relate and interpret historical events from a strictly
Hispanic perspective or that speak specifically to the Hispanic experience?

TexasTejano.com, a firm based in San Antonio, is at the forefront of Tejano history and public programming in Texas. The company has traveling exhibits and plenty
of information and educational materials telling the stories of Mexican Americans in
the state.[44] Plans are underway for the creation of a Hispanic Heritage Center of Texas
in San Antonio, but at present no such center exists at a physical location. When it
opens, it could provide the inclusive window into the Tejano experience that seems to be
lacking.

As Holcomb mentions, the rise of African American museums and their unique
interpretation of historical issues such as slavery have influenced how existing Civil
War museums and sites present those topics. Yet there are few significant Mexican-
American War sites that could be influenced by the Hispanic Heritage Center even if
it existed. Actually, the Palo Alto Battlefield near Brownsville remains the only historic
site in Texas devoted solely to Mexican-American War interpretation and education.
Until more sites and museums include exhibits or historical narratives about that war
in their programs, it will be hard to raise awareness of the topic or generate a dialogue
about its aftermath with the public.

At the time of its exhibit, the Autry Museum of Western Heritage conducted focus groups and found that both within and outside of the Mexican American community, there was little knowledge of the Mexican-American War and its legacy. But focus-group participants showed a great desire to learn. That eagerness is a good sign, though without resources to pursue their interest in the topic, the opportunity to educate is squandered. It falls to public historians to provide access to information, research, analysis, collections, and exhibits that teach students and the general public about the Mexican-American War.

Perhaps a renewed partnership with the lineage and veterans organizations that were so instrumental in creating the first monuments to the war is in order. In addition to erecting plaques in historic cemeteries, members should be active participants in the development and implementation of programming and events commemorating the Mexican-American War. The involvement of veterans organizations combined with the growing efforts of Hispanic heritage groups could finally provide a more complete presentation of the national landscape that bore the conflict and the legacy it left behind. The more public historians and academics work together to explore those aspects of the war, the more the public can learn about them in museums and heritage sites across Texas. Through dedication and education, the Mexican-American War can step out of the shadows of Texas history and receive the recognition that has eluded it.

Notes

1. Charles M. Haecker and Jeffrey G.: *Historical Archaeology of the US-Mexican War Battlefield* (College Station: Texas A&M University Press, 1997), 54–55. See also National Park Service, "Management," Palo Alto Battlefield National Historic Site, http://www.nps.gov/paal/parkmgmt/index.htm.

2. Richard Griswold del Castillo, "Los Niños Héroes," in *The United States and Mexico at War: Nineteenth-Century Expansionism and Conflict*, ed. Donald S. Frazier (New York: Macmillan, 1998), 230.

3. Steven R. Butler, "Monuments and Memorials," in Frazier, *United States and Mexico at War*, 275.

4. Richard Hoag Breithaupt Jr. *The Aztec Club of 1847: Military Society of the Mexican War. Sesquicentennial History, 1847–1997* (Los Angeles: Published by the Society, 1998), 1–7.

5. Ibid., 26–80, 755.

6. Steven R. Butler, "Veterans Organizations," in Frazier, *United States and Mexico at War*, 461.

7. Haecker and Mauck, *On the Prairie of Palo Alto*, 5, 91. See also Charles M. Robinson III, *Texas and the Mexican War: A History and a Guide* (Austin: Texas State Historical Association, 2004), 2; and Joseph Wheelan, *Invading Mexico: America's Continental Dreams and the Mexican War, 1846–1848* (New York: Carroll and Graf, 2007), 416.

8. Americans made forays into Canadian territory during the War of 1812, yet an overwhelming number of sources on the Mexican War cite Mexico as the first foreign invasion.

Perhaps that is because the 1812 army was comprised mostly of militiamen, because those ventures into Canada were generally brief and unsuccessful, or because Canada was considered a territory of Britain and not a foreign country—I am not sure. I comply with the majority of the sources in making the first-foreign-invasion claim.

9. The Nueces River is relatively close to the Rio Grande in some areas of South Texas. The implications for territory gained or lost based on those rivers, however, were considerable. The Rio Grande continues its flow across the length of modern-day Texas and up through New Mexico and Colorado, whereas the Nueces essentially peters out approximately halfway across the state. Therefore, when charting the boundary based on the flow of either river, the land disputed by Mexico and Texas included roughly half of modern-day Texas plus sections of New Mexico, Colorado, and even Wyoming. The final determination of the southern boundary was significant.

10. Otis Singletary, *The Mexican War* (Chicago: University of Chicago Press, 1960), vi–2.

11. K. Jack Bauer, *The Mexican War, 1846–1848* (New York: Macmillan, 1974), 396.

12. Richard Pyle, "19th Century Papers Shed New Light on Origin of the Associated Press," Jan. 31, 2005, Press Releases, The Associated Press, http://www.ap.org/pages/about/whatsnew/wn_013106a.html.

13. Tom Reilly, "Newspapers," in Frazier, *United States and Mexico at War*, 294.

14. Although other works were consulted, for these generalizations I am relying most heavily on Singletary, *Mexican War*, vi–5, 56–65. These interpretations likely were attempts at a more understanding and objective view of the war in contrast to early twentieth-century publications, which exhibited a nationalistic bias. Those in turn stood in contrast to the rather pessimistic accounts offered by disenchanted army officers and read by the public beginning immediately after the war.

15. Santa Anna returned to power in Mexico with US assistance. He had been living in exile in Havana when President Polk heard that he may be open to working with the United States. Polk sent a naval officer to negotiate an agreement, and the exiled dictator was quick to play along so he could return to Mexico through the American blockade. By the time Santa Anna got to the coast, two more Mexican governments had fallen. He viewed this as an opportunity to lead the nation to victory and committed to war. Robinson, *Texas and the Mexican War*, 55–56.

16. Ibid., 5.

17. See Jesus Velasco-Marquez and Richard Griswold del Castillo, "Legacy of War," in Frazier, *United States and Mexico at War*, 223–25.

18. Within a year of the war's end, gold was found in California. Had it been found only months earlier, Mexico would have reaped the rewards instead of thousands of American forty-niners. This is in addition to the silver mined in New Mexico, the oil drilled in Texas, and the general agricultural and industrial boom enjoyed by most of the American Southwest in the first half of the twentieth century.

19. John Lynch, "Causes of War," in Frazier, *United States and Mexico at War*, 85.

20. David Montejano, *Anglos and Mexicans in the Making of Texas, 1836–1986* (Austin: University of Texas Press, 1987), 26. Seguin may not have been technically forced out of Texas, but conflicts with Anglos, debts, and perceived collusion with Mexican military operations impelled him to flee to Mexico, possibly in fear for his safety.

21. Ibid., 315.

22. Arnolde de Leon, "Racism," in Frazier, *United States and Mexico at War*, 347.

23. Montejano, *Anglos and Mexicans in the Making of Texas*, 311.

24. Ibid., 38, 52.

25. Iris Wilson Engstrand, Richard Griswold del Castillo, and Elena Poniatowska, *Culture y Cultura: Consequences of the U.S.-Mexican War, 1846–1848* (Los Angeles: Autry Museum of Western Heritage, 1998), 76.

26. Humberto Garza, *The Mexican American War of 1846–1848: A Deceitful Smoke Screen* (San Jose, CA: Sun House, 2006), 4.

27. Ibid., 6–8.

28. Arnoldo De León, *They Called Them Greasers: Anglo Attitudes toward Mexicans in Texas, 1821–1900* (Austin: University of Texas Press, 1983), 75.

29. Charles C. Cumberland, "Border Raids in the Lower Rio Grande Valley—1915," *Southwestern Historical Quarterly* 57 (Jan. 1954): 290–92, 300 (quote).

30. For more about Pershing and his views on Mexico, see John Edward Weems, *To Conquer a Peace: The War between the United States and Mexico* (Garden City, NY: Doubleday, 1974). In his epilogue Weems addresses both Pershing's frustration with the Mexican government and his opinion that the best solution for peace along the border was conquering Mexico.

31. Engstrand et al., *Culture y Cultura,* 77. See also Montejano, *Anglos and Mexicans in the Making of Texas,* 316.

32. Engstrand et al., *Culture y Cultura,* 78–80.

33. Garza, *Mexican American War,* vii (quote), 6 (quote). For the California border, see ibid., 165–68.

34. Marquez and del Castillo, "Legacy of War," 225.

35. Engstrand et al., *Culture y Cultura,* 76. There was dispute over the border after a flood permanently altered the course of the Rio Grande. In December 1963 the United States and Mexico signed the Chamizal Convention, which returned 630 acres to Mexico.

36. Press Release, "Gov. Perry Signs Legislation to Place Tejano Monument on Capitol Grounds," May 29, 2009, Office of the Governor, http://governor.state.tx.us/news/press-release/12433/.

37. Abiel Abbot Livermore, *The War with Mexico Reviewed* (Boston: Crosby and Nichols, 1850; repr., Chicano Heritage Series, New York: Arno, 1976), vi.

38. Ibid., 163, 170.

39. Wheelan, *Invading Mexico,* 258, 297.

40. Frederick Merk, "Dissent in the Mexican War," in *Dissent in Three American Wars,* ed. Samuel Eliot Morrison et al. (Cambridge, MA: Harvard University Press, 1971), 39–55 (quote, 47).

41. Wheelan, *Invading Mexico,* xix.

42. Engstrand et al., *Culture y Cultura,* viii–ix.

43. Julie Holcomb, "'Tell it Like it Was': Texas, the Civil War, and Public History," in *The Fate of Texas: The Civil War and the Lone Star State,* ed. Charles D. Grear (Fayetteville: University of Arkansas Press, 2008), 182–83.

44. James M. Smallwood, Barry A. Crouch, and Larry Peacock, *Murder and Mayhem: The War of Reconstruction in Texas* (College Station: Texas A&M University, 2003), 27.

9

The Prolonged War

Texans Struggle to Win the Civil War during Reconstruction

Kenneth W. Howell

TRADITIONALLY, HISTORIANS have viewed the American Civil War (1861–65) and the Reconstruction era (1865–77) as two distinct and separate periods in US history. Though this approach provides a convenient way to understand two very complex eras, it tends to skew the general understanding of the violence that remained commonplace in the South during Reconstruction. Scholarly celebrations of the Union victory in the Civil War tend to ignore the fact that the US government ultimately failed to rehabilitate southern society in the decades following the war. A more constructive way to study these two periods is to examine them as two distinct phases of a continuous conflict between the northern and southern states lasting from 1861 to 1877.

In the first phase of the war (1861–65), the US and Confederate governments used conventional military forces to achieve their respective goals: Federal troops fought to preserve the Union, and after the Emancipation Proclamation went into effect in January 1863, to end slavery. The Confederate military fought to win southern independence and to preserve the institution of slavery. The larger population, greater industrial capabilities, and naval superiority of the northern states dictated almost from the very beginning that the Union would win what became a war of attrition.

During the second phase of the war (1865–77), sometimes referred to as the War of Reconstruction, whites organized terrorist groups and initiated a prolonged guerrilla war against Republican governments in the southern states that sought to force political and social change. Given that Radical Republicans supported federal and state legislation that would guarantee African Americans suffrage rights and other freedoms, white southerners became concerned about potential changes to their political institutions.

Thomas Nast, Worse Than Slavery. *Reproduced from* Harper's Weekly, *1874.*

They believed that suffrage for former slaves would ultimately lead to complete social and political equality for southern blacks. Perhaps more than any other southern state, Texas became a bloody battleground during this second phase of the struggle between North and South.

Shortly after the fall of the Confederacy, most Texas unionists hoped to cooperate with federal authorities and bring positive change to their state. They believed cooperation was the only way to escape punitive actions such as treason trials, martial law, and a lengthy period of military occupation. On July 17, 1865, a group of North Texas unionists met in convention at Paris, in Lamar County, to swear loyalty to the national government and to vow their willingness to follow the law. The delegates elected W. B. Gray of Titus County as their president; T. G. Wright of Red River County as their vice president; and E. L. Dohoney of Lamar County as their secretary. Gray impressed upon all the importance of cooperating with the US government. He told his fellow delegates that such cooperation might eliminate the need for military occupation and for coercive legislation. Being a realist, he counseled obedience and submission for the good of Texas. Shortly afterward, Rice Maxey motioned that the convention should create a resolutions committee to draft a document to explain their views and that copies of such a statement should be forwarded to Washington. Additionally, Maxey suggested that they should distribute copies to newspapers and to the public. The delegates agreed and voted in favor of the motion; Gray appointed Maxey as chair of the committee. Other committeemen included R. H. Taylor and Sam G. Galbraith of Fannin County; William M. Ewing, L. A. Lollar, and Joseph Smith of Hopkins County; Hardin Hart and M. H. Wright of Hunt County; Henry Jones of Titus County; and W. H. Johnson, G. W. Wright, and E. W. Miner of Lamar County. The committee produced a document stating that military rule was accepted until such time that the provisional governor was satisfied that Texans would "give evidence of their loyal dispositions to the Government of the United States, and a willingness to yield obedience to the Constitution and laws there of."[1]

It was probably fitting that such a proclamation came out of Northeast Texas, where a majority of the citizens of many counties had voted against secession. But the unionists' dreams of a peaceful reconciliation with the federal government proved to be just that—dreams. The plan of those men was the best hope for an alternate history, one that would have led to a constructive rather than destructive Reconstruction, but forces at work at the end of the war dashed all their hopes. Instead of making progress, Texas became a dark and bloody ground—the home of terrorist groups and outlaw gangs that were supported by the Democratic Party so long as the malefactors fought for the goals of the party. Even before the Paris meeting, Texas was spinning out of control.

Following Gen. Robert E. Lee's surrender to Lt. Gen. Ulysses S. Grant at Appomattox on April 9, 1865, the local and state governments in Texas collapsed, leaving vast regions in total chaos. Armed bands of former soldiers, deserters, and common criminals swarmed though various areas. For example, in Tyler lawlessness became commonplace. During the war, the town was home to various Confederate installations, including a post commissary, a wartime prison, an armory, a pharmaceutical laboratory, and a quartermaster's warehouse. Immediately following the war, local women forced their way into the laboratory, taking whatever they wished; also, desperate people with hungry families tried but failed to break into the commissary.[2] Some local men tried to steal the horses on the post, but the commanding officer held them off, while Confederates blew up the armory rather than let panicky men, who could not be trusted, secure arms and ammunition. Many area women were afraid to leave their homes for fear of robbers. Nevertheless, some did so, but most went armed and rode in groups of three or more for collective protection. Worse developments were averted when a company of Union troopers temporarily stopped in Tyler.[3] But even as the cavalrymen tried to restore order, Kate Stone, a transplanted Louisiana aristocrat temporarily living in town, reported that there were "four or five men shot or hanged within a few miles of us in a week."[4]

On June 11, unknown parties even looted the state treasury in Austin, much to the disgust of officials who vainly tried to protect the treasury and restore order to the capital. The robbers successfully made their move in the middle of the night, disappearing in the cover of darkness before anyone could react. As happened in Tyler and Austin, all across Texas mobs of men and women looted places such as Confederate commissaries, stealing all things of utilitarian value. Men swarmed over supply depots, looting them for arms, ammunition, and anything else useful. Some even robbed private homes, threatening the owners with death should they resist.[5] This early mayhem was ongoing even though Confederates still controlled the state, suggesting that this violence was not part of any organized attempt to continue the war against the federal government. Instead, locals were attempting to survive the failed economic and political systems left behind in the wake of the fallen Confederacy. Nevertheless, events would quickly unfold that would cause the southern states, especially Texas, to renew their fight against the national government.

On June 19, 1865, Maj. Gen. Gordon Granger landed in Galveston and was welcomed by area unionists. Commanding 1,800 men, the general announced that Lincoln's Emancipation Proclamation would be enforced in Texas. From the moment he reached Galveston, Granger's command was a difficult one. Given that the troops at his disposal did not even have the strength of two full regiments, he could only send small detachments to the interior, though they did go to Tyler, Marshall, Austin, and San Antonio. The general, like other commanders who were later stationed there, never had enough troops to adequately police the state, a fact that doomed would-be Reconstruction reformers like the men of Northeast Texas. Despite the fact that Union forces in Texas rose to a high of 51,000 in 1865, the number of soldiers in state drastically fell to a mere 3,000 by the end of 1866, with most of them defending the western frontier from Indian raids.[6]

Meanwhile, violence continued unabated, undercutting reformers' hopes for the era and pushing Reconstruction policies along a path bound for failure. By the late spring and summer of 1865, whites were beating, whipping, and killing black Texans. Most of the freedpeople became victims of crimes because of their new status in society; they became victims of irrational racial hatred. In many cases the perpetrators were young men, most Confederate veterans. They hated the Yankees and the outcome of the war, and in their frustration they targeted freedpeople and white unionists, the very groups that supported Reconstruction policies and who were least able to protect themselves. One historian listed the reasons why Anglos killed freedmen: "[F]reedman did not remove hat when he passed him [a white man]; Negro would not allow himself to be whipped; freedman would not allow his wife to be whipped by a white man; he [a freedman] was carrying a letter to a Freedmen's Bureau official; [one murderer killed] Negroes just to see them kick; [one white killed] because he wanted to thin out niggers a little; [freedman] did not hand over his money quick enough; [freedman] would not give up his whiskey flask."[7] Even though rational minds today consider these explanations absurd, the majority of white Texans during the late nineteenth century believed in the absolute right of white supremacy. In an atmosphere of racial hatred in which the least provocation could lead to an uncontrollable riot, whites waged war against black Texans and their white allies. Contemporaries often commented about the treatment of freedpeople and unionists.

From Paris, Mrs. L. E. Potts wrote to Pres. Andrew Johnson providing personal testimony to events unfolding in her area of the state. She reported, "I wish that my poor pen could tell you of their [freedpeople] persecutions here. They are now just out of slavery only a few months, and their masters are so angry to lose them that they are trying to persecute them back into slavery." She continued by stating that "there have never been any federal troops in here, and everything savors of rebellion. I wish we could have a few soldiers here just for a while, to let these rebels know that they have been whipped." Potts concluded her letter with a plea for the president to take some action to save the freedpeople, stating: "your good heart and wise head know best what to do. I have stated only facts; the negroes need protection here. When they work they scarcely ever get any pay; and what are they to do?" Potts, however, placed too much faith in Johnson, for he simply turned the matter over to Maj. Gen. Oliver Otis Howard, the head of the Bureau of Refugees, Freedmen, and Abandoned Lands, giving little more thought to the suffering African Americans in Texas.[8]

At about the same time that Potts wrote her letter, Bvt. Maj. Gen. George Armstrong Custer observed the activities of unrepentant rebels in East, South, and Central Texas. In the summer of 1865, General Granger ordered Custer and his regiment of cavalry from Alexandria, Louisiana, to Houston to help support his efforts in Texas. After suffering organizational problems, Custer's regiment left Alexandria on August 8, crossed the Sabine River, and made its way into Texas. While in route, Granger ordered Custer to bypass Houston and march directly to the rural community of Hempstead, where the troopers would find an abundance of grass and forage for their horses. The regiment remained stationed just outside of the small Texas town until the end of October, when it moved westward to make Austin its new headquarters.[9]

Following his service in the Lone Star State, Custer reported to the Joint Committee on Reconstruction at the first session of the Thirty-Ninth Congress in March 1866. Congress created this special committee in an effort to learn more about conditions in the South. After extensive inquiry, the committee's final report aided lawmakers in establishing more-effective policies to bring the embittered South back into the Union. Custer, like many of those who testified before the legislators, reinforced the idea that certain areas in Texas were still in a virtual state of war. He stated, "[I]n Texas it would hardly be possible to find a man who has been strictly faithful to the Union, and remained in the South, during the war. They [rebels] forced all who were truly Union men to leave the state. Those who did not were murdered. The people of the north have no conception of the number of murders that have been committed in that state during and since the war." Custer was certain that it would not be "safe for a loyal man to remain in Texas [once] . . . troops were withdrawn." When asked if he knew of any organizations there that were attempting to thwart the actions of the federal government, the officer replied: "[I]t was reported to me frequently that such organizations did exist, and I have no doubt in my mind that they have existed in the northern part of the state. I was so thoroughly convinced of the fact that I sent a considerable force into that section of the state to disperse them. The fact that such organizations did exist was confirmed by the statements, written and oral, of loyal men, and by the reports of officers sent there on duty." Perhaps the most revealing aspect of Custer's testimony came when the joint committee inquired whether Texans, if offered the opportunity to secede without war, would stay in the Union or would leave. Custer simply replied, "I think they would prefer to go out." His insights were correct. Ex-Confederates, former secessionists, and conservative Democrats wanted to remain as far removed from federal control as possible, and many were willing to continue to wage guerilla war to accomplish their purpose.[10]

Custer also made lengthy comments regarding the conditions of freedpeople in Texas, revealing that blacks suffered even greater atrocities than loyal (white) Union men. "There is a very strong feeling of hostility towards the freedmen as a general thing," stated the general. He continued, "There are exceptions, of course; but the great mass of the people there seem to look upon the freedmen as being connected with, or as being the cause of, their present condition, and they do not hesitate to improve every opportunity to inflict injuries upon [them] in order, seemingly, to punish [them] for this." According to Custer, freedpeople could not find justice in Texas courts. Whites frequently murdered the ex-slaves for the slightest provocations, and in some cases, they killed blacks for no provocations at all. The murderers were rarely brought before a judge for their heinous crimes. Even in the cases where the killers were tried, white juries acquitted them. Because of such harsh treatment, Custer surmised that the freed-people would remain "loyal without a single exception" to the federal government. He further stated that "they realize, as all Union men in the state do, that their only safety and protection lies in the general government; and they realize too, that if the troops are withdrawn, they will be still more exposed than they are now."[11]

One might wonder why whites felt that they could, with impunity, whip or kill freedpeople. After all, the South appeared to have lost the Civil War. Explanations are not that complex, and one need only look to Presidential Reconstruction to find answers. White Texans after the Civil War were afraid of northern revenge. Some who supported the Confederacy believed that they might be held accountable for their treasonous acts against the federal government. A few of the larger slaveholders, high-ranking state officials, and Confederate officers chose self-exile and left the country, some going to Mexico or Brazil, while others went to Europe.[12]

Both their fears and their escapes were premature, however; for under Abraham Lincoln and Andrew Johnson, the government's position was not to pursue charges of treason against those who voluntarily sought to destroy the Union and the Constitution by force. Additionally, the Lincoln and Johnson administrations pursued a lenient policy toward southerners. Lincoln's prescription for renewing the Union was called the "Ten Percent" plan, which required almost nothing of the defeated South. The president was willing to restore the former Confederate states to the Union when just 10 percent of their voters swore allegiance to the United States and their state governments had ratified the Thirteenth Amendment, which abolished slavery. After John Wilkes Booth murdered Lincoln, the new president, Andrew Johnson, initiated his own lenient policy of reconciliation. Both men made the decision that race relations were to be best managed at the state level; consequently, the presidential plans included few if any safe-guards for the new freedpeople.[13]

The former Confederates, including those in leadership positions in Texas, inter-preted these "lenient" plans as signs of presidential weakness, for many whites began to obstruct federal operations in the South. With a newfound confidence, they began to seek ways to retain as much of the Old South's traditions as possible, including white supremacy short of reestablishing slavery, which most people considered a dead issue after 1865. In Texas various newspaper editors even predicted that it might be possible to replace slavery with a new labor system that would retain many of the old attributes of involuntary servitude. They were correct. The answer turned out to be sharecropping, an economic institution that entrapped most poor blacks and thousands of poor whites in a state of permanent poverty, that lasted well into the twentieth century.

While Mrs. Potts and General Custer both witnessed racial atrocities after the fall of the Confederacy, economic circumstances also served as an underlying cause of violence in 1865. High prices on cotton led many planters and yeoman farmers to borrow heavily to get back into cotton production. But agrarians were too successful; a glut developed that drove prices down to approximately 50 percent of peak prices in early summer. Rather than suffer loses, many planters and farmers passed the loss down to their laborers (sharecroppers). Early Freedmen's Bureau figures suggest that about 90 percent of employers simply refused to pay wages to their workers. If the laborers complained, the landowners drove them off their property, especially when the share-croppers were freedpeople. In most of these cases, the landowner claimed that the black workers had "run off" and had therefore broken the provisions of their labor contracts, surrendering their wages in the process. When trouble with disgruntled laborers continued, the employers often paid outlaw gangs to force them off their land at gunpoint—or if that failed, to kill them. Some of the more notorious bands of outlaws engaged in this type of activity operated in Northeast Texas and were led by ruthless men such as Ben Bickerstaff, Bob Lee, and Cullen Montgomery Baker.[14]

As part of Johnson's plan of Reconstruction, he appointed provisional governors in each of the southern states to oversee the process establishing new loyal governments. Accordingly, he selected a pre–Civil War unionist, Andrew Jackson Hamilton, as the provisional governor of Texas. Hamilton's primary assignment was to call a state constitutional convention. As part of Johnson's plan, the president required each southern state to create a new constitution before it could be readmitted to the Union. Yet before a governor could call for a convention, he had to make sure that enough Union men were in place at the local level to register loyal voters. Given the true nature of anti-government sentiments in Texas, Hamilton found his job near impossible, especially considering the widespread violence waged against loyal Union men. Nevertheless, on November 15, 1865, he issued a proclamation that called on Texas voters to go to the polls on January 8, 1866, to elect a slate of delegates to a constitutional convention that would convene in Austin on February 7. Political strife soon engulfed the state as election day approached. In Ellis County one candidate stated that "if he had the power he would have swept the last Northerner off the face of God's Earth." It was reported that after these comments, the crowd cheered so loud that "glass fell out of the windows."[15] In the same county another prominent citizen stated that "if he now had the power he would sink the entire [national] Republican party forty thousand feet below the Mudsills of Hell."[16] Such political vitriol was commonplace in January 1866, and it carried over into the constitutional convention that met in February.

Delegates to the constitutional convention met between February 7 and April 2, creating a new system of government for the state. In the process they declared the secession ordinance null and void, repudiated the state debt, and recognized the end of slavery, even though they refused to officially ratify the Thirteenth Amendment. In an effort to thwart Hamilton's plan to provide the freedmen limited rights, delegates denied blacks the right to vote, hold political office, serve on juries, or give legal testimony against whites in court cases. Before adjourning, convention members set June 25 as the date for the referendum on the newly created state document and for election of new officials under its provisions.[17]

Undoubtedly, many ex-Confederate and conservative Democrats celebrated the outcome of the June 25 referendum; the voters overwhelmingly approved the new constitution and elected James Webb Throckmorton as governor. The people of Texas also elected a slate of conservative Democrats, ex-Confederates, and former secessionists to the legislature. The election of these men meant that Hamilton's plan for reconstructing the state, in essence, had failed. With conservative Democrat and ex-Confederates in office, anti-Union forces now controlled the state. The only obstacle that prevented them from absolute authority was the US military still stationed in the state, agents of the Freedmen's Bureau, and a handful of loyal unionists who were not yet willing to concede victory to pro-Confederate Democrats.[18]

Once the state government was in place, the public waited to see how a conservative legislature would deal with the new realities in Texas. Among the assembly's first actions was to create the infamous 1866 "Black Codes" that returned the freedpeople to a status that resembled antebellum slavery. Now codified, black Texans could not vote nor hold political office, could not serve on juries nor testify in cases involving whites, could not marry whites nor claim land under the Texas Homestead Law, and could not escape segregation on common carriers nor share in public school funds. An apprenticeship law potentially gave whites control of underage blacks either with parental consent or by the order of a county judge. Also heinous was the Contract Labor Code, which forced blacks to sign twelve-month contracts for jobs lasting more than one month. The labor code gave employers certain judicial rights. They could fine workers who failed to perform their work, who damaged tools, who left without permission, or who were generally disobedient.[19]

Related was the Vagrancy Code. Local authorities could issue fines to blacks who were deemed vagrants, especially if they did not have a steady job or any money in their possession. Those who could not pay the fines (which most could not) were arrested and contracted out to local businesses or landowners until their bogus "debt to society" was paid in full. The Convict-Lease Code entrapped blacks whom judges and juries sent to county jails or to the state prison. Such unfortunates could be contracted out to private employers and forced to work for little except room and board. Thus whites effectively had imposed a type of semi-slavery upon the black community, reducing the status of freedpeople to second-class citizens.[20]

By the time the legislature passed the 1866 codes, it was clear that many white Texans had not given up on the Civil War. They continued to fight it, though in a new guise: a guerrilla war in which partisans had both a military and a political role to play. Over time, from 1865 to around 1874, seventy-seven Texas counties gave birth to terrorist groups that went by many names: the Ku Klux Klan, the Knights of the White Camellia, the Knights of the Rising Son, the Red Hand, and the Ku Klux Rangers. The formation of several of these groups even preceded the founding of the historic Ku Klux Klan in Tennessee in 1866. Regardless of their chosen name, these terrorist organizations had the same goals: enforce the doctrine of white supremacy by any means necessary, including violence, and assist former Confederates in the redemption of the state, using the Democratic Party as their vehicle. Indeed, many of the terrorist groups became an informal paramilitary arm of the Democrats.[21]

Outlaw gangs also were legion and did much damage. Some became an informal second paramilitary force that used the Democratic Party and in turn were used by the party. The members of many criminal gangs wrapped themselves in the Confederate flag, proclaimed loyalty to the Lost Cause, and then proceeded to do their worst. Former Confederate Democrats tended to look the "other way" so long as such gangs only targeted freedpeople, native unionists, and the federal troops who eventually occupied various parts of the Lone Star State. For example, in Northeast Texas, gangs coalesced around such desperadoes as Benjamin Bickerstaff, Cullen Montgomery Baker, Bob Lee, Elisha Guest, Ben Griffin, Henry Farrar, John "Pomp" Duty, "Indian Bill" English, George English, John Marshall, Tom Emmitt, and a host of others. Each of these men claimed to be fighting for the Lost Cause while truly seeking plunder. Indeed, Bob Lee was once heard to say that he would fight the Yankees "from the thickets and canebrakes of Texas for a hundred years if necessary" if that is what it took to win the Civil War.[22] Their claims of fighting for the Lost Cause resonated with people in the communities where the gangs traveled, providing them with a shield of protection against federal authorities.

Terrorist Klan groups and many—but not all—outlaw bands had common characteristics. The major goal of such groups was to thwart the Reconstruction pr cess because it threatened the antebellum status quo by raising the status of freedmen. Rampant racism was a major factor, for the majority of whites believed that blacks had no rights at all and should still show much deference in all matters involving whites. Such people were willing to use persuasion, intimidation, and violence when necessary to achieve this goal. They were most willing to kill if that is what it took to defeat the proposed reforms that Reconstruction was meant to impart. The groups objected greatly to the federal government's decision to abolish slavery, Aristotle's mudsill for Western civilization of which the slaveholders of the Old South had made maximum use. Indeed, the existence of southern slavery—and the strident demand that the national government protect its expansion—was the major cause of the Civil War. The Union's victorious armies, of course, meant the end of slavery.[23]

Beginning in December 1866, congressional Republicans declared Presidential Reconstruction a failure and took steps to seize control of the process from Johnson by passing the Civil Rights Act of 1866, the Freedmen's Bureau Act, and the Fourteenth Amendment over the president's veto. In an effort to solidify its control of Reconstruction, Congress next passed the Reconstruction Acts. The first of these measures, passed on March 2, 1867, abolished the existing state governments in the former Confederate states except in Tennessee, where the state legislature had ratified the Thirteenth Amendment. Subsequent legislation divided the southern states into five military districts, instituted martial law, disenfranchised former Confederate leaders, and established procedures by which these states would create new constitutions and ensure the protection of African American civil rights.[24]

As Congress gained control of the process, white Texans claimed that Radical Republicans in Washington were attempting to dominate their state through Negro-Carpetbag-Scalawag rule. "Carpetbagger" and "scalawag" were derogatory terms: A carpetbagger was a northern migrant who came to the South after the war. Scalawags were native southerners who remained loyal to the Union and supported federal policies, especially those of Radical Republicans in Congress. In southern newspapers and posted broadsides, Texas politicians outlined how congressional Republicans intended to impose military rule over the South and to force black domination on them, changing the system of white supremacy that had been in place prior to the establishment of the Republic of Texas. In response to these perceived threats, ex-Confederates and conservative Democrats joined forces to expand the already violent guerilla war that had plagued the state.[25]

As Texas became increasingly involved in this second phase of the Civil War, many northern newspaper editors and their correspondents reported on the runaway violence in the state between 1866 and 1869. For example, New York newspapers labeled the violence in Texas as "THE NEW REBELLION" along with other headlines that read "SULPHUR SPRINGS—ARMED DESPRADOES SCOURING EASTERN TEXAS—A REIGN OF TERROR." The story that followed the headlines was based on a report by Lt. Charles Vernou, who was sent to Northeast Texas to investigate the rampant violence in that region. Vernou reported that on August 30, 1866, Cullen Baker and a party number-ing at least thirty men, including Bickerstaff and some of his men, attacked him in the Bois D'Arc Creek bottoms. The lieutenant rode away, but the desperadoes chased him for several miles before he reached a farm in Lamar County that he had bought earlier that year, escaping them by riding into some dense woods and hiding in a thicket. Not finding him, the attackers beat a black sharecropper in an attempt to force him to tell them where Vernou was. Next the brigands ordered all other sharecroppers off the place after they had gathered their portion of the crops in the field, leaving Vernou's portion to rot. The raiders then ordered all the freedmen to return (within thirty days) to their old masters and to serve them, else, as Bickerstaff threatened, they would die. Vernou said that the renegades came and went in and out of Paris as they pleased and that they intended to kill white Union men, Yankees (especially Freedmen's Bureau agents), and leading black men.[26]

Two years after the New York papers were writing about the "New Rebellion," a correspondent of the *Cincinnati Commercial,* who toured Northeast Texas in 1869, wrote: "You cannot pick up a paper in East Texas without reading of murder, assas-sinations, and robbery . . . and yet not a fourth part of the truth has been told; not one act in ten is reported. Go where you will, and you will hear of fresh murders and violence. . . . The civil authority is powerless—the military insufficient in number, while hell has transferred its capital from Pandemonium to Jefferson, and the devil is holding high carnival in Gilder, Tyler, Canton, Quitman, Boston, Marshall, and other places in Texas."[27] Other contemporary observers commented that Texas was among the most lawless and most violent of the southern states during Reconstruction. Maj. Gen. Phillip Sheridan, who commanded the Fifth Military District from 1866 to 1867 and who was angered by the unabated violence taking place in the state, was not as elo-quent as the northern reporters, muttering once that if he owned both hell and Texas, he would rent out Texas and live in hell. Republican governor Edmund J. Davis was clearer, stating that all the turmoil throughout the state amounted to a "slow" Civil War, while District Judge A. B. Norton agreed, claiming that if "it [the violence] was not a war, he wondered just what would constitute war."[28]

Perhaps the clearest evidence supporting these contemporary assessments between 1865 and 1868 is found in the Report of the Special Committee on Lawlessness and

Violence in Texas. The members of the Texas Constitutional Convention of 1868–69 created the special committee to examine and compile statistics on the violence taking place in the state during that time. Its final report, which was forwarded to the US Senate during the Fortieth Congress in July 1868, reveals that freedpeople and white unionists still remained the primary victims of criminal activities taking place within the state. Most of the murders in Texas between 1865 and 1868 were committed by desperadoes "who were either Confederate officers or soldiers, or bushwhackers, during the late war, and now constitute one of the legitimate entailments of secession and rebellion." Of the 939 murders committed in the state, whites had killed 373 freedmen, while only ten whites had been slain by freedmen. This fact alone led members to conclude that whites were involved in a race war against blacks.[29]

The committee further stated that the ex-Confederates were engaged in a war against loyal unionists of both races, believing that the "multitudes who participated in the rebellion, disappointed and saddened by their defeat, are now intensely embittered against the freedmen on account of their emancipation and enfranchisement, and on account of their devotion to the Republican party, and against loyal whites for their persistent adhesion to the Union; that they are determined to resist by every means promising success the establishment of a free republican state government; that is their purpose even by desperate measures to create such a state of alarm and terror among Union men and freedmen as to compel them to abandon the advocacy of impartial suffrage or fly from the state." In this condition of lawlessness, the committee found that free speech had been abandoned and that Republicans could only hold meetings in areas where adequate troops or armed men were stationed. In essence, former Confederates did not tolerate free discourse. As evidence to the fact that men were murdered for their political convictions, committee members made reference to the killings of prominent unionists in Uvalde, Blanco, Bell, Lamar, and Hunt Counties. Just who was committing these murders? According to the report, there were "organizations of disloyal, desperate men in several sections of the state, leagued together for the purpose of murdering prominent Unionists."[30] In fact, Texas became the murder capital of the United States. For two years in a row (1868–69), the state led the nation in the number of homicides, far ahead of the runner up, Louisiana.[31]

Between the years 1865 and 1867, there were 249 indictments for murder before the district courts. In those, only five men were convicted, and only one received the death penalty, a black man from Harris County. In many cases local law enforcement found that they were outgunned and outmanned by the terrorists in their jurisdiction. In other cases the local officers were themselves involved in the acts perpetrated against the unionists. Together these cases illustrate that animosity toward the federal government and its friends was pervasive throughout the state, and the victims frequently were unionists, federal troopers, and agents of the Freedmen's Bureau.[32]

Professional armies typically find it difficult to effectively wage a war against terrorists. Such was surely the case during Reconstruction. Professional armies are trained to fight other professional armies that follow conventional military strategy and tactics. But guerrillas and terrorists play by no rules of engagement, and their tactics vary with each new situation that develops. Able to strike quickly and then disappear, they play hell with military commanders trying to restore order. Just like the Plains Indians that caused havoc in West Texas, terrorist groups and outlaw gangs in the interior of the state used hit-and-run tactics to defeat federal forces stationed in their regions of the state. Even when law enforcers identified criminals, it seemed most easy for such people to commit devilry in one county and then vanish into another, disappearing into the state's vast landscape. Even when criminals were apprehended by local sheriffs or military commands, they were often jailed in porous buildings. Untold numbers of felons escaped incarceration and continued their criminal activities. Even when local law enforcement was able to detain the outlaws long enough for their date in court, white juries often set them free, especially in cases where the victims were African Americans or white unionists.

During the second phase of the Civil War, many areas of settled Texas experienced widespread disturbances. Military commanders had difficulty in obtaining enough soldiers to deal with the terrorist groups and the various outlaw bands. Eventually, these guerillas were able to suppress Republican voters, both black and white, contributing in part to the end of Reconstruction. Widespread violence in the state did not abate until conservative Democrats, also known as Redeemers, regained control of the state government during the early 1870s. Once the Republicans had been defeated and blacks had been relegated to second-class citizenship, terrorist groups no longer found it necessary to organize. Additionally, once Democrats took office, they began to enforce the law. Though the Democratic Party generally favored the use of violence during the early years of Reconstruction as a method of wrenching control away from the Republicans, its members now felt pressure from their constituents to bring an end to the violence. All realized that they had won the second phase of the Civil War and that they could not expect any better terms. Their task complete, Texas guerrillas and terrorists slowly melted into the landscape—hidden but not forgotten. Their victory lasted until the middle of the twentieth century, until finally the federal government resumed its original mission of reconstructing southern society, making it a place where equal rights and justice was not a dream but a reality.

Notes

1. *Marshall Texas Republican,* Aug. 4, 1865; *Clarksville Northern Standard,* July 8, 1865; Norman C. Russell, "The History of Titus County since 1860" (M.A. thesis, East Texas State Teachers College, 1937), 32–33; James M. Smallwood, Barry A. Crouch, and Larry Peacock, *Murder and Mayhem: The War of Reconstruction in Texas* (College Station: Texas A&M University Press, 2003), 27; June E. Tuck, *Civil War Shadows in Hopkins County, Texas* (Sulphur Springs, TX: Walsworth, 1993), 52–53.

2. James M. Smallwood, *Born in Dixie: The History of Smith County, Texas,* 2 vols. (Austin: Eakin, 1999), 1:237–38; Vicki Betts, *Smith County, Texas, in the Civil War* (Tyler, TX: Smith County Historical Society, 1978), 76–78.

3. Smallwood, *Born in Dixie,* 1:237–38, 259–60; Betts, *Smith County, Texas, in the Civil War,* 76–78; *Houston Tri-Weekly Telegraph,* June 7, 1865; *New York Times,* July 17, 1865; Ernest Wallace, *Texas in Turmoil* (Austin, TX: Steck-Vaughn, 1965), 139–46.

4. Kate Stone, *Brokenburn: The Journal of Kate Stone, 1861–1868,* ed. John Q. Anderson (Baton Rouge: Louisiana State University Press, 1955), 226–27.

5. *Houston Tri-Weekly Telegraph,* June 7, 1865; *New York Times,* July 17, 1865; L. Roberts to Ashbel Smith, July 15, 1865, Ashbel Smith Papers, Center for American History, University of Texas at Austin Library; James M. Smallwood, *Time of Hope, Time of Despair: Black Texans during Reconstruction* (New York: Kennikat, 1981), 25; Wallace, *Texas in Turmoil,* 139–46.

6. *Flake's Daily Bulletin,* June 28, 1865; Smallwood, *Time of Hope, Time of Despair,* 25; James Alex Baggett, "Gordon Granger," in Ron Tyler, ed., *New Handbook of Texas,* 6 vols. (Austin: Texas State Historical Association Press, 1996), 3:280. Granger's military career is discussed in Ezra J. Warner, *Generals in Blue* (Baton Rouge: Louisiana State University Press, 1964), 181. See also James Sefton, *The United States Army and Reconstruction, 1865–1877* (Baton Rouge: Louisiana State University Press, 1967), 261–62.

7. See Claude Elliott, "The Freedmen's Bureau in Texas," *Southwestern Historical Quarterly* 56 (July 1952): 6.

8. US House of Representatives, *Conditions of Affairs in Texas,* 39th Cong., 2nd sess., 1866, H. Exec. Doc. 61.

9. William L. Richter, *The Army in Texas during Reconstruction* (College Station: Texas A&M University, 1987), 19. For a brief account of Custer's career, including his time in Texas, see Brian W. Dippie, "George Armstrong Custer," *New Handbook of Texas,* 2:460; and John M. Carroll, ed., *Custer in Texas: An Uninterrupted Narrative* (New York: Sol Lewis/Liveright, 1975).

10. See US House, *Conditions of Affairs in Texas.*

11. Ibid.

12. For more information on the Confederate exodus, see Andrew Rolle, *The Lost Cause: The Confederate Exodus to Mexico* (Norman: University of Oklahoma Press, 1992); and Eugene C. Harter, *The Lost Colony of the Confederacy* (College Station: Texas A&M University Press, 2000).

13. For more information on Presidential Reconstruction, see John Pressley Carrier, "A Political History of Texas during Reconstruction, 1865–1874" (PhD diss., Vanderbilt University, 1971); Walter Tribble Chapin, "Presidential Reconstruction in Texas, 1865–1867" (M.A. thesis, North Texas State University, 1979); Nora Estelle Owens, "Presidential Reconstruction in Texas: A Case Study" (PhD diss., Auburn University, 1983); Dale Baum, *The Shattering of Texas Unionism: Politics in the Lone Star State during the Civil War Era* (Baton Rouge: Louisiana

State University Press, 1998); and Carl H. Moneyhon, *Texas after the Civil War: The Struggle of Reconstruction* (College Station: Texas A&M University Press, 2004).

14. Moneyhon, *Texas after the Civil War*, 35–36.

15. A. Wright to A. J. Hamilton, Jan. 22, 1866, Governor's Papers: A. J. Hamilton, Archives Division, Texas State Library, Austin. For more information on Governor Hamilton, see John L. Waller, *Colossal Hamilton of Texas: A Biography of Andrew Jackson Hamilton, Militant Unionist and Reconstruction Governor* (El Paso: Texas Western Press, 1968).

16. Wright to Hamilton, Jan. 22, 1866.

17. Randolph B. Campbell, *Gone to Texas: A History of the Lone Star State* (New York: Oxford University Press, 2003), 272; Moneyhon, *Texas after the Civil War*, 38–48.

18. For more on the Texas constitutional convention and the election of 1866, see Baum, *Shattering of Texas Unionism*, 124–60; and Moneyhon, *Texas after the Civil War*, 38–68.

19. Texas Secretary of State, Election Returns for 1866, Archives Division, Texas State Library, Austin. For more on the Black Codes, see Smallwood, *Time of Hope, Time of Despair*, 54–59, 64, 123–24, 130–31; Moneyhon, "Black Codes," in *New Handbook of Texas*, 1:562; and Barry A. Crouch, "'All the Vile Passions': The Texas Black Code of 1866," *Southwest Historical Quarterly* 97 (1993): 13–34.

20. Texas Secretary of State, Election Returns for 1866; Smallwood, *Time of Hope, Time of Despair*, 54–59, 64, 123–24, 130–31; Crouch, "All the Vile Passions," 13–34; Ed Ellsworth Bartholomew, *Cullen Baker: Premier Texas Gunfighter* (Houston: Frontier Press of Texas, 1954), 44.

21. For more information on these terrorist groups, see the numerous works of James M. Smallwood, Barry A. Crouch, Carl H. Moneyhon, William L. Richter, and Kenneth W. Howell.

22. Smallwood, Crouch, and Peacock, *Murder and Mayhem*, 33.

23. The best one-volume work on the causes of the Civil War is David Potter, *The Impending Crisis, 1848–1861* (New York: Harper and Row, 1976). Potter examines all of the sectional clashes from 1848 to 1861 and shows how each had slavery or its expansion as a cause. A short summary that traces the origin of the war to the eighteenth century and discusses how slavery was always there to divide the nation is James M. Smallwood, "The Predominate Cause of the Civil War Reconsidered: A Retrospective Essay," *Lincoln Herald* 89 (Winter 1987): 152–60. For more on how slavery led to the secession of Texas, see Smallwood, "The Impending Crisis: A Texas Perspective on the Causes of the Civil War," in *The Seventh Star of the Confederacy: Texas during the Civil War*, ed. Kenneth W. Howell (Denton: University of North Texas Press, 2009), 32–51.

24. For more on Congressional Reconstruction in Texas, see Moneyhon, *Texas after the Civil War*, 69–102; and Baum, *Shattering of Texas Unionism*, 180–228. Also see Carl H. Moneyhon, *Republicanism in Reconstruction Texas* (Austin: University of Texas Press, 1980).

25. For more on violence in Texas during Congressional Reconstruction, see Gregg Cantrell, "Racial Violence and Politics in Reconstruction Texas, 1867–1868," *Southwestern Historical Quarterly* 93 (Jan. 1990): 333–55; Barry A. Crouch, "A Spirit of Lawlessness: White Violence, Texas Blacks, 1865–1868," *Journal of Social History* 18 (Winter 1984): 217–32; and James M. Smallwood, "When the Klan Rode: White Terror in Reconstruction Texas," *Journal of the West* 25 (Oct. 1986): 4–13.

26. *New York Times*, Sept. 29, 1866.

27. *Cincinnati Commercial* quoted in the *Montgomery Alabama State Journal*, Jan. 30, 1869.

28. James M. Smallwood, Kenneth W. Howell, and Carol C. Taylor, *The Devil's Triangl*

Ben Bickerstaff, Northeast Texans, and the War of Reconstruction in Texas (Lufkin, TX: Best of East Texas Publishers, 2007), 17.

29. Reconstruction Convention of Texas, *Report of the Special Committee on Lawlessness and Violence in Texas* (Austin: n.p., 1870).

30. Ibid.

31. For more on the violence in Texas during Reconstruction, see Gov. Andrew J. Hamilton to Pres. Andrew Johnson, Mar. 1, 1866, Andrew Johnson Papers, Archives, Manuscript Division, Library of Congress, Washington, DC; Bvt. Capt. Charles S. Roberts to Assistant Adjutant General, Aug. 12, Nov. 12, 1867, Assistant Commissioners, Tex., Letters Received, Bureau of Refugees, Freedmen, and Abandoned Lands, RG 105, National Archives; Capt. Samuel H. Starr to Lt. Charles E. Morse, acting assistant adjutant general, Feb. 9, 1868, Letters Received, Dept. of Texas, Fifth Military District, RG 393, ibid. (a copy is also in Crouch Collection, Regional History Center, Victoria College/University of Houston–Victoria); Smallwood, "When the Klan Rode," 4–13; Smallwood, *Time of Hope, Time of Despair,* passim; Barry A. Crouch and Donaly Brice, *Cullen Montgomery Baker: Reconstruction Desperado* (Baton Rouge: Louisiana State University Press, 1997); Crouch, *The Freedmen's Bureau and Blacks in Texas* (Austin: University of Texas Press, 1992); Richter, *Army in Texas during Reconstruction;* William L. Richter, *Overreached on All Sides: Freedmen's Bureau Administration in Texas, 1865–1868* (College Station: Texas A&M University Press, 1991); Charles V. Keener, "Radical Turmoil in Texas, 1865–1868" (M.A. thesis, University of North Texas, 1971); and Rebecca A. Kosary, "Regression to Barbarism in Reconstruction Texas: An Analysis of White Violence against African-Americans from the Texas Freedmen's Bureau Records, 1865–1868" (M.A. thesis, Texas State University, 1999).

32. Reconstruction Convention, *Report of the Special Committee.*

10

The Texas Immunes in the Spanish-American War

James M. McCaffrey

O N APRIL 21, 1898, upon Pres. William McKinley's request, Congress authorized him to use US military power to bring the Cuban revolution to an end. Two days later he issued a call to the state governors to provide 125,000 men to form a temporary volunteer army to supplement the regular forces. Each governor received a quota based upon his state's population, and great enthusiasm soon manifested itself. The governor of Minnesota, for example, was certain that his forty-four counterparts would not have to call forth any of their citizens because his state could provide more than twice the total number of men requested.[1]

Nowhere was the response more immediate than in Galveston, Texas. There, within hours of the president's call, hundreds of eager men thronged a meeting at Cathedral Hall to form one of Texas' three requested regiments of infantry. The president of the University of Texas addressed the patriotic throng, as did Civil War veterans from both sides. One speaker reminded the men that, while their enthusiasm was admirable, it was not enough to win the war. He told them of his own similar feelings of boyish enthusiasm in 1861, later tempered by four hard years of war. Nevertheless, by the next day enough men had signed up to form the basis of six companies, and they had chosen 1st Lt. Charles S. Riché, of the US Army Corps of Engineers, as the commander of what they began referring to as the 1st Texas Regiment.[2]

Riché and his new command were soon disappointed to learn that Gov. Charles A. Culberson was going to fill the state's quota with men from the established state guard units. Such in fact had been the intent when the president made his call for volunteers, that the nation's national guardsmen would receive first preference. Riché's would-be warriors remained optimistic, however, that there wo⌐

be another call for volunteers, and they voted unanimously to stay organized and continue drilling for at least the next thirty days in anticipation of such an event.[3]

They did not have to wait very long for another opportunity to serve. Recognizing the dangers that tropical diseases, particularly yellow fever, presented to any occupation force in Cuba, authorities sought to recruit men who had already been exposed to these diseases and had built up immunities to them. Congress thus authorized, on May 11, 1898, the raising of ten regiments of such men. The army designated the resulting units as the 1st through the 10th US Volunteer Infantry Regiments. White officers and soldiers comprised the first six numbered regiments, while the 7th through the 10th had white company commanders and regimental officers and black enlisted men and junior officers. Riché immediately offered his fledgling command as one of the "immune" regiments, even though there had been no effort to limit enlistment to those with the requisite immunities. Nevertheless, the government accepted the regiment, and it became the 1st US Volunteer Infantry Regiment, or the 1st Immune Regiment.

The Texan reaction was not unique. When the call for immunes went out, even the unlikely states of Michigan and Wisconsin got into the excitement, each offering to provide more than enough men to fill all ten proposed regiments. Ironically, recruiters did not always meet such enthusiasm in those parts of the country where young men with the sought-for immunities might actually live. A newspaper writer in New Orleans found that "although the 'immunes' are free from yellow fever dangers, the germs of the disease seem to have played sad havoc with patriotic fervor and left them as immune from any idea of enlistment as from the fever." Ultimately, according to the same source, "Young bums, old bums, any one from anywhere that will merely state he is immune and willing to enlist will be recruited, clothed and fed."[4]

Official acceptance of Riché's command made further recruiting much easier, and all across the state prominent citizens sought to convince enough young men to enlist to form complete companies, which they would then offer to the authorities in Galveston. Juan Hart, founder and owner of the *El Paso Times,* was one such man. Others included Confederate veteran Stephen Allen of Palestine, ex–Texas Ranger Lee Hall of San Antonio, and Frank Ryan of Sherman. Each of these men sent or accompanied dozens of men to Galveston, where each of the three hoped that the reward for their public spirit would be election to the command of the company thus furnished; the recruits after all had signed up based upon their knowledge of their erstwhile recruiters and intended to continue serving under them after the

Soldier of 1st US Volunteers Immune. Courtesy George Pappas Collection, US Army Military History Institute, Carlisle, Pa.

regiment was officially organized. A. D. Sparkman recruited men in Wharton who felt so strongly about him that they held a referendum on the train to Galveston and voted unanimously to refuse enlistment and return home if anyone other than he received command of their company.[5]

The army accepted no volunteer, immune or otherwise, until he had passed a physical examination, for it did not want to bring in men who could not meet the physical demands of active campaigning and who might, because of physical limitations, be a danger to themselves and to their comrades. Normally, a physician might spend ten to fifteen minutes examining each man to ensure that he was physically capable of military service, but with so many men crowding the recruitment stations, these examinations were sometimes cursory at best. A team of doctors inspecting the men of an Illinois regiment reportedly spent no more than three minutes per man, causing an onlooker to declare that "plenty of old men, so crooked in their knees until they looked like a weather beaten shingle, toothless, as stiff as a poker, [and] blind in one eye . . . passed."[6]

In Galveston five doctors set up shop in the three-story building that served as regimental headquarters and barracks to begin the examinations. The national rejection rate was surprisingly high, hovering around 75 percent for enlistees into the regular army. Overall, the rate for the Galveston regiment ran about 21 percent. Nearsightedness was one common reason for rejection. When doctors told a recruit in New York that they were concerned about his eyesight, he rather huffily informed them that he could certainly see well enough to have once run thirty-five pool balls. (It was unlikely, however, that any Spaniards in Cuba would be as close to him as the end of his cue stick.) There were always surprises as to who failed the physical examinations. Doctors disqualified both Captains Hall and Allen due to hernias, but within less than a week, following petitions to President McKinley, both men were allowed to accept their commissions.[7]

On May 28 a recruiter arrived from Houston trying to fill out a company being raised there for another immune regiment being formed in New Orleans. His goal was to convince twenty-five Galvestonians that they would have a better chance of seeing action with the Louisiana regiment. He was able to convince eight men who had already failed their physicals for the Galveston regiment and a dozen others before he returned to Houston. Ironically, on the same day that he arrived, so too did twenty-five of his fellow Houstonians to enlist in Riché's command.[8]

On June 2 the six existing companies of the regiment marched from their temporary campsite at Beach Park to new campgrounds located between Avenue T and Avenue U east of Fifty-Third Street, and within a few days all twelve companies had moved. Naming their new home Camp Hawley, after Galveston's freshman congressman, Robert Hawley, the soldiers began settling into six-man squad tents. Camp Hawley was open to visitors on Sundays, but the men stationed there were all business during the week. Bugles roused them from their slumbers at 5:30 A.M., and after breakfast at six, there was an hour of squad drills and physical conditioning followed by an hour and a half of company drill before lunch. Then there were another couple of hours of drill between lunch and supper and an hour of battalion drill in the early evening.[9]

Meanwhile, as the men in Galveston waited for orders, the war went on without them. On June 22, American troops splashed ashore on the eastern end of Cuba. Working through the jungles, they attacked the outer defenses of Santiago de Cuba on July 1 and drove the defenders back toward the city. Two days later a Spanish naval squadron that had been anchored in Santiago Harbor made a break for the open sea and was completely demolished by US warships. The fighting in Cuba was virtually over, but there was still a possibility that the Texans might see action in Puerto Rico.

Colonel Riché's men finally received their .45-caliber single-shot rifles on July 6. These weapons had been in service for a quarter century and were no longer issued to regular troops, having been replaced by much more efficient .30-caliber repeaters. Despite their relative obsolescence, the men—after two and a half months without weapons—were glad to have them, no longer having to drill with wooden sticks. Riché requested one hundred rounds of ammunition per man for rifle training, but parsimonious officials in Washington authorized only ten rounds per man, barely enough for familiarization training, let alone marksmanship training. Nevertheless, work began immediately along the beach on a firing range that allowed bullets that missed the targets—and a great number did so—to fly harmlessly out over the Gulf of Mexico. The companies took turns, each man firing five of his precious rounds at a target 100 yards away and the other five at twice that distance. A local newspaper reporter waxed poetic over the performance of the soldiers in the first four companies. After explaining to his readers that many of these men were completely unfamiliar with firearms, that these rifles delivered a stout kick upon firing, and that the 200-yard range was "an awkward distance," still "the men showed themselves capable of becoming crack shots . . . and the thinnest Spaniards . . . would not stand a ghost of a show for escape from the men of" these companies. The records indicated, however, that even a portly Spaniard would have a fair chance of survival. The men of Companies C and E made the best showing but still only hit the eight-by-ten-inch target about 40 percent of the time, while about one of every four shots fired by the men in Companies A and B managed to hit it.[10]

A week later Riché received orders from Washington to prepare his command for immediate shipment to Cuba. New orders arrived a few days later. Now, instead of shipping out directly from the Galveston docks, the regiment was to travel by rail to New Orleans and from there ship to Cuba aboard the *City of Berlin*. The soldiers welcomed the news "like a tribe of Indians jumping the reservation with war-paint and feather decorations."[11]

The long-anticipated day finally arrived, and on the afternoon of July 21, the men all took up positions at their tents. Then at a signal from a bugle, they lowered all of the canvas to the ground and rolled up their tents for shipment, along with the rest of the regimental baggage. They slept that night in small two-man tents made from buttoned-together shelter halves that each man carried as part of his field gear. Trains waited for them in the morning at the freight terminal at the foot of 33rd Street. Although it would not have been a particularly difficult hike from camp, Galvestonians got together and chipped in money to hire streetcars to carry the troops to the station. Representatives from a tobacco company distributed chewing tobacco—"a ten-cent plug of the weed"—to every man, and while waiting to board the trains, a citizen presented the regiment with a wagonload of tasty watermelons. When their departure was delayed, the proprietors of a nearby brewery threw open its doors to them. "[T]hey went at the amber colored liquid," a newsman reported, "like it was the last they expected to get in a long time."[12]

Finally, the last of the baggage was loaded and the three trains, each bearing one of the regiment's battalions, left Galveston at intervals. Citizens in the towns through which the trains passed cheered them on their way. The residents of Palestine barbecued ten beeves and prepared enough other food for every man in the regiment to eat his fill. Then, after changing trains in Marshall, the regiment began arriving in New Orleans on the afternoon of July 23.[13]

Upon arrival in the Crescent City, Colonel Riché's regiment went into camp across the river at Gouldsboro. Also present nearby and waiting for deployment was the 2nd Immune Regiment, commanded by New Orleans's own Duncan Hood, the twenty-five-year-old son of Confederate general John Bell Hood. Plans called for both regiments to sail aboard the *City of Berlin* to Cuba for occupation duty, and boarding began on the morning of July 25. An estimated crowd of 10,000 citizens—including several hundred from Texas—was on hand to cheer the troops as they boarded the *Berlin*. One local woman bestowed a hundred barrels of distilled and a thousand sandwiches upon the Texas regiment.[14]

Officers and noncommissioned officers of Company F, 1st US Volunteers Immune. Courtesy US Army Military History Institute, Carlisle, Pa. (Acc-1898-W-1123.1).

After both regiments had boarded, army paymasters arrived with the Texans' first pay. The plan had been to distribute the money after the men were safely aboard the ship and on their way to Cuba so they would not be tempted to spend it all in the bars and brothels of New Orleans. When the ship's departure was delayed, however, many of the soldiers snuck back ashore and into the saloons of the city. About a hundred such revelers made it out before officers posted guards along the dock with orders to shoot to kill anyone attempting to get off the ship. Despite this, some two hundred Texans (and another one hundred men from Hood's regiment) missed roll call that night.[15]

Some two dozen Texans, having overindulged in alcohol, found themselves as guests of the New Orleans police that evening, but the loose incarceration—they were not put in cells but allowed to sit in the corridor—did not have the desired effect. Instead, their rowdy behavior continued. They broke the jail's water buckets, smashed tin cups, and ripped the electric light fixtures and benches out of some of the cells before the soldiers were subdued. The cells—those not already vandalized—soon were full of Texans while the police waited for guard details to come and escort them to the ship. Unfortunately, the mischief makers were no sooner gone than other raucous Texans took their places. In fact, some of the soldiers sent to retrieve the prisoners also gave in to the temptation to kick up their heels on wha they assumed was to be their last night in the States before going to Cuba. Such behavior caused one local newspaper to refer to the men of the regiment as "Riche's Roisterers."[16]

About midnight the *Berlin* pulled away from the dock and anchored in the river, making it much more challenging for the soldiers on board to get ashore. Still, however, several managed to obtain a small boat but were discovered and hauled back onboard before they could get away. Some soldiers, disappointed at not having been able to sneak off, found local citizens willing to oblige their desires when small boats pulled up alongside to sell them liquor. When the officers found out about this, they ordered all boats to keep at least forty feet away from the *Berlin* or risk being fired upon by sentries. A few of the enterprising businessmen failed to heed the warning until bullets began to hit their boats, whereupon the illicit commerce came to an end.[17]

The 2,000 soldiers packed aboard the ship were more than it had been designed to carry. A Texan commented: "One would have to hold his nose for the stench that arose from the lower decks. What ventilation we had came through little round holes about eight inches in diameter in the side of the ship. Some decks were flooded with dirty water, and the men had eaten bananas, apples, etc. and thrown the refuse on the floor. There being barely standing room, it was impossible to clean or improve the sanitary condition of the ship. Several men in the lower compartments of the ship were almost suffocated." It was under these conditions that another Texan, who had been in poor health for quite some time, became the regiment's first fatality on the night of July 26.[18]

The next day commanders of both regiments met with the quartermaster officer in charge of arranging transportation, and all agreed that the ship was not big enough to transport both regiments without risking serious health problems due to overcrowding. Colonel Riché agreed to disembark his command and wait for another vessel, expected within a few days. Back on dry land, the Texans marched into camp—dubbed "Camp Riché"—at the fairgrounds a couple of miles from the docks, pitching their shelter tents in the infield of the racetrack to await further orders. Despite the disappointment in not getting off to Cuba as planned, many of the soldiers snuck out of camp to take solace in the bright lights of the city. Their behavior was, according to a local newspaper, as if "a band of Apaches had been turned loose" on the citizenry. In one drinking establishment, several Texans climbed onto tables and began shooting at the electric lights, causing near panic among the civilian patrons, who ran through doors and jumped out windows to escape any stray shots. Before order was restored, the local police had rounded up about twenty of the men and lodged them in jail.[19]

The Texans wore khaki uniforms, which set them apart from soldiers of the other regiments camped in and around New Orleans, who sported the standard blue uniforms. Many of the men made their distinctive clothing a point of pride, but they became badges of dishonor for others. Whenever khaki-clad soldiers had too much to drink in a local saloon or got into any kind of trouble, it was an easy matter for the city police to visit Riché's camp to look for the culprits. One member of the regiment assured the readers of the Galveston newspaper that the accounts of misbehavior were greatly exaggerated, that the number of miscreants was not large. "[H]ad we been any other than a Texas regiment," he opined, "no notice would have been taken of it. There have been no wild west shows given by this regiment in New Orleans." When local newspapers began reporting on the outrageous behavior of some of the Texans, the regiment's chaplain, although admitting that not all of the men were saints, stated in their defense that "some people expect a Texan to be boisterous and unruly at times."[20]

Nevertheless, Colonel Riché ordered stricter controls at camp. He assigned fatigue duty to men caught leaving without permission and took the stripes away from any corporals or sergeants found to have done so. The men chafed at these rules. Sneaking out of camp and back in again, or "running the guards," was a time-honored challenge in military camps all across the country, and the Texans embraced the game wholeheartedly. Back at Camp Hawley it had been a simple matter to sneak away, but things were different in Louisiana. Events took a decidedly more serious turn on the night of July 31. Shortly before midnight, a sentry noticed Pvt. Thomas Smith poking his head through the fence from outside. Smith, who was from New Orleans, had snuck out of camp earlier to visit his family and was now trying to sneak back in. When the sentry momentarily looked away, Smith made his move, scampering past the guardhouse and toward his tent. When the guard turned back around, he mistook the running soldier for an escaping prisoner and ordered him to halt. When Smith kept running, the guard raised his rifle and fired. The fatal bullet ripped through Smith's left wrist and into his side; before passing out the other side, it tore through his intestines. Riché, like every other man in camp, mourned Smith's death, but the colonel exonerated the sentry from any wrongdoing. "In fact," he said, "he is worthy of commendation for obedience to instructions at such a critical time." Even the dying man himself did not hold a grudge. "The guard simply did his duty," he declared to the regimental chaplain.[21]

Colonel Riché still had no inkling about any plans for the deployment of his regiment when he cabled the War Department on August 4 to express the men's willingness to serve anywhere they were needed. A reply the next day stated that the *Berlin* was on its way back to New Orleans after having delivered the 2nd Immunes, and that "[a]s soon as she reports you will embark your regiment without further orders or instruction from here." The colonel had the message posted on a bulletin board so the men could read the good news for themselves, and excitement spread throughout the camp.[22]

While the troops waited to ship out, the August rains arrived, turning the camp into a quagmire. The soldiers dug small trenches around their tents to carry off the rainwater, but these ditches soon filled, becoming tiny moats, and the water flooded into the men's sleeping quarters. "We used to be the boys in brown," wrote one soldier after three solid days of rain, but "at present we are the boys in sticky mud and slush over our shoe-tops." He was convinced that the rain might go on forever. There was soon a growing sick list as men came down with coughs, colds, and fevers. Colonel Riché increased the number of passes issued so his men could leave camp and at least find someplace dry in which to sleep. Many simply remained in camp but took their soggy blankets into a stable to sleep.[23]

Payday rolled around again on August 6, and the officers braced for another round of drunken misbehavior. Riché tripled the guards around camp, allowing only ten men from each company to be absent at one time. Conditions were more lax in the neighboring camp of the black 9th Immunes. Soldiers there were so anxious to spend their money that some of them broke down the fence to get out. And it was not long before some of them got into trouble.[24]

The *Berlin* finally reached New Orleans on August 12, and with it came clear skies and a hot, bright sun to buoy the Texans' spirits. They expected to board her right away and be on their way to Cuba by the fifteenth. The 9th Immunes were also preparing to move. They were to take trains to Jacksonville, Florida, and go from there by ship to Cuba. Unfortunately, rumors of imminent departure caused some men in each of these units to decide for one last night on the town on Saturday.[25]

A soldier from the 9th, who according to a local newspaper was "from all accounts a pretty bad customer," got into an argument with a bar owner about the cost of a drink. He opened fire with a pistol, but did not hit anybody, before moving to another establishment. He fired other wild shots before three police officers arrived and chased him into a privy behind a barbershop. Officers repeatedly called to him to put down his gun and surrender, but he refused. Finally, as he pushed open the door and began to wave his pistol, one of the policemen shot him through the head and killed him. That night a large number of soldiers from his regiment, carrying loaded rifles, headed into the city to avenge his death. Col. Charles Crane, the regimental commander, did everything he could to talk them out of it and finally had to use his saber on two of the men to stop the brewing riot.[26]

A large group of Texans also caused trouble that night, although without fatal results. Fired up with alcohol and the rumor that one of their comrades had been assaulted by a black man, they went looking for revenge. At one point when they were denied admittance to a black brothel on Basin Street, they tried to force their way in. Police officers soon sent them on their way, but some of the men returned and fired at least one pistol shot through the front door. Many New Orleans citizens likely would be happy once both regiments were on their way to Cuba.[27]

The Texans were full of energy and excitement the following Monday as they dismantled and packed up their squad tents for shipment. They would sleep in their two-man shelter tents that night and be off for the docks bright and early the next morning. That evening, however, there was a change of plans. Riché received new orders from Adj. Gen. Henry Corbin in Washington—his regiment was not going to Cuba after all but was to return to Galveston. Corbin said that he based the change on reports in the New Orleans papers about rampant insubordination and lack of discipline among the Texans. These charges, he continued, had been verified by the report of a regular-army officer in the city. The 9th Immunes embarked on the *Berlin* instead. To add insult to injury, the 9th's bugler played "Taps" as his regiment marched past the Texans on its way to the dock.[28]

There may have been, however, more to the story. For instance, the officer filing the report on the Texans' misdeeds had originally been sent to New Orleans as the mustering officer for the 9th Immunes. Colonel Crane, that regiment's commander, had served under Corbin earlier in his career and maintained cordial relations with him. He in fact had named his camp at the fairgrounds "Camp Corbin." And one of Crane's officers was the nephew of Mrs. Corbin.[29]

The disappointed Texans broke camp before sunup on August 18 and headed for the station at Algiers. As they boarded the trains, Lt. Duble Chubb tried to lighten things up with a comedic observation. "My only regret," he said sarcastically, "is that the Hon. Erastus Grant Lincoln [an obviously made-up "black" name], a lieutenant of Crane's colored regiment, has my berth on the transport Berlin. It makes my blood boil."[30]

The 1st Immunes arrived back in Galveston the next morning and reestablished Camp Hawley. By this time the war was over, and the vast majority of men in the regiment had had their fill of the military. They wanted the regiment disbanded so they could return to civilian life. To this end a petition to Secretary of War Russell Alger began circulating that respectfully requested the disbandment of the regiment. "Now that peace is declared," it read in part, "we ask the government (the serving of which we consider a privilege and pleasure) to grant our prayer for disbandment, if such disbandment or 'mustering out' does not in the least endanger the good name of our beloved country." Almost all of the enlisted men signed this document.[31]

On September 10, new regulation-blue uniforms arrived for the men, and they were a welcome sight as the khaki clothing of most of the men was nearly worn out. Galveston's "boys in brown" were soon transformed into "boys in blue." They received their pay as well as furloughs the next day. While some of them made immediate plans to return to their homes, others could not resist the opportunity to gamble their $15.60 in the craps games that sprang up. It did not take long, at up to $5 per throw, to clean out some of them. Later in the day, as the winners accumulated more and more of their fellow soldiers' pay, the stakes went as high as $50 per throw. The losers, meanwhile, were left to figure out some way to get home.[32]

The members of the 1st US Volunteer Infantry returned to Galveston to be officially mustered out on October 28. The hospital tents at Camp Hawley, now empty of patients, served as paymaster offices, and within three hours' time, every man in the regiment had received his final pay and his official discharge. By midafternoon, the camp was empty.

These men had come forward to offer their lives in their nation's cause but, like the vast majority of the volunteer troops and through no fault of their own, never heard a shot fired in anger. The sentiments expressed by a young soldier in one of the Texas National Guard regiments probably echoed the feelings of many of Riché's men. "We left home blindly," he wrote, "knowing absolutely nothing [about] what was before us, and although we were never in any battle, it was not our fault. We volunteered at the call, we were ready, willing to go where ever we were sent, and although we never reached the battle field, yet we fought disease and death in other forms, [including] . . . mosquitoes and flees [*sic*], and in fact most every thing that there is to make life miserable. We have passed through it all, and now it is over with the experience I have passed through is worth many a dollar to me."[33]

Notes

1. Peter Mickelson, "Nationalism in Minnesota during the Spanish-American War," *Minnesota History* 41 (Spring 1968): 8.

2. "Regiment's Grand Rally," *Galveston Daily News* (hereafter *GDN*), May 8, 1898.

3. "First Texas Regiment," ibid., Apr. 30, 1898.

4. "The Galveston Regiment," ibid., May 19, 1898; "Hood's Immune Regiment," ibid., May 7, 1898 (quote).

5. "At Camp Hawley," ibid., June 17, 1898.

6. "Committee of Vigilance" of the 8th Illinois Volunteers to Editor, *Springfield Illinois Record*, Jan. 4, 1899, in Willard B. Gatewood Jr., *"Smoked Yankees" and the Struggle for Empire: Letters from Negro Soldiers, 1898–1902* (Urbana: University of Illinois Press, 1971), 216 (quote).

7. Marvin A. Kreidberg and Merton G. Henry, *History of Military Mobilization in the United States Army, 1775–1945* (Westport, CT: Greenwood, 1955), 163; "Company I Mustered In," *GDN*, May 29, 1898; "Galveston Regiment News," ibid., May 24, 1898; Charles Johnson Post, *The Little War of Private Post* (Boston: Little Brown, 1960; New York: New American Library, 1960), 112–13; "Life at Camp Hawley," *GDN*, June 11, 1898; "At Camp Hawley," ibid., June 17, 1898.

8. "Recruiting for Louisiana," *GDN*, May 29, 1898; "Mission Not a Success," ibid., May 30, 1898; "More Recruits," ibid., May 29, 1898.

9. "Camp Hawley Was Started," ibid., June 3, 1898; "At Camp Hawley," ibid., June 4, 1898.

10. "Will be Target Practice," ibid., July 11, 1898; "Life at Camp Hawley," ibid., July 16, 1898 (quotes); "'Our Colonel' Captured," ibid., July 17, 1898.

11. "Last Day of Camp Hawley," ibid., July 21, 1898.

12. The street car company made up the amount that the citizens were short. "Little White City Is Gone," *GDN*, July 22, 1898; "Last Days of Camp Hawley," ibid., July 21, 1898 (1st quote); "The Regiment Gone," ibid., July 23, 1898 (2nd quote).

13. "The Regiment Gone," July 23, 1898; "Galveston Regiment," *GDN*, July 23, 1898.

14. "The Galveston Immunes," ibid., July 26, 1898.

15. Ibid.; "The Texans Disembark," ibid., July 27, 1898.

16. "The Police Busy Holding Wild Warriors in Check Last Night," *New Orleans Daily Picayune* (hereafter *Picayune*), July 26, 1898; "Reblin [Berlin] Still in Midstream Here," ibid., July 27, 1898 (quote).

17. "Hood and Riche Regiments Here," ibid., July 26, 1898; "Aboard the Transport," ibid., July 27, 1898.

18. "Texans at Camp Houston," *GDN*, Aug. 6, 1898.

19. "Riche's Regiment Is Now in Camp on the Race Track Field," *Picayune*, July 28, 1898 (quotation); "Took in the Town," ibid., July 28, 1898.

20. "Texans at Camp Houston," *GDN*, Aug. 6, 1898 (1st quote); "Riche's Immune Regiment," ibid., July 31, 1898 (2nd quote).

21. "At Camp Riche," ibid., July 31, 1898; "Shot by a Sentinel," ibid., Aug. 2, 1898 ; "A Soldier Shot by a Sentinel," *Picayune*, Aug. 1, 1898 (1st quote).;"Riche's Regiment Will Drill Daily," ibid., Aug. 2, 1898 (2nd quote).

22. "Riche's Regiment Orders," *GDN*, Aug. 6, 1898.

23. "Riche's Immunes," ibid., Aug. 9, 1898; "The Round of the Camps," ibid., Aug. 12, 1898 (quote); "Riche's Regiment," *Picayune,* Aug. 9, 1898.

24. "The Black Boys Break Out of Camp after Being Paid Off, and Make a Little Police Record on Their Own Account Last Night," *Picayune,* Aug. 7, 1898.

25. "Riche's Regiment Preparing for the Voyage to Santiago de Cuba," ibid., Aug. 11, 1898; "Crane's Immunes Fully Equipped Now and Ready for Active Service," ibid., Aug. 11, 1898.

26. "A Black Immune Meets His Death," ibid., Aug. 13, 1898 (quote); Charles Judson Crane, *The Experiences of a Colonel of Infantry* (New York: Knickerbocker, 1923), 267–70.

27. "Terrified the Tenderloin," *Picayune,* Aug. 15, 1898.

28. "Riche's Regiment Boldly Accused," ibid., Aug. 17, 1898; "Father Kirwin on Immunes," *GDN,* Aug. 21, 1898.

29. Roger D. Cunningham. "The Black 'Immune' Regiments in the Spanish-American War." The Army Historical Foundation, accessed Sept. 24, 2008, http://www.armyhistory.org/ahf2.aspx?pgID=877&id=145&exCompID=56; Crane, *The Experiences of a Colonel of Infantry,* 267.

30. "Returning Immunes," *GDN,* Aug. 19, 1898.

31. "Trouble at Camp Hawley," ibid., Aug. 28, 1898.

32. "Pay Day at Camp Hawley," ibid., Sept. 11, 1898; "The Boys in Blue," ibid., Sept. 15, 1898; "Pay Day at Camp Hawley," ibid., Sept. 12, 1898.

33. "Texas Immunes Disbanded," ibid., Oct. 29, 1898; Arthur E. Gentzen, diary, Apr. 16, 1898, The Center for American History, University of Texas at Austin (quote).

11

Surveillance on the Border

American Intelligence and the Tejano Community during World War I

José A. Ramírez

ON MARCH 3, 1917, two days after word reached the press of the British government's interception and decoding of the soon-to-be infamous "Zimmermann note," the *New York Times* hailed Mexico's apparent rejection of German foreign secretary Arthur Zimmermann's proposal for an anti-American alliance. Nevertheless, it warned its readers, their southern neighbor and its president, Venustiano Carranza, "will still bear watching from this side of the border."[1] Owing to reports of a considerable German presence in Mexico, attitudes of this sort, along with suspicions of Mexican intrigue, persisted throughout the World War I era in the United States.[2] As wartime fears of enemy spies and saboteurs undermining the war effort gripped the public, American intelligence not only conducted operations in Mexico but also kept close track of Mexicans and Mexican Americans domestically.

Even as thousands of its sons were serving in uniform, the Tejano community found itself a prime target for surveillance because of its proximity to the US-Mexico border and the pervasive unease with all things Mexican.[3] In Texas as in many other parts of the country, concerns over the possibility of German-Mexican collusion often bordered on hysteria. Throughout the war, intelligence agencies received countless tips implicating Mexican-origin individuals in nefarious activity of one form or another. To say that many of these leads—particularly those alleging the most serious crimes—were fruitless would be an understatement. The isolated cases of disloyalty that emanated from the barrios, though, were more than enough to validate the anxieties of the most fretful citizens and public officials. Inevitably, the unique relationship between Mexico and the United States during the war ensured that these cases would receive extra attention from American intelligence.[4]

To be sure, the concern of Pres. Woodrow Wilson's administration with foreign subversives was not unfounded. Germany had targeted the United States in several of its plots since the eruption of hostilities in Europe. To hinder the flow of matériel to the Allies, German agents had in July 1916 bombed the Erie Railroad docks in New Jersey, destroying thirty-four boxcars loaded with ammunition. They had also set ablaze the Kingsland munitions factory near New York Harbor several months later. These efforts, however, were sometimes downright clumsy. In one case a German consul carelessly misplaced a briefcase containing compromising evidence of espionage on a Third Avenue elevated train in New York City. Despite its success elsewhere, German intrigue in the United States, in the words of historians D. Clayton James and Anne Sharp Wells, was "[m]ore annoying than substantial."[5]

As the Zimmermann affair made clear, it also to a large extent involved Mexico, whose president welcomed a German alliance to counter US aggression. Always looking to obstruct the shipment of American manpower and supplies to Europe, the kaiser's government coveted Mexico as a base from which to wage a campaign of espionage and sabotage against the United States. Germany also hoped to produce a second Mexican-American war by fomenting anti-Americanism among the country's various revolutionary factions and coordinating armed provocations and raids along the border. Fortunately for them, Gen. John J. Pershing's Punitive Expedition against Revolutionary general Francisco "Pancho" Villa had quickly taken on the look of a US invasion of Mexico, making an anxious Carranza more receptive to overtures from their country, from which the so-called "First Chief" hoped to obtain financial and military aid in case of war. With the Mexican president suddenly more amenable to its needs, the German secret service in 1917 moved its headquarters to Mexico and launched a series of covert activities against the United States.[6]

The American government took countermeasures against this threat south of the border, albeit with mixed results. Under the direction of the military attaché, five different US secret services—the State Department, the army, the navy, the Department of the Treasury, and the Justice Department—conducted intelligence activities in Mexico. With the assistance of French and especially British intelligence, American officials were able to learn the identity and movements of most of the German agents, in large part due to Britain's interception of several telegrams and the joint Allied effort at deciphering German secret codes. The Americans also attempted to dislodge German businesses from Mexico, a less productive endeavor impeded not only by the Germans' skill for camouflaging their activities but also by US business interests. As two-thirds of German sales in Mexico were based on

US goods, American businessmen pressured Washington to resist interfering with the free flow of commerce and to regard their German counterparts down south as "harmless."[7]

Mexican intrigue was no less a focus for the intelligence community back home. The government's surveillance team for domestic matters included the army and navy intelligence branches and the investigative arms of the State Department and Postal Service, the latter of which focused on scanning mail for disloyal and subversive content and monitoring letters, telegrams, and packages to and from Mexico and other foreign countries. Another component of this network of agencies was the Justice Department's Bureau of Investigation (later the Federal Bureau of Investigation, or FBI), which had been inspecting Mexican neutrality violations on US soil since the early days of the Mexican Revolution. After the declaration of war against Germany on April 6, 1917, the bureau simply added espionage and sabotage to previous concentrations such as arms smuggling, which itself took on an entirely new dimension now that the possibility existed of revolutionary factions—the usual culprits in such crimes—delivering weapons to Germans south of the border. In Texas surveillance was aided by the state adjutant general's creation of a special investigative unit called the Loyalty Rangers. Under the direction of W. M. Hanson, a former federal marshal for the Southern District of Texas, the Loyalty Rangers worked to improve intelligence collection along the Rio Grande. Armed with the newly passed Espionage Act, which prohibited practically anything that could be defined as aiding and abetting America's enemies, this network of intelligence agencies paid considerable attention to the Tejano community.[8]

For many intelligence officials, the impertinent statements of some individuals substantiated fears of German-Mexican intrigue. In May 1917, in the small German settlement of Guda in northern Falls County, a reputed hotbed of anti-Americanism, authorities received two separate reports of a local Mexican's boasts that "Mexicans and Germans were going to take this country."[9] In San Antonio, meanwhile, an informant of German extraction filed a report with the Bureau of Investigation detailing his recent war-related discussion with a Mexican acquaintance, who allegedly expressed a desire "to see the germans whipp the Bigmouthed 'Gringos' and give them what the[y] had coming to them" for the last several years. "Knowing me to be of German decent," the informant wrote, "he spoke very bitter against the . . . Americans," whom the Mexican argued "would only make a laughing stock out of themselfes [sic], because they had not been able to get Villa."[10] Owing to the intolerant political temperament of wartime, criticism of this sort could sometimes result in legal trouble. In April 1917, for example, law enforce-

ment officials in Mission arrested a Mexican simply for writing a letter that allegedly "abus[ed] the President and the American people in general."[11]

Obviously, in cases like these where the mail was involved, the department
that took the lead in surveillance was the post office, led by Albert S. Burleson, its
autocratic postmaster general—the war era's "foremost official enemy of dissidents,"
according to historian David M. Kennedy. Authorized by the Espionage Act to
ban from the mails any materials that violated its provisions and with the leeway to
monitor the private correspondence of most "potential subversives," Burleson ruth-
lessly wielded his considerable powers to stifle critics of the Wilson administration,
many of whom relied on the mail to circulate information.[12] The postmaster general, wrote presidential advisor Col. Edward M. House in 1918, "is in a belligerent
mood against the Germans, against labor, against the pacifists, etc. He is now the
most belligerent member of the cabinet."[13]

The post office worked in conjunction with other government agencies. The
chief postal censor, for example, headed the national Censorship Board composed
of representatives from the Navy and War Departments, the War Trade Board, and
the Committee on Public Information (CPI). Charged with the task of monitoring
incoming and outgoing international mail not already censored by England, France,
or Italy, the Censorship Board often overstepped its bounds by repeatedly review-
ing domestic correspondence, which it was supposed to do only in cases of extreme
necessity. Besides its work with the board, the post office also communicated with
other agencies by providing them with lists of banned publications. In turn, military
intelligence, the Bureau of Investigation, and even the Loyalty Rangers also conducted investigations of suspect publications sent through postal channels.[14]

Due in large part to the efforts of the post office, freedom of the press suffered
continual setbacks throughout the war. The socialist press was one of Burleson's
favorite targets. Often with little provocation, he banned some of the era's major
radical publications from the mails, initiating the decline of the American socialist
movement. The foreign-language press too fell under the heavy hand of the Wilson
administration. Following the passage of the Trading-with-the-Enemy Act in
October 1917, foreign-language papers were required to submit, at their own considerable expense, translations of any items dealing with the government, the other
belligerent powers, or the conduct of the war. The post office then took on the task
of combing them for subversive messages at its Translation Bureau in New York,
where a staff of four hundred college professors volunteered as translators. In this
environment it is therefore unsurprising that publications of all sorts of languages
and affiliations wound up toeing the administration's line for fear of losing their

second-class mailing permits, a penalty Burleson meted out freely in enforcing the press censorship provision of the Espionage Act.[15]

In the case of the Mexican press, Burleson's surveillance activities were actually sensible. As part of its intense and extensive propaganda campaign in Latin America, the German Foreign Office subsidized several Mexican newspapers—including Mexico City's *El Demócrata*, the main organ of German propaganda—in exchange for favorable coverage, an expenditure US intelligence estimated at approximately $25,000 monthly. Though costly, the operation proved successful. The War Department, for example, estimated that 90 percent of the Mexican population held anti-American attitudes during the war. The reason for this level of antipathy was clear to the Wilson administration. "With the possible exception of Spain," concluded the CPI, the US government's own propaganda arm, "German propaganda has proceeded in no other country with such resolve and malicious aggressiveness, as in Mexico."[16]

The American government took several measures to counter the pro-German Mexican media. For one thing, it issued a ban on "objectionable" newspapers such as *El Demócrata*, *La Defensa*, *El Progreso*, *Informales Inalámbricas*, and *Redención*, a prohibition that resulted in the virtual disappearance of Mexican newspapers along some parts of the border.[17] It also imposed a paper embargo on all pro-German newspapers in Mexico, causing some to close shop either permanently or temporarily. The most successful countermeasures, however, were economic sanctions—which put an end to the *Boletín de Guerra* of Progreso, Yucatán, and turned *La Opinión* of Torreón, Coahuila, over to the Allied cause—and the hindrance of shipments of pro-German newspapers through US territory. The latter move especially affected the isolated Mexican provinces in the western part of the country, much of whose mail first passed through the United States.[18]

For the most part, nothing that drastic was needed to control the Spanish-language press north of the border. In Laredo, *Evolución* was downplaying the idealistic claims of the Allies as late as March 1917, portraying the war as a traditional European power struggle. With America's entry into the conflict, however, the paper devoted itself wholeheartedly to the war effort, with its publisher, Clemente Idar, even landing a job with the CPI. Most likely because it was the organ of the local Mexican exile community, cross-town rival *El Demócrata Fronterizo* was less enthusiastic about America's role in the war, although it too eventually fell into line with the mainstream. The same was true of another Mexican-exile paper, *La Prensa* of San Antonio, which remained nominally neutral throughout the conflict but lent support to the US government by translating and publishing official

Clemente Idar, owner-editor of the Laredo daily Evolución, *in Galveston, 1928. Courtesy A. Ike Idar.*

wartime notices and lauding the exploits of Mexicans and Mexican Americans in the war effort to generate patriotism in the Tejano community. Ultimately, none of the Spanish-language newspapers from Texas were ever labeled disloyal by the post office, although it is impossible to ascertain exactly whether their propriety stemmed from true patriotism—or, in the case of exile papers, gratitude toward their adopted country—or fear of retribution from Burleson and his staff.[19]

What is certain is that at least some members of the foreign-language press were keenly aware of the ever-watchful eye of the US government. In the days leading up to the declaration of war against Germany, several pieces in *El Demócrata Fronterizo* caught the attention of intelligence officials. One informant submitted a report detailing editor and publisher Justo Cárdenas's history as a refugee from Porfirian Mexico, along with a translated excerpt from an editorial criticizing the "partisans of the war movement in the United States," including President Wilson, whom it identified as its "head."[20] Another report several days later noted how, upon instructions from Bureau of Investigation officials either to suppress the publication or seek prosecution "if practicable," the matter had been turned over to a local US marshal. "As a result of the interview I am informed that Cárdenas has promised faithfully not to again publish article of like character," the report's author noted. "I am of the opinion that like article will not appear again in *El Demócrata Fronterizo*."[21]

Interestingly, members of the Spanish-language press sometimes turned on each other. In late 1917 Clemente Idar, who had been acting as an informant for the Justice Department since at least 1916, wrote President Wilson's private secretary, Joseph P. Tumulty, Sen. Morris Sheppard of Texas, and a local Bureau of Investigation agent to inform them of how two of *Evolución*'s competitors in San Antonio—*La Prensa* and *La Revista Mexicana*—were causing trouble for the government by publishing "seditious propaganda" against the Carranza administration, a regime that was, as he pointed out, "officially recognized by us and entitled to all the considerations of our friendship."[22] In his view both papers were attempting to incite Mexicans to overthrow their current president. While perhaps tolerable during peacetime, Idar argued, such intrigue was now far too dangerous, for the country could not afford to have revolutionaries smuggle any of its precious arms and munitions south of the border. Idar was adamant in his conviction. "Disturbing the peace in Mexico, fomenting a new revolutionary movement therein and fomenting it from American territory, abusing our proverbial hospitality to refugees, means treason," he wrote.[23]

As it turned out, even the Burleson-led post office considered Idar's fears of both papers' activities overblown. "As far as I have been able to ascertain this publication has been loyal since the war was declared," opined one postal inspector about *La Prensa*. "Insofar as the war news is concerned, [it] is strictly neutral."[24] He reached the same conclusion in his evaluation of *La Revista Mexicana*. "There is no evidence tending to show disloyalty to this government on the part of the publication in question," he wrote in a report for the chief inspector.[25]

Indeed, not long after Idar brought him to the attention of the authorities, *La Prensa*'s owner, Ignacio E. Lozano, attempted to make use of a provision in the Trading-with-the-Enemy Act that exempted demonstrably "loyal" foreign-language newspapers from translation requirements. Post office records do not indicate whether or not he, like Idar, was granted such an exemption.[26] But he did receive a strong rec-ommendation from Postmaster George D. Armistead of San Antonio, who called *La Prensa*'s translation and publication of an entire CPI pamphlet "a splendid specimen of patriotic cooperation."[27]

Nevertheless, Idar continued monitoring his colleagues through the duration of the war. In the fall of 1918, *El Demócrata Fronterizo*'s criticism of the "Work or Fight" laws, which required that all able-bodied men, including noncitizens, not serving in the military be employed only in what the government considered "productive work," provoked a scathing attack from *Evolución*. In an editorial entitled "What *El Demócrata Fronterizo* Is Attempting," Idar decried Justo Cárdenas for his lack of gratitude toward his adopted country, calling him a "rabid old man . . . full of passions and hatred" who deserved only "contempt" from Laredoans. His paper's "Germanophilic Labor," the subheadline read, "Is Ineffective Because *Evolución* Constantly Watches It."[28]

The post office ensnared a few US-based Spanish-language newspapers even without Idar's assistance. In California, *El Rebelde* of Los Angeles had its second-class mailing privileges revoked for violations of the Espionage Act.[29] After publishing an anti-capitalist manifesto in his *Regeneración*, a courageous act in light of the repressive wartime atmosphere, Ricardo Flores Magón was arrested on charges of, among other things, conspiracy, mailing indecent and "un-mailable" materials, and publishing false statements that undermined the US military. He was sentenced to twenty years in prison.[30] The only Tejano newspaper to be found guilty of any of Wilson's anti-dissent laws was El Paso's *La República*, a pro-Villa publication whose "sole purpose," as Mexican ambassador Ygnacio Bonillas told Secretary of State Robert Lansing, was "to create alarm and strain the relations between Mexico and the United States."[31] After Lansing brought the paper to Burleson's attention, its editors, José Luis Velasco and Luis R. Alvarez, were arrested on the minor charge of failing to submit an English-language translation to the postmaster general.[32]

Burleson remained steadfast despite criticism for his disregard of Americans' civil liberties. His contention that "no newspaper which in its conscience is free from disloyal intent has anything to apprehend" from the Espionage Act's enforcement did not fly with his detractors.[33] Theodore Roosevelt accused the post office of using the new law for political purposes by "punishing papers which uphold the war but which told the truth about the administration's failure to conduct the war efficiently."[34] Both Herbert Croly, editor of the *New Republic,* and reformer Amos Pinchot complained directly to President Wilson. Likewise, in a letter to the president, Upton Sinclair wrote, "your Postmaster-General reveals himself a person of such pitiful and childish ignorance concerning modern movements that it is simply a calamity that [in] this crisis he should be the person to decide what may or may not be uttered in our radical press."[35] When Wilson confronted Burleson about such matters, the latter threatened resignation, prompting the president to backpedal. "Well, go ahead and do your duty," Wilson reportedly responded. Except for one single instance late in the war, Burleson was never reined in by the White House.[36]

In cases unrelated to the mail, the other agencies of the federal government's surveillance team took charge. For military intelligence, a major source of anxiety without question was the seemingly endless string of Mexican raids on American soil that had been plaguing the US-Mexico border since the early days of the Mexican Revolution. By late 1917 the problem was being compounded by widespread hunger caused largely as a result of a food-export embargo on Mexico, which, according to officials, the Germans were pointing to as evidence that the United States was attempting to starve the Mexican people. As one report noted, enemy agents were utilizing such propaganda to stir up resentment against Americans and incite Mexicans to conduct raids across the border. Whether the tactic succeeded is unknown, but raids into US territory continued well into the war era.[37]

Another major concern for intelligence officials was that foreign enemies were involved in a mass conspiracy to subvert African Americans, a worry that had existed since the prewar period. In Texas, which had the most investigations into these rumors, the scheme reportedly involved not only Germans, as in other states, but also its substantial Mexican population—the largest in the country. As some authorities claimed, Mexicans were helping lure blacks south of the border, where Germans were supposedly organizing militias and lying in wait until enough Americans went off to war before attacking the United States. The recruitment of African Americans was believed to serve a dual purpose: they could enlarge these units while simultaneously depleting the United States of essential laborers.[38]

There was no shortage of leads when it came to this issue. The day after America's entry into the war, authorities in North Texas were alerted to the presence of two Mexican recruiters who were telling local blacks that "white people [were] the cause of the Negroes being held down." In Mexico, the men supposedly professed, Carranza would offer them the chance to start their lives anew.[39] One citizen of the small Central Texas town of Buda reported that twenty-four local blacks were planning to depart for Mexico "to enlist," while another man in San Antonio told authorities of a recent conversation with a black lawyer named Campbell, whom he described as a "Slippery Coon" and an "adventurer" who kept company "with a bunch of Damage suit lawyers."[40] According to the latter account, Campbell had spoken of his plans to travel south of the Rio Grande, where he claimed to fit in. "I have ready [*sic*] in the press of certain people trying to incite our Negro population," the informant wrote, "and if this be true, don't know where a better subject could be found than this man."[41] In East Texas, meanwhile, an Anglo-American woman allegedly overheard a black preacher urging his audience to support Germany and Mexico against the United States. Because "negroes were not allowed to hold offices and not allowed to vote in some of the elections," read the report, the preacher "wished Germany would wipe up the earth" with the United States and "threat [*sic*] all Americans like Americans have been treating the negroes."[42]

Of course, some leads were more reliable than others. In April 1917, authorities in Dallas received a report that a local black man by the name of Ire Cornelius had been attending meetings headed by five "well-dressed Mexicans" who were attempting to persuade blacks to immigrate to Mexico with promises of land and social equality. Little came of the matter. As investigators discovered, the original source of the tip, Cornelius's wife, had simply been spreading rumors to produce trouble for her unsuspecting husband, who had earlier threatened to leave her.[43] There were other cases of African Americans notifying authorities about Mexican subversives. In Moody, thirty miles southwest of Waco, authorities arrested a rail hand named Joel Coronado after several of his black coworkers accused him of attempting to recruit them as soldiers for his native Mexico in case it went to war with the United States. "He told me that this country belonged to Mexico," one worker was quoted as saying, "and if us Negroes would go to Mexico with him, that with the Mexicans and the Germans we could whip the United States." Not only that, he added, "after the war the Negroes would be given some land and could have all the white women they wanted." Coronado strongly denied the accusations, which were unverifiable (and perhaps the result of a preexisting enmity between the men involved).[44]

In Dallas fears over the subversion of loyal African Americans reached their height in the spring of 1918. On May 9 Chief of Police John W. Ryan ordered all "strange" Mexicans in the city arrested on sight. "There is an organized gang of Mexican

men and women now working in Texas with the intention of getting Negroes to go
to Mexico," reported the *Dallas Morning News* the following day, justifying the draco-
nian measure. "Officers have received the intimation that the Mexican propaganda is
prompted by agents of the German Government."[45]

According to historian Theodore Kornweibel Jr., Anglo-Americans in Texas
and elsewhere vastly exaggerated the extent of these plots. In his view the widespread
rumors of Mexican recruitment efforts likely stemmed from the fresh memories of the
Plan of San Diego Rebellion of 1915—an irredentist movement led by ethnic Mexicans
that initiated an Anglo-Mexican race war in the lower Rio Grande Valley—as well as
the belief that African Americans were naïve and readily manipulated. Their supposedly childlike nature, coupled with longstanding grudges against Anglos, made them
easy prey for enemy agents in the minds of many Americans. As Kornweibel notes, it
should not be surprising that most reports of black subversion came from the southern
states, which had both the largest concentrations of African Americans and the worst
history of racial conflict in the country. With so many of their young men off fighting, Anglo southerners dreaded the possibility of Germans and Mexicans turning local
blacks against them.[46] Obviously, it is very likely that some individuals did make disloyal
statements, some of which might have involved threats of moving to Mexico to fight
against the United States, but their very utterance does not necessarily mean that any
such schemes existed beyond the realms of their imaginations. Furthermore, while it
is a certainty that some Mexicans actually did attempt to draw African Americans to
Mexico, it must also be noted that recruitment of this sort had been taking place since
the late nineteenth century, when colonization and investment opportunities south of
the border first began opening up for blacks. To automatically attach insidious motives
to these activities would require ignoring altogether a unique facet of early twentieth-
century Mexican and African American history.[47]

In any case, fears of African American subversion by Germans and Mexicans persisted until the war's conclusion. But they by no means disappeared automatically once
the last shots were fired in Europe. As Kornweibel notes, a new bogeyman in the form
of Bolshevism had appeared by then, and the anxieties of wartime transferred seamlessly
into those of the Red Scare era, with blacks now regarded by many as easy targets for
the agents of Communism.[48]

Yet another focus of the intelligence community was the monitoring of draft
opponents. In July 1917, Bureau of Investigation agents arrested four Mexicans for
propagandizing against the recruitment and enlistment of Tejanos in San Antonio.
According to officials, the men had publicly condemned the use of Mexican labor for
the construction of encampments for the military, which they believed was engaging in

an unjustified war. They had also helped distribute a circular titled *The Price We Pay,* a socialist publication that attributed US involvement in the war to capitalist greed and called for mass protests to repeal the draft law.[49]

Of course, the complicity of suspected draft opponents was not always easy to prove. Such was the case with Juan Ríos, who was also arrested in McAllen by Justice Department agents for distributing literature urging Mexican workers to return to their homeland. In preliminary hearings the Mexican citizen claimed that he had been recruiting laborers for employers in northern Mexico and pleaded ignorance of the draft laws, arguing that he had assumed such hiring practices were legal not only in Mexico but also in the United States. Further complicating the government's case, the Mexican consul in Brownsville vouched for the detainee and vowed to seek his return to Mexico.[50] Similarly, one report out of San Angelo in Tom Green County had a certain Francisco Lozano scaring fellow Mexicans with stories of the American military drafting noncitizens. Upon interrogation, though, Lozano claimed only to be repeating what a German stranger had told him earlier on the road to nearby Ballinger. Unable to challenge his account, authorities were forced to drop the matter altogether, a somewhat necessary move given their fear "of the effect it would have had on Mexicans within registering age to have detained him longer at the time."[51]

Besides, these authorities likely considered Lozano's alibi plausible, for it was widely held that such rumors—and the Mexican exodus that it produced—were the handiwork of German agents and sympathizers. "Mexicans leaving this country for fear of being drafted," read a 1918 telegram from the Southern Department to Lt. G. L. Hoff in Galveston. "Probably due to German propaganda."[52] Maj. Gen. L. R. Holbrook, commander at Fort Sam Houston in San Antonio, was less equivocal. "For several days German propagandists have been busy circulating rumors among the Mexican population about the registration," he declared in a proclamation to Mexican laborers in the United States. "These rumors are baseless, malicious, and untrue."[53]

They were also multifarious. In late 1917 panic struck Mexicans in Caldwell County after a story broke that any adult males still in the country by the start of the new year—regardless of citizenship—would be thrown into the army.[54] Other stories in Poteet, a few miles south of San Antonio, had it that anyone who registered would be drafted, and that the military was planning to send a regiment composed entirely of blacks and Mexicans to the trenches in France.[55] But perhaps the most outlandish tale came out of Laredo. There, in the summer of 1918, a rumor was making the rounds that the US government would soon be conscripting Mexican washerwomen for service in Europe.[56]

Circulating false rumors to prompt the emigration of Mexican workers, so the prevailing belief went, was one of Germany's ways of sabotaging the American war effort. "The purpose of such propaganda is obvious," wrote James A. Harley, the adjutant general of Texas, in September 1918. "Unpicked cotton fields in Texas bear out [my] department's excuse for anxiety over the situation."[57] But it was not just the agricultural industry that suffered as the state's labor supply dwindled. "Mexicans are employed in almost all trades in this part of the country," observed the *San Antonio Express,* noting how vital they were to the railroad industry as well. "The hindrance of transportation at this time would be a great detriment to the war program, as it would be impossible to move troops."[58] As Lieutenant Hoff argued, the Mexican exodus was "playing into Germany's hands" because these workers "furnish[ed] a large part of the labor . . . for the carrying on of important government work."[59]

The reasons for many Americans' belief that Mexican laborers were susceptible to German propaganda were akin to those cited in discussions of the black subversion issue. "The average Mexican," the *Austin American* stated in an editorial on the exodus, "is slow to act and think."[60] General Harley concurred. "The Mexican laboring people, or peons as they are called, are very credulous and easily deceived," he wrote. "Propagandists have found them easy prey for furthering their schemes."[61]

Some Tejanos also blamed Germans for the exodus, albeit without the use of disparaging, anti-Mexican stereotypes. One letter sent to President Wilson, signed "A Mexican from Glen Flora," complained about how Germans terrorized laborers in Wharton County.[62] The staff of *Evolución,* meanwhile, attributed the labor shortage to "German propagandists found throughout the border and their allies in the interior of the country." Now that the Wilson administration was working toward luring many refugees back from their home country, the paper asserted, the enemy was "doing everything possible to stop Mexicans from immigrating into the United States, thereby interrupting the harvest of American crops."[63]

At least initially, though, not everyone in the state was in complete unanimity about what was prompting so many to flee across the border. "It would be a mistake to conclude that the exodus is proof of any widespread German propaganda," the *Dallas Morning News*—whose views, as evidenced by their reporting on the subversion of African Americans, would later change dramatically—argued in an editorial the day after the first registration. While acknowledging that anxiety over the draft was the most likely determinant, the paper stopped short of laying the entire blame on Germans.[64]

Although it probably underestimated the extent of the German propaganda machine, the *News* was on firmer ground in its opinion that the exodus likely stemmed from several causes, as more than one incident made clear. For instance, in Mercedes authorities apprehended a man by the name of Will Anderson for disseminating misinformation about the draft among the Mexican residents of nearby Donna, his hometown. Apparently, Anderson's scheme involved conducting business with the frightened people, whom he had hoped would sell their property below market value as they rushed back to Mexico.[65] The Bureau of Investigation reported something similar in San Antonio, where unscrupulous businessmen were reportedly planning to make a profit by conveying Mexicans across the border in automobiles and trains.[66] Naturally, some individuals accused Mexicans and Germans of comparable scams. One resident of Runge in Karnes County informed authorities that a certain Eliseo Muñiz, who had previously been maligning the draft, was now transporting Mexican laborers across the Rio Grande in his automobile at ten dollars a head.[67] Another report had Germans in San Marcos, thirty miles southwest of Austin, contributing to the widespread panic in order to purchase real estate from refugees, financial speculation that carried the frightening prospect of eventually building up the kaiser's war chest.[68] Not all such incidents involved economic motives, however. According to another intelligence report, the only discernible reasons for Lawton, Oklahoma, native James T. Chancelor's crime, which involved spreading false rumors about the draft in the barrios of Fort Worth, were alcohol and a marked antipathy toward Mexicans.[69]

Ultimately, not all investigations into Mexican criminality panned out. In one case the Bureau of Investigation saw fit to review the activities of a mutual-aid society called La Liga Protectora Mexicana (Mexican Protective League), the reason likely being that any Mexican organization was a prime target for scrutiny. As it turned out, however, the league's founder, Manuel C. Gonzales, was a pillar of the community in San Antonio who would go on to serve admirably in the US Army during the war. Not surprisingly, the organization's file was a short one, with no indications of follow-up investigations of any sort.[70]

Some of the Bureau of Investigation's leads were patently false. In November 1917 J. C. Childres of Callahan County reported to Justice of the Peace J. H. Surles that a Mexican sheepherder named Martínez, who claimed to be a former officer in the Mexican Army, had recently divulged a joint German-Mexican plan to invade the United States. According to Childres, whom Surles considered "perfectly reliable," Martínez was only herding sheep as a pretext and had declared that he "would be Glad to see the time this Would Take Place [*sic*]."[71] A subsequent investigation revealed Childres to be less than trustworthy, however. In a letter to a local Bureau of Investigation agent, US Commissioner W. E. Girand noted how Martínez had taken Childres's job after the latter had been terminated for "inefficiency." Concluding that the initial report was "a piece of spite work more than anything else," Girand exonerated

Martínez, who had been taken to him for questioning, and released him from police custody.[72]

Reminiscent of the internal strife that afflicted other segments of the Tejano community, Mexicans themselves also sent authorities on futile searches. In El Paso, Justice Department agents and customs inspectors were alerted to a smuggling operation involving a woman named Carolina Pacos. Their informant, another Mexican female whose identity was kept secret in the official report, told them that Pacos was in the habit of frequenting a local grocery store owned by a suspicious Turk. There, she claimed, Pacos would purchase small amounts of ammunition and smuggle them into Mexico in her undergarments. To catch the alleged smuggler in the act, the investigative team furnished customs officers with her passport photograph and waited for her next appearance at the Stanton Street Bridge.[73] After an inspection that could only have been an embarrassing experience for all parties concerned, the Bureau of Investigation conceded that its examinations had "failed to substantiate that the woman was smuggling ammunition."[74]

Other episodes bordered on absurdity even without false leads. One such case took place in the spring of 1918 in Fort Worth, where authorities placed a Mexican native by the name of Valle, a resident of Bureau, Illinois, under arrest as a potential subversive. "Being a mexican [sic] and having with him a camera and unable to explain himself clearly," Bureau of Investigation agent F. S. Smith wrote, Valle "was considered suspicious." Such reservations diminished after officials inspected the detainee and interrogated him fully, which resulted in his release from police custody. As it turned out, Valle had simply been doing a favor for his sixteen-year-old brother, who was en route from Mexico, by meeting him in Fort Worth, from where they planned to depart for Illinois. On the elder Valle's person, Smith noted, investigators had found a Liberty Loan bond.[75]

The most ludicrous of these leads involved elements of mysticism and the supernatural. In May 1917, Bureau of Investigation agents responded to rumors that Mexicans in Austin were holding meetings to plan the bombing of the state capitol building and other local structures. The main attraction at these gatherings, they were told, was a young Mexican girl with special powers of healing and clairvoyance. In actuality their investigation turned up little more than a traveling medicine show. Sitting on a throne wearing a silk dress and a brass crown, the young soothsayer would first address the crowds about war, prophesies, and other such matters before prescribing her father's miracle salve to ailing audience members, who in gratitude would then offer whatever they could as a donation. Although the girl's father was taken into custody and charged with practicing medicine without a license, authorities were unable to find any evidence of sabotage or disloyalty. Indeed, not only were the meetings not encouraging Mexicans to return to their homeland—as some agents suspected—the little girl was actually calling on her followers to "work unceasingly in the fields and in the towns" so that "food and other supplies may be produced in abundance to help the starving people across the ocean."[76]

Examples like these illustrate a troubling aspect of the war's vigilance campaign: namely, that it was conducted at the expense of the civil liberties of thousands, perhaps even millions, of innocent Americans. Besides the post office's systematic attempts to compel loyalty from the press, authorities often harassed and intimidated suspects during the course of their investigations. Even when the suspicions of disloyalty proved false, other charges were sometimes substituted to punish surveillance targets, as evidenced by the seer episode. Of course, these charges were occasionally unsustainable too, and some suspects walked free. Nevertheless, by then local officials had subjected them to the powers of arrest, confinement, indictment, and intimidation.[77] In the words of constitutional historian Paul L. Murphy, "the story of civil liberties during World War I is a dreary, disturbing, and in some respects, shocking chapter out of the nation's past. Americans . . . stood by on the domestic scene and saw liberty and justice prostituted in ways more extreme and extensive than any other time in American history."[78]

In the end, no Mexican or Mexican American was ever found guilty of active spying in the United States, although suspected cases of espionage did sometimes land in court. In Laredo the arrest in late 1918 of a sixteen-year-old girl named Guadalupe Ledesma, who was charged with being a German agent, caused a considerable stir. Garnering attention as much for her beauty as for her legal quandary, the Mexican native stood accused of carrying messages for the Germans back and forth across the Rio Grande. However sensational, her trial was short lived. In April 1919 a federal court in Laredo found Ledesma innocent of all charges.[79]

The sole enemy agent sentenced to death during World War I was a German naval lieutenant by the name of Lothar Witzke. An experienced spy despite being a mere twenty-two years old, Witzke had orders to create a major disturbance along the US-Mexico border. To accomplish this task, he and two other agents had plans to travel to Arizona to induce the African American soldiers of the 9th and 10th Cavalry to mutiny as well as to incite waves of violent strikes among the local copper miners. Unfortunately for Witzke, his companions were both double agents, one of whom was working in conjunction with US intelligence (the other agent was operating with the British). On February 1, 1918, military-intelligence officials arrested Witzke in Nogales, Arizona. Several months later a military tribunal found him guilty of espionage and sentenced him to hang, although certain legal technicalities undermining the government's case eventually led to his sentence being commuted to life imprisonment and, in 1923, his release to Germany.[80]

Because espionage and conspiracy were so difficult to prove in court, offenses such as smuggling resulted in more convictions. With its accessibility to anyone willing to hide a few munitions on his or her person and transport them across the border, smuggling was often carried out by destitute Mexican refugees willing to risk a stint in the county jail. In other cases, however, the offenders were more-high-profile individuals, such as Herminio Mercado Abasta, a captain in Gen. Pablo Gonzales's revolutionary army, who was caught attempting to smuggle five thousand rounds of pistol cartridges into the northern Mexican town of Nuevo Laredo.[81]

In the years following the Allied victory in the war, Germany's influence in Mexico gradually faded. A few weeks after the armistice, the US government sent German leaders a note stating that "the German minister in Mexico is continuing to foment anti-American propaganda in that country." If the United States is "to take in good faith the German government's recent request for aid," the message continued, "it must request that the agitation in question cease and the German minister to Mexico be recalled immediately." Not surprisingly, Germany wasted little time in complying with the demand. Although the Nazis resumed espionage projects in Mexico during the 1930s, their success paled compared to that of the kaiser's regime.[82]

Throughout the war, disloyalty manifested itself in every part of the country. The barrios of the Lone Star State were no different. But in its surveillance of the Tejano community, American intelligence above all else acted on the widespread fears of German-Mexican collusion, fears so deep and abiding that even the shakiest of leads were pursued. For the student of history, this particular aspect of World War I merits consideration not only because of its often fascinating accounts of conspiracy and intrigue but also because of what it says about the unfavorable views of Mexicans that existed during the period. At a time when no one could afford to be considered a potential subversive, the image of the Mexican as untrustworthy gained renewed credence. The result was that the civil liberties of many innocent individuals were sacrificed on the altar of national security.

Notes

This study employs the term "Tejano" to describe any Texas resident of Mexican extraction—regardless of nationality—although, when necessary, it identifies the citizenship of certain individuals or groups. By extension, the term "Tejano community" refers to the entire Mexican-descent population in Texas, including non-US citizens.

1. *New York Times,* Mar. 3, 1917.

2. Interestingly, persons of Mexican descent also came under heavy suspicion as potential subversives during the two wars that bookended World War I. For the allegedly pro-Spanish leanings of the Tejano community during the Spanish-American War, see Arnoldo De León, *They Called Them Greasers: Anglo Attitudes toward Mexicans in Texas, 1821–1900* (Austin: University of Texas Press, 1983), 61–62n122. Mauricio Mazón discusses the equally baseless rumors of Nazi activity among Mexican-origin individuals in Los Angeles and the surrounding areas during World War II. See *The Zoot-Suit Riots: The Psychology of Symbolic Annihilation* (Austin: University of Texas Press, 1984), 103–106.

3. Approximately 5,000 Spanish-surnamed Texans served in the US military during World War I, with 5 of these men receiving medals for valorous service from the US government. Among these awardees was David Bennes Cantu Barkley, one of only four World War I servicemen from Texas—and from what we know, the first Mexican American—to receive the Medal of Honor, the highest award for bravery in the US armed forces. See José A. Ramírez, *To the Line of Fire! Mexican Texans and World War I* (College Station: Texas A&M University Press, 2009), xviii, 22, 113.

4. Few studies in Chicano historiography have focused exclusively on World War I, with the notable exceptions of Carole E. Christian, "Joining the American Mainstream: Texas's Mexican Americans During World War I," *Southwestern Historical Quarterly* 92 (Apr. 1989): 559–95; Phillip Gonzales and Ann Massman, "Loyalty Questioned: Nuevomexicanos in the Great War," *Pacific Historical Review* 75 (Nov. 2006): 629–66; and Ramírez, *To the Line of Fire!* This essay (based on the third chapter of *To the Line of Fire!*) takes a new-military-history approach to World War I. Hence, it eschews battles, generals, and other traditional fare of military historians and instead examines warfare in a broader context, in this case focusing on how wartime tensions led to heightened surveillance of Tejanos and Tejanas on the home front. Although a previously unexplored area in Chicano history, government surveillance of ethnic and racial minorities during World War I has been treated elsewhere. See, for example, Theodore Kornweibel Jr., *"Investigate Everything": Federal Efforts to Compel Black Loyalty during World War I* (Bloomington: Indiana University Press, 2002); and Mark Ellis, *Race, War, and Surveillance: African Americans and the United States Government during World War I* (Bloomington: Indiana University Press, 2001).

5. Charles H. Harris III and Louis R. Sadler, "The Witzke Affair: German Intrigue on the Mexican Border, 1917–18," *Military Review* 59 (Feb. 1979): 38; Athan Theoharis, *The FBI and American Democracy: A Brief Critical History* (Lawrence: University Press of Kansas, 2004), 21–22; William E. Leuchtenburg, *The Perils of Prosperity, 1914–32,* 2nd ed. (Chicago: University of Chicago Press, 1993), 28; D. Clayton James and Anne Sharp Wells, *America and the Great War, 1914–1920* (Wheeling, IL: Harlan Davidson, 1998), 12–13 (quote, 13).

6. Friedrich Katz, *The Secret War in Mexico: Europe, the United States, and the Mexican Revolution* (Chicago: University of Chicago Press, 1981), 328–67, 411–33, 511–16.

7. Ibid., 433–41.

8. Kornweibel, *"Investigate Everything,"* chap. 1; Texas Adjutant General, *Biennial Report of the Adjutant General of Texas from January 1, 1917 to December 31, 1918* (Austin, TX: Von Boeckmann-Jones, 1919), 63–70. The Bureau of Investigation's reports on Mexican neutrality violations—the so-called Mexican Files—number some 80,000 pages and are now available on twenty-four reels of microfilm. See also Charles H. Harris III and Louis R. Sadler, *The Border and the Revolution: Clandestine Activities of the Mexican Revolution, 1910–1920* (Silver City, NM: High-Lonesome Books, 1998), 54.

9. Report of E. T. Needham, May 2, 1917, #232–1646, r 866, M1085, RG 65, Investigative Records Relating to Mexican Neutrality Violations ("Mexican Files"), Investigative Case Files of

the Bureau of Investigation, 1908–22, 1909–21, National Archives and Records Administration (hereafter cited as Mexican Files).

10. Report of R. Panster, Aug. 17, 1917, #232–1865, r 867, ibid.

11. Report of R. L. Barnes, Apr. 30, 1917, #232–1541, r 866, ibid.

12. David M. Kennedy, *Over Here: The First World War and American Society* (New York: Oxford University Press, 1980), 26, 75 (quote).

13. Edward M. House, diary, Feb. 11, 1918, Edward M. House Papers, Sterling Library, Yale University, New Haven, CT, quoted in ibid., 75.

14. Kornweibel, *"Investigate Everything,"* 32–33. Evidence of the Loyalty Rangers' investigations of the mail can be found in W. M. Hanson to James A. Harley, Feb. 15, 1918, Box 401–573, "Correspondence," Department Correspondence, Texas Adjutant General's Department, Archives and Information Services Division, Texas State Library and Archives Commission, Austin.

15. Kennedy, *Over Here,* 25–26, 65, 77; Kornweibel, *"Investigate Everything,"* 33.

16. Katz, *Secret War in Mexico,* 441–53, 459 (quote). On February 24, 1918, *El Demócrata* claimed that almost sixty thousand Mexican citizens had been enlisted in the US military, a figure that was almost certainly inflated to heighten anti-Americanism and fears of the draft. See Fernando Saúl Alanís Enciso, *El Primer Programa Bracero y el Gobierno de México* (San Luis Potosí: El Colegio de San Luis, 1999), 55.

17. *El Demócrata Fronterizo* (Laredo, TX), Dec. 1, 1917.

18. Katz, *Secret War in Mexico,* 453–59.

19. Christian, "Joining the American Mainstream," 569–70. My assertion that no Spanish-language newspapers from Texas were ever labeled disloyal comes from examining every case file on the Tejano press in RG 28, Records Relating to the Espionage Act, World War I, 1917–21, Records of the Post Office Department, National Archives and Records Administration (hereafter cited as Post Office Records).

20. Report of Seman, Apr. 1, 1917, #232–1784, r 867, M1085, Mexican Files.

21. Report of Charles E. Breniman, Apr. 5, 1917, #232–783, r 865, ibid.

22. Apparently, the targets of Idar's surveillance during the prewar period were Mexican exiles suspected of plotting revolutionary activities from US soil. See, for example, report of C. N. Idar, Aug. 3, 1916, ibid.; and report of C. N. Idar, Aug. 19, 1916, #232–784, ibid.

23. Quoted in BI report of C. E. Breniman, Dec. 14, 1917, Case File 49490, Box 140, Post Office Records.

24. L. W. Morris to Inspector in Charge, Feb. 18, 1918, ibid.

25. L. W. Morris to Inspector in Charge, Feb. 18, 1918, Case File 50715, Box 188, ibid.

26. W. H. Lamar to Idar Publishing Company, July 12, 1918, Case File 50940, Box 211, ibid.

27. George D. Armistead to the Solicitor, Post Office Department, July 16, 1918, Case File 49490, Box 140, ibid.

28. *Laredo Evolución,* Sept. 3, 1918 (translation mine). For a critical look at the "Work or Fight" laws, see Gerald E. Shenk, *"Work or Fight!": Race, Gender, and the Draft in World War One* (New York: Palgrave Macmillan, 2005).

29. Third Assistant Postmaster General, Memo, May 8, 1918, 838.14, Folder 21, r 6, Albert Sidney Burleson Papers, Center for American History, University of Texas, Austin (hereafter cited as Burleson Papers).

30. James A. Sandos, *Rebellion in the Borderlands: Anarchism and the Plan de San Diego, 1904–1923* (Norman: University of Oklahoma Press, 1982), 167–68.

31. Ygnacio Bonilla to Robert Lansing, June 12, 1918, Case File 51091, Box 223, Post Office Records. My claim that *La República* was the only Tejano periodical to fall victim to the World War I era's anti-dissent laws, as with my earlier assertion on the question of disloyalty, comes from examining the Postal Service's Espionage Act case files.

32. Newspaper clipping, n.d. [Aug. 1918], Case File 51091, Box 223, Post Office Records.

33. Albert S. Burleson to the Editor and Publisher, Oct. 3, 1917, 838.14, Folder 21, r 6, Burleson Papers.

34. Quoted in untitled statement from Albert S. Burleson, May 31, 1918, 838.14, Folder 21, r 6, Burleson Papers.

35. Upton Sinclair to Woodrow Wilson, Oct. 22, 1917, Woodrow Wilson Papers, Library of Congress, Washington, DC, quoted in Kennedy, *Over Here*, 76.

36. Kennedy, *Over Here*, 76–78. For more on the relationship between Wilson and Burleson, see Adrian Anderson, "President Wilson's Politician: Albert Sidney Burleson of Texas," *Southwestern Historical Quarterly* 77 (Jan. 1974): 339–54.

37. *Laredo Weekly Times*, Nov. 25, Dec. 2, 1917; *San Antonio Express*, Feb. 25, 1918; PF-38/1, Mar. 22, 1918, r 16, M1474, RG 165, Geographic Index to Correspondence of the Bureau of Investigation, Records of the War Department General and Special Staffs, National Archives and Records Administration (hereafter cited as GI). The report on German propaganda in Mexico, like many other personnel files of the Military Intelligence Division that were later termed "useless," was actually destroyed as part of a series of disposal actions undertaken during the late 1920s. The Bureau of Investigation's geographic index, however, contains a short summation of its contents.

38. Kornweibel, *"Investigate Everything,"* 45–46, 49, 54. For more on a prewar episode involving the supposed recruitment of African Americans for service in Carranza's army, see James Alexander Garza, "On the Edge of a Storm: Laredo and the Mexican Revolution, 1910–1917" (MA thesis, Texas A&M International University, 1996), 86.

39. F. M. Spencer to Bureau, Apr. 9, 1917, 3057, Old German Case File, Investigative Case Files of the Bureau of Investigation, 1908–1922, 1909–1921, National Archives and Records Administration, quoted in Kornweibel, *"Investigate Everything,"* 45.

40. J. H. Rogers to B. L. Barnes, Apr. 9, 1917, #232–1608, r 866, M1085, Mexican Files.

41. Quoted in report of R. L. Barnes, May 1, 1917, #232–1635, ibid.

42. Report of R. L. Barnes, May 3, 1917, #232–1530, ibid.

43. Report of F. M. Spencer, Apr. 13, 1917, #232–1546, ibid.

44. Report of B. C. Baldwin, Apr. 24, 1917, #232–1597, ibid.

45. *Dallas Morning News*, May 10, 1918.

46. Kornweibel, *"Investigate Everything,"* 38, 44–46, 49.

47. Arnold Shankman, "The Image of Mexico and the Mexican-American in the Black Press, 1890–1935," *Journal of Ethnic Studies* 3 (Summer 1975): 43–45.

48. Kornweibel, *"Investigate Everything,"* 272. For more on this aspect of the Red Scare, see Kornweibel, *"Seeing Red": Federal Campaigns against Black Militancy, 1919–1925* (Bloomington: Indiana University Press, 1998).

49. *San Antonio Express*, July 11, 21, 1917.

50. *La Prensa* (San Antonio), Aug. 31, 1917.

51. Report of J. J. Lawrence, June 4, 1917, #232–1840, r 867, M1085, Mexican Files.

52. Quoted in *Corpus Christi Caller*, Sept. 8, 1918.

53. Quoted in *San Antonio Express,* Sept. 7, 1918.

54. Ibid., Dec. 16, 1917.

55. Report of E. H. Parker, June 15, 1917, #232–1825, r 867, M1085, Mexican Files.

56. *Laredo Weekly Times,* Sept. 1, 1918.

57. James A. Harley to O. E. Dunlap, Sept. 14, 1918, 2J396, Texas War Records Collection, 1916–19, 1940–45, Center for American History, University of Texas, Austin.

58. *San Antonio Express,* Sept. 7, 1918.

59. Quoted in *Corpus Christi Caller,* Sept. 8, 1918.

60. Quoted in *Laredo Weekly Times,* July 15, 1917.

61. Harley to Dunlap, Sept. 14, 1918.

62. 10487–1224/I–2, Aug. 22, 1918, r 16, M1474, GI.

63. *Evolución,* Sept. 8, 1918 (translation mine).

64. *Dallas Morning News,* June 6, 1917.

65. *Evolución,* June 8, 1917.

66. Report of P. López, May 25, 1917, #232–1959, r 867, M1085, Mexican Files.

67. Report of E. H. Parker, June 25, 1917, #232–1951, ibid.

68. Report of P. López, June 7, 1917, #232–1851, ibid.

69. Report of Will C. Austin, Sept. 23, 1918, #232–3344, r 871, ibid.

70. Report of William Nuenhoffer, Nov. 1, 1917, #232–967, r 867, ibid.

71. J. H. Surles to A. B. Blelaski [*sic*], Nov. 11, 1917, #232–1879, ibid.

72. W. E. Girand to W. C. Austin, Dec. 8, 1917, quoted in report of W. C. Austin, Dec. 13, 1917, #232–2403, ibid. Unfortunately, the report does not reveal what punishment, if any, Childres received for lying to investigators.

73. Report of [illegible on film] Tinlepaugh, Sept. 27, 1918, #232–1652, r 866, ibid.

74. Report of Gus T. Jones, Jan. 11, 1919, ibid. This report, which officially declares the case closed, does not reveal the fate of the informant.

75. Report of F. S. Smith, June 4, 1918, #232–3105, r 870, ibid.

76. Quoted in report of Manuel Sorola, May 20, 1917, #232–1539, r 866, ibid.; report of B. C. Baldwin, May 1, 1917, ibid.; report of B. C. Baldwin, May 16, 1917, ibid.

77. Kornweibel, *"Investigate Everything,"* 3–4, 59, 61, 67–68.

78. Paul L. Murphy, *World War I and the Origin of Civil Liberties in the United States* (New York: Norton, 1979), 15, quoted in Kornweibel, *"Investigate Everything,"* 3–4.

79. *La Prensa,* Mar. 6, 1919; *San Antonio Express,* Mar. 2, 1919; *Evolución,* Apr. 29, 1919. For more on convictions for spying under the Espionage Act, see Norman Polmar and Thomas B. Allen, *Spy Book: The Encyclopedia of Espionage* (New York: Random House, 1997), 195.

80. Harris and Saddler, "Witzke Affair," 36–50.

81. Report of Manuel Sorola, Apr. 28, 1918, #232–1870, r 867, M1085, Mexican Files; Harris and Sadler, *Border and the Revolution,* 61–62.

82. Katz, *Secret War in Mexico,* 540–49, 563 (quotes, 540). For more on Nazi intrigue in Mexico, see Stanley E. Hilton, *Hitler's Secret War in South America, 1939–1945: German Military Espionage and Allied Counterespionage in Brazil* (Baton Rouge: Louisiana State University Press, 1981). Despite its focus on Brazil—the center of Nazi espionage in the Americas until 1942—Hilton's book nonetheless contains valuable information on Mexico and other Latin American countries.

12

Texan Prisoners of the Japanese

A Study in Survival

Kelly E. Crager

AS HE LOOKED BACK on his experiences as a prisoner of the Japanese in the Second World War, Texas native Clyde Shelton explained his survival: "I never did give up. I never heard an American that was in the service say, 'I'm not going home.' He'd say, '*When* I'm going home. *When* I go home.' You never heard one say, 'I don't think I'll ever make it.' You never heard one say that—never."[1] During World War II, Shelton served in the 2nd Battalion, 131st Field Artillery Regiment, 36th "Texas" Division. Better known as Texas's "Lost Battalion," the entire unit capitulated to the Imperial Japanese Army on the island of Java in the Dutch East Indies in March 1942. This group of prisoners of war (POWs), most of whom were Texans, spent the remainder of World War II in various prison camps in Southeast Asia and in the Japanese home islands. These men labored for the duration of the war, enduring extreme overwork, malnourishment, and torture while receiving almost no medical care. Despite the deplorable and dangerous conditions they faced, 84 percent of them survived to return home at war's end, a number much higher than that of the vast majority of other groups of Allied POWs.[2] Although known for their brutal treatment of prisoners throughout the war, the Japanese were unable to break the collective spirit of this small group of Texans.

The question to be asked, then, is: What explains the high survival rate of these men when compared to other prisoners of the Japanese? Evidence gathered in the years following the war—especially oral-history interviews conducted with over one hundred survivors—suggests that, among other things, a common Texas heritage and identity helped these men bond very closely during the trying times of captivity. This shared heritage helped create a unique environment of cooperation among these men, aiding their survival. When other POW communities were breaking down internally due to individual interest and selfishness—brought on by the miserable conditions imposed by their captors—these men banded together in a collective effort to promote each others' survival and, therefore, the survival of their unit. But these men were not able to endure captivity solely because they were Texans. Although Lone Star natives have cultivated a reputation for toughness through generations, and although there is much to support this reputation, one is not predestined to survive Japanese POW camps simply because of one's place of birth. Instead various factors aided the Texans in their survival.

The story of the "Lost Battalion" begins in Depression-era Texas. A National Guard outfit prior to being mobilized in late 1940, the 2nd Battalion was made up of young men in search of income and who yearned for a break from the daily routine of rural life. This small artillery unit consisted of three firing batteries—D, E, and F from Wichita Falls, Abilene, and Jacksboro, respectively—the Headquarters Battery from Decatur, and service and medical detachments from Lubbock and Plainview. Farm foreclosures and Dustbowl conditions provided the backdrop for the times and eroded the economic future for a generation of young men. Rather than patriotism, hunger and privation proved to be the primary motivating factors for joining the National Guard. Pete Evans of Hamby, Texas, explained his decision to enlist: "Times was pretty rough. . . . I quit school [to join the National Guard]. . . . Well, we drew maybe a dollar-and-a-half a drill, I believe it was, and, of course, back in those days a dollar-and-a-half was as big as a wagon wheel. . . . It would supplement our sort of meager existence. You know, there's a lot of difference between 'poor' and '*poor*,' but we were *poor*."[3]

Peacetime service in the guard was a leisurely duty. One weekend each month, the Texans would report to the local armory for drilling and classes, only occasionally participating in field exercises. To many, these weekends were a social getaway. Kelly Bob Bramlett of Decatur compared his guard weekends to summer camp.[4] Jacksboro's Luther Prunty remembered that "it was like a vacation to go into National Guard camp."[5] Even when Pres. Franklin D. Roosevelt ordered the mobilization of the 36th Division in November 1940, few of the men believed it would seriously disrupt their lives. From November 1940 through February 1941, the 2nd Battalion made its way to Camp Bowie in Brownwood and prepared to enter national service. Lubbock's Crayton "Quaty" Gordon, an undergraduate at Texas Tech University, remembered: "To me, a year's mobilization was a type of relief from the grind of studying. . . . I thought it'd be a real big relief and something different—a change, a relaxation—from schoolwork."[6] Amarillo native George

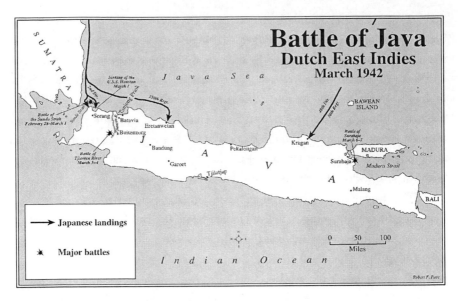

Battle of Java, March 1942. Courtesy Robert F. Pace.

Killian summed up his impression: "Well, I'm going to have a ball, you know, like always."[7]

In the summer of 1941, the 36th Division packed its gear and moved to western Louisiana to participate in further US Army training and field maneuvers. The largest of their kind prior to US entry into the war, the Louisiana Maneuvers tested the effectiveness of America's ground forces and aided in military prepared-ness. Again, there was little about their time in Louisiana that led the Texans to believe that they would face anything beyond their normal routine. Chronically short of weapons, ammunition, and transportation throughout the maneuvers, the men of the 2nd Battalion saw little value in their efforts and focused on their own small world. Service Battery's P. J. Smallwood described his time in Louisiana as an endurance test, but he did not believe that he or his unit gained much from the experience.[8] Luther Prunty recalled that he spent most of his time digging trucks out of the mud.[9]

Even after returning home to Texas in September and receiving orders to move out to bolster the defenses of the Philippines in November, the artillerymen showed their naiveté and poor grasp of world events and their place in them. The battalion had no trouble recruiting volunteers to help fill out its complement for duty overseas. Eldridge Rayburn, who transferred into the unit prior to shipping out, recalled: "There was no problem for them to get the volunteers. Everybody was looking for adventure or something different, you know. We had a year in Brownwood, and we was ready to go somewhere and do something."[10] D Battery's Max Offerle, who joined the guard to serve with this brother Oscar, said he looked forward to their new duty because it "sounded adventurous."[11] Thus, having received limited training of questionable value, the young Texans-turned-soldiers made their way for duty in the Pacific.

The Second World War came to the United States with the Japanese attack on Pearl Harbor on December 7, 1941. At the time of the attack, the 2nd Battalion was two days west of Hawaii aboard the USAT *Republic,* steaming toward the Philippines. Because of the Japanese assault on the Philippines on December 8, the *Republic* changed course for Brisbane, Australia, where the Texans offloaded and awaited their next set of orders. In early January 1942 these orders arrived, requiring the 2nd Battalion to move to Java, then a Dutch possession rich in resources coveted by the Japanese. The Texans joined the Allied defenders of the island—an uncomfortable mixture of Dutch officers, native Javanese home guards, and British and Australian forces, known by the acronym ABDACOM—to defend the island from imminent invasion.[12]

After nearly a month of Japanese air attacks to soften the island's defenses, the Imperial Japanese Army struck with a two-pronged invasion of Java on the night of February 28–March 1. The main landing force splashed ashore on the island's western tip at Bantam Bay and drove toward the capital city of Batavia, while a smaller force landed in the east near Kragan and quickly closed on the port city of Surabaja. Although outnumbering the invading forces, the ill-fated Allied defenders soon crumpled before the Japanese offensive. Two of the three US artillery batteries—D and F—saw brief but very spirited action at the Battle of Tjantien River in early March and acquitted themselves very well, while E Battery remained in the Surabaja area and vainly fought to stem the Japanese advance on that city. The Texans' performance notwithstanding, Allied defenses collapsed, and on March 8 ABDACOM commanders ordered the surrender of the island.[13]

Disappointed and dispirited with this rapid turn of events, the Texans found themselves prisoners of the Japanese—at the mercy of those known to be merciless. Frank Ficklin of Decatur remembered, "It never entered our minds that we would be prisoners of war of the Japanese."[14] Houston "Slug" Wright of F Battery expressed that he "was a discouraged dadgummed soldier."[15] Jacksboro's Lt. Huddleston Wright explained that "one of the hardest things I ever had to do was to tell my men that we were prisoners of war."[16] Certainly, they had reason to feel demoralized. The Japanese had earned a reputation for cruelty to those whom they conquered, and the Texans had little reason to believe that they would be treated any differently. Wise County's Ben Kelley explained: "I have had several incidents in my life that have been serious, but that tops them all. Number one, we didn't know what was going to happen. . . . I had heard rumors about the Japanese, that they didn't take prisoners. I had heard about their cruelty. Just the thought of being a prisoner-of-war was bad. Just the unknown itself was overwhelming. It was the worst feeling I have ever experienced in my life."[17]

Learning to adjust to life in captivity seemed to take place in stages for the young Texans. After the initial shock of surrender, the POWs in western Java were herded into a camp in Batavia, known as Bicycle Camp, while the Japanese held E Battery in the Jaarmarkt, a large market square in Surabaja. During this initial stage of their imprisonment, the men developed the means by which they would deal with the harsh realities of captivity.

At Bicycle Camp and Jaarmarkt, they encountered Japanese military discipline for the first time. The guards expected prisoners to comply with their orders immediately and completely. To fail to do so resulted in severe physical punishment. Open-handed slaps to the head were the most common and least painful of the punishments inflicted, but beatings were often administered with ax handles, rifle butts, and bamboo poles. Camp guards required prisoners to bow to them, which proved to be one of the most galling of all regulations. Grover Reichle of Jacksboro explained: "Inwardly, you hated the Japs, but you had to bow and scrape. You had to salute a Jap any time you met him if you had headwear on. Otherwise, you had to bow. Well, I always had something on my head because I didn't want to bow to them little yellow bastards."[18] Service Battery's Wade Webb described a common punishment for failing to bow: "[T]hey'd get a piece of stove wood and split it about [three or four inches in diameter]. It's got splinters and four or five edges to it. They'd put it behind a guy's knees and make him squat on it until he fainted."[19] Quaty Gordon provided his impression of a guard known as the "Brown Bomber": "[H]e was short in stature, and apparently this was something that didn't set very well with him, you know. Goddamn, he equalized it with that rifle! He'd come up there, and, man, he'd smash you upside the head with that damn rifle in the bat of an eye. . . . [H]ere's this little banty-legged devil talking to you and knocking you upside the damn head with a rifle butt, and there ain't a damn thing you can do about it."[20]

Gordon's observation is an important one: "There ain't a damn thing you can do about it." The Japanese controlled the camps, and the prisoners simply could do nothing to change it. The sooner one came to grips with this arrangement, the sooner he would learn to survive in that environment. The prisoners felt belittled by the rules, and especially by the punishments, but according to Capt. Clark Taylor of Service Battery: "You could curse a little under your breath or something, but it was something you could live with. Hell, when you would come under their rule, by dang, you would live by their rules or take their punishment. If you wanted to be bull-headed about it and not salute or stand up when they came in, and you would rather have a slapping for it, all right, you could have that. They gave the rules, and we had to live with them or take the consequences."[21]

In addition to the physical punishment exacted upon them, prisoners also learned to live in the squalid conditions of their camps. The Japanese provided food of a very poor quality, usually consisting of floor sweepings from rice warehouses; a thin, watery soup; and weevil-infested bread. Medic Raymond Reed recalled: "The rice and stew was full of worms and weevils. . . . I would pick every one out, but by the time I got through picking them out, the food was cold and tasted like hell. It didn't taste that good to start with, but when it was cold it was really bad. Finally, it wasn't a matter of picking out anything. You just looked that ol' worm in the eye and chewed him up and swallowed him. You're past that picky stage."[22] Sanitation facilities were equally abysmal as open-pit latrines teemed with disease-carrying flies and often flooded through the camps during a heavy rain. The Japanese provided almost no medical care for their prisoners and issued no medicine. Malnutrition and disease began to strike the prisoners, who were left to their own devices to provide much of their own food and medical care.[23]

Given such circumstances, the normally individualistic young Texans came to understand the importance of working with others to help promote the welfare of the unit. In both Bicycle Camp and Jaarmarkt, officers and enlisted men dispensed with the artificial distinctions of rank and dealt with each other as individuals coming together in an incredibly trying time. Lt. Ilo Hard of Itasca explained: "[I]t was not 'by-the-numbers.' . . . [The officers would try to] do the right thing at the right time. All we expected, when we talked to a man, was that he give us his undivided attention, that he'd listen to us, you know, respectfully."[24] Officers often acted as liaisons between their men and the guards to lessen the possibilities for misunderstanding and worked to protect their men from physical punishment. Both officers and enlisted men also contributed their remaining money to a community fund to secretly purchase food from local Javanese outside of the camp.

Perhaps most importantly, the men also formed small groups with their closest friends or most needy prisoners. Referred to by the survivors as "cliques," these organizations usually consisted of three to five individuals. Each man contributed to the welfare of his clique by sharing extra food with his comrades, tending to each others' medical problems when possible, aiding the most weak in their group through trying days on work details, and intervening to help end a situation that might result in a fellow prisoner being beaten or tortured. These groups formed quite naturally and were not the result of orders from their officers. In fact, it was common for officers and enlisted men to belong to the same clique. George Detre explained: "You had to form a clique to survive. It wasn't a mean thing or a means to cheat anybody or anything like that. You had to have a little clique so that you could take care of each other. If one man got sick, then you would bring his food to him and look out for him, maybe get him back on his feet again. This is the way we all operated. You had to look out for each other."[25]

The survival techniques they developed on Java would soon be put to the test. In October 1942 the Japanese began moving POWs throughout their empire to work as slave labor on numerous massive construction and mining projects. The prisoners at Bicycle Camp boarded rusting, filthy cargo ships bound for Singapore and then to Burma to aid in the construction of the infamous Burma–Thailand Death Railway. Those in Jaarmarkt were shipped to the Japanese home islands to work in the shipyards

Prisoner's sketch of POWs drilling holes in rocks for dynamiting along the Burma–Thailand Death Railway. Courtesy Oral History Program, University of North Texas.

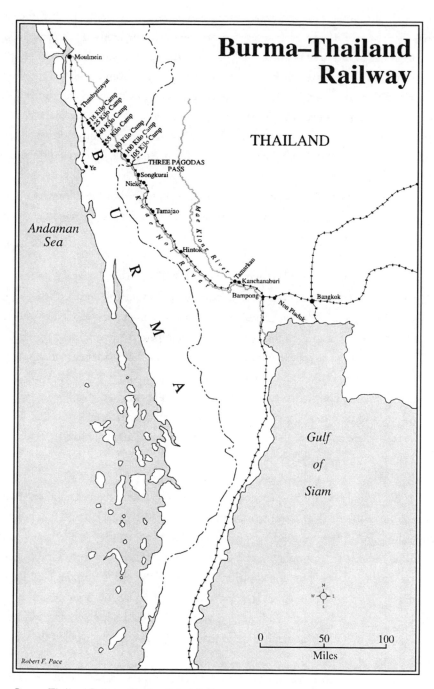

Burma–Thailand Railway. Courtesy Robert F. Pace.

and coal mines there. The transport vessels earned the moniker "hell ships" for very obvious reasons. Prisoners were severely overcrowded in the holds of the aging hulks, and each was forced to sit between the legs of the man behind him. They could not lie down for the entire trip, and the equatorial heat radiating from the ships' steel hulls, combined with the overcrowding, magnified temperatures in the holds to over 120 degrees Fahrenheit. Guards seldom allowed prisoners to climb to the main deck to relieve themselves, so most did so in the hold. Prisoners received tiny portions of rice and water each day, and their bodies continued the inevitable decline caused by malnutrition and disease.[26]

The conditions aboard the transports are best described by the unfortunate souls who endured the experience. Jack County native Lt. Julius Heinen described the process for loading prisoners:

[The guards] started people down in [the hold]. They made them take up their places and sit down. Now as they filled up the bottom [platform], then they started filling up the center, and then they started filling up the top. Now when all of that was full and you thought you were cramped, there were still men with no place to put their body that had to get down in that hold. So they made space. They just took a rifle butt and jammed it at the guy who was closest. Well, of course, his reaction was to try to get away from the rifle butt that was coming at him, and he moved backwards with as much force as he could, and that left an area where another man could get in. So you were jammed into that hold as jammed as you can possibly put people.[27]

Eddie Fung offered his impression of the *Kinkon Maru*, the hell ship that transported him and others to Singapore: "I have never read about Dante's Hell, but that comes to mind. There we were—damned near 200 of us—stuffed in that ship's hold. . . . The feeling of claustrophobia and the heat was intense. I swore to God if I ever got out of there, I would never complain about the heat again."[28] Prisoner Paul Papish lamented: "It's a horror story. . . . It was a living hell. You lived in your own filth, you ate in your own filth and the filth around you. . . . I can't understand and will never understand how a living human being can treat another living human being the way we were treated on those ships."[29]

After a miserable week's voyage on the hell ships, the POWs faced a new misery upon reaching their destination. For most of the men, it meant slave labor in the malarial jungles of Burma and Thailand, constructing a railway line through one of the most inhospitable places on earth. For the prisoners of E Battery, it meant twelve- to

Typical jungle camp for POWs. Courtesy USS Houston *Survivors Association.*

fourteen-hour days in the shipyards of Nagasaki or the coal mines near Orio. In both circumstances the Texan prisoners showed a remarkable devotion to their comrades and displayed an indomitable will to live. Throughout the remainder of the war, these men continued to work together and developed effective survival techniques to meet each new life-threatening challenge. Their experiences at this stage of captivity came to define each one of them. They reached levels of endurance they did not think possible and came to understand themselves and their fellow prisoners in ways that could only exist in the unimaginable misery of such an existence.

Upon arriving in Burma, the prisoners learned of the role the Japanese would force them to play for the remainder of the war. Due to wartime demands upon raw materials, supplies, and merchant shipping, in early 1942 Tokyo mandated that a railway be constructed connecting the rail system in Burma to that in Thailand, both of which Japan controlled. From the railhead in Thanbyuzayat, Burma, the proposed railway would wind southeast through the Burmese jungles and mountains to unite with the railway near Nieke on the Thailand plain; when completed the route would measure more than 260 miles. To hasten the railway's construction, work commenced from both ends of the line, where Japanese engineers and Korean and Japanese guards supervised an estimated 200,000 conscripted Asian laborers and 62,000 Allied prisoners of war.[30]

The geographical seclusion of the railway precluded any use of heavy equipment or machinery, so human labor alone would be responsible for its construction. Various work parties of POWs and Asian conscripts performed the innumerable backbreaking tasks necessary to build the line, all the while working under the cruel authority of their overseers. Early arrivals hacked a right of way through the heavy vegetation, felling trees and clearing underbrush with primitive hand tools. The railway necessitated a level grade throughout its length, so thousands of laborers spent their ever-increasing workdays cutting down hills, blasting through rock, and filling valleys to meet the task. Others laid the wooden ties, or "sleepers," and steel rails cannibalized from the railway systems in other Japanese-occupied territories. Menacing guards stood watch over each work party, threatening them with beatings if they failed to meet each day's quota.

On a typical workday, the Texans marched to their place on the line at daybreak and spent the rest of the daylight hours working as beasts of burden. They usually labored in groups of four men, one loosening dirt with a heavy grubbing hoe, another shoveling the loose dirt into rice sacks for the two remaining men to carry away. These two deposited the load at a common dumpsite, then returned for another load of dirt, repeating the process hundreds of times each day. Roy Armstrong of F Battery said, "I had no idea what kind of tools we was going to build [the railway] with. I have never thought about building a railroad with a basket and shovel."[31] Other men drilled holes in rocks with sledgehammers and steel bits to place dynamite for blasting, while still others brought supplies up and down the rail line.

The work and appalling treatment of the prisoners reached its nadir in the months from May through September 1943. The Japanese had redoubled their efforts to complete the railway, and their slave laborers paid the price. Food supplies dwindled during this period, but work hours increased to up to twenty hours each day; at one point the men recall working 120 days in a row. Engineers increased each day's work quota, and guards stood over their charges shouting "Speedo! Speedo!" to the English-speaking prisoners. During the so-called "speedo" campaign, monsoon rains poured all along the construction zone while severe winds lashed at the starving and overworked prisoners. The railway claimed the lives of 103 Americans during the speedo period, more than at any other time during their captivity.[32]

The heavy rains made the work on the railway exponentially more difficult. Streams and rivers flooded their banks and destroyed much of the line and bridges constructed to that point. Knee-high mud choked the worksites as the prisoners slogged through each day, striving to meet their quota. George Burns remembered: "You'd carry a basket or sack of that mud to put on [the dumpsite], and as you'd come off the dump, it would follow you down. You just couldn't make any headway."[33] Yet workers still made thousands of such trips. Luther Prunty recalled: "Sometimes I'd just pray for the rain to stop. That incessant rain! Just rain, rain, rain! It'd almost drive you off the deep end."[34] Thomas Whitehead added: "It didn't make any difference to the Japs. They had to keep going, and they did keep going. You went out and worked in the rain just like the sun was shining."[35]

When finished with a workday, the railway prisoners returned to their camps at night. Huts of bamboo-and-thatch construction served as their homes, and they slept on split-bamboo platforms with about two feet of space per man. Dirt floors in the huts became at first mired with mud in the rains but soon turned into the bases of fast-flowing streams as water ran beneath their sleeping platforms. Mosquitoes infested the huts, and all of the prisoners suffered from malaria while working on the railway. Multiple tropical and dietary diseases afflicted the men, ranging from the ever-present dysentery to beriberi, dengue fever, and pneumonia. Most also suffered from the dreaded and deadly tropical ulcers that ate away the living flesh from a man's bones, with no effective way to combat them. Adequate food and clothing became scarcer, further hastening the decline in prisoners' health. A man's illness did not prevent guards from forcing him to work each day, though; only those closest to death escaped a day's labor on the railway.[36]

Max Offerle described a heart-wrenching scene in a camp in which his desperately ill brother lay dying: "My brother died at 80 Kilo Camp. . . . This tropical ulcer

Prisoner's sketch of a burial detail, 1943. Courtesy Oral History Program, University of North Texas.

Prisoner's sketch of a POW burial site. Courtesy Oral History Program, University of North Texas.

had spread all up and down his leg, between his knee and ankle. In fact, it started eating around the bone of his leg. Right before he died, there was two inches of bone showing. Blood, pus, mucous, or whatever it was dripped down his ankle and the top of his foot, and another large ulcer was there. . . . I went over a day or two later, and Oscar was semi-conscious, and he was hot. I put his head in my lap, and he died."[37] Quaty Gordon remembered a time that has haunted him since: "There was an Australian bedded [here in a hut], and an Englishman, and myself. This Englishman died in between us, so we thought it might be a good idea not to tell anybody for a couple days so we could draw his rations. So, we split it. Then [the Englishman's corpse] got to stinking so bad that we had to tell the Japs he was dead. They started to haul him away, and he had a pretty good blanket. So, we said, 'Hell, he don't need that blanket where he's going!' So, we took turns using his blanket. God Almighty!"[38]

While death from overwork, malnutrition, or disease took the lives of untold thousands of laborers on the railway, the Texan prisoners sent to Japan suffered tremendously as well. Spartan and vermin-infested living quarters in Nagasaki offered little defense from the bitter cold of winter or intense heat of summer, and food rations became increasingly scarce. The men worked in the dangerous environment of the shipyards, risking falls from high platforms, electrocution from unsafe power tools, and the routine beatings administered by the Japanese. E Battery's Cecil Minshew described a typical beating: "[For any infraction of Japanese rules] the minimum punishment you would get—the minimum punishment—would be two licks [with a sledgehammer handle]. You'd reach over and get your ankles, and you get two licks with a sledgehammer handle [across the buttocks]. And I don't mean little licks. If you didn't move ten or fifteen feet, they hadn't done it right. Now that was the minimum punishment. But you might get two licks each day and be put in the jail, which was a wire box, with one meal a day and left there just according to the severity of the [perceived offense.]"[39] A Japanese guard discovered William Visage stealing food while at Nagasaki and beat him unmercifully. The guard became exhausted from the effort and ordered fellow prisoner Francis Gilliam to continue the beating. According to Visage: "Well, the first sergeant [Gilliam] told me when he walked up to me, 'You look like hell, Visage. All I'm going to do is hit you one time and knock you out. Whether I knock you out or not, you fall down. Fake it or something.' When he drew back and hit me then, he had tears in his eyes. He just hated to do it. Sure enough, he knocked me out. I went down, and there I lay. They didn't hit me anymore."[40]

Disease swept through the prisoners' ranks, leaving nearly all of the men suffering from the effects of malnutrition. Clyde Shelton lost over one-third of his body weight as a result of malnutrition and dysentery.[41] Cecil Minshew contracted beriberi early in his stay at Nagasaki and suffered with the disease until the war's end.[42] William Visage also contracted beriberi and described his experiences in the primitive sick bay: "I was put in the 'death room' at one time. My tonsils rotted out, and after laying in there for two or three days and suffering with a high fever . . . , I swear to this day that I was dying there. It left my throat paralyzed. I couldn't make a sound; I couldn't talk for about three months after that. I recall [fellow prisoners] teasing me in the room. They'd talk to me, and I'd try to talk back, and they'd just laugh and mock me, all in jest [to help keep his spirits up]."[43]

Given such dire circumstances, the Texan prisoners faced a simple choice: they could end their tortuous daily struggle for survival, give up hope, stop caring for themselves and for others, and wait for death to take them. Considering the misery they faced, it must have seemed like a logical and peaceful option. If they lived, they continued to work, continued to starve, and continued to watch their friends waste away and die. If they died, their suffering ended. Kelly Bob Bramlett believed that some prisoners chose this option: "You could usually tell. . . . I think a lot of them died just because they gave up. I think maybe if they'd hung on, they could have made it, but there wasn't much to hang on for them at that time."[44]

The vast majority of the prisoners chose to continue the struggle, however, and it was at this most very crucial period that their group cohesion and desire to live combined to bring them home from the war. The cliques proved vital during the most trying times in captivity. Railway prisoners gathered scraps of food to share with their most desperate comrades. After a day on the line, they came back to camp and tended to their most ill brethren. They boiled water and bathed their ulcers to help slow their spread. The ambulatory cleaned and tended to those too ill to move. Day in, day out, they performed countless acts of heroism to help ease the suffering of their fellow prisoners. It was at this point that the men combined a true desire to live with the actions necessary to help keep themselves and their friends alive.

Dan Buzzo of Headquarters Battery credited his friend Avon "Blue" Scarbrough for helping him survive. Buzzo was stricken with ulcers, malaria, pneumonia, beriberi, and dysentery and refused to eat his daily ration of rice. Scarbrough taunted him and threatened to eat Buzzo's rations, making the latter angry enough to eat the rice to spite him. After a few days of such encounters, Buzzo managed to go back to work on the line.[45] Kyle Thompson lay near death in September 1943, but his commanding officer, Winthrop "Windy" Rogers, secretly procured enough food to keep him alive through the worst of his ordeal.[46] Each night after returning from the jungle, Buzzo aided Max Offerle by massaging his atrophied legs, helping him regain his ability to walk after a few weeks. Offerle went on to explain how Keith "Zeke" Naylor came to his aid: "I had dysentery when I had this tropical ulcer, and to go to the latrine I had to crawl backwards on my knees and hands. One day I started out and had dysentery, so I messed in my pants. I was very disgusted and disheartened, and I guess I was feeling sorry for myself. So I was sitting there crying, and old 'Zeke' Naylor came in from work. He said, 'Junior, what in the world is the matter with you?' I said, 'I just dirtied my pants!' He said, 'Take the damned things off, and I'll wash them for you.' I thought that was one of the finest things a man could do for you, and I've never forgotten it."[47]

Malaria and dysentery left Clark Taylor unable to sit up or move for days. Lester Rasbury and Herschel "Dude" Cobb cut a hole in his bamboo sleeping platform for use as a toilet so he would not have to crawl to the latrine. Eldon and Ellis Schmid gave Taylor a can of condensed milk they managed to keep hidden since Bicycle Camp to help his bowels recover. Jack Cellum stole a can of salmon from the Japanese kitchen and gave it to Taylor. When the Japanese discovered Cellum's "crime," they forced him to stand at attention while they beat him for hours with bamboo poles. The weeping Taylor recalled, "They kept him there [for] at least twelve hours, and I prayed every time they hit him."[48]

These efforts, which may seem insignificant to our contemporary sensibilities, were monumental humanitarian acts for the Texan prisoners. They not only helped each other survive these hellish experiences but also instilled hope among the men, both the recipients and those who provided the care. The world had seemingly lost all measure of humanity, but these men knew that if they could hold on and try to help others when they could, they could ensure that humanity in their world still existed. This provided hope, a desire to live, and the means to effect their survival. West Texan Roger White of E Battery expressed his belief about the support he received from his fellow Texans: "They would talk about things that [we] knew about, places they went, people they knew, and so on. . . . I was from Amarillo, and I was in with a group that were just like brothers to me."[49]

The end of the war found the prisoners of E Battery in Orio, Japan, scratching out small amounts of coal from played-out mines. Most of their guards simply disappeared, gone back home to melt into the peacetime world. Those who labored on the Death Railway were scattered throughout Japanese-occupied Southeast Asia at that time, performing new labors at new sites. There were no momentous celebrations for these men when they heard the war had ended, just a joy and relief that only they can understand. Slowly, they worked to build their strength by acquiring the food and medicine that was denied them during captivity. In a few weeks' time, the US Army appeared to take the men to hospitals for observation and to tend to their long-neglected bodies. Eventually, these once-naïve young Texans made their way back to the Lone Star State to embrace their friends and loved ones again. Certainly, they would have to deal with the legacy of captivity, which took a toll on each of them in his own way, but they were now free men and determined to make a life for themselves that would not be defined by brutality but by the firm conviction that they had seen the worst of humanity and had helped defeat it by practicing the best traits humans possess.

This small group of Texan prisoners had the highest rates of survival of any nationality held by the Japanese during World War II. Although nearly 26 percent of other Allied POWs perished in Japanese hands, only 16 percent of the Texans died in captivity.[50] There are a number of reasons for this. First, the survivors determined early on in captivity that they would make the daily efforts required to keep themselves as healthy, physically and mentally, as possible. They ate rations that most people would deem inedible, washed their mess gear in boiling water before and after each meal, and bathed themselves whenever the opportunity presented itself. Again, these seem to be quite mundane activities, but in the environment in which these men found themselves, it proved vital to take these seemingly inconsequential measures to protect their health. Second, the Texans embraced a somewhat democratic form of organization that helped minimize resentment and disputes between officers and enlisted men. The rigid hierarchical POW system famously practiced by British prisoners, while beneficial in many respects, did not promote the type of unity embraced by the Texans.

Also, and very importantly, each of these men possessed an incredible desire to live. Slug Wright, who lost fifty pounds from dysentery during the speedo period, explained his determination: "This [situation] is depressing and it stinks, and I am a miserable human being, and I'm going to die. But I'm trying to live. . . . You know, it's easy as hell to die, but it's hard to live. A man can give up and go very quickly. Without the will to live, without that spark, you lost it."[51] William Visage added: "I was determined that I was going to come home. I know there was a time or two that I felt like I could die over there, but I was determined not to."[52] And according to Pete Evans: "You've got to keep your eye on the ball all the time. . . . You just have to be a pretty strong individual in order to live through all this."[53]

It is also important to keep in mind the shared Texas heritage these men possessed. Having grown up accustomed to the hardships, deprivation, and difficult labor of rural Texas during the Great Depression helped condition them for the extreme circumstances they were forced to endure in Japan and on the Death Railway. Cecil Minshew explained: "Take guys like me that grew up during the Depression, and with ten children in their family and never too much food at one meal . . . , our bodies were more adjusted to lighter diet and less nourishment. . . . The healthiest looking guys there—the ones that had been the best fed, the 'corn-fed' boys—were the ones that died. And the ol' boys that had just subsisted all their lives and lived on a hit-and-miss basis are the ones that survived."[54] Martin "Slim" Chambers, a draftee from Mexia, added: "When I came back, my granddaddy asked me: 'How was it [being a prisoner of the Japanese]?' And I told him, 'Papa, other than not seeing your folks, it was just like East Texas. The Japs worked the hell out of you and starved you to death."[55]

Perhaps the single most-significant factor explaining their high survival rate was the bond these men formed, both before and during captivity. Prior to mobilization in 1940, the 2nd Battalion was a National Guard unit. Its members were recruited from the same small towns and farms and ranches of Texas. These men knew each other, many of them for their entire lives, and it is only natural that they would put forth greater effort to help their neighbors and friends make it through the difficult times. Medic Raymond Reed believed that one must have faith in his fellow man, knowing "that they will be there when you need them most."[56] Max Offerle concurred: "You found out that you got to know men real well, some of them as well as a brother, and they did help each other a lot—especially in your little groups."[57] Speaking on this subject, Ilo Hard explained: "It's rough in a way, like the time when we went through Lubbock [en route to Camp Bowie in 1941], and these mothers and so forth would say: 'Oh, Lieutenant Hard'll take care of my boy for me.' But I'll guarantee I made every effort possible to do it, where if I hadn't known them and their mothers and everybody, I might not have made the effort."[58] Roy Armstrong spoke of the importance of these ties: "That was a main key to [survival]—a lot of it—because we helped one another. Without that, when a man's sick, he's not able to get out and get anything. You take those where they weren't bonded as close as we were, they didn't take care of one another, and they didn't make it."[59]

One cannot honestly say that being a Texan determined these men's fates. Thousands of other Asian and Allied laborers survived Japanese captivity as did those of the Lost Battalion. Many Texans died in the jungles of Burma and Thailand, and others perished in the Japanese home islands. The combination of factors that the survivors attribute to their coming home were certainly practiced by other prisoners and laborers, and many who possessed the same attributes did not survive the war. But one fact is clear: the common heritage shared by the Texans of the Lost Battalion, whether in Southeast Asia or Japan, was a major factor in creating the support system necessary to bring them home at war's end.

Notes

1. Clyde Shelton, July 27, 1987, interview transcript (OH 700), 140. All oral-history interviews cited in this study were conducted by Dr. Ronald E. Marcello and are located in the Oral History Collection, University Archives, Willis Library, University of North Texas, Denton.

2. The reported numbers of Japanese-held Allied POW deaths differ, but the 16 percent death-rate figure for the Texans is quite reliable. The overall US death rate for POWs held by the Japanese is slightly over 40 percent. See Charles A. Stenger, "American Prisoners of War in WWI, WWII, Korea, Vietnam, Persian Gulf, Somalia, Bosnia, Kosovo, and Afghanistan: Statistical Data Concerning Numbers Captured, Repatriated, and Still Alive as of January 1, 2002," prepared for the Department of Veterans Affairs Advisory Committee on Former Prisoners of War, Mental Health Strategic Group, VHA, DVA, American Ex-Prisoners of War Association, 2003. See also Gavan Daws, *Prisoners of the Japanese: POWs of World War II in the Pacific* (New York: Morrow, 1994); and Lionel Wigmore, *The Japanese Thrust*, vol. 4 of *Australia in the War of 1939–1945* (Canberra: Australian War Memorial, 1957).

3. Pete Evans, Feb. 15, 1984, interview transcript (OH 624), 2–4.

4. Kelly Bob Bramlett, Nov. 2, 1986, interview transcript (OH 345), 2.

5. Luther Prunty, Oct. 20, 1980, interview transcript (OH 689), 2–3.

6. Crayton Gordon, Jan. 31, 1977, interview transcript (OH 383), 4.

7. George Killian, Sept. 19, 1970, interview transcript (OH 56), 5.

8. P. J. Smallwood, Oct. 25, 1973, interview transcript (OH 166), 9–10.

9. Prunty interview, 8–10.

10. Eldridge Rayburn, Jan. 16, 1980, interview transcript (OH 499), 17.

11. Roy M. Offerle, Aug. 14, 1978, interview transcript (OH 457), 8.

12. ABDACOM stood for Australian, British, Dutch, American Command. The organization was further subdivided according to military branch: ABDARM (ground forces led by Dutch general Hein ter Poorten), ABDAFLOAT (naval forces under the command of US admiral Thomas C. Hart), and ABDAIR (commanded by British air marshal Richard Peirse). The combined forces were notoriously inefficient and were known to have suffered from significant branch and nationalities conflicts. Racial problems within the Dutch-commanded but largely Javanese-manned Dutch forces also played a significant role in limiting the effectiveness of the defense of Java.

13. For a full discussion of the Battle of Java, see Wigmore, *Japanese Thrust.* See also Imamura Hitoshi, *Memoirs of General Imamura*, vol. 4 of *The Japanese Experience in Indonesia: Selected Memoirs of 1942–1945* (Athens: Ohio University Center for International Studies, Center for Southeast Asian Studies, 1986).

14. Frank Ficklin, Jan. 16, 1987, interview transcript (OH 691), 18.

15. Houston Wright, Aug. 15, 1978, interview transcript (OH 466), 39.

16. Huddleston Wright, Nov. 2, 1989, interview transcript (OH 794), 42.

17. Ben Kelley, Mar. 26, 1982, interview transcript (OH 565), 41.

18. Grover Reichle, Jan. 22, 1979, interview transcript (OH 495), 59.

19. Wade Webb, Feb. 7, 1997, interview transcript (OH 1181), 90.

20. Gordon interview, 69–70.

21. Clark Taylor, Sept. 14, 1979, interview transcript (OH 491), 56.

22. Raymond Reed, Mar. 13, 1979, interview transcript (OH 486), 94.

23. "Statement of James E. Crum," Sept. 26, 1945, File 57-8-32, Box 1400, RG 153, National Archives [hereafter NA]; "In the Matter of the Japanese Failure to Provide . . . American Prisoners of War with Proper Food, Quarters, and Medical Care from April 1, 1942, to September 16, 1945: Perpetuation of Testimony of Horace E. Chumley," Nov. 20, 1945, File 52-0-8, Box 1376, ibid.

24. Ilo Hard, Mar. 26, 1980, interview transcript (OH 510), 89–93.

25. George Detre, Aug. 17, 1978, interview transcript (OH 475), 149–50. Detre was a survivor of the USS *Houston*, sunk on the night of February 28–March 1, 1942, during the Battle of Sunda Strait. The *Houston* survivors met the 2nd Battalion in Bicycle Camp in April 1942, and from this point the stories of the two groups are intricately intertwined.

26. "Case Files on Shipping, Transport Cases," Folder TR-O Misc., Box 983, RG 331, NA. For a complete discussion of Japanese transport of Allied POWs, see Gregory F. Michno, *Death on the Hellships: Prisoners at Sea in the Pacific War* (Annapolis, MD: Naval Institute Press, 2001).

27. Julius B. Heinen, Oct. 29, 1973, interview transcript (OH 174), 64–65.

28. Edward Fung, Dec. 21, 1977, interview transcript (OH 404), 76.

29. Paul E. Papish, Jan. 30, 1989, interview transcript (OH 781), 119–21. Papish was also a *Houston* survivor.

30. There are many studies of the Burma–Thailand Railway. Among the most valuable are Clifford Kinvig, *River Kwai Railway: The Story of the Burma–Siam Railroad* (London: Biddles, 1992); and Paul H. Kratoska, ed., *The Thailand–Burma Railway, 1942–1946: Documents and Selected Writings*, 6 vols. (New York: Routledge, 2006).

31. Roy G. Armstrong, Oct. 15, 1980, interview transcript (OH 530), 119.

32. *Roster, Lost Battalion Association*, 2002, 45–46. The Lost Battalion Association was

formed shortly after World War II, and its membership consists of survivors of the 2nd Battalion as well as of the sinking of the heavy cruiser USS *Houston*. The association publishes an annual newsletter (*Roster*), providing information on the group's members and detailed information on those members who were held prisoner by the Japanese.

33. George Burns, Mar. 12, 1974, interview transcript (OH 176), 86.

34. Prunty interview, 143.

35. Thomas Whitehead, Feb. 2, 1977, interview transcript (OH 366), 107–108.

36. "In the Matter of the Imprisonment under Improper Conditions of American Prisoners of War in the Kilometer Camps in Burma: Perpetuation of Testimony of Blucher S. Tharp," Nov. 30, 1945, File 57-8-57, Box 1400, RG 153, NA.

37. Offerle interview, 118–19.

38. Gordon interview, 118–19.

39. Cecil T. Minshew, Feb. 18, 1983, interview transcript (OH 597), 119.

40. William Visage, July 16–17, 1987, interview transcript (OH 698), 97–100.

41. Shelton interview, 90–91.

42. Minshew interview, 140.

43. Visage interview, 147–48.

44. Bramlett interview, 86.

45. Dan Buzzo, Feb. 11, 1998, interview transcript (OH 1245), 171.

46. Kyle O. Thompson, *A Thousand Cups of Rice: Surviving the Death Railway* (Austin, TX: Eakin, 1994), 94.

47. Offerle interview, 115–16.

48. Taylor interview, 118–19; 130.

49. Roger White, Jan. 7, 1997, interview transcript (OH 1167), 137.

50. *Roster, Lost Battalion Association,* 2002, ii. For statistics regarding death rates among other Allied prisoners, see Wigmore, *Japanese Thrust.*

51. Houston Wright interview, 129–31.

52. Visage interview, 155.

53. Evans interview, 143.

54. Minshew interview, 203–204.

55. Martin Chambers, Apr. 8, 1982, interview transcript (OH 575), 17–18.

56. *Bridgeport (TX) Index,* Nov. 11, 1990.

57. Offerle interview, 115.

58. Hard interview, 138.

59. Armstrong interview, 221.

LBJ and Vietnam Specters. *Prints and Photographs Division, Library of Congress, Washington, DC (LC-DIG-PPMSC-05883-SWANN-No. 1366).*

13

Lyndon B. Johnson's "Bitch of a War"

An Antiwar Essay

James M. Smallwood

MORE THAN 500,000 Texans served in the military during the 1960s and 1970s. Approximately 25,000 of them saw action in the Vietnam War. Of that number, 3,415 did not leave Vietnam alive. The United States collectively lost 58,159 men. About 30,000 of those died while Pres. Lyndon B. Johnson (LBJ) was at the helm, with a similar number dying during Richard Nixon's term. In addition, both North and South Vietnam lost from 3 to 5 million people each. Cambodian and Laotian dead numbered between 1.5 and 2 million, depending on the sources cited.[1] All of these people died during what President Johnson came to call "this bitch of a war." A Texan presided over the massive escalation of that conflict, which failed to bring positive results for the United States or its allies.

What was the historical context and background of the war? What was the state of the war when Johnson came to power and was forced to deal with past blunders made by others? Why did he escalate the fighting? Did he (and others) ever see that US involvement in Vietnam was folly, a mistake straight out? And did Americans learn any lessons from Vietnam, a guerrilla war to beat all guerrilla wars? To the last question, the answer is "no." The failure to learn led to the disastrous US wars in Afghanistan and Iraq, new guerrilla wars that America is finding difficult to win. Those conflicts may go the way of Vietnam, especially since the modern US Army is so thin that it hired mercenaries to perform duties associated with the conduct of the wars, including security.

Although the Vietnam War (1945–75) has been called "Mr. Johnson's War," the United States became involved in the Southeast Asian country decades before Johnson became president. A part of French Indochina, Vietnam was a land of people who had been victimized for centuries by stronger powers—one of which was the Mongol horde, another was imperial China—finally becoming independent of China only to fall to the French in 1859. The majority of Vietnamese chafed under European imperialistic rule, as the French suppressed Buddhism and replaced it with Catholicism, which became the major tolerated religion in the land; as French became the official language; and as a minority of the people became collaborators. Generally, authorities ruled for the benefit of the mother country while the majority of Vietnamese, once again, suffered from the high-handedness of foreigners.[2]

By the beginning of the twentieth century, a developing nationalist movement grew stronger, especially after the young communist Ho Chi Mihn (1890–1969) took a leadership role. Ho made several failed attempts for Vietnamese independence: during the Versailles Peace Conference after World War I, directing a nationalist movement from 1941 that targeted the Vichy French and the Japanese occupiers of his country with US help, and finally defeating a French garrison of Dien Bien Phu in 1954, forcing France to sue for peace and abandon all imperialistic authority in the region.[3]

The French withdrawal created a power vacuum that the Republican administration of Dwight D. Eisenhower rushed to fill. Talking of the "Domino Effect," Republicans argued that if Vietnam "fell" to communists, then all Indochina would "fall," threatening even Indonesia and India.[4]

Thus, the containment policy which seemed to work in Europe was extended to Southeast Asia. The Eisenhower administration propped up the already corrupt government in South Vietnam and committed about 900 armed "advisors" to train a pro-American army. Basically, South Vietnam became a client state. Subsequently, the United States refused to allow free elections in 1956 because, as Eisenhower later admitted, Ho would have likely received about 80 percent of the vote, for the Vietnamese who had not collaborated with their enemies considered him the George Washington of their country, the consensus praising him as a national hero.[5] Eisenhower's decision led to the birth of a new revolutionary movement in South Vietnam, an insurgency led by the Vietcong. In response, Emperor Bao Dai's prime minister, Ngo Dinh Diem, inaugurated a repressive campaign that resulted in the murders of approximately 12,000 suspects and in the torture of about 40,000 others.[6] That campaign only resulted in the Vietcong gaining new recruits because they were obviously fighting for national reunification and for self-determination in their homeland. Their goal was to force all imperialistic powers to leave Vietnam.[7]

As Diem was murdering and torturing his own people, he was also rigging elections and proving that the South Vietnamese government was thoroughly corrupt, a true charge that American antiwar "doves" later made. Diem's brother Ngo Dinh Nhu supervised a referendum on the leadership of the government. Effectively, the question was, should we continue the monarchy or establish a republic with Diem as president? Nhu refused to listen to US advisors who asked him to hold down the voting tally to about a realistic 60–70 percent mandate for his brother. Instead, courtesy of Nhu, Diem received just more than a 98 percent winning margin. Saigon set the record, though, where Diem won by 133 percent, a feat previously thought to be mathematically impossible, yet an impossible dream that became quite true. Americans were told that in this disgusting sham called "free elections," the United States was bringing true democracy to Vietnam, declarations later echoed in Afghanistan and Iraq.[8]

Ho Chi Mihn was patient for a time, but when patience led to nothing positive, in 1959 he committed North Vietnamese regulars to the fray and established ties with the Vietcong. That action added to the chaos south of the demarcation line. Such was the situation when John F. Kennedy (JFK) took office in 1961, a man as much a "Cold Warrior" as had been Harry S. Truman and Eisenhower. With the South Vietnamese government in danger of falling yet again, JFK committed the first US combat troops to the struggle, sending in about 16,700 men to shore up the puppet government, and also increased arms shipments despite John Kenneth Galbraith's warnings that the United States would just replace France as the imperialistic colonial power, that Vietnamese nationalists would fight on, and that American boys now would bleed and die just as the French boys had. The historical "rumor" that JFK would have withdrawn from Vietnam has no basis in fact, as witnessed by this escalation.

Although Americans were now fighting and dying, the situation remained precarious, with Ho's regulars and the Vietcong matching the US escalation. Indeed, the strength of the Vietcong rose from 5,000 in 1959 to 100,000 by late 1963.[9] Still, Gen. Paul Harkins, commanding US forces in South Vietnam, forecast a victory by Christmas of 1963. That military forecast became true for the entire course of the war: it seemed that every general was overly optimistic at best or a liar at worst, either a fool or a knave—and Americans should not have to suffer either one. Yet the generals all promised victory if only the presidents—in their turn—would send them more troops.[10] Given the position of most of the military commanders, escalation was almost certain. The only way Johnson could stop it was by withdrawing from Vietnam.

LBJ took office at a crucial time, a time of crisis spawned by the refusal of Truman, Eisenhower, and JFK to let Vietnam go, to allow that country's people their right of self-determination. Indeed, the terroristic South Vietnamese strongman Diem had just been murdered, in a plot sanctioned by JFK (who did not realize what he had sanctioned), a deed that caused even more chaos as one military regime followed another in rapid succession, each proving to be a puppet of the United States.[11] The

James M. Smallwood

government in Saigon was poised to fall unless something was done to prop it up. Johnson sought help from various advisors. In the words of Robert McNamara, LBJ inherited a "mess" that he, McNamara, would make worse because he was a pro-escalation "hawk." Another was Sen. Richard Russell (a no-escalation "dove"), who agreed with McNamara's assessment of Vietnam and even used the same term, "mess," though he meant it in a different way. Russell told LBJ: "I knew we were going to get in this sort of mess when we went in there, and I do not see how we are ever going to get out without fighting a major war with China." Then the senator gave his best advice, telling LBJ to find a strong South Vietnamese leader, put him in control, and tell him his first order had to be to ask "us" to leave, which "we" would promptly do after declaring victory. According to historian Richard Dalleck, Johnson also turned to others, one being UN Ambassador Adlai Stevenson. The ambassador said that he got the "shakes" every time he thought of Vietnam but averred that LBJ did not have much choice except to stay with the fight and escalate it if necessary.[12]

Again, another presidential administration faced a foreign-policy disaster, and a commitment of more US troops seemed the only way to "save" South Vietnam and to keep the "dominos" from falling. Certainly, LBJ was unhappy with his realistic choices, that is, either escalate or let the communists take control. That said, early on Johnson did not have Vietnam on his personal radar; he was more concerned about his Great Society program and his "War on Poverty."[13] He was not convinced that the United States should become bogged down in a land war in Southeast Asia. In the White House tapes released much later, LBJ can be heard to mutter to his advisors that he had doubts about the US presence in the middle of a hostile Asian hothouse.[14] But his military advisors, including Defense Secretary McNamara, convinced him that America must assume a larger role to avert an international disaster.

Moreover, LBJ was torn, not wanting to be in Vietnam but also not wanting to be the first president to "lose a war" (if one considers the War of 1812 a draw and if one forgets about the mid-nineteenth century's Seminole Wars in Florida). As Johnson told Henry Cabot Lodge, US ambassador to South Vietnam, and other advisors: "I am not going to lose Vietnam. I am not going to be the President who saw Southeast Asia go the way China went."[15] Thus locked into escalation, one begun by Truman and followed by Eisenhower and JFK, LBJ made Vietnam "his" war against his best judgment. Had he based his decisions on his original doubts, the United States would have had an alternate history that would have included millions of lives saved—Asians and Americans—and would have preserved millions of dollars in the treasury that could have been used to build a "Great Society." Instead of being identified as an ogre, Johnson would have been seen by history as a statesman. LBJ personally, and the United

States generally, paid a terrible price for the final judgment. Vietnam ruined the legacy Johnson left to future generations.[16]

Still hesitant about the war, LBJ acted indecisively throughout his presidency. He was ruled by inconstancy; that is, he was influenced by exactly what happened at exactly any one time. Consequently, his decision making was full of contradictions as months and then years passed. He waxed and waned repeatedly. He wanted out of the war, but no one gave him a way out—not without allowing South Vietnam to go Communist. Unfortunately, LBJ made a free independent South Vietnam his one nonnegotiable demand. Everything else he would put on the table, but not a Communist South Vietnam. As early as late November 1963, shortly after he took power and referring to loses in the Mekong Delta, he averred that America must resist Communism.

Months later, in August 1964, two North Vietnamese gunboats apparently attacked the USS *Maddox* in the Gulf of Tonkin. Two days later came another alleged attack, this one on the *Maddox* and the USS *C. Turner Joy*, both destroyers. Initial reports of the two incidents were muddled. LBJ had doubts that the attacks actually occurred and that the American sailors might have fired the first shots in the incidents. At first LBJ wanted to protest to the North Vietnamese government but to make no military retaliation for fear of drawing the Soviet Union and/or Red China into an all-out World War III. (He constantly worried about provoking a wider war throughout his entire administration, which is why he would not accept military advice to invade North Vietnam with ground troops). About the incident, still muddled, Johnson told George Ball that the sailors might "have been shooting at flying fish." LBJ wanted assurances that the incidents had really happened, that he had the truth of the matter. Again, McNamara and military advisors swore that the attacks were real and that they were unprovoked. Next they added that the president could not soft pedal the attacks, for that would show weakness and lack of resolve. The advisors said that he had no choice but to escalate the war to save South Vietnam. Although LBJ argued with them about not wanting to take irreversible actions, he ultimately accepted their advice and went before Congress.[17]

Calling the incidents "open aggression on the high seas," the president asked for broad powers in conducting a police action. But he withheld evidence that the destroyers were aiding the South Vietnamese to make clandestine attacks on North Vietnam. Congress responded with the Gulf of Tonkin Resolution, which gave the president the police power he sought; only two senators cast negative votes.[18] Opinion polls showed that LBJ had the support of a large majority of Americans, especially after he said that US aid would be limited. He vowed not to let American "boys" do all the dying when Asian "boys" ought to do their own fighting.[19]

But straightaway, inconstancy ruled. Johnson came to believe that he had to escalate US involvement. In early 1965, after an attack at Pleiku on US Marines, who at the time had only a defensive mission, LBJ followed the National Security Council's recommendation that an escalated bombing campaign on North Vietnam begin immediately. Thus began what the military dubbed Operation Rolling Thunder, which became a three-year bombardment. LBJ wanted to boost the South Vietnamese government's morale and to force North Vietnam to negotiate an end to the war. Specifically, the United States targeted North Vietnam's air defenses as well as its entire infrastructure, both military and civilian. Johnson's goals went unrealized even though the United States dropped 800 tons of bombs daily from 1965 to 1968, an amount three times more than the tonnage dropped by all World War II combatants combined. Still, Ho held out, being well supplied by China and the Soviet Union.[20]

In March 1965 LBJ received disheartening news. Several advisors told him the truth: US forces were losing ground in Vietnam. American troops controlled the cities, but the Vietcong and North Vietnam regulars controlled the countryside. McNamara and Secretary of State Dean Rusk were among others who gave the president the grim assessment, after which Johnson remarked to his wife, Lady Bird: "I can't get out, I can't finish it with what I've got. So what the hell do I do."[21] On another occasion, according to an earthy legend, the president put it another way: He said that he felt like the rancher caught out in his pasture when a horrific hailstorm developed. While being pelted and stung by the ice, he cried: "I can't run, I can't hide, and I can't make it stop." Yet LBJ had hopes for Operation Rolling Thunder. He believed that the bombing campaign would be successful, ultimately, telling one advisor that the war should be over within twelve to eighteen months. The destruction would force North Vietnam to ask for peace on US terms. Still, he continued to reject the injection of more ground troops into the fray.[22]

Believing that yet more force could accomplish US aims, LBJ's hawkish advisors worked on him as prophets of doom. The non-Communist world as we know it would end, they said, if Johnson did not escalate further. Western civilization would end, they argued. Finally giving in, LBJ committed ever-more ground troops as the weeks turned into months and the months turned into years. With 23,000 soldiers already in Vietnam as armed advisors, in March 1965 LBJ sent in two marine battalions to defend US airbases, especially at Da Nang (whose pilots were participating in Rolling Thunder) in South Vietnam. Later more men arrived for logistical support. Johnson soon added offensive operations to the marine mission and again followed a course that some of his civilian and military advisors laid out. He sent additional troops until their numbers reached 125,000 by the end of July.[23]

But the president was firm when he said there would be no ground invasion of North Vietnam, that the ground troops would fight the Vietcong and North Vietnamese regulars—but only in South Vietnam. His major concern remained what it had been all along: not wanting to provoke the Chinese or the Russians, for that could lead to World War III. In the latter part of 1965, yet more Amercians went in, but still Ho held out, still being well supplied by his Communist allies. By January 1, 1966, the United States had approximately 200,000 fighting men in Vietnam. Unfortunately, every time LBJ escalated, Ho did the same, the result being that by the end of 1967, America had committed a total of 553,000 men (some historians say more than 553,000) to "that bitch of a war," as Johnson continued to call it.[24]

Important events in 1966 had led to this continued escalation, creating more problems for LBJ and his advisors. In midyear South Vietnamese forces suffered twin defeats at Binh Gai and Dong Xoai, after which desertions increased. The native troops' morale reached a low point. Never worth much as a fighting force, the "army" of South Vietnam was worth even less after these defeats. When fighting, most of these soldiers left their guns on the ground as they ran away. Now commanding US forces, Gen. William Westmoreland raised alarms, believing the situation critical. The United States must assume a bigger role in defeating the enemy and ignore the ineptitude of South Vietnamese forces. Westmoreland's lament was, then, the reason LBJ sent more troops. The general wanted more men and more aggression in, for the most part, a hopeless situation, thereby showing why modern American generals continue to fight wars that they cannot win and soak up all the men and money that they can get.[25]

In supporting wars in the modern era, Americans are a fickle people. They do not like long wars. US participation in World War II, for example, lasted less than four years, and while it was ongoing, Americans heard, via radio and movie newsreels, patriotic reports of one Allied success after another—in North Africa, in Italy, on the Russian front, and finally in France, Germany, and in the Pacific theater, where Gen. Douglas MacArthur and Adm. Chester Nimitz "island-hopped" their way to Japan. The hot phase of the Korean War lasted less than three years, and the American public heard much mentioned of American heroism, especially during MacArthur's dramatic Inchon landing that restored the initiative to UN forces. Even the hot phase of the American Revolution lasted only from 1775 to 1781, a six-year struggle, but one in which, due to British strategy, some areas of the colonies remained at peace for most of the period. But US involvement in Vietnam had begun in 1945 and had slowly escalated over time during the administrations of Truman, Eisenhower, and JFK before LBJ built American forces in South Vietnam beyond anyone's imagination—and still the enemy fought on.

The Johnson administration was most concerned about public opinion, which is as it should be in a democracy. Yet the people seem to be ruled by the same factor that ruled LBJ: inconstancy—influenced by exactly what happens at exactly one time. Historian Robert Dalleck has measured public opinion for the duration of the Johnson presidency and found that both the people and the administration were all over the board, events shaping them instead of them shaping events to bring about a satisfactory solution to the war.[26]

In addition to being fickle, the public also has little understanding of guerrilla war, and the American war strategists have none whatsoever, a fact suggesting that the United States should avoid such warfare. Its strategists know how to fight professional armies—as in most wars of the past. But as demonstrated by Vietnam, Afghanistan, and Iraq, what the military cannot handle are suicide bombers, roadside bombs, and people holed up in rural areas who know when to surface and when to hide. And one thing more they cannot handle are people who simply refuse to quit and are quite willing to die (by the millions) for their cause. So, then, the public becomes a two-headed monster that, like George W. Bush, wants to "bring it on" but, that said, demands short wars and quick ends to guerrilla fighting while military men try to find a way to defeat partisans and fail.[27]

Such was the pattern in Vietnam. Opinion polls were positive if something good seemed to happen, but opinion turned negative if defeats came. Although many intellectuals had questioned the worth of US involvement in Vietnam from the beginning, major protests did not begin until Congress passed the Gulf of Tokin Resolution. Led mostly by college students, 25,000 people gathered in Washington, DC, to protest this action while applauding the two senators who had voted "no" on the resolution. Later protests spread to all parts of the country. In March 1965, for example, college students nationwide began to doubt the Johnson administration in a movement started at the University of Michigan, where faculty and students had "teach-ins" that raised many questions about the situation in Vietnam. Soon, "teach-ins" were being held in every state in the Union. As the conscription dragnet (the draft) swept up more and more young men in 1966, the young people increased their protests as well as learned more about warfare and about the history of Vietnam. Intellectuals and the clergy joined in, some arguing that the United States had no business intervening in a country's civil war. Others criticized the cost of the conflict, expenditures in both money and blood. Yet others held that the South Vietnamese government was so hopelessly corrupt that it had lost the support of its own people and that its army was a sham, with most of its men refusing to fight. In all, critics wanted the Johnson administration to immediately pull out of the fighting. Even LBJ's domestic program, the Great Society, suffered as the government spent more and more on war and less on the domestic "War on Poverty." There could not be both "guns and butter." Rather, there were only more guns and less butter. By 1966, the government was spending $2 billion a month in Vietnam, more than the administration spent on the "War on Poverty" in a year.

Opposition continued to build through 1966 and 1967. The author met LBJ in 1967 in a party atmosphere at the home of Marvin Watson, one of the president's closest civilian confidants. I was a graduate student, then working on my master's degree in history. Alone in a rich man's library where I had gone to temporarily escape the crowd, I heard the door open and close behind me (and heard a gruff voice telling someone to "wait out here") as I looked out a picture window at a rich man's garden, complete with night lights. Hearing the noise, I turned and saw the president; he apparently wanted a temporary escape too. I was first surprised, astounded even, to see the man up close. He was so big that he seemed to fill up the entire room, whereas, compared to him, I must have looked like a dwarf. After just a minute or so of pleasantries, LBJ asked me what the people back home in Texas were saying about him. Taking a chance, I told the truth: We loved him for the "War on Poverty" and "Great Society," but we did not support the Vietnam War. The crowd of students whom I ran with wanted him to withdraw from Vietnam. As he frowned and looked forlorn, though not angry, he said: "Tell me how, son." I did not understand then what I know now: Johnson was trapped by the Cold War mindset and by his advisors—both civilian and military—who constantly misled him. Like Truman, Eisenhower, and JFK before him, LBJ was told by a majority of the people around him that he could not let the dominos fall, could not allow another area of the world go communist.[28]

Public opinion waxed and waned as the war moved along and entered new phases. Like Johnson, the opinion polls still seemed ruled by inconstancy. They sometimes rallied for Johnson and escalation: people continued to say "yes" when news accounts suggested the war was going well, but they said "no" when they heard bad news. Put another way, like Johnson, the public was uncertain, "voting" one way when they thought the war was going well but "voting" in the opposite manner when they thought it was being lost.

The largest turnaround in public opinion occurred during the enemy's Tet Offensive of January 1968. On Vietnam's Lunar New Year holiday, which had traditionally spawned a one-day ceasefire, the Vietcong and North Vietnamese regulars attacked on a broad front that included onslaughts against a dozen US bases and more than a hundred cities and villages, of which Saigon was one. There the enemy fired on both General Westmoreland's military headquarters and the US embassy. In America many among the public stayed "glued" to their television screens while watching these battles rage. One terrible image showed a South Vietnamese officer standing in the middle of a street and shooting a handcuffed captive in the head. The scene showed murder, a war criminal exerting his ability to commit murder. Fact was that the war criminal had lost family members in the conflict, and he simply took his revenge. Nevertheless, it was still murder committed on an enemy who was bound and unarmed. What Americans saw looked as if the United States and its agents were engaged in criminal behavior and losing the war at the same time. Immediately after Tet, many more people believed that now was the time to leave Vietnam. In opinion polls, the Johnson administration lost yet more support.

The situation was made worse by the earlier "diplomacy" of Westmoreland. In late 1967 the commanding general had begun a public campaign to bolster support for the war by using several venues. Speaking to the National Press Club in November, for example, he claimed that America was winning and that he could "see" the end in sight. Viewing scenes from the Tet Offensive on television, many among the public believed that he needed glasses so that he could see the truth when it was put in front of his face. Yet Tet was not a victory for the enemy.

In fact, the US fighting men had been caught unprepared for Tet but quickly regrouped and inflicted massive losses upon the enemy. The offensive really was not a victory for Communist forces, but the damage to public opinion was done—many Americans perceived it to be a victory for the opposition. Later military reports, largely positive in nature, garnered much less attention than the scenes of a seeming defeat broadcast to all Americans who had televisions. Damage was done to Westmoreland, who was promoted out of Vietnam after undisclosed sources leaked word that, after Tet, he had called for another 206,000 troops. Flabbergasted at this, Johnson turned to his civilian advisors, one being the legendary Dean Acheson, who once favored the war but who now told the president that the military leaders "don't know what they're talking about." Another advisor who had recently replaced McNamara as secretary of defense, Clark Clifford, told LBJ that the Vietnam situation was "hopeless." Such advice the president took. He refused to further escalate the war; he would not send in any more American boys to die. For some time, LBJ had been referring to reports of US deaths in a personal way: "340 of my boys died in Vietnam today." His refusal to send more men was the president's admission that the war was lost. He now believed that even a new "surge" would only fuel the antiwar movement further and could not win the war.

The apparent never-ending war generally, and the Tet Offensive particularly, undermined LBJ's confidence. As well, he was battling a heart condition that had almost killed him in the 1950s. Then, in the presidential primary season of 1968, a major critic of the war challenged LBJ. Minnesota Democratic senator Eugene McCarthy's bid for the presidency became virtually a one-issue campaign. He held that the bloodbath in Southeast Asia had gone on long enough and should be ended immediately. Support for him started rising in the opinion polls after Tet. Many American college students embraced "Clean Gene," almost 5,000 of them rushing to New Hampshire, the first state to hold a Democratic primary in 1968. They stuffed envelops, manned phone banks, and knocked on doors, and their work was effective.

McCarthy stunned Johnson by being most competitive in the primary. McCarthy captured 42 percent of the votes, which were well placed on the political grid and gave him a large majority of delegates to the National Democratic Convention. Even though LBJ received 49 percent of the vote, the count was much less than the two-thirds majority that some analysts had predicted. Worse for Johnson, after McCarthy showed the country that perhaps the sitting president could be beaten, Robert Kennedy (always the opportunist who capitalized on the perceived weakness of an opponent) entered the primary race, and he had assets that McCarthy did not, notably a large "war chest" of money and a national organization. By this time, a number of national news magazines had called for a negotiated settlement and US withdrawal from Vietnam. Even the conservative *Wall Street Journal* now came out against the war. Much worse, Walter Cronkite of CBS—already hailed as the most trusted man in the United States—now condemned the war, saying that we could expect nothing but a stalemate that could drag on for years, a prediction that Republican Richard Nixon made sure would come true once he was president, for he was a "Cold Warrior" too. Like others, Cronkite advocated a negotiated peace. Johnson was crushed that the CBS's news anchor had taken a new, critical public stance, remarking that when he lost Walter, he lost middle America.

After New Hampshire, the nation looked to the Wisconsin primary, where twice as many students worked for their antiwar candidates. Now Kennedy was in the race and planned to campaign, like McCarthy, to end the Vietnam War. Shortly before the primary, LBJ decided that, essentially, Vietnam had destroyed him. He believed that he most likely could not win in the general elections of 1968 even if he could muster enough forces to win the Democratic nomination. On March 31, in a major national television address, Johnson shocked the country with his announcement that he would not run for reelection. He also announced that he was suspending all bombing of North Vietnam and that, during what remained of his term in office, he intended to devote all his efforts to peace negotiations.

Lady Bird Johnson told friends that after LBJ had made the announcement and moved away from his desk, he looked as though he was shedding the weight of the world from his shoulders. He seemed at peace for the first time in years. Still the legacy that remained was not good. By the time Johnson left office, more than 30,000

Americans had died in Vietnam, the US Treasury was drained, and he was surely right that Vietnam had ruined his administration and dashed his hopes of building a "Great Society"—this from a man who once said that he intended to complete "the Revolution that Franklin D. Roosevelt started." As well, the Democratic Party lost the presidency in the general elections, with Richard Nixon claiming the office.

Nixon meddled in Vietnam and hung on there for years. Finally, in 1973 the Paris Accords were signed, thereby almost ending what now seemed to be a never-ending war. With the accords, the United States, in essence, surrendered. By then at least 58,000 Americans had died in Vietnam, and 300,000 had been wounded. The war had cost at least $150 billion. The United States maintained a skeleton force in Vietnam until 1975, when North Vietnam invaded the South. Americans had to watch the embarrassing spectacle of the utter defeat of the United States, whose helicopter pilots tried to save those whom they could in the final hour. At the end, Nixon's duplicity became known. In the Paris Accords a secret pact was made by which he agreed to come to South Vietnam's rescue if the North invaded. But Congress refused to approve the spending bill that Nixon's pledge required, so he reneged. Finally, America's longest war was done. The whole disaster could have been avoided if the United States had granted the Vietnamese their right to self-determination, something that any US president could have done, post-1945.[29]

Notes

1. The data on casualties come from information compiled by the National Archives, which is available on its website; see www.archives.gov/research/military/vietnam-war/casualty-statistics.html.

2. There are a number of studies that cover the entire history of Vietnam. See, for example, Joseph Buttinger, *The Smaller Dragon: A Political History of Vietnam* (New York: Praeger, 1958); Buttinger, *Dragon Defiant: A Short History of Vietnam* (New York: Praeger, 1972); Justin J. Cornfield, *The History of Vietnam* (Westport, CT: Greenwood, 2008); Nguyen Khac, *Vietnam: A Long History* (Hanoi: Gioi, 1993); and Wendy M. Cole, *Vietnam* (Philadelphia: Chelsea House, 1997). Also see Ellen Joy Hammer, *The Struggle of Indochina, 1940–1955*, rev. ed. (Stanford: Stanford University Press, 1966); and Michael Clodfelter, *Vietnam in Military Statistics: A History of the Indochina Wars, 1772–1991* (Jefferson, NC: McFarland, 1995).

3. English-language biographies of Ho Chi Minh are almost nonexistent, but see Pierre Brocheux, *Ho Chi Minh: A Biography*, trans. Claire Duiker (New York: Cambridge University Press, 2007); and Vietnam Workers Party, *Our President Ho Chi Minh* (Hanoi: Gioi, 1976). Also see Vietnam Commission on Research, *Ho Chi Minh* (Hanoi: Gioi, 1995). For yet more on Vietnam, see George Herring's classic *America's Longest War: The United States and Vietnam, 1950 to 1975*, rev. ed. (Boston: McGraw-Hill, 2002). Although Herring obviously held that US involvement with Vietnam started in 1950, this author believes that 1945 better dates the beginning since Pres. Harry Truman sent troops to help the French retake Vietnam and began helping

the French fund their war. Also see William J. Duiker, *The Communist Road to Power in Vietnam* (Boulder, CO: Westview, 1996). For more statistics, see Clodfelter, *Vietnam in Military Statistics*. For Japanese aggression during World War II, consult US Office of Strategic Services, *Japanese Seizure of French Indochina* (Washington, DC: GPO, 1945). For more, see Jonathan Neale, *A People's History of the Vietnam War* (New York: New Press, 2003), 3–25. Also see Gabriel Kolko, *Anatomy of a War: Vietnam, the United States, and the Modern Historical Experience* (New York: Pantheon, 1985). On extending containment to Asia, see Robert M. Blum, *Drawing the Line: The Origins of American Containment Policy in East Asia* (New York: Norton, 1982); William J. Duiker, *U.S. Containment Policy and the Conflict in Indochina* (Stanford: Stanford University Press, 1994); and Robert F. Turner, *Vietnamese Communism: Its Origins and Development* (Stanford: Hoover Institution Press, 1975). For more on Truman, see Merle Miller, *Plain Speaking: An Oral Biography of Harry Truman* (New York: Putnam, 1974); William Pemberton, *Harry S. Truman: Fair Dealer and Cold Warrior* (Boston: Twayne, 1989); Glenn D. Paige, *1950: Truman's Decision; the United States Enters the Korean War* (New York: Chelsea House, 1970); and Dean Acheson, *The Korean War* (New York: Norton, 1971). For the siege/battle of Dien Bien Phu, see Richard Worth, *Dien Bien Phu* (Philadelphia: Chelsea House, 2002).

4. For more on containment, see George F. Kennan, *Containing the Soviet Union: A Critique of U.S. Policy*, eds. Terry L. Deibel and John L. Gaddis (Washington, DC: International Defense Publishers, 1987); Sheldon Anderson, *Condemned to Repeat It: The "Lessons of History" and the Making of U.S. Cold War Containment Policy* (Lanham, MD.: Lexington Books, 2008); Duiker, *U.S. Containment Policy;* and Blum, *Drawing the Line.*

5. A good source on President Eisenhower's diplomacy is Dwight D. Eisenhower, *The White House Years*, 2 vols. (New York: Doubleday, 1963–65). For his prediction about free elections in 1956, see Eisenhower, *Mandate for Change* (Garden City, NJ: Doubleday, 1963), 372.

6. Stanley Karnow, *Vietnam: A History* (New York: Penguin, 1997), 238.

7. Neale, *People's History*, 3–25.

8. Kolko, *Anatomy of a War*, 89; Karnow, *Vietnam*, 239.

9. JFK's involvement in Vietnam is reported in John M. Newman, *JFK and Vietnam: Deception, Intrigue, and the Struggle for Power* (New York: Warner Books, 1992); and Orrin Schwab, *Defending the Free World: John F. Kennedy, Lyndon Johnson, and the Vietnam War, 1961–1965* (Westport: Praeger, 1998).

10. Karnow, *Vietnam*, 326–27.

11. For more on Ngo Dinh Diem and for JFK's role in having Diem exterminated, see Seth Jacobs, *Cold War Mandarin: Ngo Dinh Diem and the Origins of America's War in Vietnam, 1950–1963* (Lanham, MD.: Rowman and Littlefield, 2006); and US Congress, Senate Committee on Foreign Relations, *U.S. Involvement in the Overthrow of Diem, 1963; a Staff Study Based on the Pentagon Papers* [prepared by Ann L. Hollick] (Washington, DC: GPO, 1972). On instability in the South Vietnamese government, see Karnow, *Vietnam*, 336–39.

12. Richard Russell quoted in Robert Dalleck, *Flawed Giant: Lyndon Johnson and His Times, 1961–1973* (New York: Oxford University Press, 1998), 144.

13. Herring, *America's Longest War*, 103; US Department of State, *Foreign Relations of the United States, Vietnam, 1961–1963* (Washington, DC: GPO, 1991), 707.

14. McGeorge Bundy, Memorandum, Aug. 13, 1964, in Bundy to LBJ, Aug. 31, 1964, LBJ Papers, LBJ Library and Museum, Austin, TX (hereafter LBJL), also published in LBJ, *Public Papers of the Presidents: Lyndon B. Johnson, Containing the Public Messages, Speeches, and Statements of the President, 1963–1964*, 2 vols. (Washington, DC: GOP, 1967), 2:1126–27.

15. Tom Wicker, *The Influence of Personality upon Politics* (New York: Morrow, 1968), 205. For more on the subject, see Brian DeMark, *Into the Quagmire* (New York: Oxford University Press, 1995).

16. Meeting on South Vietnam, Sept. 9, 1964, LBJ Papers, LBJL.

17. William Bundy, "History of the Vietnam War," 10–14, 19–22, Dean Rusk, oral history, and George Ball, oral history, LBJ Papers, LBJL; William C. Gibbons, *The U.S. Government and the Vietnam War,* vol. 2 (Washington, DC: GPO, 1986), 285–95. Bill Moyers has made it clear that Johnson originally did not want to go to war.

18. For the president's statement before Congress, see LBJ, *Public Papers of the Presidents,* 2:927–28. For more on the Gulf of Tonkin Resolution and the controversy it engendered, see Anthony Austin, *The President's War: The Story of the Tonkin Gulf Resolution and How the Nation Was Trapped into War* (Philadelphia: Lippincott, 1971); and John Galloway, *The Gulf of Tonkin Resolution* (Rutherford, NJ: Fairleigh Dickinson University Press, 1970).

19. Karnow, *Vietnam,* 340.

20. Dave Richard Palmer, *Summons of the Trumpet in Vietnam in Perspective* (San Rafael, CA: Presidio, 1978), 882; Herring, *America's Longest War,* 121; Bernard Nulty, *The Vietnam War* (New York: Barnes and Noble, 1998), 97, 261; Karnow, *Vietnam,* 468; Earl H. Tilford, *Setup: What the Air Force Did in Vietnam and Why* (Washington, DC: GPO, 1991), 89.

21. Lady Bird Johnson, *A White House Diary* (1970; rprt., Austin: University of Texas Press, 2007), 247–48.

22. Eric Goldman, *The Tragedy of Lyndon Johnson* (New York: Knopf, 1969), 477–78.

23. Gibbons, *U.S. Government and Vietnam,* 161–66; DeMark, *Into the Quagmire,* 92–94.

24. Karnow, *Vietnam,* 468.

25. For more, see Robert McNamara et al., *Argument without End: In Search of Answers to the Vietnam Tragedy* (New York: Public Affairs, 1999). McNamara eventually realized the folly of Vietnam, a folly that he helped cause. Like others, he failed to see that even a professional army of roughly 500,000 men could not defeat a nation of 34 million, most of whom (except collaborators) had a driven purpose: liberation of their country from imperial powers. The Vietnamese had fought the Mongols, the Chinese, the French, the Japanese, and other groups—including the Americans—without giving up their perceived right to self-determination.

26. Dalleck, *Flawed Giant,* 253–54, 349–50, 461, 502, 512, 522, 626.

27. For more on guerrilla warfare, see Peter MacDonald, *Giáp: The Victor in Vietnam* (New York: Norton, 1993); and Robert B. Asprey, *War in the Shadows: Guerrillas in History* (New York: Morrow, 1994).

28. Dallek captures LBJ's ambiance throughout *Flawed Giant.*

29. For the Paris Accords, see Pierre Asselin, *A Bitter Peace: Washington, Hanoi, and the Making of the Paris Agreement* (Chapel Hill: University of North Carolina Press, 2002); and Henry Kissinger, *Ending the Vietnam War: A History of America's Involvement in and Extrication from the Vietnam War* (New York: Simon and Schuster, 2003).

14

Black Paradox in the Age of Terrorism

Military Patriotism or Higher Education?

Ronald E. Goodwin

IN HIS SEMINAL treatise on blacks in the United States, W. E. B. Du Bois pondered a question that still confounds this country and particularly the black community. He asked if blacks could be accepted as Americans while still maintaining the culture and identity of Africa. Du Bois argued that such "twoness" would present a monumental challenge to blacks in the twentieth century.[1] Certainly, other immigrants have faced similar challenges, but none faced the daunting task of overcoming the legacy of slavery.

Nonetheless, the challenge of identity has not hindered African Americans from contributing to a military that forged a new nation during the American Revolution and refined the meaning of liberty during the Civil War. Today, blacks contribute to arguably the most technically advanced military the world has ever seen in the defense and preservation of democracy worldwide. In fact, the history and accomplishments of the US military inspire patriotism in those who recognize that our democracy and freedoms have come at the expense of men and women, regardless of race or ethnicity, who sacrificed in service to our nation. The images of Gen. George Washington and his ill-fed troops crossing the Delaware River as a precursor to their surprise attack against the Hessians near Trenton, New Jersey, along with the US Marines raising the Stars and Stripes during the 1945 battle of Iwo Jima serve as reminders of those sacrifices.

Unfortunately, there are other images of our democracy and freedom that we would just as soon forget. These include the images of black World War I veterans being lynched while still in uniform.[2] African Americans have served in every conflict in this nation's history and until the 1950s seldom enjoyed the benefits of the democracy for which they were fighting. In fact, Martin Luther King Jr., toward the end of his all-too-brief public career, in one of his most famous and controversial speeches, questioned if this country could continue sending the poor and minorities to foreign battlefields fighting for freedoms they frequently did not enjoy in their own country.[3]

There is no question that in the civil rights era of the 1950s and 1960s, the black community saw patriotism exhibited by military service as a means to achieve middle-class status. But the patriotism, and its inherent sacrifices, of those black men and women cannot be measured solely by the numbers who achieved the so-called American dream of homeownership in predominately white suburbs. Their patriotism should be considered also in light of the numbers who arrived home in body bags, the numbers of children who never knew their fallen parents, and the numbers of spouses left to raise children alone. In particular, the black community's relationship with this country's armed forces has been a gamble at best. On the one hand is economic opportunity and middle-class stability, while on the other is the unfortunate disillusionment and resentfulness of those surviving the loss of a loved one.

Yet the civil rights era also brought about another avenue to middle-class status for the black community. The successes of the civil rights movement led to an erosion of barriers to institutions of higher education. As a result, the numbers of blacks enrolling and graduating from universities and colleges throughout the country increased. In 1967 blacks comprised just over 23 percent of all eighteen- to twenty-four-year-old high school graduates enrolled in institutions of higher education. By 2007 that figure had increased to 40 percent.[4]

These educational statistics indicate that today's black community no longer relies upon military service as a means to economic stability. Instead, military service in this age of terrorism is an expression of the rich legacy of black patriotism to a country that continues to provide opportunities to those willing to see beyond the tangible obstacles and reach for the intangible dreams where successes, however defined, are ultimately found.

The army's Reserve Officers' Training Corps (ROTC) provides another option that combines higher education followed by military service. The Land Grant Act of 1862 (Morrill Act) not only established colleges that would specifically provide instruction in agriculture and mechanics, present-day Texas A&M University and Prairie View A&M University in Texas among them, but also a commitment to military science. Military instruction was further enhanced at civilian institutions during World War I with the passage of the National Defense Act of 1916, which provided additional resources for the training of military officers. The ROTC presence at our nation's colleges and universities played a significant role during World War II by providing more than 100,000 officers to the regular army, many of whom were black college graduates.[5]

Over one hundred years ago, during an intense period of racial discrimination, Du Bois eloquently asserted that blacks had no intentions to drastically change the United States, despite the history of racial strife. Instead, he argued that the African American "simply wishes to make it possible for a man to be both a Negro and an American, without being cursed and spit upon by his fellows, without the doors of Opportunity closed roughly in his face."[6]

In this "Age of Terrorism," the black community arguably enjoys more opportunities than at any other time in this country's history. The social, economic, and political achievements of blacks in the last few generations are too numerous to mention. But what is of significant for the African American community is the opportunity to choose the path to success, be it patriotic service in the military, the unhindered enrollment in institutions of higher education, or careers as military officers gained through ROTC training.

Therefore, the focus of this chapter will be a quantitative analysis of black Texans' enlistment trends in the US Air Force from 1996 to 2006, their enrollment trends in Texas colleges and universities, and lastly, black participation in the only wholly contained Army ROTC unit at a historically black institution of higher education, Prairie View A&M University. The air force was chosen as a particular case study because it is the only branch of the US armed services whose enlistees enter basic training in a single location: Lackland Air Force Base at San Antonio. The time period is also significant in that it represents a five-year period before and after the terror attacks of September 11, 2001 (9/11). While military service has been viewed as a means in achieving middle-class economic status by the black community, the negativity surrounding the Vietnam War coupled with the near elimination of segregation in Texas colleges and universities has opened new opportunities for social and economic advancement for black Texans.

Therefore, the principle objective here involves a determination of the influences 9/11 played in the air force enlistments and the college and university enrollments of black Texans, especially in the Army ROTC unit at Prairie View A&M University. The findings of this study will illustrate that the military enlistments varied little after the terror attacks. Likewise, there was minimal influence on the college and university enrollments and those at Prairie View's ROTC unit during the same period. This infers that the "doors of opportunity" referenced by W. E. B. Du Bois are indeed open for black Texans as the era of terrorism has not diminished the legacy of patriotism nor curtailed the opportunity to achieve higher education.

BLACK TEXANS AND THE UNITED STATES AIR FORCE

The development of computers has had a tremendous effect on demographic studies over the last twenty-five to thirty years. It is now easier to measure the movements of racial and ethnic groups spatially and temporally. At the same time, however, it has become somewhat challenging to measure "race" since the US decennial census relies upon self-identification. Furthermore, those identifying themselves as "Hispanic" have at their disposal a multitude of "race" options. For the purposes of this study, the data used for "African American/Black" are derived from the "one race" category of the 1990 and 2000 national censuses.

Black Texans constituted nearly 12 percent of the state's total population in 1990 and 2000. Texas has 254 counties, and in the 2000 census a majority (56 percent, or 1,364,344 individuals) of blacks lived in four counties: Harris (628,619), Dallas (450,557), Tarrant (185,143), and Bexar (100,025), which also represent the largest urban areas in the state.[7]

The years since the September 11 terrorist attacks on the World Trade Center and the Pentagon have not diminished the feelings of horror and rage felt throughout this country. This was an unexpected event that not only took Americans by surprise but also served as a reminder of how valuable, and vulnerable, our democracy is in the face of violent worldwide oppression. Even though Pres. George W. Bush presented the calm, in-charge demeanor expected from the leader of the free world during his immediate post-9/11 speech, the feelings of anger and rage were still present as he referred to the attacks as "despicable acts of terrorism."[8] Most Americans felt similarly, and many favored some form of immediate retaliation against a foe who would cowardly target civilians. Unfortunately, such feelings of anger and rage are often misdirected. For example, the Federal Bureau of Investigation (FBI) found itself investigating "hate crimes" against individuals with Middle Eastern characteristics in the weeks and months following the attacks.[9]

Did 9/11 evoke increased patriotism among Texans, and black Texans in particular? Measuring the influence of 9/11 on the voluntary enlistment of blacks in the US Air Force, data was obtained for the periods 1996 to 2001 and 2002 to 2006. A total of 17,572 Texans enlisted in the air force from 1996 to 2001, with 15 percent of those identifying themselves as black, 23 percent Hispanic, and the majority, 56 percent, as white.[10] The data also indicate a positive enlistment trend as all three major racial categories increased in enlistments. From 1996 to 2001, whites increased their enlistment numbers by 288, blacks by 229, and Hispanics by 358. Overall, the number of Texans enlisting in the air force increased from 2,633 to 3,359, a 28-percent increase. Yet

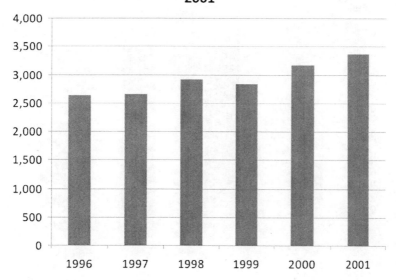

14.1
Total Air Force Enlistments from Texas, 1996-2001

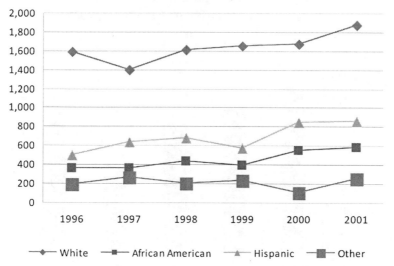

14.2
Texas Air Force Enlistments by Race, 1996-2001

White ─── African American ─── Hispanic ─── Other

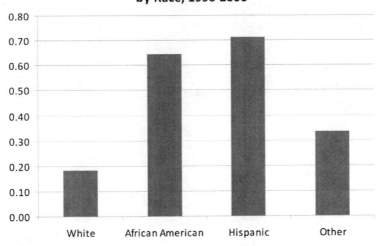

14.3

Percentage Change in Texas' Air Force Enlistments by Race, 1996-2006

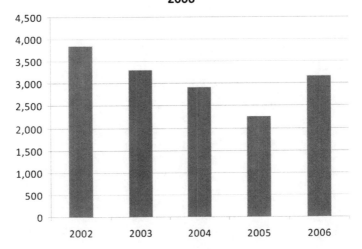

14.4

Total Air Force Enlistments from Texas, 2002-2006

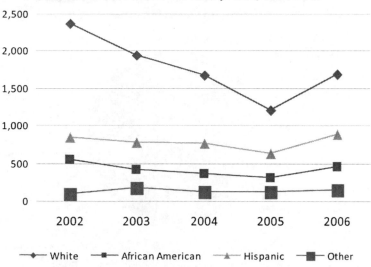

14.5

Texas Air Force Enlistments by Race, 2002-2006

━◆━ White ━■━ African American ━▲━ Hispanic ━■━ Other

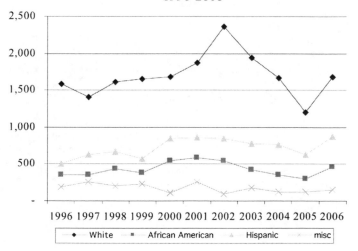

14.6

Texas Air Force Enlistees by Race, 1996-2006

━◆━ White ━✳━ African American ━▲━ Hispanic ━✕━ misc

14.7

Fall 1996 Enrollment in Four-Year Higher Education Institutions in Texas

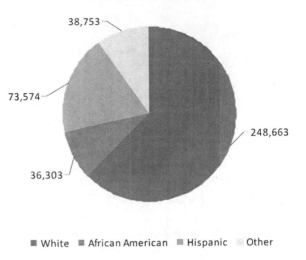

■ White ■ African American ■ Hispanic ■ Other

14.8

Percentages of Fall Enrollment in Four-Year Higher Education Institutions in Texas, 1996-2001

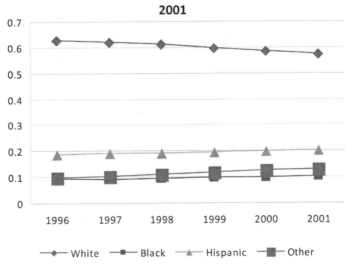

◆ White ■ Black ▲ Hispanic ■ Other

these raw numbers do not fully show the levels of the percentage increases for the racial categories. Whites only increased by 18 percent, but blacks (65 percent) and Hispanics (71 percent) experienced significant jumps in their percentages of the total air force enlistees from Texas.

There were significant increases in the state's air force enlistments across all racial categories in 2002. This data implies a significant patriotic reaction to the attacks of 9/11. But the remainder of the period, 2003 to 2006, indicates that enlistments were declining. From 2002 to 2006, the total number of Texans enlisting in the air force was 15,489, a decrease of 2,083 from the total figure from 1996 to 2001. Even though the numbers of whites increased by 14 percent between 2001 and 2002, the trend indicates the numbers of white Texans decreased between 2002 and 2005 and recovered in 2006. Conversely, the numbers of blacks and Hispanics enlisting in the air force remained fairly constant.

Overall, more than 33,000 Texans enlisted in the US Air Force during the period 1996–2006. Racially, 56 percent of those enlistees identified themselves as white, 24 percent as Hispanic, and 14 percent as black. The data illustrates a considerable percentage increase in the number of Hispanic enlistees, 74 percent, compared to the increases experienced by blacks and whites, 29 and 6 percent, respectively. The total number of air force enlistees from Texas by race illustrates that there were minimal fluctuations. Even though the enlistment of whites declined sharply by 48 percent between 2002 and 2005, that figure rebounded in 2006 by nearly 39 percent.

BLACKS TEXANS AND HIGHER EDUCATION

The Texas Higher Education Coordinating Board (THECB) is the state agency responsible for collecting and maintaining data concerning higher education in the state. THECB works in conjunction with state and higher-education officials in developing strategies and programs that provides the best access to education for all Texans.[11]

There are several assumptions that have to be accepted when evaluating demographic data from THECB. First, a majority of undergraduates fall within the "normal" college age range of eighteen to twenty-four years old. Accepting the well-documented fact that many older students matriculate at campuses throughout the state, this assumption may be the most difficult to accept when comparing to voluntary military service in the air force. Second, the demographic/racial data obtained by colleges and universities adhere to the same methodology as the military and the US census. If the methodologies are not comparable, then any results based on them will automatically be

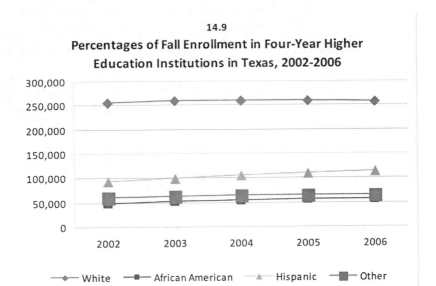

14.9
Percentages of Fall Enrollment in Four-Year Higher Education Institutions in Texas, 2002-2006

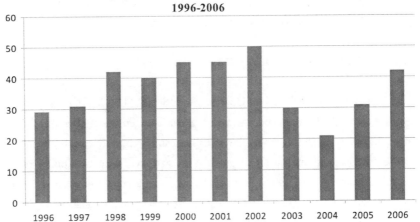

14.10
Total Fall Army ROTC Enrollments at PVAMU - Entering Cadets, 1996-2006

14.11
Total Fall Army ROTC Enrollments at PVAMU - Entering Cadets by Gender, 1996-2006

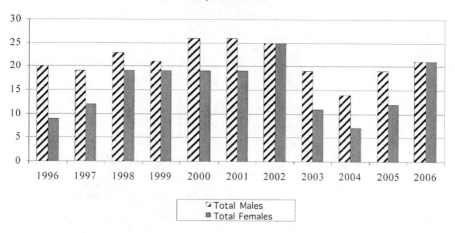

14.12
Total Fall Army ROTC Enrollments at PVAMU - Entering Male Cadets by Race, 1996-2006

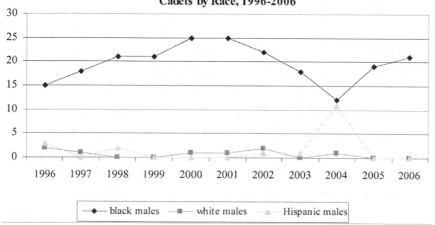

14.13
**Total Fall Army ROTC Enrollments at PVAMU - Entering Female
Cadets by Race, 1996-2006**

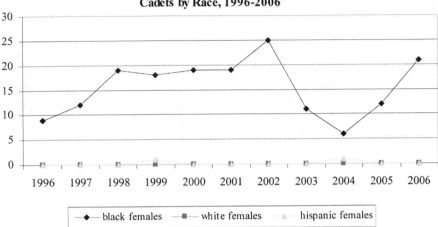

suspect. But since colleges and universities rely on self-identification of racial preference, even if the individual racial categories are different, it should provide enough similarity to the air force's method of self-identification. Finally, it must be assumed that these students are matriculating at least "half-time" during the semester in which the data was taken (usually the fall semester). This assumption is important since military service has often been viewed by the black community as a viable option to obtaining a college education. Therefore, this assumption is predicated upon the individual considering oneself primarily a student first, even if they are gainfully employed elsewhere.

The higher-education racial data used were obtained from four-year public colleges and universities in Texas. These thirty-five institutions are found in locations throughout the state and range in student population size from the University of Texas at Austin (nearly 50,000) to Sul Ross–Rio Grande College (only 948).[12]

In 1996 the data indicate that nearly 400,000 Texans enrolled in some college or university in the state. Of that figure, nearly 250,000 (63 percent) were white, compared to nearly 74,000 (19 percent) Hispanics, and just 36,000 (9 percent) blacks. The remainder have been classified as "other."[13] Through the fall reporting period in 2001, the presence of blacks and Hispanics increased by 7,214 and 12,551, respectively, while the numbers of whites decreased by 2,673. Therefore, the percentages of enrollment by race during this time period (1996–2001) illustrates fairly consistent trends positively (blacks and Hispanics) and negatively (whites). Interestingly, of the 43,517 blacks registered in Texas colleges and universities in the fall of 2001, 30 percent were found at the state's only two public historically black colleges and universities (HBCUs), Texas Southern University and Prairie View A&M University.[14]

The fall enrollment data for the period after 9/11 (2002–2006) show little deviation from the previous six years. There was only a 9-percent increase in total enrollment, from 455,719 to 497,195 students, and the percentage of blacks varied by 1 percent from 2002 to 2006 (10.5 percent in 2002 to 11.4 percent in 2006).

While the actual numbers of white enrollment increased by almost 3,000 students, the percentage of whites enrolled decreased from 2002 to 2006 from 56 to 51 percent of the total enrolled. Conversely, black and Hispanic enrollment experienced dramatic percentage increases of 16 and 22 percent, respectively. With respect to actual numbers, Hispanic students topped the 100,000 plateau in 2003 and demonstrated consistent increases in 2004–2006. Like the previous period of 1996–2001, the majority of blacks (30 percent) enrolled during 2002–2006 matriculated at either Texas Southern University or Prairie View A&M University. The number of blacks increased by just over 12,000 students, but the percentage of the total enrollment remained consistent.

BLACKS TEXANS AND PRAIRIE VIEW A&M'S ARMY ROTC UNIT

In Texas, military ROTC units are found at numerous colleges and universities. Yet the Army ROTC unit located at Prairie View A&M University (PVAMU) is the only one wholly contained at a historically black institution. Military instruction began at PVAMU in 1878, and the initial ROTC unit was organized in 1918. But due to the existing racial climate during the World War I era that reinforced the subordinate status of blacks in American society, that initial unit was classified as a junior program and carried the stigma of being deemed nonessential to the military's mission.[15]

Yet as the military's presence at PVAMU nears one hundred years, numerous ROTC-trained black Texans have enjoyed spectacular military careers, and many have achieved the rank of a general officer. Furthermore, the history of the ROTC unit at PVAMU is not only one of military achievement but also one of community change. The alumni of this storied unit have achieved success outside of the military services and served as role models during the era of segregation and beyond.

The data used in this analysis were from the Army ROTC unit at PVAMU from 1996 to 2006 and includes information related to a limited demographic profile and first-time enrollment in the corps. Between 1996 and 2006, there were 406 individuals who enrolled for the first time in the fall semester, including the baseline year of 2001. Enrollment was highest between 2000 and 2002 but saw a significant decline in 2003. Yet when omitting the baseline data of 2001, there were 187 first-time enrollees before 9/11 (1996–2000) and 174 between 2002 and 2006. This indicates that there has been a decrease in the unit's first-time cadets since the commencement of the "Age of Terrorism."

When examining the unit's enrollment by gender, of the 187 fresh cadets between 1996 and 2000, 109 were men, and black males constituted almost 92 percent. Of the remaining 78 female cadets, 99 percent were African American. Even though the total enrollment declined between 2002 and 2006, the percentage of black males increased to nearly 94 percent. While there was a decline in African American male first-time enrollments, there were greater declines in the enrollment percentages of white and Hispanic male cadets during this period. Conversely, there was a small percentage increase in female cadets between 2002 and 2006, even though blacks still comprised 99 percent of the female cadets.

The influence of establishing Army ROTC programs at HBCUs are immeasurable. These programs have become the avenue for the training of black officers into a military structure that maintained rigid segregation policies up to the beginning of the Cold War era. Furthermore, HBCUs, especially those located in the states of the former Confederacy, have been institutions where the beacon of middle-class existence shone brightest for African Americans. The "Age of Terrorism" has done little to affect the opportunities for education and military service at these schools, especially PVAMU.

CONCLUSION

The experiences of present-day black Texans in the military correspond with those of previous generations in that they recognize the obligations to a country that provides immense opportunities, even when those opportunities have been restricted by racism. Today racism is not nearly an issue to patriotic service or military success.

The average age of air force enlistees from Texas, regardless of race, corresponded with black enlistees at approximately twenty years of age. When examining the voluntary participation in the military compared to enrollment in the state's numerous public universities and colleges, it is imperative to examine the age group between eighteen and twenty-four. In 1990, blacks represented just over 13 percent of all Texans in this age group. By 2000 that figure dropped to just over 12 percent. This is significant because the percentage of blacks enlisting in the air force was only slightly higher than what was found throughout the state as a whole.

Still, the question remains: Did 9/11 evoke increased patriotism among Texans, and among black Texans in particular? The data indicates that the terror attacks had little effect on the enlistment of black Texans, who continued to voluntarily enlist at a fairly consistent rate. Yet it can be assumed that the terror attacks did influence the enlistment of white Texans as their enlistment rates dramatically increased nearly 41 percent between 2001 and 2002. But enlistments decreased by 18 percent the following year and continued to decline through 2006.

Likewise, black enrollments in Texas colleges and universities were also fairly constant with the enrollments of other races. This also implies that 9/11 had little influence in whether or not black Texans chose to enlist in the military or register for classes at the institute of higher education of their choice.

The data from the Army's ROTC unit at Prairie View A&M University indicate a slight decline (7 percent) in the overall enrollment of first-semester cadets in the five years preceding 9/11 as compared to the five years following the day the country stood still. Yet the decline of black male cadets (-8 percent) was greater than the decline in black female cadets (-2.5 percent) during this period. This implies that black females may be taking greater advantage of the opportunities provided by the army to advance a military career. Further study will be necessary to determine if black female officers from PVAMU's Army ROTC unit enjoy the same career success as their male counterparts. Nonetheless, the new environment of military preparedness has done little to diminish the belief that military service as an officer is a path to the American dream that is just as viable today as it was at the dawn of the Cold War.

Like the generations of blacks before him, Benny Goodwin Sr. enlisted in the US Air Force in 1954, at the age of eighteen, seeking a means to the middle class. Within a year he was married, and his first son arrived weeks after his twentieth birthday. He recalled with disgust the sight of "whites only" signs throughout his initial stay in San Antonio. Still, he quickly became acclimated to Texas' racial environment but found it more difficult to accept the limitations forced upon him while in uniform. Goodwin recalled that in the 1950s and 1960s, blacks in the air force were often limited in their career options. Nonetheless, he did mention serving several tours of duty in Korea and Vietnam, where only the mission mattered and race was irrelevant. After twenty years, Goodwin retired and remains patriotic of the air force and its past and current missions. Interestingly, when his son enlisted in the same branch in the early 1980s, Goodwin was able to recognize how much had changed. His son encountered none of the career limitations he had faced, illustrating the progress made in the military and the society in general since the end of Jim Crow.[16]

Likewise, Col. Jeffery Hutchinson agrees that the military is still a path to the middle class for today's black community. As a current active-duty military physician, Hutchinson has served in numerous locations and commented that he has not experienced any form of overt racism. He did mention, however, that he has observed instances where black physicians have not had the same opportunities as their white counterparts to make a "good impression."[17]

When asked if he received the same levels of respect as his white counterparts, Hutchinson also replied that he is "more quickly mistaken for an enlisted soldier" than a West Point graduate because of his race. But he did note that when in uniform, he received the respect due his rank. Hutchinson, who recently returned from a tour of duty in the Middle East, received a surprise when he landed stateside. He recalled: "My community's reaction brought me to tears. The street was lined with flags and they [his neighbors] were all waiting at my house. I did not expect it and it was extremely touching."[18]

Americans often accept the fact that the concept of democracy must be preserved and that it is worth the sacrifices that hundreds of thousands have made over the years. Even though society has not always recognized the sacrifices of its black citizens, the new millennium is opening doors of acceptance and respect for the black community. While the attacks of 9/11 have changed how Americans view themselves and the world, the levels of patriotism among black Texans in the air force has not appeared to waver at all. While many in the black community might still find it difficult to deal with Du Bois's concept of "twoness," the terror attacks have not changed their duties to the notions of democracy and freedom.

Notes

1. W. E. B. Du Bois, *The Souls of Black Folk* (New York: Penguin; Signet Classics, 1995), 45–46.

2. C. Vann Woodward, *The Strange Career of Jim Crow* (New York: Oxford University Press, 1966), 114–15.

3. Martin Luther King Jr. "Beyond Vietnam: A Time to Break Silence," Apr. 4, 1967, Information Clearing House, accessed June 2009, http://www.informationclearinghouse.info/article2564.htm.

4. Digest of Education Statistics, "Table 204. Enrollment rates of 18- to 24-year-olds in degree-granting institutions, by type of institution and sex and race/ethnicity of student: 1967 through 2007," National Center for Education Statistics, accessed Aug. 2009, http://nces.ed.gov/programs/digest/d08/tables/dt08_204.asp.

5. "UT Army ROTC History," University of Texas at Austin, accessed Nov. 2010, http://www.utexas.edu/cola/depts/arotc/cadets/History.php; "ROTC History," accessed Nov. 2010, http://www.jscc.edu/uploads/ROTC/Documents/ROTC%20HISTORY.pdf.

6. Du Bois, *Souls of Black Folk,* 45–46.

7. US Department of Commerce, Census Bureau Home Page, http://www.census.gov/.

8. "Kerry Hits Bush Reaction to 9/11 Attack News," Aug. 5, 2004, Politics, CNN.com, accessed June 2009, http://www.cnn.com/2004/ALLPOLITICS/08/05/kerry.911/. Pres. George W. Bush told the 9/11 Commission that he purposefully exhibited a calm demeanor in the days following the attacks so as not to excite the American public. Bush's entire post-9/11 speech can be viewed at Youtube.com.

9. John Harris Stevenson, "Reactions to the Attacks of 9/11," Sept. 18, 2001, *Tranquileye* (blog), http://www.tranquileye.com/blog/2001/09/reactions_to_th.html.

10. The remainder of the air force enlistees from Texas who chose to racially classify themselves did so as either Asian, American Indian, or "International."

11. Texas Higher Education Coordinating Board, accessed Jan. 7, 2009, http://www.thecb.state.tx.us/.

12. Texas Higher Education Coordinating Board, "Enrollment-Statewide by Gender and Ethnic Origin, Public University Fall 2006," accessed Jan. 7, 2009, http://www.thecb.state.tx.us/.

13. For the purposes of this analysis, "other" consists of Asians, American Indian, international, and those who decided not to self-identify their race.

14. Texas Higher Education Coordinating Board, "Enrollment-Statewide by Gender and Ethnic Origin, Public University Fall 2001," accessed Jan. 7, 2009, http://www.thecb.state.tx.us/.

15. Isaac Hampton, "The Journey of African American Officers through the Vietnam Era" (PhD diss., University of Houston, 2008), 151–52.

16. Benny Goodwin, personal interview, May 3, 2009.

17. Jeffery Hutchinson, personal interview, July 9, 2009.

18. Ibid.

Contributors

Alwyn Barr

Alwyn Barr (PhD, University of Texas) is professor of history and former chair of the department at Texas Tech University. Among his five authored books are *Black Texans: A History of African Americans in Texas, 1528–1995*, 2nd ed. (University of Oklahoma Press, 1996), and *African Texans* (Texas A&M University Press, 2004). He also has edited, with Robert A. Calvert, *Black Leaders: Texans for Their Times* (Texas State Historical Association, 1980), and has written the introduction to *Black Cowboys of Texas*, edited by Sara R. Massey (Texas A&M University Press, 2000), as well as several articles on African American history in professional journals. He is a former president of the Texas State Historical Association and a former board member of Humanities Texas.

Jimmy L. Bryan Jr.

Jimmy L. Bryan Jr. (PhD, Southern Methodist University) is assistant professor of history at Lamar University. He is the author of *More Zeal than Discretion: The Westward Adventures of Walter P. Lane* (Texas A&M University Press, 2008) and has contributed articles to *Making of the American West: People and Perspectives* (2007) and to the *Pacific Historical Review*.

Kelly E. Crager

Kelly E. Crager (PhD, University of North Texas) is head of the Oral History Project, Vietnam Center and Archive, at Texas Tech University. Crager is the author of *Hell under the Rising Sun: Texan POWs and the Building of the Burma–Thailand Death Railway* (Texas A&M University Press, 2008) and "'God Knows What's Going to Happen to Us': The 'Lost Battery' of Texas's 'Lost Battalion' during World War II," *Southwestern Historical Quarterly* (July 2008) as well as associate editor of *Heroes: Oral History Interviews with Veterans of World War II* (UNT Oral History Program, 2002).

Francis X. Galán

Francis X. Galán (PhD, Southern Methodist University, 2006) was visiting professor of history at Our Lady of the Lake University, 2008–2009. He has authored several journal articles on Los Adaes, the Spanish capital of Texas, and comparative borderlands of Louisiana-Texas and the lower Rio Grande Valley from the colonial to American Civil War periods. He is currently revising his dissertation into a book manuscript, "Forged in Blood: Spanish Los Adaes and the Arroyo Hondo Imperial Boundary of Louisiana and Texas, 1721–1773."

Ronald E. Goodwin

Ronald E. Goodwin (MA, Texas Southern University) is assistant professor of history at Prairie View A&M University. He has authored a journal article, several articles and reviews for online magazines, and a book chapter in the forthcoming anthology on the experiences of Texas slaves during the Civil War, edited by Kenneth Howell.

Charles David Grear

Charles David Grear (PhD, Texas Christian University) is assistant professor of history at Prairie View A&M University. He is author of four journal articles and five book chapters on Texas in the Civil War as well as the book *Why Texans Fought in the Civil War* (Texas A&M University Press, 2010), editor of *The Fate of Texas: The Civil War and the Lone Star State* (University of Arkansas Press, 2008), coauthor of *Beyond Myths & Legends: A Narrative History of Texas* (Abigail Press, 2008) and *The House Divided: America in the Era of the Civil War* (Abigail Press, 2011), and is the coeditor of the Civil War Campaigns in the Heartland Series for Southern Illinois University Press. He is the 2005 recipient of the Lawrence T. Jones III Award given by the Texas State Historical Association, the 2010 recipient of the Burney Parker Research Fellowship, and is currently writing a book on the Vicksburg Campaign.

Kenneth W. Howell

Kenneth W. Howell (PhD, Texas A&M University) is associate professor of history at Prairie View A&M University. Howell has written extensively on Texas and southern history, including *Texas Confederate, Reconstruction Governor: James Webb Throckmorton* (Texas A&M University Press, 2008), *The Devil's Triangle: Ben Bickerstaff, Northeast Texans, and the War of Reconstruction* (Best of East Texas Publisher, 2007), *Henderson County, Texas, 1846–1861: An Antebellum History* (Eakin Press, 1999), and several articles and book chapters. He is also editor of *The Seventh Star of the Confederacy: Texas during the Civil War* (University of North Texas, 2009),

Melanie A. Kirkland

Melanie A. Kirkland (PhD, Texas Christian University) is an adjunct instructor teaching courses in European and American history at Texas Christian University and at Tarrant County College. She is currently working on a book manuscript titled "Daughters of Athena: American Women in the Military during World War II."

James M. McCaffrey

James M. McCaffrey (PhD, University of Houston) is professor of history at the University of Houston–Downtown. Among his authored works are *Inside the Spanish-American War: A History Based on First-Person Accounts* (McFarland, 2009), *The Army in Transformation: 1790–1860* (Greenwood, 2006), and *Army of Manifest Destiny: The American Soldier in the Mexican War, 1846–1848* (New York University Press, 1992). He also has edited *Only a Private: A Texan Remembers the Civil War* (Halcyon, 2004) and *Surrounded by Dangers of All Kinds: The Mexican War Letters of Lieutenant Theodore Laidley* (University of North Texas Press, 1997) and has written the foreword to Bob Korkuc's *Finding a Fallen Hero: The Death of a Ball Turret Gunner* (University of Oklahoma Press, 2008).

Alexander Mendoza

Alex Mendoza (PhD, Texas Tech University) teaches at the University of North Texas and is the author of *Confederate Struggle for Command: General James Longstreet and the First Corps in the West* (Texas A&M Press, 2008). He has contributed book chapters on the Civil War, Texas history, and Mexican Americans for various magazines, journals, and anthologies. He is currently working on a study of the Chickamauga Campaign and a comprehensive examination of Tejanos in the American military.

Kendall Milton

Kendall Milton (MA, Texas State University–San Marcos) is curator of the Texas Heritage Museum, Hill College. She is an active member of the Texas Association of Museums and several local historical and genealogical organizations.

José A. Ramírez

José A. Ramírez (PhD, Southern Methodist University) lives in his native Laredo, Texas, where he teaches at Laredo Community College. His book *To the Line of Fire! Mexican Texans and World War I* (Texas A&M University Press, 2009) received the 2009 Robert A. Calvert Book Prize.

James M. Smallwood

James Smallwood (PhD) is emeritus professor of history at Oklahoma State University. He has also taught at Texas A&M at Commerce, Southeastern Oklahoma State University, Texas Tech University, the University of Texas at Tyler, Seton Hall University in New Jersey, and the University of Kyoto, Japan. The author of sixteen books, his *Time of Hope, Time of Despair: Black Texans during Reconstruction* (National

University Publications, 1981) won the Texas State Historical Association's Coral Tullis Award in 1982 for the best book of the year on Texas history, while *The Indian Texans* (Texas A&M University Press, 2004) won the Texas Library Association's 2005 Texas Reference Source Award. His most recent book, *The Feud that Wasn't: The Taylor Ring, Bill Sutton, John Wesley Hardin, and Violence in Texas* (Texas A&M University Press, 2008), also won the prestigious Coral Tullis Award, in 2008. Smallwood has also edited fourteen books, including ten on the writings of Will Rogers. He is a fellow of both the Texas State Historical Association and the East Texas Historical Association.

Index

CPSIA information can be obtained at www.ICGtesting.com
Printed in the USA
LVOW101620190512

282428LV00002B/2/P